THE REVELS PLAYS

Former general editors
Clifford Leech
F. David Hoeniger
E. A. J. Honigmann
Eugene M. Waith

General editors
David Bevington, Richard Dutton, Alison Findlay,
J. R. Mulryne and Helen Ostovich

DOCTOR FAUSTUS

MANCHESTER
1824

Manchester University Press

THE REVELS PLAYS

ANON   Thomas of Woodstock or King Richard the Second, Part One

BEAUMONT   The Knight of the Burning Pestle

BEAUMONT AND FLETCHER   A King and No King
Philaster, or Loves Lies a-Bleeding   The Maid's Tragedy

CHAPMAN   Bussy d'Ambois

CHAPMAN, JONSON, MARSTON   Eastward Ho

DEKKER   The Shoemaker's Holiday

FORD   Love's Sacrifice

HEYWOOD   The First and Second Parts of King Edward IV

JONSON   The Alchemist   The Devil Is an Ass
Epicene, or The Silent Woman   Every Man In His Humour
Every Man Out of His Humour   The Magnetic Lady
Poetaster   Sejanus: His Fall   The Staple of News   Volpone

LYLY   Campaspe and Sappho and Phao   Endymion
Galatea and Midas   Love's Metamorphosis   The Woman in the Moon

MARLOWE   Doctor Faustus   Edward the Second   Edward IV
The Jew of Malta   Tamburlaine the Great

MARSTON   Antonio and Mellida   Antonio's Revenge
The Malcontent

MASSINGER   The Roman Actor

MIDDLETON A Game at Chess   Michaelmas Term

MIDDLETON AND DEKKER   The Roaring Girl

MIDDLETON AND ROWLEY   The Changeling

WEBSTER   The Duchess of Malfi

THE REVELS PLAYS

DOCTOR FAUSTUS
A- and B-texts (1604, 1616)

CHRISTOPHER MARLOWE
AND HIS COLLABORATOR
AND REVISERS

edited by David Bevington
and Eric Rasmussen

MANCHESTER
UNIVERSITY PRESS

Introduction, critical apparatus, etc.
© David Bevington and Eric Rasmussen 1993

The rights of David Bevington and Eric Rasmussen to be identified as the
editors of this work has been asserted by them in accordance with the
Copyright, Designs and Patents Act 1988.

Published by Manchester University Press
Altrincham Street, Manchester, M1 7JA, UK
www.manchesteruniversitypress.co.uk

British Library Cataloguing-in-Publication Data is available

Library of Congress Cataloging-in-Publication Data is available

ISBN 978 0 7190 1643 1 paperback

First published 1993

First reprinted 1995

The publisher has no responsibility for the persistence or accuracy of
URLs for any external or third-party internet websites referred to in
this book, and does not guarantee that any content on such websites is,
or will remain, accurate or appropriate.

Typeset by Best-set Typesetter Ltd, Hong Kong
Printed and bound in Great Britain by
TJ International Ltd, Padstow, Cornwall

Contents

Illustrations

General Editors' Preface

Clifford Leech conceived of the Revels Plays as a series in the mid-1950s, modelling the project on the New Arden Shakespeare. The aim, as he wrote in 1958, was 'to apply to Shakespeare's predecessors, contemporaries and successors the methods that are now used in Shakespeare's editing'. The plays chosen were to include well-known works from the early Tudor period to about 1700, as well as others less familiar but of literary and theatrical merit: 'the plays included', Leech wrote, 'should be such as to deserve and indeed demand performance'. We owe it to Clifford Leech that the idea became reality. He set the high standards of the series, ensuring that editors of individual volumes produced work of lasting merit, equally useful for teachers and students, theatre directors and actors. Clifford Leech remained General Editor until 1971, and was succeeded by F. David Hoeniger, who retired in 1985.

Since 1985 the Revels Plays have been under the direction of four General Editors: initially David Bevington, E. A. J. Honigmann, J. R. Mulryne and E. M. Waith. E. A. J. Honigmann retired in 2000 and was succeeded by Richard Dutton. Published originally by Methuen, the series is now published by Manchester University Press, embodying essentially the same format, scholarly character and high editorial standards of the series as first conceived. The series concentrates on plays from the period 1558–1642, and includes a small number of non-dramatic works of interest to students of drama. Some slight changes have been made: for example, in editions from 1978, notes to the introduction are placed together at the end, not at the foot of the page. Collation and commentary notes continue, however, to appear on the relevant pages.

The text of each Revels play, in accordance with established practice in the series, is edited afresh from the original text of best authority (in a few instances, texts), but spelling and punctuation are modernised and speech headings are silently made consistent. Elisions in the original are also silently regularised, except where metre would be affected by the change; since 1968 the '-ed' form is used for non-syllabic terminations in past tenses and past participles ('-'d' earlier), and '-èd' for syllabic ('-ed' earlier). The editor emends, as distinct from modernises, the original only in instances where error is patent, or at least very probable, and correction persuasive. Act divisions are given only if they appear in the original or if the structure of the play clearly points to them. Those act and scene divisions not in the original are provided in small type. Square brackets are also used for any other additions to or changes in the stage directions of the original.

Revels Plays do not provide a variorum collation, but only those variants which require the critical attention of serious textual students. All departures of substance from 'copy-text' are listed, including any relineation and those changes in punctuation which involve to any degree a decision between alternative interpretations; but not such accidentals as turned letters, nor necessary additions to stage directions whose editorial nature is already made clear by the use of brackets. Press corrections in the 'copy-text' are likewise collated. Of later emendations of the text, only those are given which as alternative readings still deserve attention.

One of the hallmarks of the Revels Plays is the thoroughness of their annotations. Besides explaining the meaning of difficult words and passages, the editor provides comments on customs or usage, text or stage-business—indeed, on anything judged pertinent and helpful. Each volume contains an Index to the Commentary, in which particular attention is drawn to meanings for words not listed in *OED*, and (starting in 1996) an indexing of proper names and topics in the Introduction and Commentary.

The introduction to a Revels play assesses the authority of the 'copy-text' on which it is based, and discusses the editorial methods employed in dealing with it; the editor also considers the play's date and (where relevant) sources, together with its place in the work of the author and in the theatre of its time. Stage history is offered, and in the case of a play by an author not previously represented in the series a brief biography is given.

It is our hope that plays edited in this fashion will promote further scholarly and theatrical investigation of one the richest periods in theatrical history.

DAVID BEVINGTON
RICHARD DUTTON
J. R. MULRYNE
E. M. WAITH

Preface

This edition of the A- and B-texts of *Doctor Faustus* is intended to replace the Revels edition prepared by John D. Jump in 1962 on the basis of the B-text. We are indebted to that edition and incorporate a good number of its notes in our present editing. None the less, for reasons spelled out in our Introduction, the B-text of 1616 is no longer the text on which we would wish to base a modern-spelling edition. Indeed, the critical verdict has swung strongly in favour of the A-text in recent years, as evidenced by a spate of editions based on the edition of 1604: by David Ormerod and Christopher Wortham (1985), by Roma Gill (1989 and 1990), and by Michael Keefer (1991). Now the time has come, in our view, for an edition of both texts in full. W. W. Greg's *Parallel Texts*, 1950, remains indispensable as a scholarly edition in old spelling and with parallel passages from the 1604 and 1616 texts on facing pages, but we also believe there is a need for a reading edition of the two texts in modern spelling in which each is treated as an entity. Other Renaissance texts have appeared recently in two texts, notably *King Lear*. In our view, *Doctor Faustus* presents as compelling a case for publishing two texts as any in the canon. Increasingly, scholars and critics have come to realise that the 1604 and 1616 texts cannot be conflated into one. They are the products of strikingly different conditions of authorship and collaboration, revision and expansion, theatrical management, fashions in taste, religious and political ideology, censorship, and still more.

We have decided to edit both texts in five acts, being persuaded by the argument of G. K. Hunter (*TDR*, viii.iv (1964), 77–91) that the play was originally conceived in these terms and that the pattern is recoverable in the main. This editorial choice has the considerable advantage, among others, of making comparisons between the two texts easy and clear. For reasons spelled out in an appendix, we also move the first comic scene involving Robin and Rafe to its present location as ii.ii, from its position in the A-text after iii.i and a misplaced Chorus intended for Act iv. (A parallel scene in the B-text, involving Robin and Dick, is placed in the original text at the end of Act ii, after the show of the Seven Deadly Sins; once again, we move this scene to ii.ii.) In these significant choices we part

ix

company with all previous editors other than Michael Keefer (1991), who, though editing the A-text only with the B-text additions in an appendix, presents his A-text in acts and scenes and moves the first comic scene of Robin and Rafe to the location we also have chosen. Our editorial decisions and his were arrived at independently; our work on the entire edition was virtually ready for submission to the Manchester University Press before we were able to see his. We hope that the agreements between his edition and ours are indicative of a new consensus, not only in the editing of this play but of others as well.

Certain procedures follow as a logical consequence of editing two texts. Our collations do not attempt to list the many variations between the two texts; most collations in earlier editions that attempt to do so become cumbersome, and in our view a clearer sense of how the two texts work and differ can be derived from direct comparison. We have decided nevertheless against facing-page texts, since each play needs to be read in and for itself. We do call attention, in the commentary notes and Introduction, to the more significant variations between the two texts. We offer substantial commentary notes for the A-text, which we regard as closer to the original authors' collaborative version; B-text commentaries are limited to passages and words not occurring in the A-text. In those significant parts of the play where the A- and B-texts are close to each other, we try to avoid conflation; in our view, Keefer's generally laudable edition makes the mistake of moving back and forth for its verbal choices in a way that implies a single underlying text and procedurally seems at times arbitrary. We do, to be sure, adopt a few B-text readings in our A-text and vice versa when corruption seems unmistakable; at III.i.35, for example, Mephistopheles's 'Over the which four stately bridges lean' makes no sense without the preceding two lines about the River Tiber provided from the B-text. Such errors are easily accounted for by eyeskip or misinterpreting a difficult manuscript hand. Yet we keep to the original readings, some of them difficult, as long as they can be sensibly defended. As much as possible, then, we try to give the reader the A- and B-texts straight.

Our approach to modern spelling is, we hope, a thorough and even aggressive one, much in the spirit of Stanley Wells's *Re-editing Shakespeare for the Modern Reader* (Oxford: Clarendon, 1984). We modernise 'vilde' to 'vile' (I.i.111), 'renowmd' to 'renowned' (l. 143), 'wrackes' to 'wrecks' (l. 147), 'swowns' to ''Swounds' (I.iv.30), 'god buy' to 'goodbye' (IV.i.134), 'enow' to 'enough' (III.ii.42), and the like. The name of Faustus's constant diabolical companion, inconsistently rendered in the original texts and in many modern editions ('Mephastophilis' generally in the A-text, 'Mephostophilis' in the B-text, but also 'Mephastophilus', etc.) should, in our view, be modernised to the standard dictionary form, 'Mephistopheles'. So too with 'Beelzebub' for 'Belsabub' and 'Belzebub', even though the metre at times indicates pronunciation in three syllables. Added stage directions in square brackets are more common in our edition than in many preceding editions—not, we trust, of an impressionistic sort, but intended to give concreteness to implied gestures and stage movement where they seem clearly intended to be performed. We have expanded and normalised speech prefixes throughout.

Our collaboration on this project began in 1988 with the textual and interpretative work done by Eric Rasmussen on 'The Revision of Marlowe's *Doctor Faustus*' for his doctoral disseration at the University of Chicago (completed in 1990), under David Bevington's direction. Subsequent editorial work has been shared throughout. Bevington supplied a first draft of most of the Introduction, Commentary, and Appendix, and recast the textual introduction (with some added suggestions) from Rasmussen's textual work so that the form of the essay would be compatible with that of the rest of the Introduction. Rasmussen took initial responsibility for the texts and collations. Subsequent ideas about all parts of the project have passed back and forth, slowly transforming the result into its present form. We have shared the burdens of research and of checking for accuracy.

We wish to thank Paul Werstine and Barbara Mowat for extraordinarily insightful readings of our editorial work. Eugene Waith has been no less generous with his time and unflagging in his careful inspections. We are grateful to Gary Taylor, Leah Marcus, David Kastan, James Shapiro, James Hammersmith, Robert Kean Turner, and T. H. Howard-Hill for particular assistance. We have put so many questions to other friends that some will have to go unacknowledged here. Our thanks go to Albert Fields for permission to use some parts of David Bevington's essay entitled 'Marlowe and God' (*Explorations in Renaissance Culture*, XVII (1991), 1–38), containing a considerably different version of a part of the Introduction in this present edition. We similarly acknowledge with gratitude the use of some ideas to be published in Eric Rasmussen's essay, 'Rehabilitating the A-text of Marlowe's *Doctor Faustus*', *SB*, XLVI (1993), forthcoming. Ronnie Mulryne, Ernst Honigmann, Anita

Roy, and Juanita Bullough, among others, have been supportive as general editors of the Revels series and at the Manchester University Press.

DAVID BEVINGTON AND ERIC RASMUSSEN

Chicago and San Francisco, 1992

Abbreviations

EDITIONS AND TEXTUAL REFERENCES

A1   Quarto of 1604. *The Tragicall History of D. Faustus* (London: Thomas Bushell, 1604).

A2   Quarto of 1609. *The Tragicall History of the horrible Life and death of Doctor Faustus* (London: John Wright, 1609).

A3   Quarto of 1611 (London: John Wright, 1611).

B1   Quarto of 1616. *The Tragicall History of the Life and Death of Doctor Faustus* (London: John Wright, 1616).

B2   Quarto of 1619 (London: John Wright, 1619).

B3   Quarto of 1620 (London: John Wright, 1620).

B4   Quarto of 1624 (London: John Wright, 1624).

B5   Quarto of 1628 (London: John Wright, 1628).

B6   Quarto of 1631 (London: John Wright, 1631).

B7   Quarto of 1663. *The Tragicall History of the Life and Death of Doctor Faustus. Printed with New Additions as it is now Acted. With several new Scenes* (London: William Gilbertson, 1663).

Boas   *The Tragical History of Doctor Faustus*, ed. Frederick S. Boas (London: Methuen, 1932).

Bowers   *The Complete Works of Christopher Marlowe*, ed. Fredson Bowers, 2 vols. (Cambridge University Press, 1973).

Bullen   *The Works of Christopher Marlowe*, ed. A. H. Bullen, 3 vols. (London: J. C. Nimmo, 1885).

Cunningham   *The Works of Christopher Marlowe*, ed. Francis Cunningham (London: Chatto & Windus, 1870).

Dilke   *Old English Plays*, ed. C. W. Dilke, 6 vols. (London, 1814–15).

Dyce 1   *The Works of Christopher Marlowe*, ed. Alexander Dyce, 3 vols. (London: W. Pickering, 1850).

Dyce 2   *The Works of Christopher Marlowe*, new edition, revised and corrected, ed. Alexander Dyce (London: E. Moxon, 1858).

Ellis   *Christopher Marlowe* (Mermaid Series), ed. Havelock Ellis (London: Vizetelly and T. F. Unwin, 1887).

Gill 1   *Doctor Faustus* (New Mermaids), ed. Roma Gill (London: E. Benn, 1965).

Gill 2   *Dr Faustus* (New Mermaids), ed. Roma Gill (London: E. Benn, 1989). Based on the A-text.

Gill 3   *The Complete Works of Christopher Marlowe*. Vol. 2. *Dr Faustus*, ed. Roma Gill (Oxford: Clarendon Press, 1990).
Greg   *Marlowe's 'Doctor Faustus' 1604–1616: Parallel Texts*, ed. W. W. Greg (Oxford: Clarendon Press, 1950), and *The Tragicall History of the Life and Death of Doctor Faustus by Christopher Marlowe: A Conjectural Reconstruction*, ed. W. W. Greg (Oxford: Clarendon Press, 1950). The latter is referred to only to record emendations in the collations; all other references are to the *Parallel Texts*.
Jump   *Doctor Faustus* (The Revels Plays), ed. John D. Jump (London: Methuen, 1962, rpt. Manchester University Press, 1976).
Keefer   *Christopher Marlowe's 'Doctor Faustus': a 1604-Version Edition*, ed. Michael Keefer (Peterborough, Ont.: Broadview Press, 1991).
Kirschbaum   *The Plays of Christopher Marlowe*, ed. Leo Kirschbaum (Cleveland: World Publishing, 1962).
Ormerod–Wortham   *Christopher Marlowe, 'Dr Faustus': the A-Text*, ed. David Ormerod and Christopher Wortham (Nedlands, Australia: University of Western Australia Press, 1985).
Oxberry   *The Tragicall Historie of the Life and Death of Doctor Faustus with New Additions. Written by Ch. Mar.* [ed. W. Oxberry] (London: W. Simpkin and R. Marshall, 1818).
Ribner   *The Complete Plays of Christopher Marlowe*, ed. Irving Ribner (New York: Odyssey Press, 1963).
Robinson   *The Works of Christopher Marlowe*, ed. George Robinson, 3 vols. (London: W. Pickering, 1826).
Sleight   *The Tragical History of Doctor Faustus*, ed. A. H. Sleight (Cambridge University Press, 1928, 1936).
Tucker Brooke   *The Works of Christopher Marlowe*, ed. C. F. Tucker Brooke (Oxford: Clarendon Press, 1910).
Wagner   *Christopher Marlowe's Tragedy of Doctor Faustus*, ed. Wilhelm Wagner (London: Longman, Green, 1877).
Ward   *Old English Drama: Select Plays. Marlowe, Tragical History of Doctor Faustus; Greene, Honourable History of Friar Bacon and Friar Bungay*, ed. Adolphus William Ward (Oxford: Clarendon Press, 1878, 3rd ed., 1892).

OTHER REFERENCES

Abbott   E. A. Abbott, *A Shakespearian Grammar* (London: Macmillan, 1870, with subsequent editions).

Aristotle   Aristotle, *Nicomachean Ethics*, trans. H. Rackham; *Metaphysics*, trans. Hugh Tredennick; *The Poetics*, trans. W. H. Fyfe; *Politics*, trans. H. Rackham; *De Sensu et Sensibili* in *Parva Naturalia*, trans. W. S. Hett (Loeb Library, 1926, 1933–35, 1927, 1932, 1936).

Bakeless   John Bakeless, *The Tragicall History of Christopher Marlowe*, 2 vols. (Cambridge, Mass.: Harvard University Press, 1942).

Barber   C. L. Barber, ' "The form of Faustus' fortunes good or bad" ', *TDR*, VIII.iv (1964), 92–119.

Barnes   Barnabe Barnes, *The Devil's Charter*, ed. Jim C. Pogue (New York: Garland, 1980).

Bentley   G. E. Bentley, *The Profession of Dramatist in Shakespeare's Time, 1590–1642* (Princeton University Press, 1971).

Bevington   *Medieval Drama*, ed. David Bevington (Boston: Houghton Mifflin, 1975).

Bluestone   Max Bluestone, '*Libido Speculandi*: Doctrine and Dramaturgy in Contemporary Interpretations of Marlowe's *Doctor Faustus*', in *Reinterpretations of Elizabethan Drama*, ed. Norman Rabkin (New York: Columbia University Press, 1969), pp. 33–88.

Brockbank   J. P. Brockbank, *Marlowe: Dr. Faustus* (London: Arnold, 1962).

Calvin   *Calvin: Institutes of the Christian Religion*, ed. John T. McNeill, trans. Ford Lewis Battles. 2 vols. (Philadelphia and London: Westminster, 1960).

Cole   Douglas Cole, *Suffering and Evil in the Plays of Christopher Marlowe* (Princeton University Press, 1962).

Cornelius   R. M. Cornelius, *Christopher Marlowe's Use of the Bible* (Bern: Peter Lang, 1984).

Damnable Life   *The History of the Damnable Life and Deserved Death of Doctor John Faustus*, trans. P. F. (London: Edward White, 1592); rpt. (Hildesheim: Georg Olmes Verlag, 1985).

Dent   R. W. Dent, *Proverbial Language in English Drama Exclusive of Shakespeare, 1495–1616* (Berkeley: University of California Press, 1984).

Dido   Marlowe, *Dido, Queen of Carthage* (The Revels Plays), ed. H. J. Oliver (London: Methuen, 1968).

Edw.II   Marlowe, *Edward II*, ed. H. B. Charlton and R. D. Waller, revised by F. N. Lees (London: Methuen, 1955).

Empson   William Empson, *Faustus and the Censor: the English*

Faust-book and Marlowe's 'Doctor Faustus', ed. John Henry Jones (Oxford: B. Blackwell, 1987).

Foxe   John Foxe, *Acts and Monuments*, 2nd ed., 3 vols. (London: John Daye, 1570; new ed. by George Townsend, 3 vols., London: Seeley and Burnside, 1841).

Friedenreich   Kenneth Friedenreich, Roma Gill, and Constance B. Kuriyama, eds., *'A poet and a filthy play-maker': New Essays on Christopher Marlowe* (New York: AMS, 1988).

Gatti   Hilary Gatti, *The Renaissance Drama of Knowledge: Giordano Bruno in England* (London: Routledge, 1989).

Greene   *The Life and Complete Works in Prose and Verse of Robert Greene*, ed. Alexander B. Grosart, 15 vols. (London: The Huth Library, 1881–6). References to *Friar Bacon and Friar Bungay* are to the edition by Daniel Seltzer, Regents Renaissance Drama Series (Lincoln: University of Nebraska Press, 1963).

Henslowe   *Henslowe's Diary*, ed. R. A. Foakes and R. T. Rickert (Cambridge University Press, 1961).

Hero and Leander   Marlowe, *The Poems* (The Revels Plays), ed. Millar Maclure (London: Methuen, 1968, rpt. Manchester University Press).

Homer   Homer, *The Odyssey*, trans. A. T. Murray (Loeb Library, 1919).

Horace   Horace, *Odes and Epodes*, trans. C. E. Bennett (Loeb Library, 1914).

Jew of Malta   Marlowe, *The Jew of Malta* (The Revels Plays), ed. N. W. Bawcutt (Manchester University Press, 1978).

Justinian   *The Institutes of Justinian*, trans. J. B. Moyle (Oxford: Clarendon Press, 1969).

Kocher, *Marlowe*   Paul H. Kocher, *Christopher Marlowe: a Study of his Thought, Learning, and Character* (Chapel Hill: University of North Carolina Press, 1946).

Kocher, 'Nashe's Authorship'   'Nashe's Authorship of the Prose Scenes in *Faustus*', *MLQ*, III (1942), 17–40.

Kuriyama   Constance Brown Kuriyama, 'Dr. Greg and *Doctor Faustus*: the Supposed Originality of the 1616 Text', *ELR*, v (1975), 171–97.

Leech   Clifford Leech, *Christopher Marlowe, Poet for the Stage*, ed. Anne Lancashire (New York: AMS Press, 1986).

Levin   Harry Levin, *The Overreacher: a Study of Christopher Marlowe* (Cambridge, Mass.: Harvard University Press, 1952).

ABBREVIATIONS xvii

Loeb Library The Loeb Classical Library (Cambridge, Mass. and London: Harvard University Press and Heinemann).

Logeman H. Logeman, *Faustus-Notes* (Ghent and Amsterdam: Université de Gand, 1898).

Lucian Lucian, *Dialogues of the Dead*, trans. M. D. Macleod (Loeb Library, 1961).

Lyly *The Complete Works of John Lyly*, ed. R. Warwick Bond, 3 vols. (Oxford University Press, 1902).

Mahood M. M. Mahood, *Poetry and Humanism* (London: J. Cape, 1950).

Massacre Marlowe, *The Massacre at Paris* (The Revels Plays), ed. H. J. Oliver (London: Methuen, 1968).

Nashe *The Works of Thomas Nashe*, ed. R. B. McKerrow, rev. F. P. Wilson, 5 vols. (Oxford University Press, 1958).

OED *Oxford English Dictionary*, ed. J. A. Simpson and E. S. C. Weiner, 2nd ed. (Oxford: Clarendon Press, 1989). Numbering of definitions follows the second edition and does not always correspond with the first.

Ovid Ovid, *Metamorphoses*, trans. Frank Justus Miller; *Heroides and Amores*, trans. Grant Showerman (Loeb Library, 1916, 1921).

Ovid's Elegies Marlowe, *The Poems* (The Revels Plays), ed. Millar Maclure (London: Methuen, 1968).

Peele *The Life and Works of George Peele*, gen. ed. C. T. Prouty, 3 vols. (New Haven: Yale University Press, 1952–70).

Puttenham George Puttenham, *The Arte of English Poesie*, ed. Gladys Doidge Willcock and Alice Walker (Cambridge University Press, 1936).

Ribner Irving Ribner, 'Marlowe's "Tragicke Glass"', in *Essays on Shakespeare and Elizabethan Drama in Honor of Hardin Craig*, ed. Richard Hosley (Columbia: University of Missouri Press, 1962), pp. 91–114.

Root R. K. Root, 'Two Notes on Marlowe's *Doctor Faustus*', *ES*, XLIII (1910–11), 144–9.

Sanders Wilbur Sanders, *The Dramatist and the Received Idea: Studies in the Plays of Marlowe and Shakespeare* (Cambridge University Press, 1968).

Scot Reginald Scot, *The Discovery of Witchcraft* (London: W. Brome, 1584).

Spenser Edmund Spenser, *The Faerie Queene*, ed. J. C. Smith, 2 vols. (Oxford University Press, 1909).

SR   The Stationers' Register.
1Tamb.   Marlowe, *Tamburlaine the Great, Part One*.
2Tamb.   Marlowe, *Tamburlaine the Great, Part Two* (The Revels
Plays), ed. J. S. Cunningham (Manchester University Press,
1981).
Tydeman   William Tydeman, *'Doctor Faustus': Text and Performance*
(Basingstoke: Macmillan, 1984).
Virgil   Virgil, *Aeneid* and *Georgics*, trans. H. Rushton Fairclough
(Loeb Library, rev. ed. 1935).
Warren   Michael J. Warren, *'Doctor Faustus*: The Old Man and the
Text', *ELR*, xi (1981), 111–47.

PERIODICALS

CE   *College English*
CQ   *Critical Quarterly*
Comp.D   *Comparative Drama*
E&S   *Essays and Studies*
EIC   *Essays in Criticism*
ELH   *English Literary History*
ELR   *English Literary Renaissance*
ES   *English Studies*
JEGP   *Journal of English and Germanic Philology*
MLN   *Modern Language Notes*
MLQ   *Modern Language Quarterly*
MLR   *Modern Language Review*
MP   *Modern Philology*
MSE   *Massachusetts Studies in English*
N&Q   *Notes and Queries*
NM   *Neuphilologische Mitteilungen*
PBA   *Publications of the British Academy*
PMLA   *Publications of the Modern Language Association*
PQ   *Philological Quarterly*
Ren.D   *Renaissance Drama*
Ren.P   *Renaissance Papers*
RES   *Review of English Studies*
RORD   *Research Opportunities in Renaissance Drama*
SB   *Studies in Bibliography*
SEL   *Studies in English Literature*
SP   *Studies in Philology*
SQ   *Shakespeare Quarterly*

SSur.   *Shakespeare Survey*
TDR   *Tulane Drama Review*
TLS   *The Times Literary Supplement*
TSLL   *Texas Studies in Literature and Language*
UTQ   *University of Toronto Quarterly*

All biblical quotations are from the 1560 Geneva Bible unless other-
wise specified. Quotations from Shakespeare's plays refer to the
Bantam Shakespeare, ed. David Bevington (New York: Bantam
Books, 1988). Titles of Shakespeare's plays are abbreviated as in the
New Cambridge Shakespeare.

FOR PEGGY AND VICKY

Introduction

Among the myriad uncertainties about *Doctor Faustus*, the first is the question of when it was written and initially performed. Two dates vie for our attention, one *c*. 1588–9 and one *c*. 1592. The matter is of consequence to our view of Marlowe's career as a dramatist, for, despite their general proximity, these dates nearly span the productive career of this precocious and seemingly doomed young artist. Did Marlowe write *Doctor Faustus* shortly after his great success with the two parts of *Tamburlaine*, the second of them performed probably on 10 November 1587, or is the play perhaps his last and greatest creation before his sudden death at a Deptford tavern in May of 1593?

The case for the earlier date, generally now in critical favour, rests on a number of considerations. The anonymous play called *The Taming of a Shrew*, widely regarded as an earlier version of Shakespeare's play employing a good deal of free-wheeling plagiarism from other sources, or else a 'bad' quarto of Shakespeare's play, unquestionably takes some of its plagiarised material from *Doctor Faustus*. Even though *A Shrew* can arguably be dated any time from about 1588 to 1593, its dependence on *Doctor Faustus* tends to push back the date of the earlier play.[1] Robert Greene's *Friar Bacon and Friar Bungay*, already an old play (perhaps as early as 1589) by the time it was performed by Lord Strange's Men on 19 February 1592, seems manifestly to have been written under the influence of Marlowe, of whom Greene was openly resentful and emulous. The possibility that Greene may have pioneered in bringing a famous magician on stage seems implausible in view of Greene's other blatant attempts to capitalise on Marlowe's success, as in *Alphonsus, King of Aragon* (1587–8) and its nearly parodic depiction of the overreacher Tamburlaine. A line in *Perimedes* (SR 29 March 1588)— 'Such mad and scoffing poets that have poetical spirits, as bred of Merlin's race'—sounds like another of Greene's irritated references to Marlowe and specifically to *Doctor Faustus*. Clearly there was a new demand in 1588–9 for plays about magicians and their spectacular tricks; Anthony Munday's *John a Kent and John a*

Cumber is another of these.[2] *Doctor Faustus* may well have been the pacesetter for this fashion; even if it was not the very first, we can scarcely imagine Marlowe waiting until 1592, some four years after the height of the vogue. A *Looking-Glass for London and England*, written by Thomas Lodge and Robert Greene before August 1591, is yet another play that appears to have plagiarised material from Marlowe's play, though W. W. Greg argues the minority position that *Doctor Faustus* is the debtor. Unmistakable borrowings from *Doctor Faustus* in *A Knack to Know a Knave*, first performed on 10 June 1592, indicate that Marlowe's play was well known at least a few months before that date.[3]

'A ballad of the life and deathe of Doctur Faustus the great Cunngerer', entered in the Stationers' Register to Richard Jones on 28 February 1589, is probably essentially identical with a Faustus ballad later registered on 14 December 1674 and preserved in late seventeenth-century broadsides. This ballad, as MacD. P. Jackson shows, displays acquaintance with both Marlowe's chief source, the *Damnable Life*, and with the play itself, and may belong to a group of ballads based on plays written around 1590 including *Titus Andronicus* and *Arden of Faversham*.[4]

Doctor Faustus may have been performed in about 1588 at the Belsavage playhouse, if we can trust William Prynne's considerably later (1633) reference to 'the visible apparition of the devil on the stage at the Belsavage playhouse, in Queen Elizabeth's days, to the great amazement both of the actors and spectators, whiles they were there playing the History of Faustus, the truth of which I have heard from many now alive, who well remember it, there being some distracted with that fearful sight'.[5] The Belsavage was in use, ordinarily by the Queen's Men, until 1588 and perhaps as late as 1589; other acting companies more reliably associated with Marlowe, such as Lord Strange's Men and Pembroke's company, may also have acted there.

The case for a date in 1592 rests chiefly on the publication date of Marlowe's chief source, P. F.'s English translation of the German *Faustbuch*, under the title *The History of the Damnable Life and Deserved Death of Doctor John Faustus*. The earliest extant edition was printed by Thomas Orwin in 1592. This, however, is apparently not the first edition, since its title page speaks of its being 'newly imprinted, and in convenient places imperfect matter amended'. An entry in the Court Book of the Stationers' Register on 18 December of that year seemingly points to a now-lost edition (published by

Abel Jeffes) in May; even this need not have been the first edition. Perhaps Marlowe consulted not the extant Orwin edition but some other, quite possibly earlier in date.[6]

One way or another, Marlowe may well have had access to the *Damnable Life* before 1592. The ballad entry of 28 February 1589, whether or not it refers to the ballad preserved in seventeenth-century broadsides, does seem to suggest the existence by that date of some English version of the Faust story, for ballads of this sort ordinarily sought to exploit a phenomenon that was sensational and widely known. Since the German *Historia von D. Johann Fausten, dem weitbeschreiten Zauberer und Schwartzkünstler* was first published in 1587, with several reprints in that same year attesting to its instant popularity, we are left with only a short period of time for the story to have gained notoriety in England and for a translation to have been made by P. F.—one to which Marlowe may have had access. Paul Kocher in fact argues that an edition of the English *Damnable Life* had appeared by 1590, perhaps in November of 1589 or even a year before that, at Cambridge.[7] Harold Jantz goes still further to posit a lost Latin original of the *Faustbuch* that was perhaps widely disseminated before the German version appeared in 1587 and that Marlowe might have consulted at Cambridge.[8] A reference to Pope Sixtus in the present tense in the English *Damnable Life* might indicate that the translation was done before his death in August of 1590.[9]

Stylistically and thematically, the case for a date in 1588–9 is as strong as for 1592 and probably no stronger; as Fredson Bowers was fond of saying in cases like this, you pays your money and you takes your choice. Either Marlowe followed up his study of fortunate striving after earthly felicity in *Tamburlaine* with a more dispirited anatomy of ambition foiled by its own dark energies,[10] or he waited until after *The Jew of Malta* and *Edward II*, not to mention *The Massacre at Paris*, to give the world his most mature and exalted vision of tragic waste.[11] Since the historical evidence tends to support the earlier date, we will approach the question of Marlowe's development accordingly.

SOURCES AND BACKGROUND

Marlowe found in P. F.'s *The History of the Damnable Life and Deserved Death of Doctor John Faustus* (often referred to as the English Faust Book or EFB) a wealth of material to which he could

4 DOCTOR FAUSTUS

turn for the substance of virtually all the scenes in his play. The strong correlation between the prose source and the play in fact argues the likelihood that Marlowe, working seemingly with a collaborator,[12] conceived of the plan as a whole in which the comic scenes played an integral part. Deprived of the comedy, *Doctor Faustus* would bear an implausible relation to the *Damnable Life*.

The *Damnable Life* and its German original give us a collection of stories gathered around one Georgius of Helmstadt, who enrolled in the University of Heidelberg in 1483 and evidently later came to be known as Johann Faustus. This man had already become infamous by 1507, it seems, for on 20 August in that year the Abbot Trithemius of Würzburg wrote to Johann Virdung about a vagabond and knave calling himself 'Magister Georgius Sabellicus, Faustus junior, fons necromanticorum, astrologus, magus secundus, agromanticus, pyromanticus', and still worse. We hear a second complaint on 7 October 1513, this time in a letter from Konrad Muth, Canon at Gotha, to his friend Heinrich Urbanus, about 'a certain chiromancer named Georgius Faustus, *Hemitheus Hedelbergensis* [the demigod of Heidelberg], a mere braggart and fool'. Both 'Faustus' and 'Sabellicus' appear to be Latin cognomens in the style of many a Renaissance humanist. Possibly the name 'Faustus', meaning 'auspicious', was bestowed upon this man (whose family name is unknown) in recollection of St Clement's father, a legendary magician who engaged in a battle of devilish tricks with Simon Magus, or of the Manichean bishop with whom St Augustine engaged in debate.[13] The name Johann or John Faust may also represent a confusion with Johann Fust, an early practitioner of that sinister art known as printing. Many of the tall tales that collected around Faustus bear a generic resemblance to stories told also of Simon Magus, Roger Bacon, Empedocles, Virgil, and others, and hence are not to be taken too literally.

Marlowe and his collaborator undoubtedly relied on the *Damnable Life*'s free translation rather than on the German original. Examples of direct indebtedness to the English version for language not found in the German include the account of Virgil's tomb and of 'the highway that he cut through that mighty hill of stone in one night, the whole length of an English mile' (compare *Doctor Faustus*, A-text, III.i.13–15);[14] the description of four bridges over the River Tiber in Rome, upon one of which 'is the Castle of S. Angelo, wherein are so many great cast pieces as there are days in a year' (III.i.37–41); the fourth article of Faustus's pact with the devil,

which began as two separate articles of agreement in the German
original; Faustus's giving the Pope a box on the ear (III.i.80.2) rather
than blowing in his face as in the German version; the Pope's curse
by means of 'bell, book, and candle' (III.i.82–4); and others.[15]
Nowhere does the play rely on the German text; the spelling (in both
texts) of 'Trier' (III.i.2) corresponds with the German rather than the
Damnable Life's 'Treir', but anyone could have corrected this error.

As Harry Levin observes, the *Damnable Life* 'is at once a cautionary tale and a book of marvels, a jestbook and a theological tract'.[16]
Despite its episodic character, the work falls naturally into three
parts: Faustus's contract with the devil and his inquiries into the
secrets of the universe, his adventuresome travels and magical
demonstrations, and finally his despair and damnation. The formal
divisions of the text into 'the Second Part' at ch. 17 and 'the Third
and Last Part' at ch. 29 (out of 53 chapters in all) nearly but not
precisely demarcate such a beginning, middle, and end, since
the third part includes some episodes showing 'after what sort he
[Faustus] practised necromancy in the courts of princes' as well as
'his fearful and pitiful end'. Even so, the shape of the overall
conception is plain enough, and leaves little doubt as to why the
controversial middle of the play is so much taken up with horseplay
and entertaining spectacle.

Marlowe and his collaborator borrow many details in their adop-
tion of this tripartite scheme, including the admonition '*Homo, fuge*'
and the need 'for warm ashes' to reheat Faustus's coagulated blood
(ch. 6), his journey through the heavens and 'the principal and most
famous lands in the world' (ch. 22), including Rome and the Papal
palace, his conjuring up Alexander and his paramour, his putting
horns on the head of an obstreperous knight, his hoodwinking
a horse-courser, his providing grapes for the delectation of the
Duchess of Anholt (Vanholt in the play), his showing the spirit of
Helen of Troy to some students, his being torn apart by devils
while the students listen fearfully in an adjoining room, and much
more. To be sure, the play excises and compresses a good deal of
material. Time is radically shortened in the dramatised version
of Faustus's negotiations over his contract and in his questioning of
Mephistopheles about the universe—events that in the prose source
take place over an extended period of time. The prose account
indulges in more episodes of a spectacular nature than a stage play
could efficiently and convincingly accommodate, carrying Faustus
on a visit to hell, into the universe, and on a far more extensive

earthbound journey than in the play. Among his various pranks, Faustus conjures away the four wheels of a clown's wagon and deceives four jugglers who have cut off one another's heads and set them on again. He indulges in a 'swinish and epicurish life' by sleeping with the seven most beautiful women he has seen on his travels (ch. 53). Some of this excessive lore in the *Damnable Life* would prove irresistible to Rowley and Birde when, in 1602, Philip Henslowe decided that enough already was in fact not enough.[17] To view the original plan of the A-text against the *Damnable Life*, on the other hand, is to be persuaded of the constraint and tact exercised by Marlowe and his collaborator. The comic degeneracy was a part of the original conception, as found in the source, but it needed the discipline of dramatic form.

No less significant are the changes in *Doctor Faustus*'s presentation of its protagonist. The play explores motivation and inner conflict in a way that is largely missing in the original. The prose source is content, by and large, to relate events and to offer orthodox moral condemnation of a life from which 'all Christians may take an example and warning' (ch. 62). Some of this moralising finds its way into the play's Epilogue ('Regard his hellish fall', etc.) and else-where, and accordingly the play retains much of the source's ambiv-alence of attitude between disapproval and fascination. Yet the prose source does little to explain how Faustus got started on his career as a necromancer. We are simply told that Faustus, 'being of a naughty mind and otherwise addicted, applied not his studies, but took himself to other exercises' (ch. 1). The motivation, in so far as we can intuit it, is a combination of desires for worldly pleasure, power, and forbidden knowledge.[18] The impatience with traditional learn-ing and the rejection one by one of rhetoric, medicine, law, and theology are the play's rich elaborations. Faustus's inquiries into astronomy are far more detailed in the play than in the prose source, and manifestly more aware of current scientific controversy.

So too with the play's portrayal of inner conflict. The Good and Evil Angels, not to be found in the prose source, focus attention on Faustus's conscious choice of evil. And because Marlowe studies the matter of choice so intently, he opens up theological questions of free will and determinism that call upon a wide acquaintance with the burning theological issues of his day. The prose source, for all its patriotic Lutheran anti-Catholicism and its orthodox understanding of the power of evil set in motion when 'my Lord Lucifer fell from heaven' (ch. 14), shows virtually no interest in the great issue of what the story implies about the human condition in general and the plight of the intellectual in particular. Marlowe gives to Faustus the initiative in offering his soul to Lucifer, whereas in the source Mephistopheles is the proposer. Marlowe's protagonist perseveres in his determination, unswayed by all that he has been told about hell and damnation, whereas in the source the discussions about hell follow the signing of the contract. These reversals heighten Faustus's responsibility for his damnation and intensify the puzzle of his choice of evil. Despair is ever-present in the play, only fitfully and belatedly so in the source. The hell of the prose account is the hell of folklore, replete with fireworks and gruesome physical tortures; Marlowe's hell is the hell of theology, one grounded 'in the personal responsibility of free human choice and the inevitable consequences of that choice'.[19] The protagonist of the Damnable Life is not Everyman; our attitude towards him is one of astonishment, curiosity, and rejection. Marlowe, aiming at tragedy, puts issues of choice and reprobation at the centre of his concern.

Other sources and traditions can help illuminate the art of Doctor Faustus. Faustus's mythical ancestry is widely dispersed in Christian and classical lore. The Book of Genesis tells of humanity's first disobedience towards God, through a choice that opens the eyes of humanity to the knowledge of good and evil and thus forfeits all right to paradise. The choice is both an act of hubris and quintessentially human. In Greek mythology, Prometheus and Icarus prefigure Faustus's championship of human self-assertion and the punishment that inevitably follows.[20] Circe and Medea conversely anticipate the darker aspects of enchantment and bestial transformation. The pact with the devil is an ancient tale-type, repeatedly surfacing in such works as the twelfth-century Anglo-Norman Adam and the Legenda Aurea.[21] Theophilus of Syracuse, in the sixth century, is reported to have sold his soul to the devil for an archdeaconship, though he was saved at last by the intercession of the Virgin Mary; a version of this story appears in a play by the tenth-century nun Hrotsvitha. St Cyprian is the subject of a similar account. Apocryphal stories about Zoroaster, Moses, and Solomon credited them with magical powers; Solomon's magical ring was thought to have given him authority to control nature, animals, and spirits of all kinds.[22]

Legends such as these, widely available, were part of the tradition lying behind the Damnable Life and its German original as well as Marlowe's play. So too were the stories circulated about Simon

Magus of Samaria. Like Faustus, this legendary figure of the first century reputedly called on demons to aid him in performing miracles before the Emperor and at Rome, summoned the spirits of those long dead, debated issues of cosmology, traversed the heavens in a fiery car, turned a horse into hay, apotheosised Helen of Troy, and suffered defeat (at the hands of St Peter) when he attempted to fly up to heaven. He was reputedly a masterful rhetorician. Simon's career as a great philosopher-magician and self-indulgent sensualist was amply set forth in the second-century apocryphal *Acts of Peter* and in the fourth-century *Recognitions* of Clement of Rome, texts that Marlowe would have had no difficulty in obtaining. Whether he did so in fact is a matter of debate. Those who argue for direct indebtedness point to particular moments, such as Faustus's 'O, I'll leap up to my God! Who pulls me down?' (v.ii.77), a line that perhaps recalls Simon's boastful and failed attempt to fly. More significant for Marlowe's purposes, though harder to argue as a specific source, is Simon Magus's heroic stature and potential as a figure of tragedy.[23] Both the *Acts of Peter* and the Clementine *Recognitions* pose questions about the nature of good and evil that are given little attention in the *Damnable Life*. Certainly in any case the fall of Simon Magus captured the imagination of many painters in the Italian Renaissance, including Raphael (in a painting now at the Vatican), and the iconography was widespread in Europe. At the same time Simon Magus was, like Faustus, an ambivalent figure, both heroic and debauched; negative views of him, based in part on the equation of this Simon with the sinister necromancer of Acts viii.9–24 who attempted to buy the power of the Holy Ghost, cast Simon in the role of witch and Antichrist.

Other philosopher-magicians and heretics are in ways comparable to Faustus. Roger Bacon and Piero d'Albano are both named in the play at I.i.156, as is Virgil at III.i.13–15. Paracelsus (1493–1541) was a Swiss-born doctor who became legendary for his sympathies for rich and poor alike, his eccentric habits of dress and drink, his medical heterodoxy, his battles with university doctors, and his practising of alchemy.[24] Henry Cornelius Agrippa von Nettesheim, a renowned doctor, philosopher, and theologian, was similarly enshrined in the popular imagination chiefly as a magician whose alchemical skills opened to him the secrets of eternal youth and other forbidden knowledge. Like Faustus, his power lay in books. His *De occulta philosophia* became notorious, even before it was published, and, though he retracted what he had done in his *De vanitate* (translated into English by James Sanford in 1575 as *Of the Vanity and Uncertainty of Arts and Sciences*), he later published the *De occulta philosophia* along with the retraction, as though wanting to have it both ways. His enemies, including Philipp Melanchthon, accused him of having as his companion a devil in the shape of a dog.[25] The twelfth-century Manichean bishop named Faustus, whom St Augustine attacked so vehemently in the *Confessions* and in a tract *Against Faustus* for his dualist and Gnostic heresies, anticipated his later namesake in daring to ask whether evil is coextensive with good in the battle of creation. Giordano Bruno and John Dee had become legendary as heroic questers after knowledge of the universe.[26]

Marlowe's indebtedness to the English morality play for his portrayal of inner spiritual conflict is plainly evident in the soul-struggle, the opposition of Good Angel and Evil Angel, the temptation to evil that is both comic and serious, the contrast between Faustus and the exemplary figure of the Old Man, the oscillation between comic depravity and homiletic edification. As in *Everyman* and *Mankind*, we are shown in brief span the life of a representative erring mortal whose fall into sinfulness propels him relentlessly towards the day of judgement and death. The expository Prologue and Epilogue follow the morality tradition of laying out for the audience what it is supposed to gather from the object lesson before it. *Doctor Faustus* uses dramatic techniques found in virtually every kind of morality play. The Good and Evil Angels, seldom in fact seen on the morality stage, go back to *The Castle of Perseverance*, of the early fifteenth century—a play that Marlowe may well not have known directly. Faustus's eminence as a scholar obsessed with corrupted learning mirrors concerns of the educational moralities so dear to the hearts of sixteenth-century humanists and Calvinists like John Rastell and the anonymous author of *Nice Wanton* (1547–53). The antithetical pairing of Faustus and the Old Man as reprobate and God-fearing mortal is reminiscent of Calvinist morality plays of Elizabeth's early reign, such as *The Longer Thou Livest the More Fool Thou Art* and *Enough Is as Good as a Feast*.[27] Mephistopheles, though unlike the morality Vice in that he is not aggressively the tempter, is motivated by the Vice's malign purpose. The play's structure, medieval rather than classical, owes as much to the morality tradition as it does to the tripartite scheme of the *Damnable Life*. *Doctor Faustus* is, in Clifford Leech's words, 'both the supreme example of the genre and simultaneously the play marking the genre's ending, its merging into tragedy'.[28]

To point out such indebtedness is, at the same time, to call attention to Marlowe's extraordinary alterations, even subversions, of the form he inherited. Especially when we compare *Doctor Faustus* with an early morality like *Everyman*, we see in the earlier play a testimonial to God's promises towards frail humanity as embodied in the sacraments of the Catholic Church, whereas Marlowe portrays the anxiety of a post-Reformation intellectual whose salvation rests on the unfathomable question of faith.[29] Marlowe's play is, to be sure, closer to a number of Calvinist morality plays of the 1560s and 1570s in which similar issues of reprobation and election are prominent, but even here the Marlovian sympathy for a tragic protagonist is radically different from the alienating laughter directed at worldly fools who confirm their own innate depravity by choosing evil. Nathaniel Woodes's *The Conflict of Conscience*, with its despairing hero sympathetically modelled on the spiritual biography of one Francesco Spiera or Spira (born in 1502) and its alternative endings in repentance or damnation, is potentially closest to Marlowe's play,[30] and yet even in this instance the orthodox pattern of sin and its edifying terrible consequences is undercut by Faustus's restless questioning of the idea of a divine plan.

In a similar fashion, argues Susan Snyder, Marlowe inverts and problematises the native homiletic tradition of the saint's life. Taking the fundamental hagiographical elements of early life, conversion to the true faith, reception into the church, struggles with temptation, performance of miracles, the undergoing of mystical experiences, and holy death, *Doctor Faustus* proceeds instead to tell the life of one who is 'converted' to evil, is ritually received into a diabolical church, is tempted by the Good Angel and his own conscience, performs miraculous stunts, sees heavenly visions (of Helen of Troy, among others), and is gathered up at death by his eternal master, Lucifer. The pattern helps explain the necessity of the scenes of comic degeneracy in mid play, since they depict the kinds of bogus miracles traditionally associated with Antichrist.[31] Similarly, the *Ars moriendi* tradition offers Marlowe rich lore about preparation for death that he can at once exploit and invert; he retains in his play the central Christian scheme of salvation and its focus on judgement, while at the same time generating feelings of uncertainty and conflict towards the ideals of *contemptus mundi* upon which the *Ars moriendi* tradition necessarily rests.[32]

Marlowe's use of homiletic sources is vastly enriched by his familiarity with the controversial debates of his generation between humanistic faith in transcendence and Calvinist emphasis on human depravity. His Cambridge education exposed him to an intense revaluation of the issue of human worth and self-sufficiency. The *Oration on the Dignity of Man*, written in 1486 by Giovanni Pico della Mirandola (1463–94), offered Marlowe a spirited manifesto on behalf of human aspiration. Beginning with the questions, 'why man is the most fortunate of creatures and consequently worthy of all admiration and what precisely is that rank which is his lot in the universal chain of Being', Pico depicts his human protagonist as able 'to have whatever he chooses, to be whatever he wills'. As God explains to Adam, the latter is 'constrained by no limits, in accordance with thine own free will'. Neither mortal nor immortal, but something of both, Adam is free to 'fashion thyself into whatever shape thou shalt prefer'.[33] (Lucifer's statement to Faustus in *Doctor Faustus*, 'thou shalt turn thyself into what shape thou wilt', II.iii.172–3, is ironically close to Pico.) Hermetic magic and Cabbalism can be a means to this end of self-fashioning. The Christian humanism available to Marlowe blends a Thomistic emphasis on the limited but real capacity of the reason to approach God with a still more optimistic Neoplatonic faith, as expressed in the writings of Pico, Bruno, Ficino, Pomponazzi, and Telesio, in an almost unlimited ability to transcend earthbound limitations.[34] As Faustus exults:

O, what a world of profit and delight,
Of power, of honour, of omnipotence,
Is promised to the studious artisan! (I.i.55–7)

Yet *Doctor Faustus* is manifestly a critique of humanistic aspirations, not simply an endorsement of them. Even in the lines quoted above, we hear already the note of sensual gratification and longing for sheer power, along with the excitement. Faustus's anthropocentric daring captures the optimism of the Italian Neoplatonists, but it does not sufficiently account for the limitless depravity of human nature that is also deeply inscribed in the world of *Doctor Faustus*. St Augustine had posed long ago the question that Faustus cannot resolve: 'What can cause the will's evil, the will being the sole cause of all evil?'[35] Augustine's insistence that human nature cannot hope to know the reasons for God's rejection of some reprobate sinners was enormously influential in Reformation England among Puritans and Anglicans alike. William Perkins, fellow of Christ's College, Cambridge, when Marlowe was a student at that university, makes clear his indebtedness to St Augustine:

> The cause of the decree of God in rejecting some is unsearchable, and . . . it doth not at all depend upon any foreseen contumacy towards the grace of God offered in the Gospel. . . . For if it were otherwise, we might easily give a reason of God's decree. Augustine, epist. 105, saith very well: *Who* (saith he) *created the reprobates but God? And why, but because it pleased him? But why pleased it him? O man, who art thou that disputest with God?*[36]

Here then was a theology that rejected the very premises of Neoplatonic optimism, in that it refused to acknowledge a perfectible free will capable of self-fashioning and would not even allow that the causes for failure were knowable through human reasoning.

Certainly Doctor Faustus faces a Protestant dilemma. The stunning mood of alienation and loss that we experience in the play owes much of its force to a new sense of the isolated human soul in Luther's and Calvin's views of salvation. Both of these thinkers, and the English Church as well, denied to the individual Christian the comfort of the miraculous that had been so abundant in the medieval Catholic faith. A Homily 'Of the Worthy Receiving of the Sacraments' rejected any conception of the Holy Communion in a corporeal and magical sense; to consider it thus was 'but to dream a gross carnal feeding'.[37] The reassuring family constellation of the Trinity and the Virgin Mary, together with all the saints, progressively gave way to a more direct confrontation between the individual sinner and his or her angry God. In these circumstances, penitence became not a sacrament administered by the Church but a process of wrestling with one's conscience—a struggle at once essential to salvation and yet unmeasurable in effect. Despair, not uncommon in the turmoil of intense personal deliberation, was variously interpreted as potentially healthy (by Luther) or as a sign of predestinate evil (by Calvin).[38]

How was the individual to know whether he or she was saved or predestinately damned? The consequences were immeasurable. As the seventeenth of the Thirty-Nine Articles put it:

> As the godly consideration of predestination and our election in Christ is full of sweet, pleasant, and unspeakable comfort to godly persons . . . so, for curious and carnal persons, lacking the spirit of Christ, to have continually before their eyes the sentence of God's predestination is a most dangerous downfall, whereby the devil doth thrust them either into desperation or into recklessness of most unclean living, no less perilous than desperation.[39]

No Christian could consider these alternatives without longing for reassurance. Yet Luther and Calvin alike insisted that God's motives in this regard were unfathomable.

Luther's God is, as Paul Sellin aptly describes him, terrible and majestic, omnipotent, eternal, 'incomprehensible, inscrutable, infallible, immense, awesome, and above all hidden'.[40] We as humans cannot understand him through his works and can have no certainty of his intentions, especially in particular cases. That God has evidently decreed salvation for some mortals and damnation for others can be deduced from experience. God foreknows all that he wills, and for that reason sin must be understood to be inevitable, and yet, says Luther, 'it must be laid to the charge of our own will if we perish'.[41] The fault 'is in the will which does not receive Him'. Moreover, 'why the Majesty does not remove or change this fault of will in every man (for it is not in the power of man to do it), or why He lays this fault to the charge of the will, when man cannot avoid it, it is not lawful to ask' (pp. 191–2). God hardens the hearts of the reprobate, and yet is not himself to blame: 'God works evil in us (that is, by means of us) not through God's own fault, but by reason of our own defect'. God finds Satan's will to be evil rather than creating it so; God moves that evil which way he wills, and yet Satan 'will not cease to be evil in virtue of this movement of God' (p. 193). The question that heretically arises at this point, whether God is not ultimately the author of Satan's evil, is one that Luther will not address. Nor will he say why God will not move to virtue the hearts of the reprobate other than to say that the question 'touches on the secrets of His Majesty' (p. 195). Election or reprobation cannot depend on our merits, nor is the Church in a position to provide institutional redress; the Church is instead a community of the elect, and its sacraments are signs of a grace already abounding for those who have been chosen.

Calvin's position is alike in many respects, especially in the view of God as the awesome and unknowable author of predestination. For Calvin, as for Luther, 'it is very wicked merely to investigate the causes of God's will'.[42] Calvin accentuates this mystery by insisting on the one hand that God hardens the hearts of the reprobate and on the other hand that God's doing so is to be seen as a vital element in his plan, one that we must glorify even while perceiving that the impenitent sinner is utterly doomed by it. Far from challenging God's majesty by imputing evil to him, Calvin sees double predestination as the perfect embodiment of God's mercy and justice. Human failure is a part of God's plan. Since the grace of salvation 'was founded upon his freely given mercy, without regard to human worth', that salvation is his to bestow or not as he wishes; we may not repine that 'by his just and irreprehensible but incomprehensible judgment he has barred the door of life to those whom he has given over to damnation'.[43] Calvin's views were to be found everywhere in the official positions of the Anglican Church, as for example in the ninth of the 'Lambeth Articles' approved by Bishop Whitgift in 1595: 'It is not placed in the will or power of every man to be saved.'[44]

The consequences for humankind, and for Doctor Faustus, are sobering. If, in the Calvinist view, even Adam chose not freely but 'because he could not resist the ordinance of his God',[45] Faustus's ability to resist temptation or find contrition in his heart cannot be said to exist at all. Conscience is no certain help, since it may be only the censoring voice of one's own innate evil.

Marlowe was, as M. M. Mahood argues, 'acutely aware that he was living in an age of revolt, whose intellectuals were making the claims of self-sufficiency in innumerable ways. Marlowe may have shared in that revolt; but he had a clearer understanding than any of his contemporaries of its disastrous effects, and for this reason his tragedies record the disintegration of humanism'.[46] Marlowe was thus, as Richard Hardin puts it, 'of two minds about the sufficiency of the knowledge offered by Cicero, Isocrates, and Homer'.[47] In part this uncertainty was the result of the Lutheran–Calvinist challenge to human self-sufficiency. And nowhere in England could Marlowe have encountered a more vigorous debate between the extreme Calvinist position and its challengers than at Cambridge.[48] His Cambridge education exposed him both to a disputatious, rhetorical study of classical texts, including Aristotle, Homer, Demosthenes, Hesiod, and the like, and to exercises in the handling of scripture and doctrine.[49]

Doctor Faustus attests to a wide-ranging if impatient acquaintance with classical learning and a thorough conversance with the Bible and liturgy.[50] The play's author is well acquainted with the basics of Elizabethan psychology[51] and with Seneca.[52] In a more popular vein, Marlowe seems to be in touch with folklore tale types of the wasted wish and the foolish bargain, and is well versed in lore about witchcraft. (Faustus is clearly a witch, as defined by William Perkins: 'A witch is a magician who, either by open or secret league, wittingly and willingly consenteth to use the aid and assistance of the devil in

the working of wonders.')[53] The comic scenes, with their emphasis
on dismemberment and curing, recall the action of folk plays, especially of the swordplay type.[54] The play's vernacular roots go back to
burlesque rituals of communal gargantuan feeding as found earlier in
the *Secunda Pastorum* and other cycle plays,[55] and to country mum-
mings of the 'eldritch' type in which the grotesque comedy of false
limbs and severed heads borders on the demonic.[56] The very diver-
sity and range of Marlowe's learning ought to prepare us for a play
in which dialectical conflict and contrasting points of view form a
basic rhetorical vocabulary.

THE ORTHODOX FRAMEWORK

The polarities of Marlowe's fascination with Lutheran–Calvinist
determinism and with Italian humanism are amply evident in the
play itself, and in critical responses to it. Few plays have called
forth such a divided response. Leo Kirschbaum speaks for a large
number of orthodox readers when he declares, 'there is no more obvious Christian document in all Elizabethan drama than *Doctor
Faustus*'.[57] Conversely, Harry Levin, Paul Kocher, and Irving
Ribner speak for those who find the essence of Faustus's tragedy in
his Promethean daring and his doomed but heroic attempt to gain
for humanity some access to the secrets of the universe and some
mastery over our fate.[58] The very fact of this divided response may
be significant, suggesting as it does a sustained ambiguity for which
the dialectical form of drama is especially well suited.[59] The debate
centres on the hard question of sympathy for the protagonist. Are we
meant to assent to Faustus's doom, and is it just?

The opening Prologue, derived as we have seen from conventions
of medieval homiletic drama, certainly offers disapproving comment
that any orthodox reading of the play takes to heart. Faustus profits
in his studies in divinity, we are told, until, 'swoll'n with cunning of
a self-conceit', he strives to 'mount above his reach' on 'waxen
wings' and is brought down. His aspiration is a 'devilish exercise',
disfigured by gluttony and surfeit. 'Cursèd necromancy' means more
to this magician than 'his chiefest bliss'—presumably his immortal
soul. At the same time the image of waxen wings conjures up the
myth of Daedalus and Icarus, a story that could iconographically
signify satanic presumption or an aspiration in which humanity's
chief fault was to have challenged the prerogative of the gods. The
Chorus's insistence that the heavens have 'conspired' Faustus's over-

throw is in keeping with a legend of rebellion and its suppression. Can 'conspired' be reconciled with Christian orthodoxies of God's foreknowing and predetermining all things? The word has a flavour of its own.

In the Epilogue, as well, orthodox denunciation of one whose 'hellish fall' and 'fiendful fortune may exhort the wise / Only to wonder at unlawful things' is mixed with regret for the cutting of a branch that might have grown full straight and admiring sympathy for the artist-magician who has dared to 'practise more than heavenly power permits'. 'Power' is a resonant word in Marlowe, and here it pictures human destiny in the language of subversion and control.

From his very first appearance on stage, Faustus incessantly undercuts the potential splendour of his intellectual heterodoxy by misrepresenting the learning of which he is so intolerant. Orthodox criticism makes much of Faustus's shoddy scholarship, asking whether we can take seriously a professional scholar who confuses and misquotes his sources. His supposedly Aristotelian definition of logic, *Bene disserere est finis logices* (I.i.7), turns out to be from Ramus, and *On kai me on* (l. 12) is from the sceptic sophist Gorgias.[60] Ramus had an unsavoury reputation in some quarters for pretentious disputation and for reducing Aristotle to superficialities.[61] When Faustus rejects Galen in hopes of being able to raise the dead to life again (l. 25), he blasphemously equates himself with Christ.[62] His motives for turning to medicine are self-aggrandising, to 'Heap up gold, / And be eternised for some wondrous cure' (ll. 14–15). His sneering at jurisprudence reveals less about the unworthiness of the law itself than about Faustus's irritation at a discipline too dry and 'mercenary' for his talent. Faustus's impatience is bred as much by arrogance and misunderstanding of the traditional disciplines as by an eagerness to go beyond their bounds.

When Faustus comes to divinity, then, orthodox criticism warns us that we should be prepared for the dismissive and sophomoric demolition that he attempts. Any fool can construct a syllogism proving that, since the wages of sin is death and since we deceive ourselves if we say we have no sin, we all must die (ll. 39–47). Presumably, too, any moderately knowledgeable Christian in Marlowe's audience would have known that Faustus has rigged his syllogism by neglecting to quote in full the source of its two premises. The first should read, 'For the wages of sin is death, but the gift of God is eternal life through Jesus Christ our Lord' (Romans vi.23); the second, 'If we say we have no sin, we deceive ourselves, and truth is not in us. If we acknowledge our sins, he is faithful and just to forgive us our sins and to cleanse us from all unrighteousness' (1 John i.8–9).[63] An Elizabethan audience, used to hearing disputations on biblical texts, would presumably have been quicker than we to detect Faustus's fallacies.[64]

While we need not agree with the derisive statements of some moralistic critics that Faustus is a mere 'addle-pated pilgrim of the absolute' who 'cannot conceive of true wisdom', since he 'never recognizes the proper object of human learning, the highest human perspectives of the Augustinian teaching',[65] orthodox criticism performs a useful service by characterising Faustus's slothful intellectual habits and logical short circuits. At the least, when Faustus himself begins by postulating that 'to dispute well' is 'logic's chiefest end' (l. 8), we may be permitted to wonder if he has not cut himself off from some greater purpose. He is not only a bad Christian but a bad humanist as well. He subverts the very intellectual process by which he ought to be questing after knowledge and truth. Faustus abandons from the start his intellectual powers in favour of rationalisation. He eschews the kind of logical rigour by which humankind, in Faustus's own view, can best demonstrate its superior place in the great chain of being, and settles increasingly instead for sarcasm and hairsplitting. Perhaps his failures represent in part the failures and contradictions of humanism itself, especially what M. M. Mahood calls the 'humanistic fallacy' of creating false barriers between God and mortals whereby humankind will bring about its own undoing.[66]

Orthodox criticism usefully points out what is depraved and selfish in Faustus's seemingly public-spirited plans, although a more inclusive reading of motivation allows for some sympathy as well. His determination to clothe all the students of the public schools in silk (ll. 92–3), in direct contravention of university statutes in the English and German universities, strikes G. I. Duthie as 'not commendable but subversive, not admirable but insolent, and ridiculous as well',[67] but for a reader less enamoured of dress codes the gesture can be interpreted as a blow for academic freedom and the rights of students. Faustus's patriotic resolve to 'wall all Germany with brass' and 'chase the Prince of Parma from our land' is qualified by his simultaneous wish to 'reign sole king of all our provinces' (ll. 90–6), but even Gonzalo in *The Tempest* is guilty of a similar vanity. Faustus's pride in having 'gravelled' the pastors of the German Church and 'made the flow'ring pride of Wittenberg / Swarm to my problems' (ll. 115–17) is proof, to Kirschbaum, that Faustus suffers from 'intellectual pride to an odious degree', and that he 'relishes his inflated sense of his own abilities',[68] and yet we should remember that the Chorus credits Faustus with 'Excelling all whose sweet delight disputes / In heavenly matters of theology' (Prologue. 18–19). So too with other charges levelled at Faustus that he is cowardly, deluded, egocentric, emotionally and intellectually unstable, and so on. Faustus is presented to us as either the 'aspiring titan' or the 'self-deluded fool',[69] or perhaps both.

Faustus's essential folly is that he exchanges his eternal soul for twenty-four short years of frivolous and self-indulgent pleasure. In orthodox terms, he does so because he is guilty of pride, the most deadly of the Seven Deadly Sins. Since the treatment of pride in the moral theology of Marlowe's age was such a commonplace, Martin Versfeld argues, an Elizabethan audience would understand that Faustus's sin is to 'claim for himself what belongs properly to God', as Satan did before him. Faustus 'does not wish to admit the authority of created order and therefore of things over his mind'.[70] Lucifer's very name reminds us of the once-bright 'Prince of the East' whose fall through pride, as understood in exegetical tradition, serves as the great archetype for Faustus's spiritual biography.[71] His 'usurpation upon the Deity' amounts to a repudiation of humanity, in Roland Frye's view, not an attempted emancipation of it, since Faustus vaingloriously chooses to emulate God as a rival and to preoccupy himself with his own 'ascension above humanity'.[72] Pride is the essential link between Faustus's sin and the original sin of Adam in the Garden of Eden.[73]

Pride can assume various guises, and is multiformly linked to other forms of sinfulness. Gerard Cox's argument that Faustus is guilty of all the so-called 'sins of the Holy Ghost'—presumption, despair, impenitence, obstinacy, resistance to known truth, and envy of a brother's spiritual good—sees presumption, or pride, as the first and most inclusive of these sins.[74] Similarly, to argue that Faustus's fatal sin is despair[75] is to acknowledge the inseparable link between presumption and despair; the arrogance of believing oneself self-fashioned and complete without God gives way easily to despairing of God's love. Even so, pride has its ambiguous aspect as well. When James Smith and J. C. Maxwell astutely observe in Faustus's temperament the particular kind of pride that goes under the name of 'curiosity',[76] they point to something in him that is certainly obsessive and debased but is also quintessentially human and deserving of sympathy. Who would wish to be human and not 'curious'?

Because the Seven Deadly Sins are so closely related to one another in traditional scholastic exegesis and are so theatrically present in *Doctor Faustus*, orthodox critics are able to illustrate abundantly the link between Faustus and all of the Deadly Sins. Lorraine Stock, while not denying the primacy of pride, argues that Faustus's sinfulness manifests itself in behavioural terms as gluttony, much as Adam and Eve manifested their disobedience through their eating of the forbidden fruit. Verbal metaphors in the play of devouring and of surfeit draw upon iconographical traditions showing gluttony to be 'the fault of Adam' and the repudiation of gluttony the first victory of Christ's temptation in the wilderness. Marlowe's depiction of Faustus's gluttony is thus 'theologically sound'.[77] Other critics have made similar cases for sloth, lechery, and cupidity,[78] along with the sins already mentioned above. Gluttony, avarice (cupidity), and disobedience (pride), symbolising flesh, world, and devil, were all proposed by medieval exegetes as the cause of Adam's original sin.[79] The comic scenes (many of them by Marlowe's collaborator) are especially rich in parodic representations of the Seven Deadly Sins, both in their actual appearance on stage (II.iii.107.1 ff.) and in jests about shoulders of mutton, wenches' plackets, greedy servants, carousing church dignitaries, and the like.[80]

The desire of orthodox critics to know precisely when Faustus is damned can take on at times the exaggerated dimensions of a dispute about theology rather than a play. James Smith contends that when Faustus signs the contract, 'at that moment, and without delay, he plunges to spiritual death'.[81] W. W. Greg, essentially in agreement, asks if the wording of Faustus's contract, according to which Faustus is made 'a spirit in form and substance' (II.i.97), does not indicate the end of meaningful choice for Faustus; devils are persistently called 'spirits' in the play, and if Faustus is in effect a devil after affixing his signature he is beyond redemption. When the Evil Angel insists to Faustus that 'Thou art a spirit. God cannot pity thee' (II.iii.13), he seems to argue an inflexible link between being a 'spirit' and being irrevocably damned. Helen too is a spirit, Greg notes, and so when Faustus takes her as his paramour he commits the sin of demoniality, or bodily intercourse with demons, thereby confirming his state of irredeemable depravity.[82] Roma Gill, accepting Greg's argument in the main but noting that the Old Man does not give up in his attempts to counsel Faustus until Faustus vows to take Helen as his paramour (v.i.110 ff.), argues that the moment of irreversible damnation occurs precisely at this point.[83]

Yet for many, Greg's Calvinist interpretation must do battle with the
repeated insistence that it is 'never too late' to repent (see, for
example, II.iii.12 and 79, and v.i.36–57), while Gill's search for a
point of irreversibility late in the play rests on the questionable
supposition that the Old Man and the Good Angel would abandon
their efforts simply because Faustus embraces his paramour and thus
allows Helen literally to suck forth his soul (v.i.94). Surely in the
theatre the struggle for damnation or salvation runs through the
play; to award Faustus irrecoverably to the devil at some earlier
point satisfies Calvinist theology at the expense of dramatic tension
and uncertainty.[84]

On the central issue of divine justice in Faustus's damnation, the
orthodox view is that *Doctor Faustus* does not differ materially in its
theology from Genesis, St Augustine, Dante, or Milton. Heaven and
hell of course exist. If hell is both a place of physical torment and a
state of mind, Protestant theology stands ready to explain that
the physical tortures of the damned may partly be understood as
metaphor, since, in view of our limited human understanding, hell
needs to be 'figuratively expressed to us by physical things', such as
unquenchable fire and the gnawing of worms at the heart. When
Calvin puts the matter this way, however, he in no way means to
deny the reality of hell, which is above all a condition of separation
from God.[85] Faustus is, like Adam, fully informed of the consequences of his choice. And, although he (abetted by the Evil
Angel) cries out towards the end that he cannot repent, and that his
guilt is too great for God to pardon, such despair is his own. His will
is in bondage to evil, in just the way that the Wittenberg reformers,
Luther and Melanchthon, explain that it will surely be for any
reprobate whose sin is lack of faith.[86]

Despair is, in medieval tradition, a sin that may well prove fatal,
for it denies God's power to forgive. In despairing, Faustus re-enacts
the crime of Judas, who sinned like many a frail mortal in selling
Christ but who then refused to accept that he could be pardoned for
his crime.[87] And if Judas's crime of selling the Lord was forgivable,
Faustus's must be also. His failure to repent is his supreme act of
folly, certainly no less so than his pact with the devil. Faustus sees
even in his last hours Christ's blood streaming in the firmament
(v.ii.78), confirming the Old Man's vision of an angel that hovers
over Faustus's head 'And with a vial full of precious grace / Offers to
pour the same into thy soul' (v.i.55–6). The last debate about
salvation is not between the Good and Evil Angels but between

the Old Man and Faustus himself. It is Faustus who, in his own
intransigence, pronounces sentence: 'Damned art thou, Faustus,
damned! Despair and die!' (v.i.49). He does so partly out of terror
for what Mephistopheles will surely do to him otherwise; fear is,
after all, the obverse of Faustus's love of pleasure. His cravenness
in asking that Mephistopheles torment the Old Man for tempting
Faustus to good is one last sign of his deeply corrupted nature.
Perhaps it is this action, more than Faustus's resolution to take a
paramour, that persuades the Old Man finally to abandon the cause
of one who excludes 'the grace of heaven' and flies 'the throne of His
tribunal seat' (v.i.112–13).

The central problem with most orthodox interpretations of *Doctor
Faustus* is that they often verge on lack of sympathy, even open
hostility. To the extent that Faustus is a negative object lesson, we
are distanced from him. The result is, for the purposes of tragedy, a
diminished protagonist and a conventionalised 'message' that can
sound reductively homiletic. Methodologically, as Harriet Hawkins
observes, the case for orthodoxy is often predictable and boring, and
is one that can be applied to any literary work of past centuries:
the critic explains away seeming heterodoxy by pointing to a basic
morality-play or exegetical structure underlying the play according
to which the rebel stands condemned, thereby awakening in an
Elizabethan audience its expected and normal response to a traditionally hierarchical world picture. The formulaic method works
against individuality of texts and of audiences, and in effect joins
forces with Plato in his unwillingness to admire on stage or in poetry
any behaviour that in our daily lives we would consider deplorable.[88]

At its best, orthodox interpretation endeavours to meet these
criticisms. One strategy is to enlarge the meaning of 'orthodox', as in
Moelwyn Merchant's argument that contradiction and duality are
the essence of any Renaissance (or even medieval) vision of humankind. Nowhere does Marlowe show himself 'more characteristically
at the meeting-point of medieval and Renaissance values', says
Merchant, 'than in his constant examination of man's "striving after
knowledge infinite" and his continuous awareness that inordinate
aspiration leads perversely to triviality'.[89] The vision of Faustus as
fool need not then deprive him of tragic stature, for human fate can
be defined universally in tragic terms of doomed aspiration. Robert
West, in his investigation of witchcraft in the play, makes the case
for a Faustus who is undeniably besotted, impetuous, self-indulgent,
even stupid, but whose daring is 'sustained by no common means,

and at infinite cost'. Demonology offers nothing morally redemptive
in Faustus's defence, but it does seem appropriate to a protagonist
who is 'a man of stature' and whose fate 'is dramatically moving'.[90]
We do assent to Faustus's damnation, in West's view, because
Faustus is offered and then denies the chance of salvation that is
open to any Christian, but the assent is to a doom both 'deserved'
and 'tragic'. West and Merchant alike reach for universality in the
tragic protagonist, a universality that we can regard with sympathy
even while we perceive that it is couched in terms of the orthodoxies
of a Renaissance world view. We must now examine more heterodox
arguments that ask if Marlowe does in fact assent to the divine
retribution that is so plainly registered in the play's final action.

Those critics like Una Ellis-Fermor and Irving Ribner who sympathise with Faustus's challenging of divine authority at the risk of
eternal punishment sometimes begin by viewing *Doctor Faustus* in
the context of Marlowe's other plays, especially the two parts of
Tamburlaine. Although Faustus ends in limitation and failure, he is
like Tamburlaine a person of humble origins who dares to assert his
individual will in defiance of the gods. To Irving Ribner, the comparison shows *Doctor Faustus* to be no Christian morality play. To be
sure, *Doctor Faustus* depicts a Christian religious cosmos in extensive
detail, but does so without offering any sense of goodness or justice
in that system. The play is instead, says Ribner, a protest against a
system that imposes 'a limitation upon the aspirations of man,
holding him in subjection and bondage, denying him at last even
the comfort of Christ's blood, and dooming him to the most terrible destruction'. Even if we grant that Faustus degenerates into a
trivialiser of his magic powers and a cowering wretch, this is not to
say 'that the order of things which decrees such human deteriora-
tion as the price of aspiration beyond arbitrary limits is affirmed
by Marlowe as a good and just one'. The play is 'essentially anti-
Christian' in its extraordinarily pessimistic statement 'of the futility
of human aspiration'.[91] Even if *Doctor Faustus* is a later and more
troubled play than *Tamburlaine*, perhaps even a recantation, we can
at least see that Faustus shares with Tamburlaine the temperament
of an overreacher in a cosmic battle between gods and men.[92] If in
Doctor Faustus 'Marlowe denies the possibility of that harmony
between ambition and salvation, between heroic *virtù* and Christian

virtue, which he once postulated in *1 Tamburlaine* but in which he could no longer believe',[93] the change of heart does not necessarily bring Marlowe any closer to acceptance of orthodox Christianity than in the earlier play.

Any such view of *Doctor Faustus* as a pessimistic and sceptical statement postulates a deeply personal meaning on the part of its author. The biographical hypothesis is problematic, in part because of the uncertain reliability of the so-called Baines note and other testimonials to Marlowe's heterodoxy at the end of his life[94] and in part because of the danger of making too simplified an equation between biography and art. These hazards do not, however, deter those critics who respond deeply to what they feel to be an unmistakably Marlovian presence in all his plays and especially in this one. Ellis-Fermor reads the play as an expression of Marlowe's own agony of loss.[95] So does Paul Kocher, for whom Marlowe's own heterodoxy is, on the whole, beyond doubt. In Kocher's view, *Doctor Faustus* 'stands in a succession of other dramas of decisively anti-Christian colouring written by a man of violently anti-Christian beliefs'. Marlowe really had only one great theme, argues Kocher, and that was himself. Kocher's Marlowe is a militantly anti-Christian person in whom there nevertheless remain, 'no doubt repressed and scorned, strong vestiges of the old beliefs in which he had been educated since infancy'. The result is 'an inner religious conflict which manifests itself frequently in his plays'.[96] What we find in *Doctor Faustus*, according to Kocher, is a persistent voice of doubt that works against the orthodox cosmic framework. Faustus's derisive rejoinder to Mephistopheles, 'Come, I think hell's a fable' (II.i.130), and the Evil Angel's dismissal of prayers as 'illusions, fruits of lunacy, / That makes men foolish that do trust them most' (ll. 18–19), have the same note of bravado that we hear in the Baines note and the Kyd letters. They are of course the utterances of deluded or vicious characters, and they are amply answered in the play's debate, but they do attest to the presence of 'contrary systems of value'.[97] Ribner similarly contends that 'the play is not a mirror of Christian certainty but of agnostic intellectual confusion'.[98]

The question of interpretation, then, becomes one of arguing how we are to 'read' the orthodoxy that governs the plot of *Doctor Faustus*. Kocher offers a clever if unprovable argument: the orthodoxy, though 'real' enough in the world of the play, is essentially a convenient cover for a dramatist who wishes to indulge in protest against that orthodoxy. The theme of spiritual conflict, waged according to the rules of the Christian world view, 'allows Marlowe congenial opportunities of blaspheming without fear of being called to account. Through Faustus he can utter strictures on prayer, on Hell, on the harshness of Christian dogma, and then cover them safely with the usual orthodox replies'.[99] Marlowe never overthrows the Christian world picture with his 'iconoclastic sallies', in Kocher's view, but he does unsettle the audience by asking uncomfortable questions about the supposed justice of the system. This is no doubt persuasive to those who view Marlowe as a sceptic, but it will seem like a circular argument to orthodox readers for whom Faustus's iconoclasm is a convincing demonstration of his fitness for damnation. Can heterodox interpretation find a surer basis than this upon which to build a sceptical reading?

Simon Shepherd adroitly addresses the question by asking whether Marlowe's use of surprisingly modern dramaturgical techniques of alienation and montage (thus partly anticipating Brecht and Eisenstein) does not undermine the authority of the play's dramatic form in such a way as to make the 'message' of the text more 'complex and opaque' than 'single and normative'. What constitutes authority in this play? The only physical sign of heaven (found in the B-text only) 'is also an emblem of state control, a throne'. The Good Angel exhorts Faustus to read the Scriptures (1.i.75), but 'reading in the play is marked as a problem'. The play problematises experience too as a guarantor of certainty; indeed, in the last analysis all truths are seen as beyond human knowledge and the power of language to explain truth adequately. In the theatre we hear the magnificent poetry and witness the scenic illusion, but are afforded no normative fixed point in the play's staging by which to resolve sceptical questioning. Cohesion is perhaps a will o' the wisp as an interpretive goal; unsettling contradictions and ambiguities may give us a truer glimpse of the play's restless uncertainty about the ultimate authority of divine truth.[100] This poststructuralist reading will perhaps not win many adherents among those who are out of sympathy with recent criticism, but it has the great advantage of addressing a distinctively contradictory quality in Marlowe's dramatic writing.

The uncertainty of fixed meaning encourages a reading of *Doctor Faustus* as 'almost the spiritual autobiography of an age' in a richly complex sense defined for us by Wilbur Sanders: Faustus, as a 'man of the Renaissance', stands 'at the centre of a vast network of conflicting ideas', his mind 'half free, half bound', neither essentially medieval nor modern. Even if his humanism seems deficient in its lack of humane breadth and generosity, it lacks nothing in the way of excitement and challenge; he is seriously committed 'to thought, experiment, living, discussion, discovery'.[101] Faustus is, like Oedipus (whose curiosity also destroyed him), a problem solver. Having been 'ravished' by Aristotle's *Analytics*, Faustus wants no more to do with philosophy because he has 'attained the end' (1.i.10). He has likewise achieved the end of curing the human body of its ills (1. 18), and so the conquering of death (in an age constantly threatened by plague) is the only new endeavour open to him; if to dare so is blasphemous, let that be God's problem. Law strikes Faustus as too 'illiberal' (1. 36)—a word that evokes the ideal of the Liberal Arts. His rejection of divinity is of course opprobrious and sophomoric, but one motive at least is the scholar's impatient desire to move on to new and controversial fields that can hold out to the 'studious artisan' the promise of 'profit and delight' (ll. 55–7)—the time-honoured goals of Horace's *dulce et utile*. Faustus's prolonged encounter with the four traditional university disciplines,[102] then, has left him unsatisfied in a number of ways that might make sense to a one-time Cambridge student: the scholar finds himself desiring more power in the real world, more of its wealth and comfort, and more areas of knowledge he can conquer.

Orthodox scholars correctly insist that we listen to the Good Angel's reproofs, but we must listen to the Evil Angel as well, for he is given equal time and equal presence in the theatre. He offers Faustus a 'famous art' by which a man can be 'on earth as Jove is in the sky, / Lord and commander of these elements' (ll. 76–9). This is blasphemy, of course, but not very different in its optimism from Tamburlaine's 'Is it not passing brave to be a king / And ride in triumph through Persepolis' (Part I, II.v.53–4). The poetry commands a vital kind of assent, that of our wonderment at the vastness of the speaker's dream. Faustus is flirting dangerously with magic, but are we sure that we can distinguish between magic and poetry? Can we fail to sympathise with the artist who finds philosophy, law, medicine, and theology odious and harsh in comparison with the ravishing prospect of Lapland giants or of young women who display 'more beauty in their airy brows / Than in the white breasts of the Queen of Love' (1.i.108–11, 128–31)? If Faustus is an epicure he is also an adventurer, one who delights as much in the seven hills of Rome as he does in discomfiting the Pope. And in the theatre our own journey is no less one of delight and discovery.

Faustus's conjuration of Mephistopheles has of course its ludicrous aspect. He spouts mumbo-jumbo, jests coarsely about friars' robes as best suited to the devil, and learns that Mephistopheles has come on his own accord to win the soul of one who has racked the name of God (I.iii.48) rather than in response to the power of Faustus's magic. The folly of Faustus's aspiration is apparent, and his sceptical refusal to be terrified of damnation (1. 60) is manifestly indefensible in view of Mephistopheles's plain assurance that damnation lies in wait for whose who abjure the Scriptures. Indeed, even before he signs the contract Faustus imperfectly knows that he will be damned, and enters into the agreement as much out of a conviction that God does not love him as out of desire for honour and wealth (II.i.1–21). The confusion of aims, the unhappiness even before the prize is first achieved, are poignantly real. Yet this negative vision is offset to a significant degree by the intrepidity with which Faustus stabs his arm and perseveres in his bad bargain when divine warning—*Homo, fuge*—appears visibly before him. And the intrepidity is inspired, in part at least, by his intellectual curiosity. The first use he wishes to make of his ill-gotten power is to ask more questions about hell.

Faustus thinks hell 'a fable' (II.i.130), or thinks so at times. How can he maintain such a position in view of Mephistopheles's wry assurance that experience will convince him of the contrary (1. 131), and Mephistopheles's vivid accounts of hell as an absence from God that terrifies the soul even to think about (I.iii.78–84)? No question haunts Faustus more than that of hell's existence and its nature. He believes himself damned to hell one moment and scoffs at the idea of hell the next. Possibly it is the corporeal image of physical suffering that poses the greatest challenge to his imperfect understanding, for the torments of hell are at once intellectually incredible to him and personally terrifying to one who will suffer them if they are real. Mephistopheles's answers, for all their startling candour, create uncertainty for Faustus because they do seem to allow a kind of hell that an intellectual might actually enjoy. Hell is evidently a place where one can dispute with colleagues. 'Nay, an this be hell', rejoins Faustus, 'I'll willingly be damned here. What? Walking, disputing, etc.?' (II.i.141–3). One might say that at this moment Faustus's idea of hell is of a university made up of congenial sceptics like himself. For one who cannot will himself to believe in God, at least in a God who offers mercy to sinners like himself, this will do very nicely. As long as those frightening stories of pain after life are 'trifles and mere old wives' tales' (l. 138), Faustus has found the very condition that his intellectual premises have dictated. When he longs for books to increase his knowledge of and control over the heavens and all things on earth, they are given to him (II.i.162 ff.).

Faustus's inquiries into astronomy are at the heart of the play and of any sceptical interpretation of it. His questioning of the universe goes into far more detail than is suggested in Marlowe's chief source, the *Damnable Life*, and examines issues on which Renaissance thinkers were sharply divided. It is true of course that Faustus learns nothing he did not know before, thus seeming to confirm the orthodox view that he is simply prying into the unknowable and the illusory; indeed, most of the play's astronomical lore could have been found in the third volume of Pierre de la Primaudaye's *The French Academy*, not published in England until after Marlowe's death but available in French. Still, we must understand that his investigations take Marlowe where sceptical minds were at debate. Francis Johnson shows that Marlowe raises problems 'inspired by the disagreement among the astronomical textbooks then current at Cambridge, and has the answers given by Mephistopheles accord with the doctrine expounded by the unconventional rather than the more orthodox authorities'. That is, Marlowe does not rely on the conventional system of ten spheres within the empyrean of neo-Aristotelian cosmology, but chooses instead a system of eight spheres within the empyrean that was espoused by the 'skeptical, empirical school among Renaissance astronomical writers' including Augustinus Ricius (or Ricci), Orintius Finaeus (or Finé), John Dee, and Agrippa.[103]

How much more did Marlowe know or suspect about the new astronomy, especially the Copernican revolution? Dee had quite a reputation in England as a heterodox thinker, and Marlowe seems to have known his work. Marlowe must also have been acquainted with the opinions on Copernicus of Richard Harvey, Thomas Harriott, and Giordano Bruno (who visited England). Thomas Digges's writings were published in the 1570s. Only three years after Marlowe's death, Thomas Nashe referred familiarly to Copernicus as the author 'who held that the sun remains immovable in the center of the world, and that the earth is moved about the sun'.[104] Marlowe does not allude to the Copernican sun-centred system in his play, but he does give his audience reason to wonder if the whole truth has yet been told.

Faustus's discourse with Mephistopheles on astronomy breathes with impatience to know more and with an intellectual conviction that more is there to be learned if ignorance, superstition, and divine prohibition can be swept aside. Even the controversial and modified Ptolemaic system that Mephistopheles lays before Faustus embodies 'slender trifles Wagner can decide' and 'freshmen's suppositions' (II.iii.49–56). There is something not only insultingly elementary about Mephistopheles's whole lecture, which Faustus can interrupt and finish himself, but something fishy. How is this cosmology to explain why we have not 'conjunctions, oppositions, aspects, eclipses all at one time, but in some years we have more, in some less' (ll. 62–5)? This is the question that, in the later sixteenth century, tested the adequacy of the Ptolemaic system itself. Why do the planets move at times in a retrograde direction, creating, especially for Mars and the inner planets, mathematical anomalies that made the whole look increasingly absurd? Tycho Brahe's complex elaborations of the epicycles needed to make the Ptolemaic system work were devised precisely to answer the question posed by Faustus in his insistence that Mephistopheles tell him something new.

What answer does Faustus get from Mephistopheles? '*Per inaequalem motum respectu totius*', 'because of inequal motion with respect to the whole' (l. 65). Oddly, this interchange has received almost no attention in critical discussions of Marlowe's sceptical astronomy. Even Pierre Tibi, who recognises that Mephistopheles's answer is a thundering cliché ('il y a là, pour un esprit de l'époque, l'équivalent d'un truisme'), is content to be surprised that Faustus is so easily satisfied.[105] But is he? Faustus's 'Well, I am answered' (l. 66) can be read in a much more despondent sense than mere satisfaction. An intellectual has sold his soul partly to know what to make of the erratic occurrences of 'conjunctions, oppositions, aspects, eclipses' and has been fobbed off with the pabulum that he heard years before at university lectures. His weary answer to Mephistopheles can be taken to mean, 'Well, I should have known.' The answer in no way concedes that a more detailed and indeed revolutionary explanation might not be there if one knew how to unlock the secret.

We cannot be certain what an Elizabethan audience would have made of such a possibility. Presumably some viewers would have concluded in orthodox terms that Faustus is only asking after vanities that will destroy his soul, much as, even in the latter half of the seventeenth century, Milton's Adam is persuaded to abandon his astronomical inquiries. But Marlowe is not Milton. In view of all that Dee and others were writing in the years when *Doctor Faustus* first appeared, Marlowe may well be inviting his audience to wonder if the orthodox cosmology of the age is a hoax, or at least a long-perpetuated human error no longer able to explain the mysterious movements of the inner planets. If Mephistopheles stands behind the proposition that an earth-centred theory of cosmology is all ye know on earth and all ye need to know, where else is one to turn for enlightenment? The implication that God himself will allow no more to be said on the subject leaves one with the painful choice of deciding that one has indeed run up against the limits of truth itself or that a great unknowable conspiracy is at work—the one that 'conspired' Faustus's overthrow (Prologue, l. 22). Faustus retreats from this virtually unthinkable heresy, longing to find spiritual rest in the belief that God made the world (II.iii.66, 73), but he knows that his own intellectual restlessness can no longer leave the matter alone and that he is damned.

Heretical notions of divine conspiracy, once raised, do not quickly go away. They question the justice of Faustus's damnation. Although the Christian doctrine of salvation is plainly manifest in the Good Angel's insistence that it is never too late to repent and in the Old Man's vision of an angel hovering over Faustus's head 'with a vial full of precious grace' (v.i.54–5), there is always a catch. It is never too late 'if Faustus can repent' (II.iii.79). Much virtue in *if*! The B-text reading, 'if Faustus will repent', shifts the emphasis perhaps to Faustus's corrupted will, but either reading suggests that Faustus is simply unable to will himself to repent. As Faustus himself put it, earlier in the same scene, 'My heart's so hardened I cannot repent' (l. 18). What does Marlowe's play make of this critical problem of the unwilling will? Christian doctrine of course has an answer, especially as formulated by the Wittenberg reformers and Calvin: God hardens the hearts of those whom he rejects. As we have seen, this difficult issue leads in Calvinist theology to a non-answer: we must accept God's unfathomable will. Because grace is God's gift, he may give it or withhold it as he wills in perfect justice. Faustus embodies all the characteristic failings of the reprobate; his deeds are manifest signs of his ungodliness, and they deserve, in Calvinist terms, the punishment they receive. But does Marlowe assent to such a view? Non-answers are precisely what his protagonist, Faustus, cannot abide. In the same way that Faustus is bitterly disappointed to learn that the heavens' astronomical secrets will not be opened to him, he is crushed by his perception that heaven's

mercy, offered to all who penitently turn to God, is not for him. The
Good Angel tries to teach him otherwise, but the lesson is one that
Faustus cannot will himself to believe in true faith.

It isn't as though Faustus doesn't long fitfully for a better relation
with God. 'When I behold the heavens, then I repent', he concludes
at one point (II.iii.1). Does this mean only that he wishes he were
out of a bad bargain? As though by way of answer, Faustus repeats
the idea in the form of a determination: 'I will renounce this magic
and repent' (l. 11). He must mean 'repent' in its salvific sense, for
the Good Angel enters at this point to urge him on: 'Faustus, repent
yet, God will pity thee'. (Compare the B-text's punctuation, 'Faustus,
repent, yet God will pity thee.') To the Evil Angel's charge that he
is a 'spirit' who cannot be pitied, Faustus has the correct answer: 'Be
I a devil, yet God may pity me' (l. 15). A short while later he
calls out, 'Ah, Christ, my Saviour, / Seek [B-text: 'Help'] to save
distressèd Faustus' soul!' (ll. 82–3). As several commentators have
observed, Christ does not answer this call for help; Lucifer appears
instead with Beelzebub and Mephistopheles.[106] Certainly it is no
coincidence that Lucifer thus makes his first entrance in the play (in
the A-text version; the B-text has introduced him in I.iii); this is a
moment of spiritual crisis, and heavy reinforcements are needed.
Does the absence of Christ at this critical juncture suggest a conspiracy in heaven? Not necessarily; the orthodox explanation might
be that we all have to be left to face the devil alone, as was Christ in
the wilderness, and that in any event the Good Angel continues to
urge Faustus to repent. We are left none the less with the perception
that God (Christ) is starkly absent from the play,[107] and that in his
separation from God Faustus finds repentance seemingly impossible.

All that is required of Faustus is that he believe and repent. But
how can the sceptical mind will itself to believe? The play itself,
through its endless uncertainties, re-enacts the mood of doubt and
questioning that afflicts the mind of Faustus. In a sense he never
really tries to repent, for he knows his own disposition too well.
Curiositas is at once his bane and his most essential self. To accept
things as they are would be to deny his very identity. Character
is fate. *Doctor Faustus* is the biography of a man, perhaps like
Marlowe, who has tasted the heady pleasures of heterodoxy and has
then reconsidered the basic teachings of his Christian upbringing
only to discover that its gifts are no longer open to him. They are
denied him not simply because he is a sinner who has made a pact
with the devil, but because his mind and will have embraced the

agnostic spirit of questioning even the most sacred of authorities. Faustus partly hates what he sees in the rebel he has become, but he cannot—perhaps for solid reasons—persuade himself that he is a rebel without a cause. What is he to make of a God that has given him an inquisitive mind and a grasping, acquisitive instinct only to punish him for being what he is? If, as in *Tamburlaine*, the very Nature who 'framed us of four elements' does 'teach us all to have aspiring minds' and to strive perversely after infinitude (Part I, II.vii.18-20), can the human condition be anything but damned in its confrontation with a heavenly power that conspires our overthrow?

MAGIC AND POETRY

The very persistence of rival interpretations of *Doctor Faustus* as orthodox and as heterodox would seem to suggest that neither can wholly invalidate the other, and that both are to an important extent 'true'. This is especially so in the theatre, where the dramatist has the advantage of speaking through various and incompatible voices. Surely Marlowe, dialectically trained at Cambridge and in the London theatres, was steeped in the tradition of 'the Tudor play of mind' that Joel Altman has so aptly demonstrated throughout the sixteenth century.[108] Faustus himself delights in debate—not always admirably, to be sure, but with such vivacity that controversial topics are continually laid before us. Everything that the Good Angel says produces an equal and opposite reaction from the Evil Angel; so too with the Old Man and Faustus, Faustus's cohorts in magic and his compassionate fellow students, prayers to Christ and conjurations of the devil, tragic action and burlesque comedy. The antithesis of voices generates an anxiety that is both theological and artistic. Faustus's often flippant agnosticism is not simply his own pathway to hell; it is also, for Marlowe, a shifting point of view from which to explore uncertainties.

Increasingly, as a result, the most persuasive criticism about *Doctor Faustus* has spoken of its 'complementary' aspects, of 'multiplicity of vision', 'ambivalent effect', 'dualism', 'dilemma', 'paradox', 'oxymoron', 'divided response', 'double view', and the like.[109] Ambiguity has value in such art because human nature itself is essentially ambiguous.[110] Ambiguity helps us see how the anarchic impulse of the self-aggrandising and narcissistic fantasy collides with a prohibition. The obsessive blasphemy, the perverse and infantile desire for power and sensual gratification, are ultimately rebuked, but in such a way that the prohibition becomes a denial of life itself.[111] Faustus becomes, in Stephen Greenblatt's terms, a quintessential Marlovian hero struggling to invent himself, embarking on a pursuit of knowledge that progressively destroys and violates as he squeezes dry and then discards the world's resources. His longing to be autochthonous and to make an end of his endeavours ('*Consummatum est*') propels him towards a perverse and self-destructive re-enactment of Christ's archetypal role as the fulfilment of being. Such an identity is one that can be achieved only as the parodic and blasphemous expression of 'a perverse, despairing faith'. Even Faustus's self-destructive and horrible suffering marks 'an ambiguous equation of himself with Christ, first as God, then as dying man'.[112]

The ambivalent response has the effect, as Robert Ornstein observes, of denying to the play the 'tragic acceptance' that we find in other Renaissance dramatists. Death is for Marlowe 'a metaphysical outrage which annihilates the meaning of existence', and so the Marlovian hero, who begins as a lover of the world he would remake, ends in nihilism and despair. We are not allowed to 'rejoice in the human' (much less in human self-sufficiency) because Marlowe considers 'that which is merely human' to be 'worthless'. At the same time, the ambivalent response generates a strong identification between audience and protagonist. For all his pettiness, Faustus is a man whose 'primal disobedience is a Promethean impulse'. His questioning mind 'threatens the divinely established order', to the extent that heaven and hell are mobilised for battle. And, argues Ornstein, Faustus does grow in moral awareness. His arrogance collapses in the face of what he learns; his fall 'is a moral education and discovery'. When he finds the presence of God unbearable and turns despairingly from the wrathful deity and father, we sympathise with the plight of one who knows that God will save the Old Man but not Faustus. We understand the theological basis for such a judgement, but we are struck with Faustus's perception that the ethic of heaven is fundamentally inhuman, that is, beyond human reach and entirely antithetical to the humanity of which the incarnated Christ is (for Faustus) an ironic symbol. A humane sense of loss and impotence lies at the heart of the play's tragic experience, whatever the Epilogue may say by way of orthodox explanation.[113]

Yet if Faustus is a tragic failure, he is also an artist, as was his creator. Faustus's magic shows, like those of Prospero, do what dramatic presentations regularly do: call up shadows from the past, entertain audiences with spectacle, and 'eternise' beauty, honour, and achievement. Faustus begs Helen to 'make me immortal with a kiss' and simultaneously immortalises her with some of the most often-quoted lines in all literature: 'Was this the face that launched a thousand ships / And burnt the topless towers of Ilium?' (v.i.91–3). In this power to bestow such fame, Faustus is also Marlowe. Is Faustus then Marlowe's portrait of the artist as a young man who is given twenty-four years to find out what art can do? Does Marlowe's view of his own art take shape in the play's ambiguous exploration of forbidden magic and its relation to poetry and drama?

The question does not encourage a happy view of Marlowe's self-examination as artist. Patrick Cheney argues well that Faustus turns to magic, 'at least in part, because he believes magic will offer him the incarnation of heavenly beauty', but ultimately fails to achieve the synthesis forged by some Neoplatonic poets (such as Edmund Spenser) in which love is indeed the true magic; instead, magic becomes for Faustus a means 'not merely for acquiring forbidden knowledge, but also for fulfilling forbidden desires', a 'demonic drive for lust and power'.[114] Something has gone fatally wrong with the very project to which the artist has committed himself. The immortality that Faustus longs for in Helen's kiss is the immortality of ravishing art, all right, but it is based, as Philip Traci shows, upon 'the creative-destructive power that launches ships and destroys the topless towers'. Helen, in her function as the last achievement of Faustus's art, is both a whorish demon and the subject of the play's most poignantly erotic poetry. She is famous as the cause of a war that in turn inspired some of the greatest literature ever written. Surely this unstable vision is not unrelated to Faustus's 'artistic and creative conjuring, that results in the loss of his soul'.[115] Faustus sells his soul not only to hear blind Homer sing to him (ii.iii.26) but also to become Paris in his own person, to combat with weak Menelaus and wound Achilles in the heel (v.i.98–102)—in other words, to reinhabit the world of classical mythology that shone so brightly in Marlowe's imagination and yet also embodied the polytheism, demonology, and sexual licence that were so vehemently denounced by Tertullian and other Christian apologists.[116] No wonder Faustus invokes during his last moments the idea of Pythagoras's metempsychosis (v.ii.107), for it encapsulates the dream through which Faustus as artist has projected his own imagination into an exquisite but morally ambiguous past. Yet even if the parallel of magician and playwright bespeaks the artist's disappoint-

ment at having created beautiful but unreal spectacles (such as that
of Alexander and his paramour), and even if the dramatist chafes at
the necessity of creating his magical dreams out of crude sideshow
effects like firecrackers and detachable legs,[117] we can still stand in
wonder at the extravagant daring of Marlowe's attempt and resonate
to the poetic splendour of an artist figure who, with terror and
uncertainty but with a growing conviction that there can be no
turning back, sacrifices his soul to art.[118]

Perhaps, then, as Neil Forsyth also argues, we are meant to see
magic and art as the Cleopatra for whom this wretched Antony loses
the world in order that he may be subsumed, even immolated, into
the apocalypse of his own self-destructive vision. As in *Antony and
Cleopatra*, the 'radical instability' of a quest for beauty that is both
seductive and annihilating tests 'the very notion of *limit* or *term*'.[119]
Faustus's impulse to confound hell in Elysium (I.iii.61) even generates for us an uncertainty as to where Faustus will spend eternity,
for manifestly in one sense he is immortalised in a work of art where
he continues to be delighted and terrified by his power to conjure up
images. David Palmer eloquently sums up this persuasive view
of *Doctor Faustus* as itself a kind of enchantment, one in which
Marlowe's ability to transform theatrical chicanery into 'moments of
poetic rapture and tragic grandeur' constitutes his supreme achievement. The magic of poetry depends, moreover, on the kind of
theatre for which Marlowe wrote. Marlowe's stage is exciting
'precisely because it is not true to nature in the respects laid down by
Sidney'; its freedom from the constricting bonds of mimesis, assisted
by the unlocalised setting, enables the playwright to transform narrative source material into a dramatic experience that holds the
spectators, 'as literally as possible, spellbound'. Surely, argues
Palmer, 'Marlowe's disregard of probability is at one with Faustus'
flouting of divine commandment, and Faustus' demonic power
over nature is both image and source of the drama's hold upon its
spectators'. Marlowe's 'secret and anarchic fantasies, thinly veiled in
good Protestant sentiment', appeal to us on the simplest level as 'a
kind of wish-fulfilment or indulged fantasy'.[120] This present essay
asks whether the perennial debate between orthodox and heterodox
readings of *Doctor Faustus* cannot best be resolved in the terms of art
and magic with which Marlowe broods upon his own ambiguous
achievement. Ultimately the dangerous enchantment of art in this
play exacts a terrible price of the magician protagonist, and we are
asked (by the Epilogue) to reassert the self-control of moral judge-

ment that must accompany our own return to our daily lives; but this very need to put the genie back in the bottle attests to the subversive energy released by the theatrical experience of this play.

GENRE AND STRUCTURE

Whether we consider *Doctor Faustus* to be orthodox or heterodox or something of both has an important bearing on our view of its genre. Is it a tragedy of negative example with an unsympathetic protagonist, or a tragedy of undeserved punishment (both of which types are criticised by Aristotle),[121] or something more mixed? The play's non-Aristotelian blend of comic and tragic, its disregard of all the so-called 'unities' of classical precept, and its indebtedness to a native morality tradition all suggest that we approach Marlowe as an experimenter who, for all his classical training, is formulating a tragic pattern of his own in which a deeply flawed but sympathetic protagonist is perceived to be both ludicrous and noble, petty and heroic.

Whether Aristotelian concepts of tragic error, hubris, reversal, discovery, and catharsis can be of critical use in analysing this play, especially in view of Marlowe's turning to native homiletic models, is an issue on which readers are divided. To M. M. Mahood, Faustus's tragic error or *hamartia* is his attempt to solve the dilemmas of his existence by selling his soul and then by seeking the stoical companionship of the 'old philosophers' as a way of ennobling his despair; the pride he invests in these solutions is part of his hubris. The moment of reversal or *peripeteia* occurs when he is on the verge of spiritual recovery and cries out to Christ as his saviour, only to be greeted by the arch-fiend Lucifer instead of a divine messenger.[122] In this reading, Faustus is an embittered Oedipus, one whose crime is a violent act of usurpation against the father and whose recognition or *anagnorisis* is to discover that he is miserable in the simple fact of being human. The will of the heavens, inscrutable to him at first, must be fulfilled, and at his expense.

The comparison of Faustus and Oedipus yields many stark contrasts, however, and to that extent the terms of Aristotelian definition must be seen to be of limited usefulness.[123] Faustus is self-infatuated, arrogant, and sensual in ways that Oedipus is not. The supposed reversal of Lucifer's appearing to Faustus is a bitterly ironic one, if it can be called a reversal at all, since destiny reasserts itself and nothing changes for the protagonist. Indeed, since Faustus never accepts the wisdom of God's plan, there can be no reversal in the form of a last-minute recantation.[124] Catharsis is similarly jeopardised by the spectre of divine injustice, or at least something inadequately explained. In *Oedipus*, we know that we are to accept the mysteriousness of things as Oedipus does, and celebrate the wisdom of a supernal authority unshaken by human doubt. Why do the gods doom Oedipus to kill his father and marry with his mother? We never know, but we agree that what must be shall be. Why is Faustus destined to be what he is? We are invited to consider a very different and deeply sardonic response: 'What doctrine call you this, *Che serà, serà*, / What will be, shall be?' (i.i.49–50).

The distinctively English tragedy that emerges from such a consideration evades any single attempt at naming. Its extraordinary tensions may arise in part from the way it (consciously or unconsciously) rearranges and subverts Aristotelian norms of tragedy, juxtaposing the punitive tragedy of a bad man with a more ennobling tragic vision of one who wrestles with his fate, and arousing expectations of reversal and cathartic acceptance only to problematise them. In historical terms, the play can be seen as a Protestant Christian tragedy that makes a significant contribution to English Renaissance drama by discovering in the Protestant concept of damnation a genuinely aesthetic potential. The play anticipates *Macbeth* in this regard, as Richard Waswo demonstrates, by its depiction of a man who sees the good and yet chooses evil. When Faustus and Macbeth 'choose and act against knowledge and conscience they become psychologically incapable of repentance—not because God or Christ is unwilling or unable to forgive, but because they have rejected the means by which they could be made psychologically capable'.[125] Such an analysis helps redefine *hamartia* in Christian terms and thereby make it amenable to Renaissance dramatists. Robert Heilman has a name for this: in his view, *Doctor Faustus* is a 'tragedy of knowledge', whose protagonist exhibits in his aspiration and folly both the 'heroic dimensions essential to the tragic protagonist' and the hubris of pride and sinfulness. The tragedy of knowledge, then, is that human intellectuality contains within itself a hubris that necessarily 'destroys the understanding of the nature and limitations of knowledge'.[126]

Is *Doctor Faustus* a 'Christian tragedy'? The very phrase is a contradiction in terms, as has often been pointed out,[127] since tragedy cannot constrict itself within the parameters of a Christian story that is, in Dante's terms, a divine comedy. Despite the contradictions, however, Richard Sewall argues that the term 'is permissible and, I think, useful, to indicate the new dimensions and tensions introduced into human life by Christianity and which perforce entered into the Elizabethan tragic synthesis'.[128] Sewall calls to his aid W. H. Auden's distinction between the Greek 'tragedy of necessity' and the Christian 'tragedy of possibility': at the end of a Greek tragedy we say, 'What a pity it had to be this way', whereas at the end of a Christian tragedy we say, 'What a pity it had to be this way when it might have been otherwise'.[129] In this sense, argues Sewall, Faustus is close to Dostoevsky's tragic heroes in being torn between the desire to exploit a new mastery over the world and guilt-ridden allegiance to traditional values. Faustus is, like many of Dostoevsky's protagonists, a criminal in the eyes of society, 'the first modern tragic man, part believer, part unbeliever, vacillating between independence and dependence upon God, now arrogant and confident, now anxious and worried, justified yet horribly unjustified'. He does not abase himself, as a Christian might, but resists his fate and clings to a doomed life.[130] The 'tragedy of possibility' mocks him with the illusion of a new freedom he may not have, but it also defines what is generically new in Marlowe's play. If we understand 'Christian tragedy' in this ironic sense, the concept is critically useful.

On what does the unity of such a tragedy depend, or does it in fact have a unity? Since the play is manifestly non-classical in the way it organises its material, juxtaposing and inverting what Marlowe found in his sources as Faustus veers back and forth from serious inquiry to frivolity, unity must be sought paradoxically in the contradictions and struggles of the play's protagonist, in what Nicholas Brooke calls the bitter irony of Faustus's blasphemous protest 'against the monstrous nature of a world where man is created to want to be at his finest precisely what he is not allowed to be'. The play's unity of vision lies in its perception that man's nature 'is in direct opposition to his fate'.[131]

Yet even those critics who respond to Faustus's tragedy as a whole are often troubled by the play's seeming lack of a proper middle. In Cleanth Brooks's view, Faustus appears to have little to do after he has signed his fateful bargain 'except to fill in the time before the mortgage falls due and the devil comes to collect the forfeited soul'. The lack of any fixed tragic structure allows the playwright (or his collaborator and later revisers) to 'stuff in comedy and farce' at this point 'more or less *ad libitum*'. Faustus is a man 'all dressed up with no place to go'.[132] Can answers be found to this key structural problem?

One persuasive reply looks to the practicalities of theatre, especially as theatre evolved in late medieval England. Morality drama experimented extensively in the sixteenth century with formulas of contrast between serious action and burlesque parody. Moreover, as Nigel Alexander notes, in any age a good comedian knows 'that it matters a great deal what he puts in as filler'. The middle of the play is needed to make clear to the audience the nature of Faustus's danger and folly. It does so by generating what Alexander calls the 'logic of suspense', making use of rapid transitions to sharpen the audience's awareness of Faustus's approaching destiny. The Seven Deadly Sins entertain Faustus with 'a representation of the bonds which will fetter him until his destruction at the end of the play'. The low comedy scenes are much more than parody; they are tied together by a symbolic imagery of evil that suspensefully reminds us of the 'consequences of following passion wherever it leads'.[133] They give objective form to the dilemma in which Faustus is caught, between his knowledge that grace is truly offered to the penitent and his own conviction that he cannot repent.

Equally persuasive is the argument that *Doctor Faustus*, for all its mix of comic and tragic, moves (in both its A- and B-texts) through a regular five-act structure. The B-text is in fact divided into five acts; the A-text, though obscured by textual difficulties and the decision of most modern editors to present the A-text in scenes, lends itself to the five-act division employed in Keefer's and this present edition. Act I is expository; Act II centres on the signing of the contract that sets the tragedy on its inexorable course; Act III is spent in Rome, Act IV in the courts of Germany; Act V is the dénouement. As George Hunter argues, a 'single and significant line of development' connects these points as we move from initial excitement in Act I to Faustus's being balked from his pursuit of astronomy in Act II to his being distracted into sightseeing and sensual indulgence as his intellectual quest falters. The subplot material meantime operates through parody, not in a feeble modern sense but through the 'multiple presentation of serious themes'.[134] All in all, then, the genre and structure of *Doctor Faustus* are most clearly evident when they are measured sympathetically against the traditions of a native English theatre rather than being subjected to a superimposed Aristotelian analysis.

STYLE AND IMAGERY

A play in which a magician sells his soul to hear blind Homer sing to him (among other wonders) is certain to be filled with both exultation and uncertainty directed towards the enormous potential of poetic language for good and evil. Faustus turns to magic in the hope that it will offer him heavenly beauty incarnated, only to discover that in his hands the power of language is converted into demonic lust. Marlowe, too, is embarked on a subversive quest, one that both exalts poetic rapture and unravels the very rhetorical and dramaturgical elements out of which the artist creates images.[135] Dialectic, antithesis, and ambivalence are essential modes in *Doctor Faustus*, for it is through them that Marlowe projects his clash of ideologies.

Contrasts abound in the play's discourse. On the one hand, Caroline Spurgeon finds an 'imaginative preoccupation with the dazzling heights and vast spaces of the universe . . . a magnificent surging upward thrust and aspiration'. Marlowe seems 'more familiar with the starry courts of heaven than with the green fields of earth'.[136] At the opposite extreme are the clowns' coarse jests about shoulders of mutton and wenches' plackets, the devils' display of fireworks, and Faustus's own abuse of language. His fascination with logic, derived no doubt from Marlowe's own intellectual experience at Cambridge, shows what is simultaneously exalted and debased in Faustus's view of human aspiration through language. Faustus wilfully misinterprets Ramus's idea that disputing well is 'logic's chiefest end' (i.i.8) to mean that disputation should be an end in itself rather than a means to salvation. Consequently, the syllogism becomes in Faustus's hands mere sophistical argument, and flagrantly deceptive. Increasingly, too, he abandons the test of experience and settles instead for sarcasm and rationalisation.[137] Yet since Mephistopheles and his fellow devils are also capable of linguistic cunning, the very project of language through which Faustus dares to assert human greatness is doomed by his perversion of the gift of language. As William Blackburn insists, 'not magic, but the magician, is on trial here'; the play 'is Marlowe's metaphor, not for the failure of language as an instrument of transformation, but for man's failure to understand it and use it wisely'.[138] At the same time, we are invited to sympathise with a protagonist who discovers to his cost the ambiguous power of speech.

Marlowe's mastery of the traditional arts of rhetoric leaves little doubt as to the thoroughness of his training. When he writes in the argumentative mode, as Frederick Burwick demonstrates, Marlowe turns to figures of speech that express choice: affirming that one speaks the truth (*orcos*), deliberating with oneself what to do or say (*aporia*), asking and answering one's own questions (*anthypophora*), and many more. He is especially effective in his use of rhetorical figures of repetition. The repetition of syntactic elements in chiastic order (*antimetabole*) is nicely illustrated in the following:

> *Faustus.* How comes it then that thou art out of hell?
> *Mephistopheles.* Why, this is hell, nor am I out of it. (I.iii.77–8)

Repetitions of equal sound, length, and grammatical function (*parison, isocolon,* alliteration, and the like) come as effortlessly to Marlowe as to the early Shakespeare:

> To give me whatsoever I shall ask,
> To tell me whatsoever I demand,
> To slay mine enemies and aid my friends,
> And always be obedient to my will. (I.iii.96–9)[139]

Yet this pyrotechnic versatility of style affords no solid ground of meaning for the protagonist. Even the Christian assurances that seem so absolute in the world of the play—eternal joy and felicity, pardon, penitence—dissolve before his eyes and leave in their wake an angry God stretching out his arm and bending his ireful brows (v.ii.83). What seems so plain is, for Faustus, impossible.

The diction of *Doctor Faustus*, as T. McAlindon has shown, characteristically embodies duality of meaning. 'Resolute' is an important word for Faustus, as it was for Tamburlaine, but in this protagonist it bespeaks a woeful contrast between boast and fulfilment. Faustus repeatedly undertakes to 'Resolve me of all ambiguities' (I.i.82), but comes instead to occupy a world where to be resolved is to disintegrate or dissolve. Images of congealing and melting, evoked by mythological allusions to 'waxen wings', reinforce a pattern of dissolution that ends (in the B-text, at any rate) in a literal dismemberment of Faustus's body by devils. The word 'perform' ambivalently suggests both active accomplishment and illusory fabrication of dramatic spectacles. A 'deed' is both something Faustus longs to accomplish and a document by which all will be undone.[140] As in *Macbeth*, words promise so much only to 'betray 's in deepest consequence'. At the same time, the extraordinary density of language in *Doctor Faustus* makes possible a

INTRODUCTION   41

flexibility and subtlety of characterisation not to be found in earlier
Elizabethan drama; for the first time, says Wolfgang Clemen, we can
see 'how Faustus thinks while he speaks'.[141]

Punning and other wordplay assume metaphysical dimensions in
these circumstances. Language is seductive in this guise; if punning
is 'the fatal Cleopatra' for which Shakespeare was content to lose the
world,[142] Marlowe seems no less ready to embrace (as Neil Forsyth
puts it) a 'radically unstable language where the boundaries between words constantly shift'. The very name of Helen, always an
ambivalent figure in classical tradition since the time of Euripides,
may resonate with suggestions of the 'hell' that Faustus is so ready to
'confound' in Elysium (I.iii.61).[143] Much of the wordplay is chop
logic, as when Wagner interprets 'God in heaven knows' to mean,
conventionally, 'No one knows', or, more radically, 'God knows,
and so may I' (I.ii.6–8). The wordplay is related to an irony that
operates not only at the level of cosmic incongruity but in arresting
verbal figures. 'Learn thou of Faustus manly fortitude' (I.iii.87),
Faustus patronisingly reassures Mephistopheles at one point, leaving
us to ponder, as we do in *Macbeth*, what it is to be a man.

Recurrent verbal images of inversion and parody, often explicitly
religious in their terminology, subvert the orderly cosmos upon
which the play is premised. Valdes assures Faustus that the nations
of the world will 'canonise' those who excel in magic (I.i.122).
Faustus boasts of the 'virtue' in his 'heavenly words' (I.iii.28).
Mephistopheles urges Faustus to 'pray devoutly to the prince of hell'
(I.iii.55).[144] Pursuing an unholy parallel between himself and Christ,
Faustus longs for power to bring the dead to life again (I.i.25), cries
out '*Consummatum est*' when he has finished signing away his soul
(II.i.74), forms a partnership with Mephistopheles that recalls the
fellowship of Christ and his disciples, enacts miracles, shares with
his fellow scholars a blasphemous last supper, and so on.[145] Yet such
parallels are not simply denunciatory in their effect. Images of discovery, of ransacking the oceans for orient pearl (I.i.85), of bringing
back 'the golden fleece / That yearly stuffs old Philip's treasury'
(I.i.133–4), of mining 'the massy entrails of the earth' (I.i.149)
condemn Faustus as a sybarite, of course, but the magic of the
poetry cannot be conjured away by simple moral denunciation. Plato
was right to fear that such poetry often undoes what it purports to
do.

In the theatre, the verbal imagery is reinforced by a compelling
visual dimension. What does it mean to 'look up' in *Doctor Faustus*?

The play's imagery of aspiration draws our attention to the dominance of the vertical dimension. The flight of Icarus, the topless
towers of Ilium, the star-threatening 'aspiring top' of Venice's
temple (III.i.18) all remind us that Faustus 'Did mount himself to
scale Olympus' top', where, seated in a dragon-drawn chariot, he
can see the planets and the stars.[146] Moreover, in the Elizabethan
theatre these verbalised pictures are yoked to our visual perception that the 'heavens' are above and hell beneath. The theatrical
spectacle reinforces a disjunction between 'height' and 'depth', as
Johan Birringer argues; 'this visual allegory can be proved against
the background of the stage business in the play, especially in
Faustus' relation to "heaven" and "hell" and to the diabolical trinity
overlooking his desperate attempt to flee from himself'.[147] Faustus
looks up to see Christ's blood streaming in the firmament and hopes
that his soul 'may but ascend to heaven' (v.ii.95), but he knows that
hell beckons instead (l. 88). In the theatre, Faustus's interest in
the movements of the heavenly spheres takes on a spatial dimension.
Similarly, the devices and props used to stage this play take on
imagistic value: the theatrical business of 'discovery', the books in
Faustus's study, the stage blood that is identified imagistically with
his soul, and many others all contribute to a vertical and antithetical
balance around which the play is visually organised.[148] All aspects of
style and imagery, then—the debased logic, the rhetorical bag of
tricks affording no sure foundation, the ambivalent diction, the
subverted visual images in the theatre—reinforce a reading of *Doctor
Faustus* in which magic and poetry are at once the immortal achievement through which the play lives and the source of disillusionment
and despair.

STAGING AND THEMES IN THE 1616 QUARTO

The analysis presented thus far has been based on the A1 Quarto of
1604, for reasons outlined in the discussion on text. There are in fact
two different early versions, however, and we must consider in what
ways the later text, the B1 Quarto of 1616, invites a different
interpretation from that of the earlier text. One place to begin is with
staging, since the later text adds extensive material and thereby
places new demands upon the playing space.

   Most of the scenes presented in common by the two texts, to be
sure, do not differ materially in their staging requirements. In both
texts, Faustus begins '*in his study*', having perhaps been 'discovered'

there as the Prologue draws aside a curtain or otherwise gestures towards Faustus as the Prologue exits. The phrase 'Enter Faustus in his study' in the A-text probably does not ask for different staging from the B-text's 'Faustus in his study'; the use of the word 'Enter' for the action of 'discovering' a character in this fashion is well attested to in the Elizabethan theatre.[149] Probably Faustus is intended, in both texts, to come forward from the 'discovery area' so that he can be clearly seen and heard on the Elizabethan stage, though he must also be seen in relation to the books and other artefacts of his study that are perhaps illustrated in the 1616 title-page woodcut.[150]

The study is in any event a recurrent location of thematic significance. Faustus appears there thrice in the play's first half, where he converses with Wagner, Valdes and Cornelius, the Good and Evil Angels, Mephistopheles, Lucifer, Beelzebub, and the Seven Deadly Sins. We are probably meant to imagine him there sleeping 'in his chair' (A-text; in the B-text he 'sits to sleep') during his encounter with the Horse-courser after his return 'To Wittenberg' (A-text, IV.i.105 ff.) from his travels. The play's final action takes place there; a banquet is served 'into Faustus's study' by devils (B-text, V.i.o.1–2; compare A-text V.i.8), and the three scholars eventually retire 'into the next room' (A-text, V.ii.56). In both texts, then, Faustus's study serves as the locus of his 'devilish exercises' and their terrible consequences.

Away from Wittenberg as well, staging requirements are often similar when the two texts essentially agree. The A-text's stage directions for the scene in the Pope's chamber are more explicit than the B-text's—'The Pope crosseth himself', 'Cross again and Faustus hits him a box of the ear'—but are implicit in the B-text's dialogue. The clowns vex the Vintner with a stolen 'silver goblet' (A) or a 'cup' (B). The Horse-courser enters 'wet'. Mephistopheles carries out Faustus's magical trick at the court of the Duke of Vanholt by fetching 'the grapes', probably exiting and re-entering here and on similar errands for Faustus even when the stage directions are sparse. When Faustus despairs, Mephistopheles 'gives him a dagger' (A-text, V.i.51.1, B-text, V.i.54.1). Helen 'passeth over the stage', explicitly escorted by Mephistopheles in the B-text (V.i.26.2–3; see also l. 93.1), implicitly so in the A-text (ll. 25.2–3 and 90.1).[151]

On the other hand, the B-text additions generally call for more characters on stage, more props and special effects, and more exploitation of physical space. Whereas in the A-text Faustus enters 'to conjure' alone (I.iii), B specifies 'Thunder' and 'Enter Lucifer and four *devils'*. The B-text's scenes in Rome add to the cast Bruno, the German pope; Raymond, King of Hungary; two Cardinals of France and Padua (whereas the A-text has one Cardinal of Lorraine); the Archbishop of Rheims; Monks and Friars (whereas the A-text has Friars only); and Lords. At the Emperor's court we are introduced to the Duke of Saxony, Martino, Frederick, and two speaking Soldiers who take part in an attempted ambush of Faustus, in addition to Benvolio (the equivalent of the A-text's unnamed Knight). The B-text's dumbshow of Alexander and his paramour adds King Darius as a mute. Beelzebub, silent in the A-text, is a speaker in the B-text. A Carter and a Hostess add to the scenes of ribaldry and carousing at the Emperor's court, and two mute Cupids accompany Helen in her second appearance in the B-text. Added extras such as soldiers swell the numbers still further. At the beginning of Act v, the B-text brings on devils carrying a banquet to Faustus's study.

These added persons contribute to elaborate ceremonial processions in the B-text, as when the Cardinals and Bishops enter '*some bearing crosiers, some the pillars*', with Monks and Friars '*singing their procession*' followed by the Pope and the King of Hungary '*with Bruno led in chains*' (III.i.88.1–6). The Emperor Alexander overthrows Darius in dumbshow, to the accompaniment of trumpets and other '*music*' (IV.i.102.1–9). Sennets and other fanfares announcing the arrival and departure of dignitaries are more common than in the A-text (see III.i.97.1, III.ii.0.1, IV.i.47.3, and IV.i.102.2). A devil plays a drum (IV.ii.105.1) in a scene not found in the A-text. Fireworks displays are sometimes specified in the B-text for scenes not included in the A-text, as when Mephistopheles sets upon the ambushing soldiers with '*fireworks*' and drives them out (IV.ii.105.3–4). Extra props are required, such as the false head used to convey the illusion of Faustus's decapitation. The horns bestowed on the Knight in the A-text sprout into a small forest of horns for Benvolio and his associates in the B-text (IV.iii.0.3).

As Bernard Beckerman notes, the B-text displays a pattern of redundancy: that of occasionally dividing up the A-text's speeches to accommodate more speakers. When Lucifer arrives to warn Faustus about his wavering loyalty, for example (II.iii), the A-text gives ll. 90–3 entirely to Lucifer, whereas the B-text assigns the material to Beelzebub and Lucifer in alternating single lines. The phenomenon is part of a larger move in the B-text to augment the number of devils on stage, as when Lucifer and four devils are silently added to I.iii and when the three chief devils are brought on in Faustus's final scene. The effect, both theologically and theatrically, is to increase the odds against Faustus and to foredoom his attempts at self-determined action. The choric presence of devils in I.iii, II.iii, and V.ii lends a chillingly sardonic atmosphere while also encouraging visual spectacle.[152]

Along with its increased requirements in casting and in use of stage properties, the B-text also makes new demands on theatrical space. The A-text, as Glynne Wickham shows, could have been performed on a raised and removable platform standing in front of a dressing room from which it was separated by a wooden or canvas partition featuring two doors. The A-text does not require a terrace or gallery above rear stage, nor is there need yet for a throne to be raised and lowered by means of machinery housed in a permanent 'heavens' supported by pillars.[153] (Of course the theatrical building where the A-text was performed may in fact have had gallery, pillars, and heavens even though they are not called for in this instance.) The B-text, on the other hand, makes elaborate provision for acting 'above'. Benvolio enters 'above at a window, in his night-cap, buttoning' when he is awakened from a drunken sleep by his comrades in order to see Faustus's magic tricks (IV.i.23.1. S.D.). Benvolio will be content, he declares, to 'thrust my head out at a window' to 'see this sport' (ll. 38, 44). Later in the scene, Faustus points amusedly to the strange beast that 'thrusts his head out at window' (ll. 120–3), now awakening with 'two spreading horns' fastened upon his head. Presumably Benvolio is still at this upper location when he is attacked by a kennel of diabolical hounds and has to beg to be relieved from his torment (ll. 150–63).

The final act in the B-text places considerable stress on vertical movement and position. Lucifer, entering at the start of V.ii with Beelzebub and Mephistopheles (none of whom enters at this point in the A-text), describes how 'from infernal Dis do we ascend / To view the subjects of our monarchy' (V.ii.1–2). Even if one cannot be entirely confident that they enter 'above', the language of elevation is suggestive.[154] Certainly, in any case, vertical movement is mandated for the final moments of the B-text version. A throne descends, presumably by means of machinery in the 'heavens', to tantalise Faustus with a glimpse of the indescribable bliss he has forfeited; he would have sat 'In yonder throne', the Good Angel tells him, whereas now 'The jaws of hell are open to receive thee' (V.ii.111–20). The Good Angel directs Faustus's gaze to 'those bright shining saints' who occupy the heavenly throne (l. 117), presumably represented by live actors or by painted figures. Hell is then *'discovered'* at the back of the playing area by the Bad Angel so that Faustus (and presumably the audience) can let their eyes 'with horror stare / Into that vast perpetual torture-house' (ll. 121–2). Images appear of 'damnèd souls' tossed 'On burning forks' and of bodies that 'boil in lead'—possibly on a painted backcloth[155] or by means of some more vivid representation. An 'ever-burning chair' dominates this gruesome stage picture in place of the heavenly throne, now evidently retracted into the 'heavens'.

The B-text makes a good deal of Faustus's physical dismemberment at the moment of his death, thereby bringing to fulfilment a pattern of a dismemberment evoked in both texts of the play, as in the Evil Angel's ominous warning, 'If thou repent, devils shall [will] tear thee in pieces' (A II.iii.80, B II.iii.81), in Mephistopheles's similar threat, 'Revolt, or I'll in piecemeal tear thy flesh' (A v.i.69, B v.i.71), in the Horse-courser's pulling off Faustus's leg, and (in the B-text only) Benvolio and his friends' striking off of Faustus's head. The A-text does not explain how Faustus dies; the B-text is, characteristically, more conscious of theatrical effect and indebted to the *Damnable Life* for its materials,[156] even if it does not indicate specifically what sorts of theatrical illusions (if any) are to accompany the Second Scholar's horrified observation, 'See, here are Faustus' limbs, / All torn asunder by the hand of death', and the Third Scholar's pointed reference to devils that 'have torn him thus' (v.iii.6–9).

Throughout, the B-text makes more spectacular use of the stage than does the A-text. Entrances and exits *'at several doors'* or *'several ways'*, that is, at separate doors, are routine.[157] More elaborately, when Benvolio concocts a plot to ambush Faustus, instructing his companions to 'hie thee to the grove, / And place our servants and our followers / Close in an ambush there behind the trees' (IV.ii.16–18), Faustus is able to triumph over them with an unusual piece of stage business. 'Base peasants, stand!' he exults. 'For lo, these trees remove at my command / And stand as bulwarks 'twixt yourselves and me / To shield me from your hated treachery' (ll. 100–3). However this effect was carried out, we have little reason to suppose that the dramatists who wrote this scene (or the entrepreneur, Henslowe, who paid for it) would have settled for miming. The whole point seems to be to add opportunities for tangible effects, including (in this episode alone) a severed head, a small army of devils who drive off the ambushers, and the 'brutish shapes' (IV.iii.24) in which Benvolio and his fellows return. Comic situations that manifestly have proved their stageworthiness in the A-text, such as Faustus's revenge on the scornful Knight and his tricking of the Horse-courser, are similarly extended through horseplay, sight gags, the introduction of new characters (Martino, Frederick, the Carter, the Hostess), and a good deal of narrative repetition.[158]

Thematically, the B-text moves intentionally in the direction of the jingoistic anti-papal feeling that was plentifully available to the revisers in the *Damnable Life* and in John Foxe's *Acts and Monuments*. The motif is there in the A-text, of course, in Faustus's determination to 'wall all Germany with brass' and 'chase the Prince of Parma from our land' (I.i.90–5), and especially in the practical joking in the Pope's chamber, but we can see that Henslowe asked for more of this. We are given a rival German pope, Bruno, as the foil to the Italian pope, in an elaborate plot of rescue. The battle is joined between Germany and Rome, as it was in Luther's day and had been so previously in the reign of Frederick Barbarossa (alluded to at B III.i.137), with obvious application to the England of Henry VIII and Elizabeth I. The plot affords Faustus an opportunity to play more pranks, in this case by disguising himself and Mephistopheles as cardinals who are given custody of Bruno and are thus able to spirit him off to Germany. Faustus is an anti-papal hero in the B-text.[159] The indebtedness of the Bruno episode to John Foxe's *Acts and Monuments* is all the more interesting in view of Foxe's influence on the Lutheran intrigue in *When You See Me You Know Me* (1603–5)—a play by the same Samuel Rowley whom Henslowe paid for some of the 1602 additions.[160]

Critics and editors need to be keenly aware of differences between the two texts. The excessive reliance until recently on the B-text has had the unfortunate effect of giving us what Michael Keefer aptly calls 'a general relapse from the tragic ironies of the A-version in the direction of the more grotesque features of the Faustbook'.[161] Faustus's use of verbal magic, so carefully dramatised in the A-text as he moves from a gloating sense of his own near-omnipotence to helplessness and despair, is replaced in the B-text by an incoherent delight in stage trickery and a demonstration of control and mastery when Faustus ought to be seen as increasingly out of control. Critical differences such as these between the two texts offer confirming evidence that the A-text is close to the Marlovian original and that the B-text trivialises the very nature of Faustus's tragic experience by its endless appetite for stage contrivance.

Whether the B-text and its revisions embrace a consistent shift in theology, or whether the new emphases are at least partly inadvertent, is a difficult matter to decide. Certainly in either case criticism must learn not to obfuscate theological issues by conflating the two texts. The B-text gives us a Faustus whose freedom of choice is markedly reduced. Mephistopheles's gloating claim, ''Twas I that, when thou wert i'the way to heaven, / Dammed up thy passage. When thou took'st the book / To view the Scriptures, then I turned the leaves / And led thine eye' (v.ii.98–101), has the effect of transforming a renowned scholar 'into a puppet whose very act of reading is determined by the devil', as Martha Rozett puts the matter.[162] The beginning of v.ii in the B-text, in which Lucifer, Mephistopheles, and Beelzebub converse about the 'lasting damnation' they bring to inflict upon Faustus's soul, and their assurance that 'The time is come / Which makes it forfeit' (ll. 5–7), has a similar effect of pronouncing final sentence before the drama has fully run its course.[163] The B-text omits the pity-evoking cries of Faustus in the A-text—'See, see where Christ's blood streams in the firmament!' and 'Yet for Christ's sake, whose blood hath ransomed me' (v.ii.78 and 100)—and gives us instead pious moralising by the Good and Bad Angels: 'O, what will all thy riches, pleasures, pomps / Avail thee now?' (v.ii.108–9). Overall, then, the A-text is more consistent in its Christian content and is more suspenseful in its conclusion, while the B-text, as Michael Warren puts it, 'appears to reflect a Christianity which is less intellectual, more homely, more timid, superstitious even', and more piously confident in its 'cautionary morality' that God 'will withdraw divine grace in anger against a great sinner'.[164] The B-text has an unmistakable point of view of its own, but it is one that relies intensively on theatrical stunts and accordingly gives us an inconsistent Faustus of admirable magical powers and of deplorable blasphemy—the double Faustus, in other words, of the *Damnable Life*.

THE PLAY IN PERFORMANCE

The first recorded performance of *Doctor Faustus* was on 30 September 1594, by the Lord Admiral's Men. This company had just separated itself from a joint arrangement with the Lord Chamberlain's Men in June of that year and had taken up acting at the Rose Theatre, where the September performance must have taken place. The play was surely not new on that occasion and was not so marked by Philip Henslowe as part of his entry of receiving 'iij^ll xij^s' for 'docter ffostose'.[165] It may possibly have been performed at the Belsavage playhouse in 1588 or so; William Prynne, writing in 1633, tells of the 'visible apparition of the devil on the stage' at that theatre during a performance of 'the History of Faustus', and the Belsavage may not have been used after 1589 (see 'Date', p. 2). Thomas Middleton's reference to the appearance of devils 'in Dr. Faustus when the old Theatre cracked and frighted the audience' might possibly point to performance at the so-called Theatre in Shoreditch in 1590–1 or as late as 1594, where the Admiral's Men performed, though the description may simply echo the language of a fictional performance narrated in *The Second Report of Dr. John Faustus*, 1594.[166] Whether the play may have been performed instead by Pembroke's Men or Lord Strange's Men, both of which companies acted other plays by Marlowe, cannot be determined. In any event the play was in the possession of the Admiral's Men a year or so after Marlowe's death.

Edward Alleyn, playing Faustus in 'a surplice / With a cross upon his breast', according to one account[167] (thus accentuating in visual terms the irony of his defection from the study of divinity), was a huge success. Henslowe's *Diary* records six more performances before the end of 1594, three more in January and February of the next year, four more in the remainder of 1595, seven in 1596, and one on 5 January 1597.[168] The takings were generally handsome: 44 shillings for the first of these performances, 33s and 38s for the next two, 52s on 27 December of the first year, and lesser amounts on other dates until, on the final two occasions, the revenue had diminished to 9s and 5s. When the Admiral's Men combined with Pembroke's Men in the autumn of 1597 at the Rose, they put on another revival (October) but without mention in Henslowe's *Diary*. The Admiral's Men became the Earl of Nottingham's Men when their patron received that title in the autumn of 1597, and so the fact that the title-page of the 1604 quarto describes the play as having been 'acted by the Right Honourable the Earl of Nottingham his Servants' would seem to imply more performances between late 1597 and the accession to the throne of James I in 1603, when the company assumed the name of Prince Henry's Men. Henslowe's payments to Birde and Rowley for additions in 1602 certainly confirm that the play was not only still in the repertory but was considered a viable commercial property.

A company of English players acted some version of *Doctor*

Faustus in Graz, Austria, in January 1608. English 'comedians' performed '*eine tragoedia von Dr. Faust*' at Dresden on 7 July 1626. Since on both occasions *The Jew of Malta* was also performed, the Faust play is likely to have been Marlowe's. English actors are known to have travelled in Germany. Presumably their productions relied heavily on exaggerated stage business and spectacle.[169] The continued popularity of the play in England until 1642 is attested to by the publication of as many as nine quartos between 1604 and 1631 and by indications that Prince Charles's Men were still performing the play at the Fortune Theatre a year or so before the closing of the theatres. (On one occasion a member of the audience threw a tobacco pipe at Mephistopheles, to which the actor replied that he hoped 'e'er long' to see the fellow 'as bad as I am', that is, the 'son of a whore'.)[170]

What were performances like, however, and what had become of the text? The references by Middleton and Prynne to strange diabolical phenomena in the theatre suggest the notoriety of the play and the pleasurable terror audiences seem to have enjoyed in their uncertainty as to whether all the devils on stage were real or not. So does an account of a performance of a Faustus play of uncertain date at Exeter in which the actors on a sudden 'were all dashed, every one hearkening other in the ear, for they were all persuaded there was one devil too many amongst them'—a story so worth telling that it was retold by John Aubrey in 1673 with Edward Alleyn as one of the seven thus unpleasantly surprised.[171] Narratives like these are too suspiciously like one another to offer hard evidence as to staging (a similar story was told from a Roman Catholic point of view about a play that had given offence to the Church in 1586),[172] but they do attest to an attitude that encouraged spectacular additions to *Doctor Faustus* in performance. The title-page woodcut in the early B-text editions gives an arresting visual impression of what seems to have fascinated audiences: Faustus with a book in one hand and a conjuring wand in the other, in doctor's robes, surrounded by a circle of astrological figures; a globe and Faustus's books arrayed against the wall, along with representations of the cross; and facing Doctor Faustus, dominating the foreground of the illustration, a hideous, physically distorted, black, and winged devil. Not surprisingly, Henslowe's *Diary* for 1598 lists among the stage properties in the company's inventory 'j dragon in fostes'.

Here was the scary business that spectators paid for, and we can hardly doubt that Henslowe and the acting company added to the play what they thought would please. John Melton's account of a performance at the Fortune Theatre by Palgrave's Men (formerly Prince Henry's Men), as set down in his *The Astrologaster, or, The Figure-caster* (1620), gives a vivid explanation of why men 'go to the Fortune in Golding Lane to see the tragedy of *Doctor Faustus*':

> There indeed a man may behold shag-haired devils run roaring over the stage with squibs in their mouths, while drummers make thunder in the tiring-house and the twelve-penny hirelings make artificial lightning in their heavens.[173]

The continued popularity into the early 1640s of such a production, with its superstitious appeals and magic shows, may have added to the Puritans' reasons for wishing to close the theatres.[174]

'To the Red Bull, where we saw *Dr Faustus*, but so wretchedly and poorly done that we were sick of it', wrote Samuel Pepys on 20 May 1662. Although often performed in the Restoration, the play lived on in a degenerated form. The version that Pepys complained about, and that was acted at least once more in 1662, was probably the text that appeared in print in 1663, 'As it is now acted with several new scenes', and may also have served as the script for a performance on 28 September 1675 by the Duke of York's company in the presence of royalty. Thomas Betterton played Faustus and William Mountford played Mephistopheles, according to marginal notes in a copy of the 1663 text.[175] Edward Phillips, writing an account of Marlowe in that same year, wryly comments that 'of all that he hath written to the stage, his *D. Faustus* hath made the greatest noise with its devils and suchlike tragical sport'.[176] The sentiment is echoed some fourteen years later, in 1687, by William Winstanley: 'None made such a great noise as his comedy of *Doctor Faustus*, with his devils and suchlike tragical sport, which pleased much the humours of the vulgar'.[177] Marlowe's play had become a 'comedy', and even its tragical action was 'sport' aimed to please the crowd.

As with many of Shakespeare's plays in the Restoration and eighteenth century, *Doctor Faustus* eventually yielded, even in its degenerate form, to adaptations that bore only an occasional resemblance to the original. William Mountfort's farcical *The Life and Death of Doctor Faustus* retained the business of the Seven Deadly Sins, the discomfiture of the Pope, and the tricking of the Horse-courser, along with a mutilated version of the opening and closing scenes, but focused mainly on added material from *The Humours of*

Harlequin and Scaramouche. The resulting pastiche was acted at the Queen's Theatre in Dorset Garden in 1688 and perhaps earlier, was then revived at the theatre in Lincoln's Inn Fields, and appeared in print in 1697.[178]

Mountfort's version inspired in turn two rival pantomimes that were first performed in 1723: John Thurmond's *Harlequin Dr. Faustus* (published in 1724) at Drury Lane, and *The Necromancer, or Harlequin Doctor Faustus* (for whom no author is assigned) at Lincoln's Inn Fields. This twin phenomenon was enough to draw the wrath of Alexander Pope, who deplored, in his notes to the *Dunciad*, the fact that persons 'of the first quality in England' frequented these wretched contrivances 'to the twentieth and thirtieth time' during the season of 1726 and 1727.[179] In the *Dunciad* itself, Pope satirically catalogues the wonders that a gull like Colley Cibber would have seen on such an occasion:

> [He] looked and saw a sable sorcerer rise,
> Swift to whose hand a wingèd volume flies.
> All sudden, gorgons hiss and dragons glare,
> And ten-horned fiends and giants rush to war.
> Hell rises, heav'n descends and dance on earth;
> Gods, imps, and monsters, music, rage, and mirth,
> A fire, a jig, a battle, and a ball,
> Till one wide conflagration swallows all. (III.229–36)

Not only did the two legitimate playhouses of London rival each other 'in showing the burnings of hellfire in *Dr. Faustus*' (note to III.310), but Martin Powell's puppet theatre, lodged under the Covent Garden piazzas, took up the Faustus mania as well.

The play itself disappeared from the stage. When a semblance of it reappeared in December of 1885 at the Lyceum Theatre, it showed the influence of Goethe's *Faust* and especially of the operatic treatments by Gounod and others that Goethe's poem had inspired. Indeed, the production by W. G. Wills, with Henry Irving as Mephistopheles, was markedly operatic in its use of ponderous and verisimilar scenery, its reduction of the number of scenes to accommodate the massive sets, and its focus on the emotional experience of the major characters. In fact, *Doctor Faustus* is so built around a dominating central character that it provided a suitable vehicle for acting companies operating under the actor managers; what it lacked in the way of a leading female role could be provided by Goethe and his followers. Herbert Beerbohm Tree, at His Majesty's Theatre in 1908, took full advantage of the opulent style of late nineteenth-century staging to mount a spectacular production based on a freely adapted text.

As with many another Elizabethan play, movement away from heavy sets and adapted texts towards a more authentically Tudor mode of production began under the auspices of the Elizabethan Stage Society at St George's Hall, under the direction of William Poel. *Doctor Faustus* first appeared there on 2 and 4 July 1896, on a reproduction of the stage of the Fortune playhouse. In the centre of his platform stage, Poel erected a curtained raised structure in the semblance of the pageant stages of the medieval cycle plays. During the final scene, Faustus's fellow scholars stepped outside this structure on to the main platform and knelt there, 'giving the effect of kneeling figures in the lower lights of a stained-glass window'.[180] The text (an amalgam of A and B) was notably closer to Marlowe than in the productions of Wills and (some years later) Tree, though the comedy was still curtailed. A. C. Swinburne wrote a prologue for the occasion. The Elizabethan Stage Society performed the play again at the Court Theatre in October of 1904 and at Terry's Theatre in December, followed by a six-week tour of England and Scotland.[181]

Germany too made an important early contribution to experimental theatre, beginning on 16 and 17 December 1903, with a production by the Heidelberger Hebbelverein, under the general direction of Ernst Leopold Stahl, that used an undecorated stage. Further productions followed at Göttingen, Essen, and Frankfurt in 1910, at Hamburg in 1911, and at a meeting of the German Shakespeare Society in 1928 for which a new unpublished translation took as its basis the 1604 A1 quarto with some borrowings from the 1616 B1 quarto.[182]

Interest in textual restoration and in staging conditions approximating those of the Elizabethan theatre found a natural haven in the university world, and so we should not be surprised to see a number of academic performances in the early years of rediscovery. The success of a production at Cambridge University in 1907, with Rupert Brooke and George Mallory (later a famous mountain-climber) among the members of its cast, led to the foundation of the Marlowe Dramatic Society in 1908. At Princeton, also in 1907, the Chaucer scholar Robert K. Root supervised a production. Williams College put on the play on four occasions in May and June of 1908, and twice again in 1912. Bakeless and Jump record further performances on campus.[183]

Suddenly, it seemed, *Doctor Faustus* was playable again after the centuries of neglect.[184] A major event of the 1930s was Orson Welles's successful production at the Maxine Elliott Theatre, New York, in 1936–7, on a projecting stage, with Welles in the title role, Jack Carter as Mephistopheles, and Joseph Cotton also in the cast. This production, sponsored by the New Deal's WPA (Work Projects Administration), enjoyed a run of some six months, and gave a major impetus to Welles's career. When Welles revived the play in Paris in 1950, he chose as his Helen the famous black singer Eartha Kitt, who told a *Life Magazine* reporter, evidently without irony, of her big moment with Faustus: 'I made him immortal with a kiss'.[185] The music was by Duke Ellington, and the version of the text was very much Welles's own. This production was part of Welles's project to show that American actors, directors, and film makers could do the plays of the English Renaissance in a distinctively American style rather than competing with British productions solely on their terms.[186]

Artistic recognition by the leading centres of Elizabethan revival, the Old Vic and the Shakespeare Memorial Theatre in Stratford-upon-Avon, came in the 1940s. The Old Vic staged *Doctor Faustus* on 16 May 1944 in a theatre let to the company by the Liverpool repertory theatre, under the direction of John Moody, with D. A. Clarke-Smith as Faustus and Noel Willman as Mephistopheles. At Stratford in 1946, Walter Hudd put on a largely uncut B-text *Doctor Faustus* with Robert Harris as Faustus, Hugh Griffith as Mephistopheles, and David King-Wood as the Chorus; in 1947, Paul Scofield took over the part of Mephistopheles and Michael Golden that of the Chorus. The set employed a permanent inner stage for Faustus's study, with separate levels for heaven and hell.[187] For the Old Vic's production on 7 October 1948, director John Burrell chose Cedric Hardwicke to play Faustus and Robert Eddison to play Mephistopheles. The results were disappointing to a number of critics, but at least the play had become a part of the standard repertory.[188]

In the 1960s, in an era of growing East–West tension and American involvement in Vietnam, productions of *Doctor Faustus* often took on a more polemical cast than had been seen before and explored controversial aspects of a play that had been interpreted in a fairly traditional way as a Christian tragedy of evil. Michael Benthall's Old Vic production at the Assembly Hall, Edinburgh, in 1961 was, to be sure, still recognisably Elizabethan in its period costuming, with scholars' habits for Faustus (Paul Daneman) and his fellow students, stubby horns and a goatee for Mephistopheles (Michael Goodliffe), and the like. Yet Benthall chose these traditional icons with a view to subverting them. Visual oppositions explored new dimensions of contrast between ceremonial solemnity (as in papal Rome) and the banality of Faustus's practical joking. As the *Punch* reviewer noted, 'the pageant of the interrupted papal meeting is staged with magnificence . . . [so that] the contrast between the fusty study and the riot of colour when he gets loose as a magician is extremely effective'.[189] Visual juxtaposition and iconoclastic violence of this kind, amply justified by Marlowe's text, were to prove well suited to the 1960s.

Jerzy Grotowski's 1963 production in his Theatre Laboratory in Opole, Poland, carried revisionism about as far as it could go. Grotowski reordered the quarto texts into a 'montage', taking out some scenes to make room for newly invented ones and presenting the whole as a flashback recalled during the last hour of Faustus's life. The set consisted of two long, bare tables running the length of a rectangular, low theatre about forty by fifteen feet in dimension, with one smaller table at one end of the room and with seating for no more than sixty spectators. In this austerely monastic world, Grotowski's Faustus was a martyr who, perceiving God's laws to be nothing more than 'traps contradicting morality and truth', rebelled against divine authority in order to redeem his own self-consciousness, his soul. Mephistopheles's first appearance to the kneeling Faustus was an inverted scene from the Annunciation in which Mephistopheles, 'a soaring angel', sang his lines to the accompaniment of an angelic choir. Faustus had to undergo a masochistic mortification and baptism in a 'river' (the space between the tables) before he could sign the contract and thereby dedicate himself to the purity of a new life. Mephistopheles, now identifiably female, comforted Faustus in her lap, thereby invoking the familiar icon of the Pietà. Faustus received new vestments amid liturgical gestures. When his 'devil-wife' was brought to him, Faustus examined the parts of her body as though they were the planets and other secrets of nature. Having begun to suspect that the devil was in God's service, Faustus underwent a series of temptations by Mephistopheles in which the latter, doubling also as the Good and Bad Angels, dressed as a Jesuit and acted like a police informer. The comic characters, who began the play sitting among the spectators, represented by their talk of beer and whores 'the banality that marks

our everyday life'. When Lucifer paraded before Faustus the Seven
Deadly Sins, all played by the 'double Mephistophilis', Faustus
absolved them as Christ absolved Mary Magdalene. His miracle at
Rome was to convert the Pope into a humble man; at the court of
Charles V, he turned Benvolio into a little child. At his last supper
Helen began to make love to Faustus, gave birth at once to a baby,
and then became herself a 'wailing infant' greedily at suck. Faustus's
last monologue was his 'most outrageous provocation of God', leaving him the moral victor but at 'the full price of that victory: eternal
martyrdom in hell where all is taken from him, even his dignity'.[190]
The contemporary relevance of Grotowski's interpretation gained
from the audience's awareness that Auschwitz was only sixty miles
away.

Although few directors of the 1960s followed the calculated
revisionism of Grotowski to such lengths, the play thrived on the
political and social disillusionment of the era. Nevill Coghill's 1966
production of *Doctor Faustus* at the Playhouse, Oxford, for the
Oxford University Dramatic Society (who had performed the play
under Coghill's direction in 1957), used irony and juxtaposition to
undermine the seeming orthodoxy of the play's Christian framework. Rather than condescend to the comic scene in the Pope's
chamber as feeble theatrical gimcrackery, Coghill treated it as an
occasion for anti-authoritarian violence and blasphemy. The Holy
Father and the Cardinal of Lorraine became parodic copies of
Lucifer (David McIntosh) and Beelzebub (Jeremy Eccles). These
two devils emerged 'luridly out of darkness, enskied perhaps, but
far from sainted'; Mephistopheles (Andreas Teuber) unexpectedly
erupted from behind the shoulder of Faustus.[191] Richard Burton as
Faustus was low-key and conversational, 'a surprisingly dim little
man', a 'bandy-legged little scholar seizing on magic to act out his
frustrated sensual fantasies'.[192] Burton's deliberately unheroic performance was at its best in conveying the sense of wasted opportunity in Faustus's practical joking. Elizabeth Taylor's part of Helen
required her to learn no lines; she was simply there, the quintessential twentieth-century movie goddess, visibly a bit overweight,
playing opposite an actor of extraordinary if dissipated talent
who had graciously come back to Oxford perhaps to enshrine his
tempestuous and deteriorating relationship with Taylor in a moment
of supreme artistic irony. Small wonder that Burton's line, 'Was this
the face that launched a thousand ships?', rang with such intensity.
Viewed reflexively in relation to an unspoken story of disillusioning

love and fading career—a subtext that necessarily impinged upon every aspect of the production—this *Doctor Faustus* was destined to become a fable for the theatre of our times. A film version, co-directed by Burton and Coghill, appeared in 1967.[193]

The threatening presence of the Seven Deadly Sins gave to Clifford Williams's 1968 Royal Shakespeare Company Stratford production (based for the most part on the A-text) an aura of ominous destiny in a distinctively modern idiom. Williams's 'weird skeletal figures' were portentous embodiments of decay lying in wait for the protagonist and finally claiming him at his death. Nigel Alexander describes the production's final scene:

> Faustus finished his final speech grovelling in abject terror on the ground. The clock finished striking. Nothing happened. After a long moment Faustus raised his head and looked round the totally empty stage. He started to laugh. As he reached the hysteria of relief, the back wall of the stage gave way and fell forward in sections revealing an ominous red glow and a set of spikes like the dragon's teeth of the Siegfried Line. The denizens of hell emerged with a kind of slow continuous shuffle until Faustus was surrounded by a circle of these skeletal figures — including the seven deadly sins. He was then seized and carried shrieking through the teeth of hell mouth which closed leaving the wall of Faustus's study again intact.[194]

This Bosch image of diabolical creatures 'boiling over Faustus' agonised body' aptly concluded a play about a man who 'sees bodies rotting and decomposing as objects of beauty and desire'.[195] Bosch and Lucas Cranach provided the visual inspiration for Abd' Elkader Farrah's set and for a tantalising glimpse of a naked Maggie Wright as Helen of Troy. Magical effects included grape pips that exploded when Mephistopheles spat them out, a turban that belched smoke, and a hand that suddenly emerged from a plate of food. Eric Porter was sonorous and fierce-eyed as Faustus; Terrence Hardiman, handsomely young and yet ravaged by torment, 'as quiet and powerful as a coiled spring', was hauntingly bitter as Mephistopheles.[196] The show toured six cities in the United States in early 1969.

Gareth Morgan's production in 1970 for the Royal Shakespeare Company's Theatregoround troupe at Dublin's Abbey Theatre and later at Stratford and the RSC's Roundhouse (also on tour) was consciously unheroic and small-scale. Morgan cut the text to about two and a half hours and doubled forty-nine roles for twelve players. The set was a many-sided grey platform with blocks for furniture; the costumes began in uniform black with an occasional colourful cloak; the acting space was a small lit circle. This austerity and drabness accorded with Morgan's view of his protagonist as a pygmy in the cosmic scale of things—a giant among men, perhaps, but just another sucker in the devil's book. David Waller's Faustus was thus a slightly flabby Northerner of foghorn voice and burly manner, in over his depth, while Alan Howard's Mephistopheles was a figure of fallen greatness now forced to confront his eternal loss of heavenly bliss and his contempt for the duped human being he must serve for a time. The tricks these two played on their victims became increasingly joyless and tawdry. Huge carnival heads for the Deadly Sins, slapstick of the Laurel and Hardy vintage (not excluding the custard pie), and underscoring of sexual double entendre all accentuated the gulf between Faustus's learned ambitions and the crudity of his achievements. In his final moments, Faustus was not hauled off stage by devils but simply dropped to the ground the cloak he had assumed at the play's beginning, thus conveying in a simple gesture the parting of his soul and body. Taut, bleak, unromanticised throughout, Morgan's *Faustus* was a Brechtian parable about alienation.[197]

John Barton, directing *Faustus* for the Royal Shakespeare Company at Nottingham, Newcastle, the Lyceum (Edinburgh), the Aldwych, Stratford, and elsewhere in 1974–5, chose to deglamorise his protagonist by cutting extensively, by adding nearly six hundred lines of his own derived from Marlowe's source, and by conflating the original A and B texts. Barton took out most of the farce to achieve a unity of tone, located all of the action in Faustus's study, and made considerable use of the *Damnable Life* to underscore the play's theology of damnation. The resulting focus on Faustus's inner life was not an ennobling one, despite the absence of low comic action calculated to make him look trivial. As John Barber observed, the effect was to strangle the play's hedonistic exuberances, the wonders of Faustus's European travels, and the zest of his impertinent discomfiting of the Pope, in favour of a depiction of interiorised schizophrenia.[198] In Ian McKellen's portrayal this Faustus was a mental invalid, nursing a diseased ego and confronting in his study the dilemmas of his intellectual arrogance. The two attending angels were glove puppets operated by him; Helen was a marionette in a blonde wig, mask, and nightdress, carried in by Mephistopheles (Emrys Jones). The Deadly Sins too were marionettes, described by Michael Billington as 'wispy, trailing, Bunraku-like creatures that underline the illusory nature of Faustus's pleasure'.[199] Spiritual debate and the lusts of the flesh were thus illusions of theatre, though no less real for being perceived from the inside of Faustus's brain. Hell was understood to be not merely a story-book place of grotesque physical torture but, as Mephistopheles insists, a state of mind. In the same vein, the orientation of good and evil was paradoxically reversed by theatrical sleight of hand: Mephistopheles at one point urged Faustus to turn to God, and the play's choruses spelling out the lesson of spiritual failure were given to Lucifer and his fellow devils. Faustus visibly twitched under the force of being possessed; at his final damnation, his lifeless body sunk from its chair to leave behind an empty, shroud-like scholar's robe. One could well imagine, as Robert Cushman observed, that 'the whole moral system which Faustus transgresses is diabolically controlled'.[200] The overall effect was of 'a nightmare of blindness and appetite'.[201]

Modern interpretation need not, to be sure, adopt the wholesale cutting and rewriting used by John Barton in 1974. Taking the B-text pretty much as it stands, Adrian Noble's production at the Royal Exchange Theatre in Manchester, 1981, found plenty of theatrical links between the scenes of spiritual struggle and those of buffoonery. The production's beginning, for example, was attentive to the academic and clerical setting: a bell tolled as the lights went down, the chorus was spoken by a bell-ringer, Faustus (Ben Kingsley) broke away from divine service to contemplate his books, Valdes and Cornelius arrived as fellow dons, the Good and Evil Angels wore black gowns. When Wagner came on to banter saucily with the two scholars in the manner of a college scout, the continuity between his chop logic and Faustus's sic probo was manifest. The Balioll and Belcher who tormented the clowns were 'evil-faced choirboys armed with rods' on black bicycles. Faustus smirkingly asked a have a 'wife' and was rewarded with a seeming beauty in a white gown and veil, only to encounter beneath her inviting crinoline the painfully biting mouth of a simian mask. The broad horseplay of Robin and Dick with Faustus's stolen conjuring book was placed, as in this edition, right after Faustus's encounter with the 'hot whore', thus clarifying a juxtaposition that is lost in the misarranged B-text (and in the A-text as well). Lechery entered in a procession of the Deadly Sins pushing Sloth in a pram. Faustus took impish pleasure in hitting the Pope's face with a meringue, in impersonating the Cardinals, and in freeing Bruno. Mephistopheles (James Maxwell) provided continuity between 'low' and 'high'

scenes by taking an active if invisible part in Robin's conjurations,
turning the pages of Robin's book as he had previously done for
Faustus, helping Robin to pronounce hard words like 'Demogorgon',
and whispering temptations and encouragements in Robin's ear. The
overall effect, as Russell Jackson wrote, was 'not reductive irony,
showing Faustus squandering his powers on trivial shows, but an
impression of the honour, pleasure and pageantry' he enjoyed. The
'ultimate emptiness of these amusements' was thus 'the greater
for their temporary satisfaction'. Faustus's three encounters with
women ('hot whore', Lechery, and Helen) were 'properly reminiscent of one another'. The production lent support 'to the contention
that Marlowe was a good judge of theatrical effect and that the
shows—if not the language—of the middle part of *Faustus* have
variety and richness'.[202]

Two productions perhaps best illustrate the trend of recent years
towards a nightmare of estrangement and disillusionment. The first
is that of Christopher Fettes at the Lyric Studio, Hammersmith, in
February 1980, later at the Fortune Theatre, featuring John Aubrey
as Faustus, with a 'black box' setting, ethereal supernatural effects
behind a white gauze curtain rear-stage, and an all-male cast (Helen
was a young man in a filmy trouser suit) reminiscent of Grotowski's
Polish production in 1963. The second is that of Barry Kyle for the
Royal Shakespeare Company at the Swan Theatre, Stratford-upon-
Avon, in 1989. In an austere and monochromatic set designed by
Ashley Martin-Davis, performed swiftly without intermission, Kyle's
interpretation was homoerotic, voyeuristic, and vividly iconoclastic.
A recurrent motif was that of defiled sanctity. Faustus (Gerard
Murphy) collected his blood in a chalice, greeted his 'wife' to
the strains of a 'Sanctus', collapsed among his tormentors in the
iconographical posture of the Pietà, and descended finally to hell in a
cruciform cage. Mephistopheles in his first appearance was dressed
not as a monk but as Christ, complete with stigmata and crown of
thorns.[203] An all-male Chorus adopted a protean range of functions:
it emerged from the underworld to open the play, dispersed into
various other dramatic roles, officiated as fellow-students at Faustus's
rejection of the traditional academic disciplines, acted out the
pageant of the Deadly Sins as a single group with agitated body
language (Wrath hissing, Envy standing apart, Gluttony staggering),
writhed half-naked as devils or angels, groaned when the words
'God' or 'heaven' were spoken, and came together once again for the
final chorus. Their metatheatrical omnipresence underscored a sense

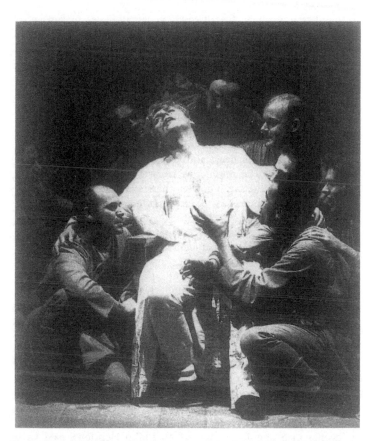

From the Royal Shakespeare Company production of *Doctor Faustus* at the Swan Theatre, Stratford-upon-Avon, 1989, directed by Barry Kyle. Faustus (Gerard Murphy) collapses among his tormentors, including Mephistopheles (David Bradley). Courtesy of the Royal Shakespeare Company. Photograph by Donald Cooper

of an inner unreality, of a diseased imagination, of masturbatory fantasies, of hallucinatory egotism and fears of impotence. Faustus's companions were metamorphosed, as Michael Billington observed, from robed scholars into red devils who clawed and caressed his body 'as in an erotic dream'.[204] Helen was played by a manifestly masculine actor; Faustus and Mephistopheles were often physically close. Devils appeared through the panels of the grey-walled chamber to gape at the virile Helen conjured up for Faustus's delectation. David Bradley's Mephistopheles was no less striking: saturnine, reptilian, cadaverous, insinuating, glacial, moving stiffly in his cassock (in Michael Schmidt's phrase) as if 'carrying Hell with him in his bones', watching Faustus 'like a ferret'.[205] Using Peter Brook's principle of creating magic 'from the resources of the stage', Kyle thus fashioned a Faustus who embodied 'the hero's internal drama'.[206] In productions like these, *Doctor Faustus* has come into its own as a script (or scripts) that can make eminent theatrical sense on today's stage.[207]

THE A- AND B-TEXTS

Doctor Faustus exists in two early versions. The first, the so-called 'A-text', was first printed by Valentine Simmes for Thomas Bushell in quarto (A1) in 1604, some three years after Bushell had entered in the Stationers' Register on 7 January 1601 'A booke called the plaie of Doctor Faustus'. The edition of 1604 was reprinted in 1609 (A2) by George Eld for John Wright (the play being then assigned by Bushell to Wright on 13 September 1610) and in 1611 (A3), again by Eld for Wright. Publication came after years of theatrical success and revision (see 'The Play in Performance'), including the 'adicyones in doctor fostes' for which Philip Henslowe paid £4 to William Birde (or Borne) and Samuel Rowley on 22 November 1602.[208]

The second version of *Faustus*, the so-called 'B-text', first appeared in quarto in 1616 (B1) as printed for John Wright, and was then reprinted at least six times, in 1619 (B2), 1620 (B3), 1624 (B4), 1628 (B5, discovered in the late 1940s), and 1631 (B6, known as B5 before the discovery of the 1628 quarto). Except for the phrase 'With new Additions' inserted into the title-page of B2 and carried forward into subsequent editions, the title-pages are essentially identical. The B2 compositors seem also to have consulted A1 occasionally. None of the reprints of the A-text or the B-text offers evidence of authoritative readings. Nor does a debased version printed in 1663 for William Gilbertson after the play had been assigned to Gilbertson by John Wright's brother Edward. The substantial differences between the A-text and the B-text, on the other hand, pose an immense problem. The B-text omits a few short speeches or episodes totalling 36 lines in the A-text, provides new passages totalling 676 lines, and introduces thousands of verbal changes. Are these changes the result in part of the additions by Birde and Rowley? What is the nature of the copy underlying the two early versions? Editorial practice has veered back and forth. The earliest editors of *Doctor Faustus*—Dilke (1814), Oxberry (1818), and Robinson (1826)—followed the B-text. Most nineteenth- and early twenteth-century editors—Dyce (1850), Wagner (1877), Ward (1878), Bullen (1885), Ellis (1887), and Tucker Brooke (1910)—rejected what they took to be the Birde–Rowley revisions of the B-text in favour of the A-text. Even Cunningham, while basing his 1870 edition on the B-text, allowed the A-text to be closer to Marlowe's original. The B-text, however, regained the field under the championship of Boas (1932), Kirschbaum (1946 and 1962), and Greg (1950), who insisted that the A-text was a so-called 'bad quarto' put together from memory, in which the missing passages could be explained as cuts for performance on tour or as memory lapses. Greg even argued that the fuller B-text gives us substantially the original play rather than the Birde–Rowley additions. Bowers (1952, 1973) allowed that the B-text did include the Birde–Rowley additions but insisted notwithstanding that the A-text is 'a reconstruction from memory' by a group of actors 'of the play as originally performed' while the B-text is derived from 'an authoritative manuscript, very likely the foul papers'.[209] Other editors who based their work on the B-text include Jump (1962), Ribner (1963), and Gill (in her 1965 edition).

Troublesome problems remained unresolved by the hypothesis of memorial reconstruction and preference for the B-text, however. As Bowers conceded, the A-text reporter would have had to suffer a 'complete blackout' in order to leave out the scenes that are entirely missing from the A-text.[210] Greg had already conceded that portions of the B-text rely heavily on A3 and its unauthoritative variants that had been introduced for the first time into A2 or A3. The Birde–Rowley additions, now generally allowed to form a substantial part of the B-text, cannot be part of the original. For these reasons and more, current opinion has shifted once more in favour of the

A-text, in the work of C. L. Barber (1964), Constance Kuriyama (1975), Michael Warren (1981), Roma Gill (in her 1989 and 1990 editions), Stephen Greenblatt (1980), various theatre directors, Ormerod and Wortham (1985), and Keefer (1991).[211] This present edition wishes to support with new evidence the current critical rehabilitation of the A-text, and indeed to go beyond recent work by challenging the still-lingering orthodoxy[212] that the A-text betrays signs of having been memorially reconstructed. What follows here is a condensed and modified account of the argument, presented more fully in Eric Rasmussen's *A Textual Companion to 'Doctor Faustus'* and elsewhere,[213] that the A-text is set from an authorial manuscript composed of interleaved scenes by two dramatists, while the B-text represents a mix of authorial and theatrical provenances that included extensive revision in 1602 and possibly afterwards.

The A-text
The criteria that Kirschbaum and Greg apply to show that the A-text is memorially reconstructed are essentially all reversible. A memorially reconstructed text, they argue, will reveal itself through transposition, misremembering, recollection or anticipation, assimilation, insertion of corrective phrases, and the dividing of the speech of one character among two or more speakers or the combining of two or more characters' speeches into one speech. But how are we to know, for example, whether a presumed A-text reporter inaccurately divided his text between two speakers at I.iv.40–1 ('*Robin.* No, no, here, take your gridirons again. *Wagner.* Truly, I'll none of them') or whether the B-text revisers simply reassigned two speeches to one actor ('*Robin.* Here, take your guilders. I'll none of 'em')?[214] Greg finds both anticipation and recollection in the purportedly sloppy work of the A-text reporter;[215] do not these opposite phenomena cancel each other out as evidence as to which text is revising which? Assimilation works in the same ambivalent way, in favour of either the A-text's original simplicity ('a bottle of hay', IV.i.154, 171, 187) or of the B-text's more authentically varied expression ('a little straw', 'a bottle of hay', 'a bundle of hay', IV.iv.31–44). What Greg calls the insertion of corrective phrases may be editorial or theatrical revision, or simply eyeskip on the part of the A-text compositor. Moreover, in Renaissance texts where we can reliably determine the process by which revision took place, as in Thomas Dekker's 'new written' version (folio 12v) of Anthony Munday's original (folio 11v) in the manuscript *Sir Thomas More*, the original

version nicely illustrates what we would call recollection, anticipation, transposition, dividing of speeches, and assimilation of Dekker's language if we were to imagine for a moment that the original was the revision.[216] Assertions of the B-text's general superiority to the A-text in the tragic sections[217] rest on considerations of taste. Both texts supply readings that are manifestly superior to those of the other text; the improved readings in the B-text can often be accounted for as corrections of obvious error and the A-text compositors' difficulty with their manuscript copy. The manifest shortness for a Renaissance tragedy of the A-text, we will argue, may well be the result of lost manuscript material; in any case, the B-text additions, most of them by Birde and Rowley, do not piece out that part of the play that most readers and viewers regard as part of the original.

Where the two texts report similar incidents, the A-text gives a more reliable account than does the B-text of the playwrights' chief source, the *Damnable Life*. In the description of Rome (III.i.1–43), for example, Greg's hypothesis of memorial reconstruction is unable to explain the A-text's nearly perfect recollection of detail, including 'four' bridges over the Tiber (l. 35), whereas the B-text mistakenly reads 'two'. The A-text version of Faustus's visit to the Emperor (IV.i) is manifestly so much closer to the *Damnable Life* that Greg is forced to hypothesise a complete memory failure on the part of the A-text reporter that left him no expedient other than to turn to the *Damnable Life* and paraphrase it literally.[218] Similarly, Greg can only suppose it to be 'an accident' (p. 377) that the wording of Faustus's conversation with the Duchess of Vanholt is closer to the *Damnable Life* in the A-text than in the B-text: the former literally reproduces such phrases as 'some dainties' and 'I will not hide from you' (IV.ii.6–10), whereas the B-text version gives us paraphrases like 'things' and 'I will make known unto you' (IV.vi.12–15). No 'accident' in reporting could convert such paraphrases into the exact language of the source.

Another argument in favour of the primacy of the A-text is that other plays from the 1590s seem to echo its language at points where the B-text readings are dissimilar. In the anonymous *The Taming of a Shrew* (SR May 1594), now generally viewed as a memorially reconstructed version of Shakespeare's *The Taming of the Shrew* (or, by a few textual scholars, as Shakespeare's source), a speaker declares, 'I take no great delight in it . . . You should command a greater thing than that' (vi.10–17), much as Faustus says to the Duchess of

Vanholt, 'it may be, madam, you take no delight in this . . . Were it
a greater thing than this, so it would content you, you should have
it' (A-text, IV.ii.4–16). The B-text reads quite differently. And since
A Shrew plagiarises freely from other plays as well, including
Tamburlaine, the likelihood is small that the A-text is the borrower.
A Shrew also picks up the unusual word 'pickedevants' from the A-
text at I.iv.3, though in other respects the first two speeches in the
B-text are markedly closer to *A Shrew* than are the comparable
A-text lines, suggesting either that in this instance at least the B-text
provides comic language that was heard on stage in the early 1590s
or possibly that the plagiarist of *A Shrew* is the same Samuel Rowley
who later received payment from Henslowe for revising parts of
Faustus.[219] Other seeming echoes of the A-text appear in *Mucedorus*
(*c.* 1588–98)[220] and *A Looking-Glass for London and England*
(*c.* 1587–91); compare, for example, 'Then may I count myself I
think a tall man, that am able to kill a devil' in *A Looking-Glass*
(ll. 1733–4) with the A-text's 'Say I should kill one of them, what
would folks say? "Do ye see yonder tall fellow in the round slop? He
has killed the devil." So should I be called "Kill devil" all the parish
over' (I.iv.49–52). (The B-text says nothing about killing the
devil.)[221] Individual parallels of this sort are reversible as evidence of
borrowing, and not much critical weight can be attached to them,
but in view of the derivative nature of *A Shrew* and *A Looking-Glass*,
the evidence may provide further cumulative support for the
hypothesis that some version of the A-text was being performed
in the early 1590s.

If the A-text, then, is prior to the B-text and cannot be shown to
have been memorially reconstructed, what sort of printer's copy lies
behind it? Recognising that the traditional categories of 'good' and
'bad' quartos, 'foul papers', 'promptbooks' or 'playbooks', and the
like have been cast into suspicion by the recent researches of Paul
Werstine and William B. Long, and that the terms 'foul draught'
and 'foul papers' occur only rarely in Renaissance usage,[222] we wish
to argue that prompters and bookkeepers did none the less sometimes impose theatrical regularisations upon scripts acquired by
the acting companies and that, however sporadic those theatrical
markings appear to have been, we should be able to recognise
on balance a difference between texts based largely on authorial
manuscripts and those based on playhouse documents like the playbook. The striking fact for our present purposes, in any event, is
that all the supposed characteristics of authorial papers identified by

Greg—loose ends and false starts, inconsistency in the designation of characters by means of stage directions and in speech prefixes, and indefinite or permissive stage directions[223]—are identifiable in the A-text of *Doctor Faustus*.

Take for example false starts and second thoughts, which in Greg's view are the most indisputable evidence of authorial copy, and which are incompatible in any case with a theory of memorial reconstruction even if, as seems possible, false starts may sometimes be attributable to scribal copying.[224] The A-text offers a double ending of III.ii in which the clowns mockingly conjure Mephistopheles; he enters twice (without exiting) and twice transforms the clowns into beasts. Greg is obliged at this point to suppose that his reporter first reconstructed from memory the scene as it was originally staged, but that the acting company, dissatisfied with this ending for the scene, had someone other than the reporter write a new conclusion, leaving both in the manuscript as alternatives for performance. Even Greg admits that the motive for such a revision is not clear. A false-start hypothesis, on the other hand, proposes more simply that the compositor, working with authorial papers or a copy closely based on them, failed to ignore a deletion mark for the first version. The B-text, derived evidently from a script that incorporated some theatrical practice, deletes the first ending in favour of the second.

The A-text contains permissive stage directions, such as we find in *Romeo and Juliet* ('*Enter three or four Citizens*', I.i.72.1) and elsewhere in texts often ascribed to authorial papers. Faustus enters in the fifth act '*with two or three* SCHOLARS' (v.i.8.1). The B-text uses the same phrasing. We can more easily argue that the partly theatrical manuscript upon which B was based simply failed to regularise this feature, or that the scribe preparing printer's copy for the B-text (see below) relied on a copy of A3 at this point, than that a hypothetical A-text reporter, witnessing a stage performance in which a specific number of scholars must have appeared in v.i, would then coincidentally invent the same permissive phrase that had been set down in the B-text manuscript. And although vague numbering in stage directions can occur in texts usually thought to be memorially reconstructed (such as Shakespeare's *The First Part of the Contention*), they are perhaps more likely to do so in referring to silent extras like lords and soldiers than in the case of three speaking scholars in *Doctor Faustus*. Other imprecise references to 'scholars' and 'devils' occur at I.iii.23.2 and 27.1, v.i.113.1, and v.ii.0.1 and 120.1.[225]

Information on the composition and printing of the 1604 quarto offers more concrete evidence that the A-text was based on authorial papers. Two compositors worked for Valentine Simmes on this black-letter quarto. There may have been a break in the printing process between sheets D and E, since, as Robert Ford Welsh observes, the two skeleton-formes used throughout are reversed on sheet E,[226] and since sheets E and F have only 36 lines per page whereas the previous sheets all have 37; moreover, the final sheet F features a new watermark. Although these changes invite the speculation that the work was shared by two printing shops, the presence of this watermark in another book (Q3 of *1 Henry IV*) printed by Simmes in 1604, and the use throughout sheets A–F of the same black-letter fount with recurrent pieces of identifiable type, strongly indicate that the whole book was printed in Simmes's shop rather than being shared with another printer. The evidence also supports Bowers's contention that sheet A was not cast off and set last, but was instead the first to be composed.[227]

Although attempts to link at least one of A1's two compositors (labelled by Welsh as X and Y) with compositors working for Simmes on other books have not been entirely convincing,[228] we can reasonably distinguish their work on A1. Compositor X abbreviates speech headings and punctuates them with a period, uses an upper-case *E* in *Exit* directions, prefers *-ea-* spellings in words like *year*, *dear*, and *chear*, prefers *bloud* over *blood*, and uses *-ll* spellings in words like *will*, *shall*, and *hell*. Compositor Y frequently uses un-abbreviated and unstopped speech headings or abbreviated speech headings punctuated with a colon. He prefers the lower-case *e* for *exit* directions, *-ee-* spellings in words like *yeer*, *deer*, and *cheer*, prefers *blood* over *bloud*, and uses single *-l* spellings in words like *wil*, *shal*, and *hel*. From these differences we determine that Compositor X set A2r–B2r, B3v, B4v 37–C2r 24, C3r 28–C3v 30, C4v 16–37, D1r 28–D3r 8, E2r 12–E3r 5, E3v 29–E4v 11, and F1v 6–36; in the present edition, these passages correspond to Prologue–I.iii.75, I.iv.34–67, II.i.61–151, II.iii.44–83, II.iii.142–62, III.i.0.1–100.2 and the Chorus to Act IV, IV.1.136–95, V.i.17–69, and V.ii.13–45. Compositor Y set the rest.

Stint assignments by Welsh and Bowers differ in a few details,[229] but in all such assignments a remarkable fact emerges: the two compositors generally do not begin or end at the beginning of a new page or sheet. Instead, they frequently change in mid-page, some-times at the beginning of a new scene (III.i, III.ii, and IV.ii) or at the entrance of a character within a scene (II.i.151.1–2, II.iii.83.1). They also shift stints in mid page where no scene break or entrance occurs. Moreover, a study of recurrence of broken type, undertaken for this present edition, even allowing for the difficulty of such a study of a single printed copy and of relying chiefly on the evidence of types from sheet C recurring in sheet E, confirms Bowers's hypothesis that the two compositors were setting from two type-cases and setting simultaneously—this despite what may have been the more normal practice of setting in turn when two or more compositors worked on a book.[230] Even though two compositors using two type-cases could conceivably have worked by turns, the combined evidence of distinctive compositor punctuation and spellings, together with the recurrence of identifiable type, offers substantial proof of simultanous setting.[231] What are we to make of a practice that, as Bowers observes, is 'so consistent and so odd as to call for explanation'?[232]

The best explanation is Bowers's own conjecture, that the two compositors 'were setting from manuscript that had not been cast off but where arbitrary joins could be marked at readily identifiable points' (II.146–7), allowing the compositors to set not complete pages but galley stints that were then transferred on to the imposing stone and there divided into pages, by formes, at the time of imposition. Such an unusual practice, requiring compositorial shifts in mid page, strongly suggests that the two compositors were handed batches of manuscript that could not be cast off in the usual manner. And since a number of the 'readily identifiable points' marking new stints are at scene breaks or important entrances, we might well suppose that at least some fresh scenes began on a new manuscript page. The only type of manuscript likely to feature such a characteristic, as Bowers observes elsewhere, is 'the foul papers of a collaboration'.[233]

Such a likelihood has important consequences for the A-text of *Doctor Faustus*. It confirms the probability that we are dealing with authorial copy, not a reported text, unless we improbably hypothesise two reporters whose work was then interleaved for the compositors. As a procedure for dealing with authorial collaboration, on the other hand, the sort of copy proposed here has manifest advantages. It supposes the assignment of various portions of the play to two dramatists. It offers a ready explanation for the apparent misjoining and misplacing of scenes—a marked feature of the A-text, where a very long scene in Act II involving Faustus and

Mephistopheles and then the Seven Deadly Sins seems to require division into two separated scenes (and is indeed thus divided in the B-text), and where two linked clowning scenes awkwardly feature comic characters (Robin and Rafe) who must exit at the end of the first scene only to reappear immediately in the second. (See Appendix for a discussion of the editors' solution in this present edition by moving the first comic scene between Robin and Rafe to the middle of Act II.) The B-text shows signs of having struggled with the A-text's mis-shuffling of scenes, albeit with imperfect success.

Above all, the present explanation suggests that in the A-text we have something resembling what Marlowe and a collaborator wrote, even if their separate portions may have been interleaved incorrectly at times and some material may have been lost. The hypothesis of a joint authorial manuscript may give us insight into how the collaboration proceeded.

Collaborative authorship
Scholars have long suspected that Marlowe wrote the serious and tragic portions of *Doctor Faustus*, by and large, and that a collaborator took responsibility for the comic horseplay. We support that view. Possibly Marlowe had already collaborated in the writing of *Tamburlaine*, as the printer Richard Jones's 'To the Gentlemen Readers' suggests by its reference to some 'fond and frivolous' material that he has chosen to excise from Part I. Certainly the normal Renaissance practice was for collaborating dramatists to divide their labour by scenes,[234] and the authors of *Doctor Faustus* seem to have been no exception. Our analysis of the frequency of function-words like 'for', 'from', 'here', 'how', 'if', 'in', 'now', 'out', 'so', 'some', 'than', 'then', 'this', 'to', and 'which' suggests that Marlowe was responsible for the Prologue, I.i, I.iii, II.i, II.iii, V.i to the end, and perhaps the Choruses to Acts III and IV, with a collaborator taking on the rest. Word-frequency tests are of course only matters of statistical probability, and are particularly subject to hazard in small samples like the Choruses or portions of larger scenes like the appearance of the Seven Deadly Sins (which, taken by itself, falls within the normal range of Marlowe's use of function-words). Even as a speculation, none the less, the test is remarkable for the extent to which it assigns most of the comic scenes to a collaborator.[235]

Renaissance playwrights working together on a play generally worked apart. Occasional contradictions between the serious and comic scenes of *Doctor Faustus* seem to confirm Greg's supposition that Marlowe 'planned the whole' and then farmed out certain scenes to another dramatist who worked with only an imprecise knowledge of what Marlowe was up to.[236] When Mephistopheles is conjured up by Robin, his annoyance at being summoned 'From Constantinople . . . Only for pleasure of these damnèd slaves' (III.ii.33–5) contradicts his earlier insistence, to Faustus, that he was not raised by Faustus's conjuring speeches but came of his 'own accord' (I.iii.44–55).[237] Nor have we heard any mention of Constantinople in the accounts of Faustus's travels, though it does appear prominently in the source to which the collaborator was evidently directed, the *Damnable Life* (ch. 22). Quite plausibly, then, the collaborator was given the assignment of dramatising certain episodes from the *Damnable Life*, such as the scene at the Emperor's court (ch. 29–30), the Horse-courser episode (ch. 34), and the scene at the Duke of Vanholt's court (ch. 39), along with the invented comic horseplay of Wagner and the clowns.

We have seen that Compositors X and Y, working simultaneously, did not cast off their copy in a way that allowed them to set whole pages consistently; instead, they sometimes began their stints in mid page and at scene breaks or important new entrances where a change of author seems indicated. The irregularity of this procedure suggests that the printers' copy was a composite authorial manuscript compiled of separate scenes. The misplacement of at least one comic scene adds to the plausibility of this hypothesis. So does the misplacement of one chorus (which must have been written on a separate page) and the possible loss of others. When we add to this the consideration that the Admiral's Men sold four plays from their repertory to London publishers in 1600–1, all of them apparently dramatists' manuscripts,[238] we perceive the likelihood that Thomas Bushell too, in January of 1601, obtained his copy of *Doctor Faustus* from the Admiral's Men and Henslowe not as a reported text but as the original manuscript of Marlowe and his collaborator. These are the papers Henslowe would have found expendable once a fair copy had been made into a playbook, and all the more so if, as seems virtually certain, he was at the point of ordering new additions from Birde and Rowley. The *Doctor Faustus* he evidently sold in 1601 was an outdated text.

Who was Marlowe's collaborator? Samuel Rowley, whom Henslowe paid for revisions of *Doctor Faustus* in 1602, seems to have been born around 1575 and would thus have been too young in

1588–9. So was Thomas Dekker, born in 1572. Neither emerges as a working playwright until 1598.[239] Thomas Nashe is a more interesting candidate, since, as Paul Kocher has urged, suggestive parallels do occur, especially in the farcical depiction of a papal feast (Nashe's *Lenten Stuff*, 1597) and in a conjuring up of a great figure from the past (*The Unfortunate Traveller*, 1594).[240] Such resemblances, however, can be accounted for by the fact that Nashe was writing well after Marlowe's play had become famous on stage. Verbal parallels and recurring rare words like 'pickedevants', '*Qui mihi discipulus*', 'stavesacre', 'Mistress Minx', and 'hey-pass', found nowhere else in Marlowe, are tantalising, but 'rare word' tests are of limited validity in dealing with authors of unusually large vocabularies like Shakespeare and Nashe.[241] Too many of Nashe's distinctive stylistic traits noted by R. B. McKerrow, such as the separation of an adverbial phrase from the adjective to which it belongs, boisterous compound words, Italianate verbs ending in -*ize*, and a predilection for the qualifying 'almost', are missing from the collaborator's scenes in the A-text of *Doctor Faustus*. A possible candidate not heretofore proposed is Henry Porter, Marlowe's contemporary at Cambridge and a dramatist for the Admiral's Men at the time Marlowe was writing *Tamburlaine* and *Doctor Faustus*, whose repeated use of the phrase 'Do you hear?' in *The Two Angry Women of Abington*, c. 1587–8 (ll. 2049–51, 2119–20), markedly more so than in other plays of the period, is liberally sprinkled in the A-text of *Doctor Faustus* (as at I.iv.20–69). This is only a very speculative possibility, however. What seems more certain is that Marlowe did have a collaborator.

The B-text
Samuel Rowley, one of the revisers of *Doctor Faustus* in 1602, seems to have left his distinctive mark on some of the B-text additions. His trick of completing a verse line with an adjective terminating in -*al*, prominently visible in Rowley's only known play, *When You See Me You Know Me* (1603–5), is also notable in Faustus's rescue of Bruno from Rome (B-text, III.i.57–III.ii.57). Moreover, these Bruno scenes are derived from John Foxe's *Acts and Monuments*, a source to which Rowley turned for his scenes of Lutheran intrigue in *When You See Me*.[242]

Other stylistic characteristics tend cumulatively to distinguish the B-text additions in Acts IV and V dealing with Frederick, Martino, Benvolio, the Clowns, and so on from those parts of the play where

the A-text and B-text are more nearly in agreement. Such characteristics include the liberal use of rhymed couplets, clumsy joins,
and three instances of the contraction *i'the*, a form that appears to
have been extremely rare before 1599.[243] Some dramatist other than
Rowley must have helped with these B-text additions, since one
marked stylistic feature of IV.i–iii and V.ii—the shift from one
speaker to another in the middle of a verse line (some ten occurrences in these 235 added lines)—is almost wholly absent (one
occurrence) in the passages from III.i and ii attributed to Rowley.
Similarly, the trick of referring to Faustus as 'the doctor' occurs
twice in IV.i and several times in the additional prose scenes, as
well as at V.iii.5, but never in the original A-text or in the scenes
suggested for Rowley. William Birde (or Borne) may be the reviser
here, since Henslowe paid him and Rowley for additions in 1602,
but in the absence of any identifiable writing we have no way of
testing Birde's authorship of any part of *Doctor Faustus*. Birde and
Rowley may also have revised some of the original scenes.[244]

Birde and Rowley were not the only revisers responsible for the
B-text's many alterations. Marlowe and his collaborator may have
done some rewriting; few authors could resist the opportunity to
introduce verbal changes whenever they had to copy a text.[245] Any
identifiable changes of this sort would bear strong authority. On the
other hand, the play was produced and revived over a long period of
time after Marlowe's death, providing irresistible opportunities for
revisions that are non-authorial.[246] The alteration of the A-text's
'Tha⊤ yearly stuffs old Philip's treasury' at I.i.134 to the past tense,
'That yearly stuffed old Philip's treasury' in the B-text, may have
been introduced by the 1602 revisers to reflect the death of Philip II
of Spain in 1598. If, as seems likely, Henslowe would pay his
playwrights only for fair copy manuscripts,[247] Birde and Rowley
may have had reason to copy the whole, with plentiful opportunity
to reword even those passages they took more or less as they found
them. A seeming echo from *Hamlet* in 'He took his rouse with
stoups of Rhenish wine' (B IV.i.19; compare *Hamlet*, I.iv.8–10) may
or may not point to a date right around 1602; the indebtedness could
be later. If Benvolio's comment at IV.ii.27, 'But yet my heart's more
ponderous than my head', owes something to the Folio version of
Cordelia's aside in *King Lear*—'And yet not so, since I am sure
my love's / More ponderous than my tongue' (I.i.77–8), and if
Shakespeare is the originator of this phrase rather than the copier,
we could be dealing with a revision as late as 1609–10, since the

earlier quarto version (1608) of *Lear* differs significantly. Verbal alterations in the B-text can generally be explained without positing the involvement of the original dramatists.

Some readings of the B-text are derived from the A3 quarto of 1611. Marked agreements in spellings (e.g., 'Magitian'), orthographic features ('In stead', 'some time'), and shared substantive readings ('subtle Sillogismes') demonstrate with certainty that B1 was in some way influenced by A3. Yet B1 does not seem to have been set directly from a copy of A3; as Bowers shows, certain misreadings suggest a reliance on handwritten copy ('Sworne' for 'Swarme', 'Lopland' for 'Lapland', 'desir'd' for 'desire' and the like), while others show the compositor persisting in a misreading ('euening Starres' for 'erring Starres', I.iii.12 and II.iii.42) that would have been clear to him in printed copy. The very regularity of the compositors' stints in B1, and the apparent ease with which copy was cast off, suggest that the two compositors were not dealing with a mix of manuscript and annotated quarto copy. Bowers posits instead a scribe who made a fresh copy for the printer, sometimes using an example of A3 as his central authority when its text was close to his manuscript and otherwise consulting it on occasion.[248] In any case, B1 was substantially influenced by A3 and hence was derived in part from A1.

Theatrical markings of the sort normally recorded in Renaissance playbooks have left their imprint on the B-text. Bowers posits that the printers' copy for B1 was a transcript of the original authors' foul papers along with an infusion of A3 readings and the revisions of 1602. But might not some of this material have passed through theatrical hands? Consider, for example, the duplicate stage direction at the end of III.ii in the B-text, '*Beat the* FRIARS, *fling firework among them, and exeunt*', together with another '*Exeunt*' at the right margin. A1 provides only the original direction, sightly varied in its wording. Greg and Bowers merely suppose that B1's version represents the work of a copyist or editor preparing the manuscript for the printer,[249] but a copyist would have no motive to make such a duplication whereas a bookkeeper would be following normal playhouse practice. In the extant manuscript of Massinger's *Believe as You List* (1631), for example, the bookkeeper frequently repeats in the margin, apparently to facilitate prompting, entry directions that he leaves standing in the text. Greg elsewhere agrees that 'the repetition of stage directions' in printed texts 'points to prompt copy'.[250] Similarly, the tendency of the B-text to print mid-scene entrances over to the right rather than centred as in the A-text may reflect playhouse practice, as in the playbook manuscript of the anonymous *Charlemagne* (1584–c. 1605).[251] Certainly the 1602 additions are attentive to practical staging matters like thunder, music, processions, exeunts 'several ways', action 'above', descents from the 'heavens', and the like (see 'Staging and Themes in the 1616 Quarto', above). The B-text sometimes uses the theatrical imperative in stage directions, such as '*Music sound*' at v.i.26.2 in place of the A-text's descriptive '*Music sounds*'.

We do not wish to argue that the B-text represents a theatrical manuscript throughout. Its erroneous placement of the A-text's Chorus to Act III and its unconvincing placement of the first comic scene between Robin and Rafe (the latter renamed Dick) point to an unsuccessful literary or editorial attempt to solve the A-text's arrangement of scenes that any bookkeeper would have found intolerable. Several departures in the B-text from the A-text certainly do not seem theatrically derived, such as the omission of entry and exit directions found in the A-text (Prologue. 27, I.iv.39.1), the omission of the word '*Enter*' (I.i.0.1, IV.i.47.3), the inconsistent naming of the Bad Angel as '*Spirit*' (I.i.68.1) and '*Euill An.*' (II.i.14) in contrast with the A-text's consistent use of '*Evil Angel*', stage directions with vague proper names and descriptions of action where the A-text is more precise (B I.iv.36.1, II.iii.78.1, IV.iv.28.1), and declarative stage directions in place of the A-text's imperatives (B II.i.146.1, IV.iv.28.1, and IV.iv.37). Some of the B-text's theatrical features cited in the previous paragraph, such as attentiveness to sound effects and processions, could well have been written in by the revising authors rather than the bookkeeper. We do argue, on the other hand, that certain features pointing to an intermittent playhouse influence should not be ignored in an attempt to reconstruct the nature and evolution of printers' copy for the 1616 quarto. A play that had undergone at least one major revision for a revival might well be expected to show some effects of adaptation for practical use in the theatre, and we believe this to be the case with *Doctor Faustus*.

Evidence of censorship in the B-text further confirms a view that this text is a compilation of materials written and revised at different times and with varying degrees of theatrical annotation. The additions attributable to Birde and Rowley in 1602 introduce many strong profanities, such as ''Snails' (II.ii.11), 'By Lady' (III.iii.38), ''Lounds' (IV.i.87, 132, 138 and 150, IV.ii.67, and IV.iii.13, variously spelled in the original), and "Sblood' (iv.i.152 and 164). Censorship of such oaths was not necessary for publication even in 1616, after the parliamentary act of 1606 forbidding the use on stage of 'the holy name of God or of Christ Jesus, or of the Holy Ghost or of the Trinity'; that act was directed at theatrical performance, and John Wright, the publisher of B1 in 1616, had already published A2 of *Doctor Faustus* in 1609 and A3 in 1611 with no evidence of censorship. On the other hand, some of the play's original scenes have been censored in B1. Two references to Christ are deleted (A v.ii.78 and 100), though some others remain. Mephistopheles's advice to 'abjure the Trinity' (A i.iii.54) becomes 'abjure all godliness' (B i.iii.51). Several references to God are removed or altered to the less objectionable 'heaven' (A ii.i.10, 25, 78, v.ii.77, 82, 85, 98, 120). The offensive ''Swounds' at i.iv.30 in the A-text disappears in the B-text, directly contradicting the practice of the B-text revisers with their 'Zounds' and ''Zons'. If Gary Taylor is right in insisting that excision of profanity is a sign of a theatrically-based text altered for performance after 1606,[252] we ought to view this censorship as an attempt to prepare a version of the original play for a stage revival well after the 1602 revision. Yet the scribe Ralph Crane, we now know, rewrote and took out some offensive language in a fairly unsystematic and 'literary' way as he copied,[253] and some at least of the expurgations in *Doctor Faustus* sound as if motivated by the imprecise notions of taste and decorum of a scribe. 'Tush' is systematically expunged (at A ii.i.138, ii.iii.49 and 55). 'Tut', possibly confused with 'tush', disappears at ii.iii.167,[254] even while other seemingly more offensive profanities are allowed to stand. We cannot be certain, then, that any alterations of profanity took place after 1606 in order to ready the text for performance. We can be reasonably certain of two things: first, that the 1602 revisers, who introduced profanity with abandon, were not the censors of the original part of the play, and second, that no one ever assembled or transcribed a manuscript of the B-text with a consistent approach to profanity. The B-text seems to represent a compilation of various kinds of copy produced on at least three occasions: at the time of original composition, in 1602, and at some other time.

What kind of copy, then, was provided to the printers of B1 in 1616? T. H. Howard-Hill posits in the case of the Folio *King Lear* that the scribe commissioned to prepare printers' copy used a copy of a quarto (Q2 in this instance) as a means of interpreting the manuscript playbook when he found it hard to decipher.[255] Perhaps a similar hypothesis can be applied to *Doctor Faustus* B1. Some time between 1611 and 1616, the publisher John Wright presumably hired someone to make up printers' copy for a new and expanded edition of the play Wright had published in its shorter form in 1609 (A2) and 1611 (A3). The preparer of this printers' copy must have been given a copy of A3, together with some manuscript version of the play—either a playbook that, because it had been added to at various times for different revivals of the play, contained both censored and uncensored scenes together with erroneous placement of a Chorus and a comic scene, or else, as Bowers argues, the foul papers of Marlowe and his original collaborator along with the 1602 revisions. Something like the former hypothesis seems more plausible to the present editors, since it better allows for various chronological layers of addition and revision after 1602.[256] The possibility of some revision as late as 1608–16 is perhaps reinforced by the fact that the *Damnable Life* was reprinted in 1608 and that the added scenes about Benvolio draw heavily upon this source (though it was of course available in earlier editions), whereas the added scenes about Bruno and the German Emperor are derived chiefly from Foxe's *Acts and Monuments*. Some such hypothesis about the mixed copy lying behind *Doctor Faustus* B1, in any event, can account for many of B1's most salient features: (*a*) strong evidence that B1 was set throughout from manuscript copy; (*b*) equally strong evidence of influence from A3; (*c*) a sprinkling of authoritative readings in B1 that are not in A3; (*d*) new material in B1 from an independent manuscript source; and (*e*) misplacement of a comic scene and the Chorus to Act III, despite literary attempts to solve the misarrangement of the A-text.

The consequences for editors of *Doctor Faustus* seem clear. Because the B-text incorporates a thorough if intermittent reworking of concept and language, it deserves to be treated as a text by itself. All the evidence adduced here, on the other hand, points to the A-text as closer in most ways to the original work of Marlowe and his collaborator (though the B-text remains an important witness in critical editing and offers a few clearly superior readings, along with a host of indifferent variants that may in some cases be authorial). Editors and critics alike need to be wary of claims based on a conflated text. Both texts of *Doctor Faustus* continue to deserve our divided attention.

NOTES

Date

1 W. W. Greg, ed., Marlowe's 'Doctor Faustus' 1604–1616: Parallel Texts (Oxford: Clarendon, 1950), pp. 5 ff., provides much useful information on dating, though he chooses to argue for a date in 1592.

2 I. A. Shapiro, 'The Significance of a Date', SSur. VIII (1955), 100–5.

3 Curt A. Zimansky, 'Marlowe's Faustus: the Date Again', PQ, XLI (1962), 181–7. On A Looking-Glass, see Constance Brown Kuriyama, 'Dr. Greg and Doctor Faustus: the Supposed Originality of the 1616 Text', ELR, V (1975), 171–97, pp. 181 ff.; Greg, p. 53; and William Empson, Faustus and the Censor (Oxford: B. Blackwell, 1987), pp. 185–95.

4 MacD. P. Jackson, 'Three Old Ballads and the Date of Doctor Faustus', Journal of the Australasian Universities, Language and Literature Association, XXXVI (1971), 187–200.

5 William Prynne, Histrio-Mastix (1633), pt. i, p. 556.

6 Greg, pp. 5 ff.; John Henry Jones, 'The Earliest English Faust Book', forthcoming.

7 Paul H. Kocher, 'The English Faust Book and the Date of Marlowe's Faustus', MLN, LV (1940), 95–101, 'The Early Date for Marlowe's Faustus', MLN, LVIII (1943), 539–42, and 'Some Nashe Marginalia Concerning Marlowe', MLN, LVII (1942), 45–9. See Greg, pp. 5–6, for a counterargument.

8 Harold Jantz, 'An Elizabethan Statement on the Origin of the German Faust Book', JEGP, LI (1952), 137–53.

9 Philip Mason Palmer and Robert Pattison More, The Sources of the Faust Tradition, from Simon Magus to Lessing (Oxford University Press, 1936), p. 177. Empson, pp. 92–5, argues that publication in 1592 was delayed through censorship and that the translation is earlier.

10 Those who argue for an early date on the basis of stylistic and other affinities between Tamburlaine and Doctor Faustus include Jeremy Collier, The History of English Dramatic Poetry to the Time of Shakespeare, 3 vols. (London: John Murray, 1831), III.126–30; M. M. Mahood, Poetry and Humanism (London: J. Cape, 1950), p. 66; Robert Knoll, Christopher Marlowe (New York: Twayne, 1969), p. 70; and J. B. Steane, Marlowe: a Critical Study (Cambridge University Press, 1965), pp. 118–19.

11 In favour of the later date on stylistic grounds, among others, are Frederick S. Boas, Christopher Marlowe: a Biographical and Critical Study (Oxford: Clarendon, 1940), and Greg, pp. 5 ff.

Sources and background

12 See below, 'The A- and B-texts', for an analysis of collaboration on the A-text. In this Introduction we often speak of 'Marlowe' as the dramatist

as a matter of convenience, and because Marlowe was responsible for the more 'serious' and 'tragic' parts of the play, but the collaborative nature of the playwrights' task should be understood to be implicit in the discussion throughout.

13 See John Bakeless, *The Tragicall History of Christopher Marlowe*, 2 vols. (Cambridge, Mass.: Harvard University Press, 1942), ch. viii; Palmer and More, *The Sources of the Faust Tradition*, p. 87; Michael Keefer, ed., *Christopher Marlowe's 'Doctor Faustus'* (Peterborough: Broadview, 1991), pp. xxxiii–xxxvii; Keefer, 'Right Eye and Left Heel: Ideological Origins of the Legend of Faustus', *Mosaic*, XXII (1989), 79–94; and P. W. F. Brown, 'St. Clement and Dr. Foster', *N&Q*, CXCIX, n.s. I (1954), 140–1, for what is known about the historical Faustus.

14 Citations throughout are to the A-text unless otherwise specified.

15 John D. Jump, ed., *Doctor Faustus*. The Revels Plays (London: Methuen, 1962), pp. xxxviii–xxxix.

16 Harry Levin, *The Overreacher* (Cambridge, Mass.: Harvard University Press, 1952), p. 110. John Henry Jones gives an extensive account of the *Damnable Life* in his Introduction to Empson, pp. 12–36.

17 See, for example, in the B-text additions at III.iii.53–5, a reference to 'the Great Turk's court', an episode from the *Damnable Life* that is not in the original play.

18 Sara Munson Deats, '*Doctor Faustus*: From Chapbook to Tragedy', *Essays in Literature*, III (1976), 3–16; James A. Reynolds, 'Marlowe's *Dr. Faustus*: "Be a divine in show" and "When all is done, divinity is best"', *American Notes and Queries*, XIII (1975), 131–3; and Erich Heller, 'Faust's Damnation: the Morality of Knowledge', *The Listener*, LXVII (1962), 59–61.

19 Douglas Cole, *Suffering and Evil in the Plays of Christopher Marlowe* (Princeton University Press, 1962), pp. 203, 207–8. See also Arieh Sachs, 'The Religious Despair of Doctor Faustus', *JEGP*, LXIII (1964), 625–47, and Butler Waugh, 'Deep and Surface Structure in Traditional and Sophisticated Literature: Faust', *South Atlantic Bulletin*, XXX.iii (1968), 14–17.

20 Erich Kahler, 'Doctor Faustus from Adam to Sartre', *Comp.D*, I (1967), 75–92.

21 Wolfgang S. Seiferth, 'The Concept of the Devil and the Myth of the Pact in Literature Prior to Goethe', *Monatshefte*, XLIV (1952), 271–89.

22 J. P. Brockbank, *Marlowe: Dr. Faustus* (London: Arnold, 1962), pp. 12–13; David Woodman, *White Magic and Renaissance Drama* (Rutherford: Fairleigh Dickinson University Press, 1973), pp. 35–49.

23 Beatrice Daw Brown, 'Marlowe, Faustus, and Simon Magus', *PMLA*, LIV (1939), 82–121; Keefer, pp. xxxix–xli; and Brockbank, pp. 10–11. Paul H. Kocher, 'The Witchcraft Basis in Marlowe's *Faustus*', *MP*, XXXVIII (1940), 9–36, discounts the likelihood of direct influence on Marlowe by the Simon Magus texts here discussed, since the elements

linking Faustus and Simon are widely distributed in witchcraft lore.
24 Ailene S. Goodman, 'Alchemistic Diabolism in the *Faust* of Marlowe
   and Goethe', *Journal of Evolutionary Psychology*, V (1984), 166–70.
25 Michael Hattaway, 'The Theology of Marlowe's *Doctor Faustus*', *Ren.D*,
   n.s. III (1970), 51–78. On Marlowe's probable familiarity with general
   witchcraft traditions as recorded in Reginald Scot's *The Discovery of
   Witchcraft* (1584) and similar tracts, see Kocher in note 23 above; Robert
   H. West, *The Invisible World: a Study of Pneumatology in Elizabethan
   Drama* (Athens, Ga.: University of Georgia Press, 1939), passim; West,
   'The Impatient Magic of Dr. Faustus', *ELR*, IV (1974), 218–40; and
   Keefer, pp. xxxviii–xxxix.
26 Brockbank, pp. 9–13; Claude J. Summers and Ted-Larry Pebworth,
   'The Conversion of St. Augustine and the B-Text of *Doctor Faustus*',
   Renaissance and Renascences in Western Literature, I.ii (1979), 1–8; David
   Ormerod and Christopher Wortham, eds., *Christopher Marlowe, 'Dr
   Faustus': the A-Text* (Nedlands: University of Western Australia Press,
   1985), pp. li–liii; Hilary Gatti, *The Renaissance Drama of Knowledge:
   Giordano Bruno in England* (London: Routledge, 1989), pp. 74–113;
   Frances A. Yates, *The Occult Philosophy in the Elizabethan Age* (London:
   Routledge, 1979), pp. 92–3; and Eleanor Grace Clark, 'Atheism and the
   Bruno Scandal in *Doctor Faustus*', *Ralegh and Marlowe: a Study in
   Elizabethan Fustian* (New York: Fordham University Press, 1941), pp.
   338–89.
27 David Bevington, *From 'Mankind' to Marlowe* (Cambridge, Mass.:
   Harvard University Press, 1962).
28 Clifford Leech, '*Faustus*: a Moral Play?', *Christopher Marlowe, Poet for
   the Stage*, ed. Anne Lancashire (New York: AMS Press, 1986), pp.
   100–20. See also Malcolm Kelsall, *Christopher Marlowe* (Leiden: E. J.
   Brill, 1981), pp. 154–80.
29 David Kaula, 'Time and the Timeless in *Everyman* and *Dr. Faustus*',
   CE, XXII (1960), 9–14.
30 Lily B. Campbell, '*Doctor Faustus*: a Case of Conscience', *PMLA*, LXVII
   (1952), 219–39, Arieh Sachs, 'The Religious Despair of Doctor
   Faustus', *JEGP*, LXIII (1964), 625–47, and Helen Gardner, 'Milton's
   "Satan" and the Theme of Damnation in Elizabethan Tragedy', *E&S*,
   n.s. I (1948), 46–66. On the resemblance of *Doctor Faustus* to a
   seventeenth-century play by Tirso de Molina, dealing similarly with
   religious despair, see R. H. Bowers, 'Marlowe's *Dr. Faustus*, Tirso's *El
   Condenado por Desconfiado*, and the Secret Cause', *Costerus*, IV (1972),
   9–27.
31 Susan Snyder, 'Marlowe's *Doctor Faustus* as an Inverted Saint's Life',
   SP, LXIII (1966), 565–77.
32 Beach Langston, 'Marlowe's *Faustus* and the *Ars Moriendi* Tradition', *A
   Tribute to George Coffin Taylor: Studies and Essays*, ed. Arnold Williams
   (Chapel Hill: University of North Carolina Press, 1952), pp. 148–67.

INTRODUCTION   81

33 Giovanni Pico della Mirandola, *Oration on the Dignity of Man*, trans.
Elizabeth Livermore Forbes, in *The Renaissance Philosophy of Man*, ed.
Ernst Cassirer, Paul O. Kristeller, and J. H. Randall, Jr. (Chicago and
London: University of Chicago Press, 1948), pp. 223–54, esp. pp.
223–5. Discussed in William Blackburn, '"Heavenly Words":
Marlowe's Faustus as a Renaissance Magician', *English Studies in
Canada*, IV.i (1978), 1–14, and Wilbur Sanders, *The Dramatist and the
Received Idea: Studies in the Plays of Marlowe and Shakespeare*
(Cambridge University Press, 1968), p. 209.

34 L. T. Fitz, 'Humanism Questioned: a Study of Four Renaissance
Characters', *English Studies in Canada*, V.iv (1979), 388–405; Gatti, pp.
75 ff.; and John S. Mebane, *Renaissance Magic and the Return of the
Golden Age: the Occult Tradition and Marlowe, Jonson, and Shakespeare*
(Lincoln: University of Nebraska Press, 1989), pp. 113–36.

35 Quoted in Brockbank, p. 56.

36 William Perkins, *A Golden Chain: or, The Description of Theology* (1591),
in *Works* (Cambridge: John Legat, 1600), p. 173. Quoted in Sanders, p.
244.

37 *Second Tome of Homilies*, in Clifford W. Dugmore, *The Mass and the
English Reformers* (London: Macmillan, 1958), p. 233. Discussed in C.
L. Barber, '"The form of Faustus' fortunes good or bad"', *TDR*,
VIII.iv (1964), 92–119. The homily was sanctioned by the Convocation
of Canterbury in 1563.

38 Susan Snyder, 'The Left Hand of God: Despair in Medieval and
Renaissance Tradition', *Studies in the Renaissance*, XII (1965), 18–59,
and Pauline Honderich, 'John Calvin and Doctor Faustus', *MLR*, LXVIII
(1973), 1–13. Lily B. Campbell, '*Doctor Faustus*: a Case of Conscience',
PMLA, LXVII (1952), 219–39, sees in the play a highly topical concern
with Calvinist issues of reprobation.

39 Charles Hardwick, *A History of the Articles of Religion* (Cambridge: John
Deighton, 1851, rev. ed. London: G. Bell, 1904), appendix III, p. 313.
Discussed in Barber, p. 105.

40 Paul R. Sellin, 'The Hidden God: Reformation Awe in Renaissance
English Literature', *The Darker Vision of the Renaissance: Beyond the
Fields of Reason*, ed. Robert S. Kinsman (Berkeley: University of
California Press, 1974), pp. 147–96. The whole of this paragraph is
much indebted to Sellin's article.

41 *Martin Luther: Selections from His Writings*, ed. John Dillenberger (New
York: Doubleday, 1961), p. 191. Subsequent page references to Luther
are to this edition.

42 *Calvin: Institutes of the Christian Religion*, ed. John T. McNeill and
trans. Ford Lewis Battles, Library of Christian Classics, vols. XX and
XXI (Philadelphia and London: Westminster, 1960), III.xxiii.2 (XXI,
949). Discussed in Sellin, 'The Hidden God', p. 170.

43 Calvin, *Institutes*, III.xxi.7 (XXI.930–1). Quoted in Sanders, p. 244.

44 Edgar C. S. Gibson, *The Thirty-Nine Articles of the Church of England*, 4th ed. rev. (London, 1904), p. 476. Quoted in Sanders, p. 246.

45 Arthur Dent, *The Opening of Heaven Gates; or, The Ready Way to Everlasting Life* (London, 1611), p. 37. Dent cites Calvin on p. 75 for the idea that human will depends entirely on God's ordinance. Discussed in Sanders, p. 245.

46 Mahood, *Poetry and Humanism*, pp. 86–7.

47 Richard F. Hardin, 'Marlowe and the Fruits of Scholarism', *PQ*, LXIII (1984), 387–400.

48 Pauline Honderich, 'John Calvin and Doctor Faustus', *MLR*, LXVIII (1973), p. 5. See also Roy T. Eriksen, *'The Forme of Faustus' Fortunes': a Study of the Tragedie of Doctor Faustus (1616)* (Oslo: Solum Forlag; New Jersey: Humanities Press International, 1987), pp. 26–34.

49 Hardin, 'Marlowe and the Fruits of Scholarism', p. 388.

50 R. M. Cornelius, *Christopher Marlowe's Use of the Bible* (Bern: Peter Lang, 1984), passim.

51 Carroll Camden, Jr., 'Marlowe and Elizabethan Psychology', *PQ*, VIII (1929), 69–78.

52 T. M. Pearce, 'Jasper Heywood and Marlowe's *Doctor Faustus*', *N&Q*, CXCVII (1952), 200–1, and Allan H. Gilbert, ' "A Thousand Ships" ', *MLN*, LXVI (1951), 4–5.

53 L. T. Fitz, ' "More Than Thou Hast Wit to Ask": Marlowe's Faustus as Numskull', *Folklore*, LXXXVIII (1977), 215–19, and Paul H. Kocher, 'The Witchcraft Basis in Marlowe's *Faustus*', *MP*, XXXVIII (1940), 9–36, quoting (from a later edition of 1617) William Perkins, *A Discourse of the Damned Art of Witchcraft* (London, 1608), p. 167. See also Barbara Howard Traister, *Heavenly Necromancers: the Magician in English Renaissance Drama* (Columbia: University of Missouri Press, 1984), pp. 89–107.

54 Thomas Pettitt, 'The Folk-Play in Marlowe's *Doctor Faustus*', *Folklore*, XCI (1980), 72–7. Oral-formulaic elements are stressed in Pettitt, 'Formulaic Dramaturgy in *Doctor Faustus*', in Friendenreich et al., pp. 167–91.

55 Robert Weimann, *Shakespeare and the Popular Tradition in the Theater: Studies in the Social Dimension of Dramatic Form and Function* (Baltimore: Johns Hopkins University Press, 1978), pp. 183–4, 201–3.

56 Muriel C. Bradbrook, 'Marlowe's *Doctor Faustus* and the Eldritch Tradition', *Essays on Shakespeare and Elizabethan Drama in Honor of Hardin Craig*, ed. Richard Hosley (Columbia: University of Missouri Press, 1962), pp. 83–90.

The orthodox framework

57 Leo Kirschbaum, 'Marlowe's *Faustus*: a Reconsideration', *RES*, XIX (1943), 225–41. See also James T. F. Tanner, '*Doctor Faustus* as Orthodox Christian Sermon', *The Dickinson Review*, II.i (1969), 23–31,

and Margaret Ann O'Brien, 'Christian Belief in *Doctor Faustus*', *ELH*, XXXVII (1970), 1–11.

58 Levin, *The Overreacher*, pp. 121–32, Paul H. Kocher, *Christopher Marlowe: a Study of His Thought, Learning, and Character* (Chapel Hill: University of North Carolina Press, 1946), and Irving Ribner, 'Marlowe's "Tragicke Glasse" ', *Essays on Shakespeare and Elizabethan Drama in Honor of Hardin Craig*, ed. Richard Hosley (Columbia: University of Missouri Press, 1962), pp. 91–114. Earlier enthusiasts for Marlowe's humanism include Francis Cunningham, ed., *The Works of Christopher Marlowe* (London: Chatto & Windus, 1870), p. xiv, W. Wagner, ed., *Christopher Marlowe's Tragedy of Doctor Faustus* (London: Longman, Green, 1877), pp. xxxiii–xxxiv, Havelock Ellis, ed., *Christopher Marlowe*, Mermaid Series (London: Unwin, 1887), pp. xxxviii–xli, and George Santayana, *Three Philosophical Poets: Lucretius, Dante, and Goethe* (Cambridge, Mass.: Harvard University Press, 1910), pp. 145–53. For a judicious brief history of the debate between orthodox and Romantic critics, see Irving Ribner, 'Marlowe and the Critics', *TDR*, VIII.iv (1964), 211–24.

59 See, for example, Max Bluestone, '*Libido Speculandi*: Doctrine and Dramaturgy in Contemporary Interpretations of Marlowe's *Doctor Faustus*', *Reinterpretations of Elizabethan Drama*, ed. Norman Rabkin (New York: Columbia University Press, 1969), pp. 33–88.

60 A. L. French, 'The Philosophy of *Dr. Faustus*', *EIC*, XX (1970), 123–42. For a reply, see James Jensen, 'Heroic Convention and *Dr. Faustus*', *EIC*, XXI (1971), 101–6.

61 Gerald Morgan, 'Harlequin Faustus: Marlowe's Comedy of Hell', *Humanities Association Bulletin*, XVIII.i (1967), 22–34.

62 Melvin Storm, 'Faustus' First Soliloquy: the End of Every Art', *MSE*, VIII.iv (1982), 40–9.

63 R. W. Ingram, ' "Pride in Learning goeth before a fall": Dr. Faustus' Opening Soliloquy', *Mosaic*, XIII.i (1979), 73–80.

64 Joseph T. McCullen, 'Dr Faustus and Renaissance Learning', *MLR*, LI (1956), 6–16, and Celia Barnes, 'Matthew Parker's Pastoral Training and Marlowe's *Doctor Faustus*', *Comp.D*, XV (1981), 258–67.

65 Morgan, 'Harlequin Faustus', p. 31, and James A. Reynolds, 'Faustus' Flawed Learning', *ES*, LVII (1976), 329–36.

66 Mahood, *Poetry and Humanism*, p. 104. See also L. T. Fitz, 'Humanism Questioned', *English Studies in Canada*, V.iv (1979), 388–9; Phoebe S. Spinrad, 'The Dilettante's Lie in *Doctor Faustus*', *TSLL*, XXIV (1982), 243–54; and A. N. Okerlund, 'The Intellectual Folly of Dr. Faustus', *SP*, LXXIV (1977), 258–78.

67 G. I. Duthie, 'Some Observations on Marlowe's *Doctor Faustus*', *Archiv für das Studium der neueren Sprachen und Literaturen*, CCIII (1966), 81–96. See also Adolphus W. Ward, ed., *Old English Drama: Select Plays. Marlowe, Tragical History of Doctor Faustus; Greene, Honourable History*

of Friar Bacon and Friar Bungay (Oxford: Clarendon, 3rd ed., 1892, 4th ed., 1901), pp. 137–8.

68 Leo Kirschbaum, 'Marlowe's Faustus: a Reconsideration', *RES*, XIX (1943), 231.

69 Robert Ornstein, 'The Comic Synthesis in *Doctor Faustus*', *ELH*, XXII (1955), 165–72. Judith Weil astutely studies 'The Tragic Folly of Doctor Faustus' in the tradition of Erasmus's *The Praise of Folly*, Rabelais, and Richard Hooker's 'A Learned Discourse of Justification, Works, and How the Foundation of Faith is Overthrown' (*Christopher Marlowe: Merlin's Prophet*, Cambridge University Press, 1977, pp. 50–81).

70 Martin Versfeld, 'Some Remarks on Marlowe's *Faustus*', *English Studies in Africa*, I (1958), 134–43.

71 Anne Hargrove, '*Lucifer Prince of the East* and the Fall of Marlowe's Dr. Faustus', *NM*, LXXXIV (1983), 206–13.

72 Roland M. Frye, 'Marlowe's *Doctor Faustus*: the Repudiation of Humanity', *South Atlantic Quarterly*, LV (1956), 322–8.

73 Cole, *Suffering and Evil*, pp. 230, 234, and J. B. Steane, *Marlowe: a Critical Study* (Cambridge University Press, 1965), p. 134.

74 Gerard H. Cox III, 'Marlowe's *Doctor Faustus* and "Sin against the Holy Ghost"', *Huntington Library Quarterly*, XXXVI (1973), 119–37.

75 John C. McCloskey, 'The Theme of Despair in Marlowe's *Faustus*', *CE*, IV (1942–3), 110–13.

76 James Smith, 'Marlowe's *Doctor Faustus*', *Scrutiny*, VIII (1939), 36–55, and J. C. Maxwell, 'The Sin of Faustus', *The Wind and the Rain*, IV (1947), 47–52.

77 Lorraine Kochanske Stock, 'Medieval *Gula* in Marlowe's *Doctor Faustus*', *Bulletin of Research in the Humanities*, LXXXV (1982), 372–85.

78 Joseph T. McCullen, 'Dr Faustus and Renaissance Learning', *MLR*, LI (1956), 6–16; John B. Cutts, *The Left Hand of God: a Critical Interpretation of the Plays of Christopher Marlowe* (Haddenfield, N.J.: Haddenfield House, 1973), pp. 136–7, 145; and Margaret Ann O'Brien, 'Christian Belief in *Doctor Faustus*', *ELH*, XXXVII (1970), 3.

79 Morton Bloomfield, *The Seven Deadly Sins* (East Lansing: Michigan State University Press), p. 382, n. 16. See also Sherman Hawkins, 'The Education of Faustus', *SEL*, VI (1966), 193–209.

80 See Russell and Clare Goldfarb, 'The Seven Deadly Deadly Sins in *Doctor Faustus*', *College Language Association Journal*, XIII (1969–70), 350–63.

81 James Smith, 'Marlowe's *Doctor Faustus*', *Scrutiny*, VIII (1939), 53.

82 W. W. Greg, 'The Damnation of Faustus', *MLR*, XLI (1946), 97–107. For a response, see Frank Manley, 'The Nature of Faustus', *MP*, LXVI (1969), 218–31.

83 Roma Gill, ed. *Doctor Faustus*, New Mermaids (London: E. Benn, 1965), Introduction, p. xxvi.

84 T. W. Craik, 'Faustus' Damnation Reconsidered', *Ren.D*, n.s. II (1969), 189–96. E. A. J. Honigmann, 'Ten Problems in *Dr Faustus*', in a Festschrift for G. K. Hunter, *The Arts of Performance in Elizabethan and Early Stuart Drama*, ed. M. Biggs, Philip Edwards, Inga-Stina Ewbank, and Eugene M. Waith (Edinburgh University Press, 1991), similarly wonders if editors and scholars are not attempting to be too dogmatic about a matter that Marlowe approaches with a calculated 'technique of uncertainty'. Nicolas Kiessling, 'Doctor Faustus and the Sin of Demoniality', *SEL*, XV (1975), 205–11, offers evidence that even demoniality was not considered a mortal sin 'beyond repentance'. Malcolm Pittock, 'God's Mercy is Infinite: Faustus's Last Soliloquy', *ES*, LXV (1984), 302–11, believes that Faustus is damned not before his last soliloquy 'but during it'.

85 Calvin, *Institutes*, III.xxv.12; discussed in C. A. Patrides, 'Renaissance and Modern Views on Hell', *Harvard Theological Review*, LVII (1964), 217–36. See also Leech, *Christopher Marlowe*, pp. 83–99.

86 Clifford Davidson, 'Doctor Faustus of Wittenberg', *SP*, LIX (1962), 514–23.

87 Joseph Westlund, 'The Orthodox Christian Framework of Marlowe's *Faustus*', *SEL*, III (1963), 191–205.

88 Harriet Hawkins, 'The Morality of Elizabethan Drama: Some Footnotes to Plato', *English Renaissance Studies Presented to Dame Helen Gardner in Honour of Her Seventieth Birthday*, ed. John Carey (Oxford: Clarendon Press, 1980), pp. 14–26.

89 W. Moelwyn Merchant, 'Marlowe the Orthodox', in Brian Morris, ed., *Christopher Marlowe*, Mermaid Critical Commentaries (London: E. Benn, 1968), pp. 177–92.

90 Robert H. West, 'The Impatient Magic of Dr. Faustus', *ELR*, IV (1974), 218–40.

Humanist aspiration

91 Ribner, 'Marlowe's "Tragicke Glasse"', pp. 91–114. See also Una Ellis-Fermor, *Christopher Marlowe* (London: Methuen, 1927, rpt. Archon, 1967), pp. 61–87, Philip Henderson, *And Morning in His Eyes* (London: Boriswood, 1937), pp. 310–12, and F. S. Boas, *Christopher Marlowe* (Oxford: Clarendon, 1940), p. 211. Empson, *Faustus and the Censor*, passim, speculates that the original uncensored play was more heterodox than what survives, with Faustus outwitting Mephistopheles (who is really only a 'Middle Spirit' of neither heaven nor hell, acting as a double agent pretending to serve Lucifer) and thereby escaping punishment.

92 Levin, *The Overreacher*.

93 Christopher R. Fanta, *Marlowe's 'Agonists': an Approach to the Ambiguity of His Plays* (Cambridge, Mass.: Harvard University Press, 1970), p. 40.

86   DOCTOR FAUSTUS

See Paul H. Kocher, 'Marlowe's Atheist Lecture', *JEGP*, xxxix (1940), 98–106, and 'Backgrounds for Marlowe's Atheist Lecture', *PQ*, xx (1941), 304–24.
95 Ellis-Fermor, *Christopher Marlowe*, p. 62.
96 Paul H. Kocher, 'Christopher Marlowe: Individualist', *UTQ*, xvii (1947–8), 111–20. Constance Kuriyama similarly traces Faustus's intense fear and mistrust of God, his feelings of emptiness and unworthiness, to a re-enactment of Marlowe's own difficulty with a hostile, threatening father (*Hammer or Anvil: Psychological Patterns in Christopher Marlowe's Plays*, New Brunswick: Rutgers University Press, 1980, pp. 95–135). Edward Snow sees a pattern of 'oral-narcissistic dilemma' in Faustus's compulsive gluttony, his fear of and longing for dismemberment, his psychic aggression and passive longing for ravishment and self-extinction ('Marlowe's *Doctor Faustus* and the Ends of Desire', *Two Renaissance Mythmakers: Christopher Marlowe and Ben Jonson*, ed. Alvin Kernan, Selected Papers from the English Institute, 1975–6, Baltimore: Johns Hopkins University Press, 1977, pp. 70–110). C. L. Barber similarly applies Freud's definition of perversion—namely, an attempt 'by repeating a way of using the body in relation to a certain limited sexual object, to recover or continue in adult life the meaning of a relationship fixed on this action and object in childhood'—to a recurrent motif of orality (' "The form of Faustus' fortunes good or bad" ', pp. 110–13). For a Jungian reading of *Doctor Faustus* in terms of the anima, see Kenneth L. Golden, 'Myth, Psychology, and Marlowe's *Doctor Faustus*', *College Literature*, xii (1985), 202–10. Clarence Green, '*Doctor Faustus*: Tragedy of Individualism', *Science and Society*, x (1946), 275–82, reads Faustus in terms of a 'psychopathic solipsism' not unlike that of the Nietzschean aristocratic superman. Kay Stockholder sees Faustus as 'a man whose sexual and erotic energies have been diverted into the successful pursuit of knowledge and fame, and who is therefore left with a vague feeling of unsatisfied emptiness'—a feeling that incessantly drives him to associate women and sexuality with forbidden magic (' "Within the massy entrailes of the earth": Faustus's Relation to Women', in Friedenreich et al., pp. 203–19). Philip K. Wion studies Faustus's anxieties and defences in the context of Ernest Becker's *The Denial of Death*, an approach that enables us 'to recognize and understand ambivalent and contradictory feeling' such as fear of mutilation and fantasies of sexual possession of a figure unconsciously equated with the mother ('Marlowe's *Doctor Faustus*, the Oedipus Complex, and the Denial of Death', *Colby Library Quarterly*, xvi (1980), 190–204).
97 Kocher, 'Christopher Marlowe: Individualist', pp. 111–20.
98 Ribner, 'Marlowe's "Tragicke Glasse" ', p. 110.
99 Kocher, *Christopher Marlowe*, p. 104.
100 Simon Shepherd, *Marlowe and the Politics of the Elizabethan Theatre*

(New York: St Martin's Press, 1986), pp. 14, 54, 96–8. See also
Johannes H. Birringer, *Marlowe's 'Dr Faustus' and 'Tamburlaine'*
(Frankfurt: Peter Lang, 1984), passim.
101 Sanders, pp. 208–9. See also Charles G. Masinton, *Christopher
Marlowe's Tragic Vision: a Study in Damnation* (Athens: Ohio University
Press, 1972), pp. 113–59, esp. pp. 113 and 125. Christopher Ricks
('*Doctor Faustus* and Hell on Earth', *EIC*, XXXV (1985), 101–20) aptly
makes the point that with the bubonic plague constantly threatening
London in the 1580s and 1590s, Faustus's bargain for half a lifetime of
assured existence is not as nugatory as some orthodox critics claim.
102 For a comparison of Faustus's rejection of the four disciplines with a
similar situation in Rabelais's *Tiers Livre*, more useful as an analogue
than as a source, see Lawrence V. Ryan, 'Panurge and the Faustian
Dilemma', *Stanford Literature Review*, II (1985), 147–63.
103 Francis R. Johnson, 'Marlowe's Astronomy and Renaissance
Skepticism', *ELH*, XIII (1946), 241–54, and 'Marlowe's "Imperiall
Heaven"', *ELH*, XII (1945), 35–44. On *The French Academy*, see
Brockbank, pp. 47–8. Marlowe presumably had access to Agrippa's *Of
the Vanity and Uncertainty of Arts and Sciences*, since it was translated
into English by 1580.
104 Nashe, *Have With You to Saffron Walden* (1596), ed. McKerrow, III.94.
See J. O. Halliwell, ed., *The Private Diary of Dr. John Dee* (London:
Camden Society, 1842); Charlotte Fell Smith, *John Dee (1527–1608)*
(London: Constable, 1909); H. W. Herrington, 'Christopher Marlowe—
Rationalist', *Essays in Memory of Barrett Wendell*, ed. William R. Castle
Jr. (Cambridge, Mass.: Harvard University Press, 1926), pp. 121–52,
esp. p. 135; and Michael Hattaway, 'The Theology of Marlowe's *Doctor
Faustus*', *Ren.D*, n.s. III (1970), 51–78. On Bruno and Marlowe, see
Roy T. Eriksen, '*The Forme of Faustus' Fortunes*' (Oslo: Solum, 1987),
pp. 59–94, and Gatti, pp. 74–113.
105 Pierre Tibi, '*Doctor Faustus* et la Cosmologie de Marlowe', *Revue des
Langues Vivantes*, XL (1974), 212–27.
106 See Bluestone, '*Libido Speculandi*', pp. 66–9.
107 Michel Poirier, *Christopher Marlowe* (London: Chatto & Windus, 1951),
p. 141.

Magic and poetry
108 Joel Altman, *The Tudor Play of Mind* (Berkeley: University of California
Press, 1978).
109 Bluestone, '*Libido Speculandi*', pp. 36–7; William W. French, 'Double
View in *Doctor Faustus*', *West Virginia University Philological Papers*, XVII
(1970), 3–15; Sidney R. Homan, Jr., 'Chapman and Marlowe: the
Paradoxical Hero and the Divided Response', *JEGP*, LXVIII (1969),
391–406; Homan, '*Doctor Faustus*, Dekker's *Old Fortunatus*, and the

Morality Plays', *MLQ*, XXVI (1965), 497–505; Arthur Mizener, 'The Tragedy of Marlowe's *Doctor Faustus*', *CE*, V (1943–4), 70–5; JoAnne M. Podis, 'The Concept of Divinity in *Doctor Faustus*', *Theatre Annual*, XXVII (1971–2), 89–102; H. Röhrman, *Marlowe and Shakespeare: a Thematic Exposition of Some of Their Plays* (Arnhem: Van Loghum Slaterus, 1952), pp. 28–43; Kristian Smidt, 'Two Aspects of Ambition in Elizabethan Tragedy: *Doctor Faustus* and *Macbeth*', *ES*, L (1969), 235–48; and Claude J. Summers, *Christopher Marlowe and the Politics of Power* (Salzburg: Institut für Englische Sprache und Literatur, 1974), pp. 117–31. Catherine Belsey, *Critical Practice* (London: Methuen, 1980), sees *Faustus* as an 'interrogative text' that 'refuses a single point of view'.

110 Frank Manley, 'The Nature of Faustus', *MP*, LVI (1968–9), 218–31, and King-Kok Cheung, 'The Dialectic of Despair in *Doctor Faustus*', in Friedenreich et al., pp. 193–201.

111 L. C. Knights, 'The Strange Case of Christopher Marlowe', *Further Explorations* (London: Chatto & Windus, 1965), pp. 75–98. Jonathan Dollimore argues that 'a discovery of limits which ostensibly forecloses subversive questioning in fact provokes it' (*Radical Tragedy: Religion, Ideology and Power in the Drama of Shakespeare and His Contemporaries*, University of Chicago Press, 1984, p. 110).

112 Stephen Greenblatt, 'Marlowe and the Will to Absolute Play', *Renaissance Self-Fashioning: From More to Shakespeare* (University of Chicago Press, 1980), pp. 193–221.

113 Robert Ornstein, 'Marlowe and God: the Tragic Theology of *Dr. Faustus*', *PMLA*, LXXXIII (1968), 1378–85.

114 Patrick Cheney, 'Love and Magic in *Doctor Faustus*: Marlowe's Indictment of Spenserian Idealism', *Mosaic*, XVII.iv (1984), 93–109.

115 Philip J. Traci, 'Marlowe's Faustus as Artist: a Suggestion About a Theme in the Play', *Ren.P 1966* (1967), 3–9.

116 T. McAlindon, 'Classical Mythology and Christian Tradition in Marlowe's *Doctor Faustus*', *PMLA*, LXXXI (1966), 214–23.

117 Alvin Kernan, 'The Plays and the Playwrights', in *The Revels History of Drama in English*, gen. eds. Clifford Leech and T. W. Craik, vol. 3, 1576–1613 (London: Methuen, 1975), pp. 346–53.

118 Traci, 'Marlowe's Faustus as Artist', p. 9.

119 Neil Forsyth, 'Heavenly Helen', *Études de Lettres*, IV (1987), 11–21.

120 D. J. Palmer, 'Magic and Poetry in *Doctor Faustus*', *CQ*, VI (1964), 56–67. See also A. Bartlett Giamatti, 'Marlowe: the Arts of Illusion', *Yale Review*, LXI (1972), 530–43.

Genre and structure
121 Aristotle, *Poetics*, ch. xiii.
122 M. M. Mahood, *Poetry and Humanism*, pp. 107 and 110. See also T. McAlindon, *English Renaissance Tragedy* (Vancouver: University of British Columbia Press, 1986), pp. 131–2.

123 Richard Waswo, 'Damnation, Protestant Style: Macbeth, Faustus, and Christian Tragedy', *Journal of Medieval and Renaissance Studies*, IV (1974), 63–99.
124 Thomas Stroup, '*Doctor Faustus* and *Hamlet*: Contrasting Kinds of Christian Tragedy', *Comp.D*, V (1971–2), 243–53.
125 Waswo, pp. 63–99.
126 Robert Heilman, 'The Tragedy of Knowledge: Marlowe's Treatment of Faustus', *Quarterly Review of Literature*, II (1946), 316–32.
127 Laurence Michel, 'The Possibility of a Christian Tragedy', *Thought*, XXXI (autumn 1956), 403–28. See also Richard Sewall, *The Vision of Tragedy* (New Haven: Yale University Press, 1959), p. 159, n. 58.
128 Sewall, *The Vision of Tragedy*, pp. 57–67, 159.
129 W. H. Auden, 'The Christian Tragic Hero', *New York Times Book Review*, 16 December 1945, p. 1.
130 Sewall, *The Vision of Tragedy*, pp. 63–7.
131 Nicholas Brooke, 'The Moral Tragedy of *Dr Faustus*', *Cambridge Journal*, VII (1952), 662–87, rpt. in *Critics on Marlowe*, ed. Judith O'Neill (Coral Gables: University of Miami Press, 1969), pp. 93–114.
132 Cleanth Brooks, 'The Unity of Marlowe's *Doctor Faustus*', *To Nevill Coghill from Friends*, ed. J. Lawlor and W. H. Auden (London: Faber, 1966), pp. 109–24.
133 Nigel Alexander, 'The Performance of Christopher Marlowe's *Dr Faustus*', *PBA*, LVII (1971), 331–49. On structure in morality drama, see David Bevington, *From 'Mankind' to Marlowe* (Cambridge, Mass., Harvard University Press, 1962), passim. See also Richard Levin, *The Multiple Plot in English Renaissance Drama* (University of Chicago Press, 1971), pp. 119–23.
134 G. K. Hunter, 'Five-Act Structure in *Doctor Faustus*', *TDR*, VIII.iv (1964), 77–91. The objection to merely scenic division on the part of most editors was made earlier by Boas, p. vi. See also Susan Snyder, 'Marlowe's *Doctor Faustus* as an Inverted Saint's Life', *SP*, LXIII (1966), 571–4; Robert Ornstein, 'The Comic Synthesis in *Doctor Faustus*', *ELH*, XXII (1955), 165–72; John H. Crabtree, Jr., 'The Comedy in Marlowe's *Dr. Faustus*', *Furman Studies*, IX.i (1961), 1–9; Charles N. Beall, 'Definition of Theme by Unconsecutive Event: Structure as Induction in Marlowe's *Doctor Faustus*', *Ren.P 1962* (1963), 53–61; Clifford Leech, 'Marlowe's Humor', *Essays on Shakespeare and Elizabethan Drama in Honor of Hardin Craig*, ed. Richard Hosley (Columbia: University of Missouri Press, 1962), p. 70; Warren D. Smith, 'The Nature of Evil in *Doctor Faustus*', *MLR*, LX (1965), 171–5; Sherman Hawkins, 'The Education of Faustus', *SEL*, VI (1966), 193–209; Mutsumi Nozaki, 'The Comic Sense in Marlowe Reconsidered', *Shakespeare Studies* (Japan), IX (1970–1), 1–27; and Linda Wyman, 'How Plot and Sub-plot Unite in Marlowe's *Faustus*', *College English Association Critic*, XXXVII.i (1974), 14–16.

Style and imagery

135 Johan H. Birringer, 'The Daemonic Flight of Dr. Faustus: Hope and/or Escape?', *MSE*, VIII.iii (1982), 17–26. See also Virginia Mary Meehan, *Christopher Marlowe: Poet and Playwright* (The Hague: Mouton, 1974), pp. 72–7.

136 Caroline Spurgeon, *Shakespeare's Imagery and What It Tells Us* (New York: Macmillan, 1935), p. 13. Discussed in Jeffrey P. Hart, 'Prospero and Faustus', *Boston University Studies in English*, II (1956–7), 197–206. In a similar vein, Harry Morris stresses the wonderment and awe that are projected through images of seeking and seeing ('Marlowe's Poetry', *TDR*, VIII.iv (1964), 134–54).

137 A. N. Okerlund, 'The Intellectual Folly of Dr. Faustus', *SP*, LXXIV (1977), 258–78.

138 William Blackburn, '"Heavenly Words": Marlowe's Faustus as a Renaissance Magician', *English Studies in Canada*, IV.i (1978), 1–14.

139 Frederick Burwick, 'Marlowe's *Doctor Faustus*: Two Manners, the Argumentative and the Passionate', *NM*, LXX (1969), 121–45. See also R. T. Eriksen, 'Mnemonics and Giordano Bruno's Magical Art of Composition', *Cahiers Élisabéthains*, XX (1981), 3–10. For examples of *epizeuxis*, or emphatic repetition, see V.ii.5, 25–6, 29–34, 58, 116, 120, etc., and F. P. Wilson, *Marlowe and the Early Shakespeare* (Oxford: Clarendon, 1953), p. 83.

140 T. McAlindon, 'The Ironic Vision: Diction and Theme in Marlowe's *Doctor Faustus*', *RES*, n.s. XXXII (1981), 9–41.

141 Quoted in Robert Weimann, *Shakespeare and the Popular Tradition in the Theater*, p. 201. See also Wolfgang Clemen, *English Tragedy before Shakespeare: the Development of Dramatic Speech*, trans. T. S. Dorsch (London: Methuen, 1961, originally published in German in 1955), pp. 147–54.

142 Samuel Johnson, *Preface to The Plays of William Shakespeare* (1765).

143 Neil Forsyth, 'Heavenly Helen', *Études de Lettres*, IV (1987), 11–21.

144 Douglas Cole, *Suffering and Evil*, p. 209.

145 Sara Munson Deats, 'Ironic Biblical Allusions in Marlowe's *Doctor Faustus*', *Medievalia et Humanistica*, n.s. X (1981), 203–16.

146 Rowland Wymer, '"When I Behold the Heavens": a Reading of *Doctor Faustus*', *ES*, LXVII (1986), 505–10. See also T. McAlindon, *English Renaissance Tragedy*, pp. 123–4.

147 Birringer, 'The Daemonic Flight of Dr. Faustus', *MSE*, VIII (1982), 22. Jan Kott discusses the 'polytheatricality' of *Faustus* in 'The Two Hells of *Doctor Faustus*: a Polytheatrical Vision', in *The Bottom Translation: Marlowe and Shakespeare and the Carnival Tradition*, trans. Daniela Miedzyrzecka and Lillian Vallee (Evanston: Northwestern University Press, 1987), pp. 1–27.

148 David Hard Zucker, *Stage and Image in the Plays of Christopher Marlowe* (Salzburg: Institut für Englische Sprache und Literatur, 1972), pp.

143–76; Felix Bosonnet, *The Function of Stage Properties in Christopher Marlowe's Plays* (Bern: Francke Verlag, 1978), pp. 58–80; Jocelyn Powell, 'Marlowe's Spectacle', *TDR*, VIII.iv (1964), 195–210, p. 199; and Leonard H. Frey, 'Antithetical Balance in the Opening and Close of *Doctor Faustus*', *MLQ*, XXIV (1963), 350–3. For a dramaturgical analysis of binary structure in the play, see Bernard Beckerman, 'Scene Patterns in *Doctor Faustus* and *Richard III*', in *Shakespeare and His Contemporaries: Essays in Comparison*, ed. E. A. J. Honigmann (Manchester University Press, 1986), pp. 31–41.

Staging and themes in the 1616 quarto

149 See, for example, John Lyly, *Sappho and Phao* (III.iii.0ff.), and *2H6*, III. ii.146 ff.
150 Felix Bosonnet, *The Function of Stage Properties in Christopher Marlowe's Plays* (1978), pp. 58–60.
151 Allardyce Nicoll, 'Passing Over the Stage', *SSur. XII* (1959), 47–55.
152 Bernard Beckerman, 'Scene Patterns in *Doctor Faustus* and *Richard III*.'
153 Glynne Wickham, 'Exeunt to the Cave: Notes on the Staging of Marlowe's Plays', *TDR*, VIII.iv (1964), 186. John Astington, on the other hand, shows that Wickham is wrong in claiming that no theatres had the capability before 1600 to make descents and ascents from the heavens by means of winch machinery; see 'Descent Machinery in the Playhouses', *Medieval and Renaissance Drama in England*, II (1985), 119–33.
154 A weakness in Bowers's decision to stage the second appearance of the Old Man (found only in the A-text) 'aloof', since the Old Man does not interact with Faustus directly on this occasion, is that the A-text does not provide elsewhere for action above. For a persuasive visual reading of the final scenes in the A- and B-texts, see Alan Dessen, *Elizabethan Stage Conventions and Modern Interpreters* (Cambridge University Press, 1984), pp. 146–9. Discussed in William Tydeman and Vivien Thomas, *Christopher Marlowe: a Guide Through the Critical Maze* (Bristol Classical Press, 1989), pp. 36–55.
155 Jump, p. 99.
156 E. A. J. Honigmann, 'Ten Problems in *Dr. Faustus*', in a Festschrift for G. K. Hunter, *The Arts of Performance in Elizabethan and Early Stuart Drama*, ed. M. Biggs, Philip Edwards, Inga-Stina Ewbank, and Eugene M. Waith (Edinburgh University Press, 1991).
157 See II.iii.174.1, IV.i.0.1–2 and 102.2–3, IV.ii.105.1–IV.iii.0, and V.ii.103.2 ff.
158 Kuriyama, 'Dr. Greg and *Doctor Faustus*', pp. 178 and 186.
159 Clifford Davidson, 'Doctor Faustus at Rome', *SEL*, IX (1969), 231–9.
160 L. M. Oliver, 'Rowley, Foxe, and the *Faustus* Additions', *MLN*, LX (1945), 391–4. Discussed in Kuriyama, 'Dr. Greg and *Doctor Faustus*', p. 191. Leah Marcus's argument, in 'Textual Indeterminacy and

Ideological Difference: the Case of *Doctor Faustus*', *Ren.D*, n.s. XX (1989), 1–29, that the B-text revisers are pro-imperial, internationalist, and Anglican in support of James I's foreign policy of reversing hostility towards Spain and the Empire, overstates the ideological differences between the two texts; even in the B-text, we find popular ideals of Protestant national self-determination that would have appealed to Londoners who were wary of James's new foreign policy and toleration of Catholicism. The 1602 additions predate, in any case, James's accession in 1603. Still, Marcus rightly calls attention to the importance of seeing the B-text revision in the context of a changing political environment.

161 Michael H. Keefer, 'Verbal Magic and the Problem of the A and B Texts of *Doctor Faustus*', *JEGP*, LXXXII (1983), 324–46.

162 Martha Tuck Rozett, *The Doctrine of Election and the Emergence of Elizabethan Tragedy* (Princeton University Press, 1984), p. 238.

163 Ormerod and Wortham, pp. xli–xlv, similarly make the point that Faustus's and Mephistopheles's power to transform is only illusory in the A-text, whereas the B-text 'characteristically places no limitation on the actual power of Mephostophiles'. They argue that the pact is more binding in the B-text, and that the devils accordingly have no difficulty in exacting their due. Empson, pp. 165–78, argues that the B-text additions in Act V were added at the command of a censor, to ensure that an audience would be certain of Faustus's punishment in hell.

164 Michael J. Warren, '*Doctor Faustus*: the Old Man and the Text', *ELR*, XI (1981), 111–47.

The play in performance

165 *Henslowe's Diary*, ed. R. A. Foakes and R. T. Rickert (Cambridge University Press, 1961), p. 24.

166 Eric Rasmussen, '*The Black Book* and the Date of *Doctor Faustus*', *N&Q*, CCXXXV, n.s. XXXVII (1990), 168–70; Bakeless, I.298; Greg, p. 9; and Jump, p. xxiii. See Barbara Cooper, 'An Ur-Faustus?', *N&Q*, CCIV, n.s. VI (1959), 66–8, whose argument for an Ur-Faustus rests on the unnecessary supposition that the 'cracking' of the theatre referred to in the *Black Book* points to an earthquake.

167 'The Knave of Clubs', 1609, sig. D3, in *The Complete Works of Samuel Rowlands, 1598–1628*, 3 vols. (Glasgow: for the Hunterian Club, 1880), II.29. Alleyn's inventory around 1598 mentions 'faustus Jerkin [and] his clok'; Henslowe's inventory of March 1598 lists 'the sittie of Rome' (*Henslowe's Diary*, pp. 293 and 319).

168 The complete record is laid out in Bakeless, I.297, along with much data used in the early part of this present essay on stage history. On the unusual nature of Henslowe's paying for additions in 1602, see Roslyn L. Knutson, 'Influence of the Repertory System on the Revival and

Revision of *The Spanish Tragedy* and *Dr. Faustus'*, *ELR*, XVIII (1988), 257–74.

169 E. K. Chambers, *The Elizabethan Stage*, 4 vols. (Oxford: Clarendon, 1923), II.281; Johannes Meissner, *Die englischen Comoedianten zur Zeit Shakespeares in Oesterreich* (Vienna: C. Konegan, 1884), p. 90; Albert Cohn, *Shakespeare in Germany in the Sixteenth and Seventeenth Centuries* (London and Berlin: Asher, 1865), pp. lxxxiii, xciii, cxv–cxviii; and Bakeless, I.302.

170 G. E. Bentley, *The Jacobean and Caroline Stages*, 5 vols. (Oxford: Clarendon, 1941–56), I.318–19, and Jump, p. lix. Jump's essay on 'The Stage-History of the Play', pp. lviii–lxiii, contains much information also presented in this current essay.

171 Chambers, *Elizabethan Stage*, III.424, citing one J. G. R., who bases the story on a manuscript note on 'the last page of a book in my possession, printed by Vautrollier' in 1585 (*Gentleman's Magazine*, 2nd series, XXXIV, 1850, p. 234); and John Aubrey, *The Natural History and Antiquities of the County of Surrey* (London: for E. Curll, 1718–19), I.190. Aubrey incorrectly assigns the episode to one of Shakespeare's plays.

172 Winifred Smith, 'Anti-Catholic Propaganda in Elizabethan London', *MP*, XXVIII (1930–1), 208–12.

173 John Melton, *The Astrologaster, or, The Figure-caster* (1620), p. 31; ed. C. F. Tucker Brooke, *Transactions of the Connecticut Academy of Arts and Sciences*, XV (1921–2), 375.

174 For a refreshingly sceptical view of the supposed Puritan hostility to the stage in the 1640s, see David Kastan, 'The Summer of '42: the Closing of the Theaters and the English Revolution', in *Proud Majesty Made a Subject: Representation and Authority in Early Modern England* (London: Routledge, announced for 1992).

175 Leslie Hotson, *The Commonwealth and Restoration Stage* (Cambridge, Mass.: Harvard University Press, 1928), pp. 178–9; Allardyce Nicoll, *A History of English Drama 1660–1900*, 4th ed., 6 vols. (Cambridge University Press, 1952–9), I.310, 348; Bakeless, I.301; and Jump, p. lx.

176 Edward Phillips, *Theatrum Poetarum, or, A Complete Collection of the Poets*, 2 vols. (London: for Charles Smith, 1675), II.25.

177 William Winstanley, *The Lives of the Most Famous English Poets* (London: H. Clark for S. Manship, 1687), p. 134.

178 Bakeless, I.301–2; Jump, p. lxi.

179 *The Dunciad Variorum*, in *The Poems of Alexander Pope*, ed. John Butt (New Haven: Yale University Press, 1963), bk. III, note to l. 229.

180 Percy Simpson, 'Marlowe's *Tragical History of Doctor Faustus'*, *E&S*, XIV (1929), 20–34.

181 Robert Speaight, *William Poel and the Elizabethan Revival* (London: Heinemann, 1954), pp. 113–19; Bakeless, I.305; and Jump, p. lxi.

182 Bakeless, I.303–5.

94　DOCTOR FAUSTUS

183 Bakeless, 1.303–5, and Jump, p. lxi, mentioning performances at the Carnegie Institute in 1921, at Yale in 1932, at Stanford in 1934, at Cambridge, England (not by the Marlowe Dramatic Society) in 1924 and 1934, and subsequently at Dartmouth and Brown. Robert Frost directed a production while teaching at Pinkerton Academy; see Robert H. Fleissner, *The Prince and the Professor: the Wittenberg Connection in Marlowe, Shakespeare, Goethe, and Frost* (Heidelberg: Carl Winter, 1986), p. xii.

184 Ben Greet staged *Faustus* at the Garden Theatre, New York, in 1910; Sam Hune produced it at the Detroit Arts and Crafts Theatre in 1918. A Cleveland production of 1922 was revived for the opening of the new Francis E. Drury Theatre and ran throughout the season of 1927–8. In England, in 1924, a project to erect a memorial to Christopher Marlowe at Canterbury was supported by a dramatic reading from Marlowe's plays under the direction of William Poel. Next year, on 25 October, the Phoenix Society staged *Faustus* at London's New Oxford Theatre on an open, uncluttered stage, with some of the farcical slapstick reintroduced. Nugent Monck's Norwich Maddermarket Theatre, so pioneering in the experimental staging of a number of Shakespeare's plays, gave three performances of *Faustus* at Chapter House, Canterbury, during the Festival of Music and Drama there in 1929. See Bakeless, 1.304–6, and Jump, pp. lxi–lxii.

185 Barber, 'The form of Faustus' fortunes good or bad', p. 105.

186 Another American *Faustus*, directed by Walter Armitage, played at New Orleans and Atlanta in late spring and summer of 1937. Further revivals took place in England in 1937, at the Tavistock Little Theatre, and on 12 March 1940 at the Rudolf Steiner Hall. See Bakeless, 1.304, and Jump, p. lxii.

187 *Birmingham Gazette*, 13 July 1946; *Wolverhampton Express & Star*, 10 April 1947.

188 Notable productions of the 1950s included a cut version taken on tour by the Compass Players in 1950, under the direction of John Crockett, and a performance on 6 April 1956 at the Tower, Canonbury, by the Tavistock Repertory Company. See Jump, pp. lxii–lxiii.

189 Quoted in John Russell Brown, 'Marlowe and the Actors', *TDR*, VIII.iv (1964), 155–73. See also A. D. Wraight, *In Search of Christopher Marlowe: a Pictorial Biography* (London: Macdonald, 1965), pp. 322–5, and William Tydeman, *'Doctor Faustus': Text and Performance* (Basingstoke: Macmillan, 1984), pp. 53 ff.

190 Jerzy Grotowski, *'Doctor Faustus* in Poland', translated by Richard Schechner, *TDR*, VIII.iv (1964), 120–33. See also Johnnes H. Birringer, 'Between Body and Language: "Writing" the Damnation of Faustus', *Theatre Journal*, XXXVI (1984), 335–55. A production by Charles Marowitz at the Glasgow Citizens' Theatre in the late 1960s featured a long refectory table or reading desk like that used by Grotowski (Tydeman, p. 50).

191 Harold Hobson, 'All This and Helen, Too', *Sunday Times*, 20 February 1966, p. 29.

192 J. C. Trewin, *Birmingham Post*, 28 June 1968; Irving Wardle, *The Times*, 29 June.

193 See H. W. Matalene, III, 'Marlowe's *Faustus* and the Comforts of Academicism', *ELH*, XXXIX (1972), 495–519, esp. pp. 499–500; J. C. Trewin, '*Dr. Faustus*', *Birmingham Post*, 15 February 1966; and Tydeman, pp. 60 ff.

194 Nigel Alexander, 'The Performance of Christopher Marlowe's *Dr. Faustus*', *PBA*, LVII (1971), 331–49, esp. pp. 340–1.

195 *Observer*, 20 June 1968, and *Sunday Times*, 30 June. See also Tydeman, pp. 53 ff.

196 Irving Wardle, *The Times*, 29 June 1968; *Observer*, 30 June; Rosemary Say, *Sunday Telegraph*, 30 June; B. A. Young, *Financial Times*, 28 June; *Birmingham Mail*, 28 June.

197 Maureen O'Farrell, *Evening Press (Dublin)*, 11 March 1970; Eric Shorter, *Daily Telegraph*, 25 June; J. C. Trewin, *Birmingham Post*, 25 June; Peter Fiddick, *Guardian*, 26 June; John Peter, *Sunday Times*, 29 November.

198 John Barber, *Daily Telegraph*, 9 September 1974, and Tydeman, pp. 62 ff.

199 Michael Billington, *Guardian*, 7 September. See also Alan Riddell, *Daily Telegraph*, 1 September, and Charles Lewsen, *The Times*, 27 August.

200 Robert Cushman, *Observer*, 1 September 1974.

201 Irving Wardle, *The Times*, 7 September 1974. At Chicago's Court Theatre, in the autumn of 1988, under the direction of Nicholas Rudall, the Seven Deadly Sins were puppets fashioned unexpectedly to no single scale and operated by Brechtian stagehands in black leotards. Envy, lean as a rake, was eight feet tall, whereas Sloth was a dismal little chap who could scarcely stay awake long enough to say his lines, and Lechery was a porcine fat lady from a carnival show who crossed and recrossed her well-exposed legs.

202 Russell Jackson, '*Doctor Faustus* in Manchester', *CQ*, XXIII.iv (winter 1981), 3–9. In a similar vein, Ronald Huebert's production for the Dalhousie Dramatic Society in 1978 conceived of Faustus as a man who, by losing his respect for 'the objects of experience' in the very act of desiring, tries 'to reduce them to properties or puppets under his control'. Faustus was a 'spiritual junkie', for whom the renunciation of desire would be 'to annihilate the person he has become'. Huebert was influenced by Edward Snow's '*Doctor Faustus* and the Ends of Desire'. See Ronald Huebert, 'Tobacco and Boys and Marlowe', *Sewanee Review*, XC (1984), 206–24.

203 On Fettes's production, see Tydeman, pp. 50, 63 ff. On the Kyle production, see Irving Wardle, *The Times*, 12 May 1989; John Gross, *Sunday Telegraph*, 14 May; Michael Coveney, *Financial Times*, 12 May.

204 Michael Billington, *Guardian*, 12 May 1989.
205 Michael Schmidt, *Daily Telegraph*, 12 May 1989. See also Kate Kellaway, *Sunday Observer*, 14 May; John Peter, *Sunday Times*, 14 May; Margaret Ingram, *Stratford-upon-Avon Herald*, 2 June.
206 Michael Billington, *Guardian*, 12 May 1989.
207 In recent years, *Faustus* has enjoyed considerable popularity at universities and in experimental theatres, often in radically transformed versions. A checklist of 'Renaissance Drama Productions', begun by G. K. Hunter in 1972–3 and continued in 1977 and afterwards by Tony Howard and published in *Research Opportunities in Renaissance Drama*, indicates that the play was performed at Clare College, Cambridge on 4 December 1975; at St Peter's College, Oxford, in the summer of 1976; at the Perth Repertory Theatre on 10–27 November 1976 (directed and adapted by Andrew McKinnon), with free cuts and new material added from the Faust legend; at the Young Vic in the autumn of 1977, with hand glove puppets for the human figures and more elaborate demons for the Deadly Sins, while three puppeteers divided the text among them (Hunter, *RORD*, XIX (1976), 86; Tony Howard, *RORD*, XX (1977), 68–9; *The Stage*, 27 September 1977); at the Arts Centre, York (York Theatre Royal Company, directed by Alan Drury), lasting ninety minutes and featuring two Faustuses, one of whom, a confirmed alcoholic, 'sat in his ubiquitous hell with his back to the audience' throughout the performance and saw the events of his life flash before his eyes (Howard, *RORD*, XX (1977), 69–70); at Mary Washington College in Virginia in February of 1977, with a lot of doubling and a short film and electronic sound track to depict hell; at the Belgrade Theatre Company in Coventry, March 1978, under the direction of Andrew Tuckey, in a condensed version and minimalist set owing much to Grotowski and Charles Marowitz; at the Oxford Playhouse in November of 1978 (directed by Jeremy Howe) in which devils played all the roles, dressing themselves from an on-stage costume rack; at Pembroke College, Cambridge, in November 1979 (directed by Richard Spaul), featuring a Mephistopheles who played all the other parts for Faustus as an hour-long series of dream-temptations (Howard, *RORD*, XX (1977), 70–1; XXI (1978), 66–7; XXII (1979), 78; Bernard Levin, *Sunday Times*, 5 March 1978, p. 38); at the Lyric Theatre, Hammersmith, in February and March of 1980 (directed by Christopher Fettes) in which Faustus encountered Helen to the accompaniment of Wagner's *liebestod* and at last was stripped and dismembered while the music of Bach swelled and the voice of Richard Nixon could be heard speaking to the astronauts on the moon; at the Jesus College chapel in October of 1980, with many carnival effects including two huge figures of the Good and Bad Angels flanking the choir-screen, a Pope who was farcically deaf and drunk, a boxing match between Alexander and Darius, and the chiming of the chapel bell to mark Faustus's final hour

(Howard, *RORD*, XXIII (1980), 60–3; *Guardian*, 26 February and 29 March 1980); at the Swan Theatre, Worcester, in April of 1982, with added nightclub songs for the Seven Deadly Sins and a slideshow illustrating the accomplishments of science, including a moon landing and a nuclear Armageddon; at the Nottingham Playhouse in May of 1983 (directed by Michael Winter and Jeremy Howe) with an all-male transvestite and homosexual cast that included giggling monks, a Lucifer of both beauty and malevolence, reptilian monster-demons out of science fiction, a vampish paramour for Alexander, and a 'maiden-aunt' Mephistopheles; during the Edinburgh Festival of August 1986, with a four-member Cambridge-based touring company and a Faustus who acted out all the Deadly Sins himself under Mephistopheles's hypnotic suggestion; and again at the Edinburgh Festival in production by the St Magnus Players from Orkney, with such inventive staging effects as 'a large pair of cage-like balances from which the Good and Evil Angels strove for dominance, Minotaur and eagle-headed demons, and a large fishing net in which the cast of devils caught and smothered Faustus at the end' (Howard, *RORD*, XXVI (1983), 82–3 and XXIX (1986–7), 60–1; *Guardian*, 6 April 1982). For still other notices of other university and experimental productions, see the reports on 'Renaissance Drama Productions' in *RORD*.

Faustus has also had quite a career on radio. Data provided to Bakeless (1.305) by the National Broadcasting Company lists performances on 16 October 1931, 17 October 1932, 30 September 1933, 28 January 1935, 15 January 1937, 12 September 1937, 6 November 1938, and 3 November 1940. The British Broadcasting Company, according to data provided to Jump, sponsored ten presentations between 1929 and 1962, one of which was a performance by the OUDS on 13 April 1934. The roster of actors in the British broadcasts is a distinguished one, including Ion Swinley, William Devlin, Robert Donat, Ralph Richardson, Alec Guinness, Robert Harris, and Stephen Murphy in the role of Faustus and Robert Farquharson, Marius Goring, Ernest Milton, Laidman Browne, Peter Ustinov, and Esmé Percy as Mephistopheles. Jump (p. lxiii) also mentions three television performances in Great Britain, one directed by Stephen Harrison on 22 June 1947 with David King-Wood as Faustus and Hugh Griffith (repeating a role he had undertaken at Stratford in 1946) as Mephistopheles, a second directed by Ronald Eyre for schools on 21 February 1958 with William Squire and James Maxwell in the leading roles, and a third on 7 and 14 November 1961, also directed by Eyre but with Alan Dobie as Faustus.

The A- and B-texts

208 Greg, pp. 11–12. Fredson Bowers's speculation (p. 124) about a lost earlier edition during the years 1601–4 seems unlikely in view of the

evidence presented below as to A1's having been set directly from manuscript copy.

209 Leo Kirschbaum, 'The Good and Bad Quartos of *Doctor Faustus*', *The Library*, 4th series, XXVI (1946), 272–94; Greg, pp. 63–97; Bowers, 'The Text of Marlowe's *Faustus*', *MP*, XLIX (1952), 195–204, esp. p. 197; and Bowers, II.125–7.

210 Fredson Bowers, 'Marlowe's *Doctor Faustus*: the 1602 Additions', *SB*, XXVI (1973), 1–18, esp. p. 7.

211 Barber, p. 93n.; Kuriyama, pp. 171–97; Warren, pp. 111–47; Gill 3, pp. 141–3; Stephen Greenblatt, *Renaissance Self-Fashioning*, p. 290; Ormerod–Wortham, pp. xxv–xxix; and Keefer, pp. xi–xxii, who argues that the swing from the B-text to the A-text represents an ideological shift from a de-historicised Christian orthodoxy and belief in autonomous authorship to a more heterodox validation of multiple and ambivalent meanings found in textual and theatrical variants. (A more detailed version of this argument is in Michael Keefer, 'History and the Canon: the Case of *Doctor Faustus*', *UTQ*, LVI (1987), 498–522.) Gill 3 (p. xi) offers her view that the A-text is 'founded on the manuscript used as a prompt-book by the Admiral's Men for their earliest performances', but gives no reasons for excluding the possibility of authorial 'foul' papers. Empson, p. 192, dismisses the entire hypothesis of memorial construction as 'that romantic darling of the modern expert'.

212 Ormerod–Wortham, p. xxvii; Keefer, p. xii.

213 Eric Rasmussen, *A Textual Companion to 'Doctor Faustus'* (Manchester University Press, forthcoming). See also Rasmussen, 'Rehabilitating the A-text of Marlowe's *Doctor Faustus*', *SB*, XLVI (1993), forthcoming; ' "Who gave thee power to change a line?" The Revision of Marlowe's *Doctor Faustus*' (Ph.D. dissertation, University of Chicago, 1990).

214 Compare also II.iii.90–3 in the A-text, spoken by Lucifer, and II.iii.91–5 in the B-text, divided between Beelzebub and Lucifer.

215 Greg, pp. 54–5, argues that the A-text at II.iii.106 and 176 recalls the B-text at II.iii.94, and that the A-text at I.iv.25–7 anticipates the B-text some six lines later. See also Kirschbaum, 'The Good and Bad Quartos of *Doctor Faustus*', pp. 282–3.

216 BL MS Harley 7368. For transposition, see Dekker's 'an English honourd Poett' into 'or honord English poet'; for recollection, see Munday's 'observe me Sirrah' and the identical phrase in Dekker's text some nine lines earlier; etc. On folios 12v and 13r, Dekker divides a speech by Erasmus into two speeches by Surrey and Erasmus.

217 Bowers, II.127.

218 Greg, p. 363. Bowers, II.134, n. 1, comments: 'To posit memorial failure in A every time a stylistically distinctive scene appears in B is a desperate expedient.'

219 H. Dugdale Sykes, 'The Authorship of *The Taming of a Shrew, The Famous Victories of Henry V*, and the Additions to Marlowe's *Faustus*', in

Sidelights on Elizabethan Drama (Oxford University Press, 1924), pp. 49–78.

220 Compare *Mucedorus*: 'I, your pot?' and 'I'll cap [arrest] thee for my pot', etc., xii.36–52, in C. R. Baskervill et al., eds., *Elizabethan and Stuart Plays* (New York: Holt, 1934), with the A-text at III.ii.10–27.

221 Compare also *A Looking-Glass*, ed. Tetsumaro Hayashi (Metuchen, N. J.: Scarecrow Press, 1970), ll. 433 and 2054 ff., with the A-text's v.i.31–2 and v.ii.84–8, and the B-text's v.ii.154–9. See Kenneth Muir, 'The Chronology of Marlowe's Plays', *Proceedings of the Leeds Philosophical and Literary Society*, v (1938–43), 345–56, esp. pp. 353–4.

222 Paul Werstine, '"Foul Papers" and "Prompt-books": Printer's Copy for Shakespeare's *Comedy of Errors*', *SB*, XXXIX (1988), 232–46, and 'Narratives about Printed Shakespeare Texts: "Foul Papers" and "Bad" Quartos', *SQ*, XLI (1990), 65–86; and William B. Long, 'Stage-Directions: a Misinterpreted Factor in Determining Textual Provenance', *Text*, II (1985), 121–37. The phrase 'foul draught' appears in John Hardesty's 'The Publisher to the Reader' in his 1653 edition of Henry Killigrew's *The Conspiracy (Pallantus and Eudora)*, sig. A2r; the term 'foul papers' appears in a transcript of John Fletcher's *Bonduca* made by the bookkeeper Edward Knight. See also the Shakespeare First Folio, preliminaries, sig. A3r; the Beaumont and Fletcher Folio of 1647, sig. A4r; G. E. Bentley, *The Profession of Player in Shakespeare's Time, 1590–1642* (Princeton University Press, 1984), pp. 38–42; Fredson Bowers, *On Editing Shakespeare* (Charlottesville: University Press of Virginia, 1966), pp. 13, 107–8, 186–7; and E. A. J. Honigmann, *The Stability of Shakespeare's Text* (London: E. Arnold, 1965), pp. 17–18. The present editors are moreover indebted to Paul Werstine, in private conversation.

223 Greg, *The Shakespeare First Folio* (Oxford: Clarendon, 1955), p. 142.

224 *Ibid.*, pp. 37 8. Evidences of scribal false starts, pointed out to the present editors by Paul Werstine, are to be found in *The Captive Lady*, Malone Society Reprints, 1982, pp. 52–3, ll. 1613 ff., and in *The Fatal Marriage*, Malone Society Reprints, 1958–9, pp. 84 and 88, folios 156b and 157b.

225 See Paul Werstine, 'McKerrow's "Suggestion" and Twentieth-Century Shakespeare Criticism', *Ren.D*, XIX (1989), 149–73.

226 Robert Ford Welsh, 'The Printing of the Early Editions of Marlowe's Plays' (Ph.D. dissertation, Duke University, 1964), pp. 85–126.

227 Bowers, II.146.

228 W. Craig Ferguson, 'The Compositors of *Henry IV, Part 2, Much Ado About Nothing, The Shoemakers' Holiday*, and *The First Part of the Contention*', *SB*, XIII (1960), 19–29; Alan Craven, 'Simmes' Compositor A and Five Shakespeare Quartos', *SB*, XXVI (1973), 37–60, 'The Reliability of Simmes's Compositor A', *SB*, XXXII (1979), 186–97, and 'Two Valentine Simmes Compositors', *Papers of the Bibliographical*

Society of America, LXVII (1974), 163–6; Charlton Hinman, Introduction to the Shakespeare Quarto Facsimile of *Richard II* (Oxford: Clarendon, 1966), p. xiv; and Bowers, II.145n., 146. See Peter Blayney's caveat about making too much of similar habits of spelling found a year or so apart, even in the same printing house, in *The Texts of 'King Lear' and Their Origins* (Cambridge University Press, 1982), p. 155.

229 Welsh, 'The Printing of the Early Editions of Marlowe's Plays', and Bowers, II.145–6.

230 D. F. McKenzie, 'Printers of the Mind: Some Notes on Bibliographical Theories and Printing-House Practices', *SB*, XXII (1969), 1–75, p. 18.

231 Rasmussen, *A Textual Companion to 'Doctor Faustus'*, and 'Rehabilitating the A-Text'.

232 Bowers, II.147.

233 Bowers, 'The Text of Marlowe's *Faustus*', *MP*, XLIX (1952), 195–204, esp. p. 199, n. 6. Further evidence that dramatists working in collaboration would use separate sheets for their acts or scenes is to be found in a libel suit brought by Benjamin Garfield over the portrayal of his mother-in-law in the subplot of *Keep the Widow Waking*, to which Dekker responded that he only 'wrote two sheets of paper containing the first act'; cited by G. E. Bentley, *The Profession of Dramatist in Shakespeare's Time, 1590–1642* (Princeton University Press, 1971), p. 233.

234 Bentley, *The Profession of Dramatist*, p. 228.

235 See the word-frequency data and discussion thereof in Rasmussen's *'Doctor Faustus': A Textual Companion*. Greg, pp. 138–9, comes to essentially similar conclusions about authorship assignment in the B-text, though, given the revised character of the B-text, he tends to divide up individual scenes into Marlovian and non-Marlovian portions; for example, he assigns III.i.1–23 and 30–45 to Marlowe. He assigns all of I.ii to Marlowe. Bowers, II.155–8, regards I.ii in both texts as Marlowe's but the description in III.i.1–56 as by the collaborator. Probably I.ii and the beginning of III.i are more problematic in regard to authorship than other scenes of the play. The word-frequency word tests used in the present study are those developed by Frederick Mosteller and David Wallace, *Inference and Disputed Authorship: the Federalist* (Reading, Mass.: Addison-Wesley, 1964).

236 Greg, 'The Damnation of Faustus', *MLR*, XLI (1946), 97–107, esp. p. 99. On the use of different sources by Fletcher and Shakespeare in their collaboration, see G. R. Proudfoot, ed., *The Two Noble Kinsmen*, Regents Renaissance Drama series (Lincoln: University of Nebraska Press, 1970), p. xix; and see Thomas Nashe, *Lenten Stuff*, ed. McKerrow, III.154, for Nashe's complaint that his collaborator on *The Isle of Dogs*, Ben Jonson, did not have 'the least guess of my drift or scope'.

237 Noted by C. F. Tucker Brooke, ed., *The Works of Christopher Marlowe* (Oxford: Clarendon, 1910), p. 141.

238 *The Downfall* and *The Death of Robert Earl of Huntington*, *Look About You*, and *The Shoemakers' Holiday*.

239 A supposed record of payment to Dekker in 1597 for additions to *Faustus* turns out to be a Collier forgery. See Tucker Brooke, ed., *Works*, p. 141.

240 Paul Kocher, 'Nashe's Authorship of the Prose Scenes in *Faustus*', *MLQ*, III (1942), 17–40. Gill 3, pp. xviii–xxi, also believes Nashe to be the author of the comic scenes, in collaboration with the comic actor John Adams.

241 See Donald Foster, ' "Shall I Die" Post Mortem: Defining Shakespeare', *SQ*, XXXVIII (1987), 58–77, esp. p. 64.

242 Leslie Oliver, 'Rowley, Foxe, and the *Faustus* Additions', *MLN*, LX (1945), 391–4. On the universal supposition today that the B-text additions incorporate the work of Birde and Rowley, see for example Roma Gill's review of Bowers's edition of the *Complete Works*, in *RES*, n.s. XXV (1974), 459–64; Kuriyama, pp. 171–97; and Warren, pp. 111–47. Greg's argument (p. 28) that some at least of the B-text additions must be before 1600–1 since the episode of the three knights, Benvolio, Frederick, and Martino is seemingly alluded to in *The Merry Wives*' mention of 'three *Germane*-diuels; three *Doctor Faustasses*' (IV.v.66–7 ff.) can be countered by Bowers's observation (II.136–7) that Shakespeare's comedy was certainly revised after the bad quarto text of January 1602.

243 Bowers, II.133–4; David Lake, 'Three Seventeenth-Century Revisions: *Thomas of Woodstock*, *The Jew of Malta*, and *Faustus B*', *N&Q*, n.s. XXX (1983), 133–43, esp. p. 143.

244 Bowers, II.134–5, and 'Marlowe's *Doctor Faustus*: the 1602 Additions', *SB*, XXVI (1973), 1–18, points especially to the two comic scenes involving Robin and Rafe (now renamed Dick), the expanded chorus to Act III, the scene with the German Emperor incorporating Bruno and naming the knight as Benvolio, the transferring of some material from the Horse-courser episode to the Clowns' tavern scene, a revised soliloquy for Wagner at V.i.1–9 in the B-text, and revision of the Old Man's role in V.i, omitting the devils' attack on him.

245 Bowers, *On Editing Shakespeare*, p. 19; E. A. J. Honigmann, *The Stability of Shakespeare's Text*, passim.

246 Bentley, *The Profession of Dramatist*, p. 263.

247 Bowers, *On Editing Shakespeare*, p. 15.

248 Bowers, II.128 and 149, refuting Greg's argument, pp. 63–73, that several passages of B1 were printed from A3.

249 Greg, p. 75; Bowers, II.141. Greg's dismissal of playbook influence on the B-text depends chiefly on the superiority of A's version of V.i.26–32, including a three-line 'addition' of ll. 28–30 not present in B; a report of the B-text could hardly provide these splendid lines if they had not been part of the presumed original, and so Greg postulates authorial revision in A at this point (pp. 80–1). If on the other hand the A-text represents

102 DOCTOR FAUSTUS

an authorial manuscript rather than a reported text, as argued in this edition, A's superiority is easily accounted for. Bowers simply asserts that the general characteristics of the original manuscript, apart from the 1602 additions, 'do not suggest a promptbook' (II.140); however, the examples that we adduce here to suggest playbook characteristics are not limited to the 1602 additions. Gill 3 (pp. xi, 143) asserts her view that both the B-text and the A-text were based on promptbooks, but gives no textual argument.

250 Greg, *The Shakespeare First Folio*, p. 138.

251 See W. W. Greg, ed., *Dramatic Documents from the Elizabethan Playhouses*, 2 vols. (Oxford: Clarendon, 1931), II.207. Sample mid-scene entering stage directions in the B-text that are printed to the right are at I.i.63, I.i.98.1, and I.ii.2.1. A few others remain centred, as at I.i.68.1. The A-text prints a similar stage direction to the right at II.i.29.1. The practice seems not to have been printing-house style, since Eld's shop printed A2 and A3 for Wright with centred mid-scene entrance directions and then printed B1 with most mid-scene directions over to the right. Interestingly, the practice of centring is also to be found in a manuscript fragment of *Massacre at Paris* now owned by the Folger Library. Arguments in favour of the fragment's authenticity, put forward by J. Q. Adams, 'The Massacre at Paris Leaf', *The Library*, 4th series, XIV (1934), 447–69 and J. M. Nosworthy, 'The Marlowe Manuscript', *The Library*, 4th series, XXVI (1946), 158–71, have been countered by, among others, R. E. Alton in the *TLS*, 26 April 1974, p. 528.

252 Gary Taylor, 'Zwounds Revisited: Theatrical, Editorial, and Literary Expurgation', in *Shakespeare Reshaped* (Oxford University Press, forthcoming). See also Janet Clare, '*Art Made Tongue-Tied by Authority*': *Elizabethan and Jacobean Dramatic Censorship* (Manchester University Press, 1990), pp. 27–30, 104–6.

253 T. H. Howard-Hill, 'Shakespeare's Earliest Editor: Ralph Crane', *SSur*. *XLIV* (1992), 113–29, lending some indirect support for Greg's insistence on 'a purely literary tradition of expurgation' (*The Shakespeare First Folio*, p. 152). See Howard-Hill's edition of *A Game at Chess*, Malone Society Reprints, 1990.

254 Bowers, II.247, n. 524.

255 T. H. Howard-Hill, 'The Problem of Manuscript Copy for Folio *King Lear*', *The Library*, 6th series, IV (1982), 1–24.

256 Additions were sometimes made to Renaissance playbooks without returning the altered document to the Master of Revels; Henry Glapthorne's *The Lady Mother*, licensed on 15 October 1635, affords an instance. See Greg, ed., *Dramatic Documents from the Elizabethan Playhouses*, II.306.

DOCTOR FAUSTUS
A-text (1604)

THE
TRAGICALL
History of D. Faustus.

As it hath bene Acted by the Right
Honorable the Earle of Nottingham his seruants.

Written by Ch. Marl.

LONDON
Printed by V. S. for Thomas Bushell. 1604.

Title-page of the Quarto (A1) of 1604. Courtesy of the Bodleian Library,
Oxford, Malone 233(3).

[DRAMATIS PERSONAE

THE CHORUS.
DOCTOR JOHN FAUSTUS.
WAGNER.
GOOD ANGEL.
EVIL ANGEL.   5
VALDES.
CORNELIUS.
THREE SCHOLARS.
MEPHISTOPHELES.
ROBIN, *the Clown.*   10
DEVILS.
RAFE.
LUCIFER.
BEELZEBUB.
PRIDE.   ⎫   15
COVETOUSNESS.   ⎪
WRATH.   ⎪
ENVY.   ⎬ *The Seven Deadly Sins*
GLUTTONY.   ⎪
SLOTH.   ⎪   20
LECHERY.   ⎭
THE POPE.
THE CARDINAL OF LORRAINE.
FRIARS.
A VINTNER.   25
THE EMPEROR OF GERMANY, CHARLES V.
A KNIGHT.
ATTENDANTS.
ALEXANDER THE GREAT. ⎫ *Spirits*
HIS PARAMOUR.   ⎭   30
A HORSE-COURSER.
THE DUKE OF VANHOLT.
THE DUCHESS OF VANHOLT.
HELEN OF TROY, *a spirit.*
AN OLD MAN.]   35

DRAMATIS PERSONAE.1–35.] *Dyce 1 (in hierarchical order); not in A1.*

The Tragical History of Doctor Faustus (A-text)

[Prologue]

(Enter CHORUS.*)*

Chorus. Not marching now in fields of Trasimene
Where Mars did mate the Carthaginians,
Nor sporting in the dalliance of love
In courts of kings where state is overturned,
Nor in the pomp of proud audacious deeds,   5
Intends our muse to daunt his heavenly verse.
Only this, gentlemen: we must perform
The form of Faustus' fortunes, good or bad.

1. s.h. *Chorus*] Oxberry; *not in* A1.

---

1. *fields of Trasimene*] the battlefield near Lake Trasimenus or Trasimeno in Italy, north of Rome, where the Carthaginian general Hannibal defeated the Romans in 217 BC. In ll. 1–5, Marlowe announces his intention of turning away from the heroic and political themes that had occupied his attention in *Dido* and *Tamburlaine*. We have no evidence that he wrote a play about Hannibal.
   2. *mate*] side with, ally himself with (*OED*, v.² 4). *OED* must be in error in quoting this passage to illustrate the meaning 'to overcome, defeat, subdue' (v.¹ 2); as Keefer notes, Livy's *Historiae*, xxii.1.8–12 (trans. B. O. Foster, Loeb Library, 1961), describes terrifying portents preceding the battle (prominently figuring Mars) which utterly demoralised the Romans, not the Carthaginians.
   4. *state*] government; pomp and ceremony.
   6. *our muse*] our poet, one under the guidance of a Muse (*OED*, sb.¹ 2c.); a standard Renaissance metonymy. Compare *Sonn.*, xxi.1–2: 'So is it not with me as with that muse, / Stirred by a painted beauty to his verse.'
   daunt] control (*OED*, v. 3), or perhaps 'jade, tire, exhaust'; compare 'overcome, tame, quell' (*OED*, v. 1–4). Greg may well be right that A1's *daunt* is a 'mere misprint' for the 'undoubtedly correct' *vaunt* of B1, but Tucker Brooke points out that *daunt* is supported by *1Tamb.*, III.ii.86: 'my daunted thoughts', and by *Hero and Leander*, IV.334: 'god of undaunted verse' ('Notes on Marlowe's *Doctor Faustus*', *PQ*, XII (1933), 17). The present edition generally tries to preserve distinctions between the A-text and the B-text when the individual readings are at all defensible.
   7–8. *perform / The form*] The verbal repetition is characteristic of Marlowe. Compare *2Tamb.*, III.v.27: 'brandishing their brands', and v.iii.7: 'pitch their pitchy tents'.
   8. *form*] shape, representation.

106

To patient judgements we appeal our plaud,
And speak for Faustus in his infancy.
Now is he born, his parents base of stock,
In Germany, within a town called Rhode.
Of riper years to Wittenberg he went,
Whereas his kinsmen chiefly brought him up.
So soon he profits in divinity,
The fruitful plot of scholarism graced,
That shortly he was graced with doctor's name,
Excelling all whose sweet delight disputes
In heavenly matters of theology;
Till, swoll'n with cunning of a self-conceit,   20

12. Rhode] *Boas; Rhodes A1.*   13, *and throughout.* Wittenberg] *A3;*
Wertenberg or Wertenberge throughout A1.

9. *appeal our plaud*] appeal (as to a higher tribunal) our deserving of
applause.
12. *Rhode*] Roda, in modern times Stadtroda, near Weimar, in the Duchy
of Saxe-Altenberg.
13. *Wittenberg*] The A-text's *Wertenberg* may represent a common confusion of Wittenberg with the Duchy of Württemberg, where in Knittlingen,
according to some accounts, the historical Faustus was born (Logeman, p. 7).
The *Damnable Life* provides one instance of spelling Faustus's place of
residence as *Wirtenberg* (ch. 8), and Marlowe may conceivably have derived
his spelling from there, though the normal spelling throughout the *Damnable
Life* is *Wittenberg*. The name intended in the present passage would appear to
be *Wittenberg*, famous as the university with which Martin Luther and
Philipp Melanchthon were associated. On the other hand, Württemberg and
its University of Tübingen were well known for left-wing Protestantism in
opposition to the more orthodox Lutheranism of Wittenberg. Leah Marcus,
'Textual Indeterminacy and Ideological Difference: the Case of *Doctor
Faustus*', *Ren.D*, XX (1989), 1–29, argues for a theologically meaningful
difference between the A- and B-texts. See 1.i.91n.
14. *Whereas*] where. Marlowe also employs this obsolete and fairly rare
usage (*OED*, 1, Abbott 135) in *2Tamb*., III.ii.66, V.iii.132.
brought him up] supported him.
15–16. *divinity . . . graced*] theology, the fruitful area of human study
graced by the learning of the universities, or by Faustus, or by its own divine
subject (A. Goldman, *N&Q*, n.s. XI (1964), 264).
17. *graced*] 'Marlowe had in mind the Cambridge official "grace" per-
mitting a candidate to proceed to his degree. His own name appears in the
Grace Book in 1584 for the B.A., and in 1587 for the M.A.' (Boas).
18. *whose . . . disputes*] who sweetly delight in disputing (Wagner). Sometimes emended (as by Bowers) to 'whose sweet delight's dispute', whose
sweet delight is dispute.
20–2.] The image seems to conflate Daedalus, as the 'cunning' maker of

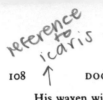

His waxen wings did mount above his reach,
And melting heavens conspired his overthrow.
For, falling to a devilish exercise,
And glutted more with learning's golden gifts,
He surfeits upon cursèd necromancy;   25
Nothing so sweet as magic is to him,
Which he prefers before his chiefest bliss.
And this the man that in his study sits.   *Exit.*

25. necromancy] *A1* (Negromancy); *similarly at I.i.52, 107, etc.*

---

wings, with Icarus, who mounted above his reach (Ovid, *Metamorphoses*, viii.183–235).

20.] Compare John Udall's 1589 sermon on pride: 'We see the whole world so carried away in pride and presumption, that every man swelleth in his own conceit' (*The Combat between Christ and the Devil: Four Sermons*, London: T. Man, 1589, fol. F2).

cunning] (*a*) erudition (*b*) expertness, cleverness (*c*) skill in magic (*d*) skilful deceit, craft (*OED*, sb. 1–5).

22. *melting heavens*] The lack of a comma following *melting* may be simply an error in A1; B1 surely gives the better reading. But the A1 reading is defensible in a transitive sense of 'melting': the heavens do not melt themselves, but have the power to melt the waxen wings.

heavens . . . overthrow] Compare *1Tamb.*, IV.ii.10–11: 'sooner burn the glorious frame of heaven / Than it should so conspire my overthrow'.

23. *falling*] The image juxtaposes the myth of Daedalus and Icarus just cited (ll. 21–2) with the Christian story of Lucifer's falling into sin and hell when he rebelled against God. 'Falling to', in the sense of 'beginning to eat' (compare III.i.61 below, Shakespeare's *R2*, v.v.98, 'My lord, will't please you to fall to?', and *OED*, 'fall', 98c), also anticipates 'glutted', 'surfeits', and 'sweet' in the next three lines. (See Michael Mangan, *Christopher Marlowe: Doctor Faustus*, Harmondsworth: Penguin Books, 1987, p. 29.)

25. *necromancy*] The A1 spelling, *negromancy*, probably represents a common medieval confusion. The word as thus spelled was popularly derived from the Latin *nigro* (*niger*) + *mantia*, black magic or divination. More accurately, *necromancy*, from *necromantia*, means the art of revealing future events through communication with the dead (*OED*).

27. *prefers before*] Compare Marlowe's translation of *Ovid's Elegies*, II.iv.19: 'Before Callimachus one prefers me far', and *Oth.*, I.iii.189: 'preferring you before her father'.

his chiefest bliss] i.e., his hope of salvation.

28.] Evidently, Faustus is visible *in his study* before the speaker of the Prologue leaves the stage. As to whether the effect is created by a *discovery*, that is, by the Prologue pulling back a curtain in front of a space backstage, as most editors assume, and whether (as seems likely) the *mise-en-scène* must also permit Faustus to come forward on to the main stage, see Introduction, pp. 42–3. Perhaps the woodcut illustration of several early editions, showing Faustus conjuring in front of a windowed wall where a hanging globe, a bookshelf with three books, and some other objects are visible (see p. 200), gives some idea of what his study looked like in the theatre.

Act I

Enter FAUSTUS *in his study.*

Faustus. Settle thy studies, Faustus, and begin
    To sound the depth of that thou wilt profess.
    Having commenced, be a divine in show,
    Yet level at the end of every art,
    And live and die in Aristotle's works.
    Sweet <u>*Analytics*</u>, 'tis thou hast ravished me! 5

[handwritten annotation: he loves magic before his own salvation. italicized to keep meter.]

1.i.6. *Analytics*] *A1 (Anulatikes).*

1.i.1–50.] Compare Euphues's resolve to abandon the wanton dissipations of Naples for the life of a scholar: 'Philosophy, physic, divinity, shall be my study. O, the hidden secrets of nature, the express image of moral virtues, the equal balance of justice, the medicines to heal all diseases, how they begin to delight me! The *Axioms* of Aristotle, the *Maxims* of Justinian, the *Aphorisms* of Galen, have suddenly made such a breach into my mind that I seem only to desire them which did only erst detest them' (ed. Bond, 1.241; first noted in Morris William Croll and Harry Clemons's edition of *Euphues*, London: Routledge, 1916, p. 85). Although the occasion of this speech certainly differs from that of Faustus in that Euphues is returning to a life of scholarly discipline, the list of books cited by the two speakers is similar enough to demonstrate the way in which the names of Aristotle, Justinian, and Galen resonated in the intellectual life of the 1570s and 1580s. Marlowe must have been familiar with Lyly's notoriously successful work published in 1578 and 1580. See ll. 16–37 and note below for parallel language that makes a strong case for Marlowe's direct indebtedness.

    1. *Settle*] place in order, fix securely; clarify, consolidate; come to a fixed conclusion on.

    2. *that*] that which.

    profess] (*a*) claim to be an expert in (*b*) teach (*OED*, v. 5, 6).

    3. *commenced*] (*a*) begun (*b*) taken the degree of Master or Doctor (*OED*, v. 1, 4).

    in show] in appearance only.

    4. *level*] aim.

    end] (*a*) purpose (*b*) utmost limit.

    art] discipline.

    6. Analytics] 'the name given to two works by Aristotle on the nature of proof in argument' (Jump).

[*He reads.*] *Bene disserere est finis logices.*
Is to dispute well logic's chiefest end?
Affords this art no greater miracle?
Then read no more; thou hast attained the end.   10
A greater subject fitteth Faustus' wit.
Bid *On kai me on* farewell. Galen, come!
Seeing *ubi desinit philosophus, ibi incipit medicus,*
Be a physician, Faustus. Heap up gold,
And be eternised for some wondrous cure.   15
[*He reads.*] *Summum bonum medicinae sanitas:*

7, 16. S.D. *He reads*] *Kirschbaum (subst.); not in A1.*   7. *logices*] *B4; logicis A1.*   8–9. end? / Affords . . . miracle?] *B1;* end / Affoords . . . myracle: *A1.*
12. *On kai me on*] *Bullen; Oncaymaeon A1; Oeconomy A2–3, B1.*

7.] translated in the following line. On Marlowe's quoting from Ramus's Ciceronian *Dialecticae* instead of Aristotle, see Introduction, p. 16, and Ward.
11. *wit*] intelligence, understanding.
12. On kai me on] being and not being. Again, not from Aristotle but from Gorgias of Leontini, as cited by Sextus Empiricus, *Adversus Mathematicos*, vii.66 (Jump). Latin editions of Sextus Empiricus appeared in 1562 and 1569 (Keefer). According to Ormerod–Wortham, the phrase appears also in the writings of a Cambridge Ramist named Alexander Richardson. See Introduction, p. 16.
Galen] Claudius Galenus (AD 129–99), the famous Greek physician, was considered the leading authority on medicine; his works were widely consulted during the medieval period and early Renaissance. Even Falstaff claims to have read Galen (*2H4*, 1.ii.115–16).
13. ubi . . . medicus] where the philosopher ends, the physician begins. This sentence, not from Galen but from Aristotle's *De Sensu et Sensibili*, 436a, was a favourite of Renaissance writers (see Dent P252.11).
15. *eternised*] immortalised, made famous for ever (*OED*, v. 3). Compare *1Tamb.*, 1.ii.72–3: 'Even as thou hopest to be eternised / By living Asia's mighty emperor'.
16–37.] Compare *Euphues*: 'If thou be so nice that thou canst no way brook the practice of physic, or so unwise that thou wilt not beat thy brains about the institutes of the law, confer all thy study, all thy time, all thy treasure to the attaining of the sacred and sincere knowledge of divinity' (ed. Bond, 1.251–2). The previously unnoticed similarities here of a progression from 'physic' (ll. 17, 27) to the 'institutes of the law' (compare ll. 32–3) to 'divinity' (l. 37) by means of 'study' (l. 34) suggest a direct indebtedness to Lyly. See ll. 1–50n.
16.] The greatest good of medicine is health. Faustus offers a free translation in the following line. From Aristotle's *Nicomachean Ethics*, 1094.a.8 (i.3). Keefer also compares *Politics* 1258a (1.iii.19–22).

The end of physic is our body's health.
Why Faustus, hast thou not attained that end?
Is not thy common talk sound aphorisms?
Are not thy bills hung up as monuments,   20
Whereby whole cities have escaped the plague
And thousand desp'rate maladies been eased?
Yet art thou still but Faustus, and a man.
Wouldst thou make man to live eternally?
Or, being dead, raise them to life again?   25
Then this profession were to be esteemed.
Physic, farewell! Where is Justinian?
[*He reads.*] *Si una eademque res legatur duobus,*
Alter rem, alter valorem rei, etc.

22. eased?] *Dyce 1*; easde, *A1*; cur'd? *B1*.   28, 31, 39, 42. S.D. *He reads*]
Dyce 1 (subst.); not in A1.   28. *legatur*] *Dilke; legatus A1*.

17. *physic*] medicine.
19. *sound aphorisms*] trustworthy medical precepts. The original medical
sense, derived from the *Aphorisms* of the fifth century BC Greek physician
Hippocrates, persists in the present usage along with the broader definition of
'any principle or precept expressed in few words' to which the word was
evidently applied. *OED*, 'aphorism', 2, by citing the present line only in the
broader sense, misleadingly suggests that the original meaning has been lost.
Sound is conceivably an error for *found* (Ward).
20. *bills*] prescriptions, advertisements (*OED*, sb.¹ 5b, 8a).
monuments] i.e., records of the accomplishments of a famous man.
21. *the plague*] i.e., any of a number of epidemic infectious diseases.
22. *eased*] The B-text's *cured* is an equally viable reading, as with many
variants between the two texts.
24. *man*] B1's *men* agrees better with *them* in l. 25.
24–5.] On the blasphemous analogy to Christ's raising of Lazarus from
the dead, see Introduction, pp. 16, 41.
27. *Justinian*] Roman Emperor AD 527–65, whose supreme achievement
was the great codification of Roman Law in the *Institutes*.
28–9.] If one and the same thing is given as a legacy to two persons, one
shall have the thing, the other the value of the thing. The original in the
Institutes, II.xx, reads as follows: '*Si eadem res duobus legata . . . scinditur inter
eos legatum*', 'If the same thing is given as a legacy to two persons . . . each is
entitled to only a half.' The change, which would be hard to hear in Latin in
the playhouse, may be nothing more than an approximation of memory;
either legal principle illustrates the dry legal subtleties of 'paltry legacies'
complained about in the next line. Marlowe is no more likely to have looked
up his Justinian for accurate quotation than he is to have consulted Aristotle
in the original.

A pretty case of paltry legacies!   30
[*He reads.*] *Exhaereditare filium non potest pater nisi*—
Such is the subject of the Institute
And universal body of the Church.
His study fits a mercenary drudge
Who aims at nothing but external trash—   35
Too servile and illiberal for me.
When all is done, divinity is best.
Jerome's Bible, Faustus, view it well.
[*He reads.*] *Stipendium peccati mors est.* Ha!

31. *Exhaereditare*] Dyce *1*; *Ex haereditari A1*; *Exhereditari A2-3*.   36. Too
servile] *B1*; The deuill *A1*.   39-40. *Stipendium* . . . etc.] *divided here this
ed.; one line in A1.*

---

30. *pretty*] fine, admirable; said ironically (*OED*, adj. 3c). B1's *petty* seems
manifestly superior in the legalistic context of the line, and the error, if it is
one, would be easy, but the A1 reading can be defended.
   case] in the legal sense (*OED*, sb.¹ 6), with perhaps a pun on 'receptacle'
(*OED*, sb.² 1) to contain either wills or the laws, or 'a brace, a pair' (*OED*,
sb.² 8). The punning adds to Faustus's scornful tone.
   31.] A father cannot disinherit his son unless—. The original in the
Institutes, II.xiii, is as follows: '*masculos vero postumos, id est et deinceps, placuit
non aliter recte exheredari, nisi nominatum exheredentur*', 'male family heirs born
after the making of the will, sons and other lineal descendants, are held not
to be properly disinherited unless they are disinherited specially'. As at ll.
28-9, the inexactness of the quotation may be owing to imprecise memory
rather than deliberate alteration.
   33. *Church*] This reading is perhaps defensible, since canon law relied
extensively on Justinian's *Institutes*, as any student at Wittenberg or
Cambridge would have known (Ormerod-Wortham). The B-text's substitu-
tion of *law* is understandable and perhaps correct.
   34. *His study*] the study of Justinian. The B-text reading, *This study*, has
perhaps more logical force, but the A-text reading is defensible. See Abbott
228.
   36. *Too servile*] The A1 reading, *The deuill*, is difficult to justify, whereas
the B1 reading is too persuasive to be explained as a compositor's guesswork.
Conversely, with five letters in common in the same order—*T, e, u, i, l*—a
manuscript *Too seruile* could have been misread as *The deuill*.
   illiberal] not befitting one acquainted with the liberal arts (*OED*, adj. 1);
menial.
   37. *When all is done*] after all. A common expression (Dent A211.1).
   38. *Jerome's Bible*] The Vulgate or Latin translation codified by St Jerome
in the fourth century remained the canonical scriptural text for Western
Christendom until the Reformation, and for the Roman Catholic Church
until considerably later. *Jerome's* perhaps requires three syllables.
   39. *Stipendium* . . . *est*] Romans vi.23. Faustus translates in l. 41, but does
not quote fairly or in full; see ll. 42-3n.

Stipendium, etc.   40
The reward of sin is death. That's hard.
[*He reads.*] *Si peccasse negamus, fallimur*
Et nulla est in nobis veritas.
If we say that we have no sin,
We deceive ourselves, and there's no truth in us.   45
Why then belike we must sin,
And so consequently die.
Ay, we must die an everlasting death.
What doctrine call you this, *Che serà, serà*, → predestination
What will be, shall be? Divinity, adieu!   calvinism 50
                    [*He picks up a book of magic.*]
These metaphysics of magicians

42–3.] *divided as in Boas; one line in A1.*   50.1. S.D.] *Kirschbaum*
(subst.); not in A1.

40. *etc.*] Unlike its use at l. 29 above where 'etc.' is part of the spoken text,
here it seems to be an indication of repetition. Greg thinks that Faustus
'murmurs the words over to himself' before giving his translation.
42–3.] 1 John i.8. As Cornelius points out, Faustus's English rendering
(ll. 44–5) is close to the wording in various English bibles, but his Latin does
not coincide with either the Vulgate or any known sixteenth-century Latin
Bible (p. 237). The verse was very familiar because of its inclusion in the
Order for Morning Prayer in *The Book of Common Prayer* (D. E. Dreher,
N&Q, n.s. xxx (1983), 143–4). More seriously, here and in l. 39 Faustus
chooses not to quote the full biblical passages in which God's promises to
those who truly repent are made clear. See Introduction, pp. 16–17.
46. *belike*] in all likelihood.
49. *Che serà, serà*] Dent (M1331) traces this still-popular sentiment back to
at least 1471 in England ('*Homo proponit . . . deus disponit*', 'Man proposes,
God disposes', '*Quy serra serra*') and finds several sixteenth-century uses. His
earliest citations of the English version, 'What will be shall be', are in Peele's
Edward I, c. 1591 (*Works*, ed. Prouty, scene xii, l. 1923) and here in *Faustus*.
Compare *Edw.II*, IV.vi.94: 'That shall be, shall be.'
51. *metaphysics*] occult or magical lore—an obsolete definition assigned
by the *OED* to Marlowe alone (sb. 2), though *metaphysical*, as the *OED*
notes, is common in the English Renaissance in the sense of 'supernatural,
transnatural'. Compare *2Tamb.*, IV.ii.63–4: 'Tempered by science
metaphysical / And spells of magic from the mouths of spirits'. In this
regard, the *OED* cites a common misinterpretation based on a false understanding of *meta* as meaning 'beyond' or 'transcending'; hence in this case
metaphysics comes to mean 'the science of things transcending what is
physical or natural', rather than the science that treats 'of the first principles
of things'.

And necromantic books are heavenly,
Lines, circles, signs, letters, and characters—
Ay, these are those that Faustus most desires.
O, what a world of profit and delight,   55
Of power, of honour, of omnipotence,
Is promised to the studious artisan!
All things that move between the quiet poles
Shall be at my command. Emperors and kings
Are but obeyed in their several provinces,   60
Nor can they raise the wind or rend the clouds;
But his dominion that exceeds in this
Stretcheth as far as doth the mind of man.
A sound magician is a mighty god.
Here, Faustus, try thy brains to gain a deity.   65
Wagner!

---

53. signs] *Greg;* sceanes *A1.*

52.] Faustus claims that the necromantic books can give the excellence
and delight that properly belongs to heaven (*OED,* 'heavenly', adj. 4).
  53.] The language here anticipates Faustus's actual conjuring in i.iii by
means of a *circle* (i.iii.8) that he evidently draws around himself to ward off
evil spirits, as we see in the famous woodcut illustration (see p. 200); by *letters*
from Jehovah's name that are 'forward and backward anagrammatised' (l. 9);
and by '*characters* of *signs* and erring stars', i.e., planets, 'By which the spirits
are enforced to rise' (ll. 12–13). *Characters* are cabbalistic signs or emblems
such as the astrological symbols for the planets (*OED,* sb. 5). *Lines* may here
be simply a part of what Faustus draws around him, though lines are also
used in geomancy, the art of divination through signs derived from the earth;
the usual method was to jot down lines and dots at random and then interpret
them.
  57. *studious artisan*] one who practises and cultivates this art (*OED,*
'artisan', 1, citing this line as the first instance).
  58. *quiet poles*] motionless poles of the universe.
  60. *several*] respective.
  61.] Compare Jeremiah x.13: 'He giveth by his voice the multitude of
waters in the heaven, and he causeth the clouds to ascend from the ends of
the earth: he turneth lightnings to rain, and bringeth forth the wind out
of his treasures' (Cornelius, p. 238). Faustus's implied comparison of his own
prowess with the powers ascribed by Jeremiah to God alone is, of course,
blasphemous—a hubris that is confirmed in l. 64.
  62.] but the sovereign authority of one who excels in this art.
  65. *try*] (*a*) use, apply, experiment with (*b*) subject to severe test or strain
(*OED,* v. 10, 11). Most editors accept the B1 reading *tire;* Greg dismisses *try*
as 'too banal for consideration'. But Bowers points out that Marlowe uses *try*
several times in similar contexts (see I.i.167, I.iii.6, and I.iii.15). Compare

FAUSTUS, A-TEXT (1604)   115

Enter WAGNER.

Commend me to my dearest friends,
The German Valdes and Cornelius.
Request them earnestly to visit me.
Wagner. I will, sir.   *Exit.*
Faustus. Their conference will be a greater help to me   70
Than all my labours, plod I ne'er so fast.

Enter the GOOD ANGEL *and the* EVIL ANGEL.

Good Angel. O Faustus, lay that damnèd book aside
    And gaze not on it, lest it tempt thy soul
    And heap God's heavy wrath upon thy head!
    Read, read the Scriptures. That is blasphemy.   75
Evil Angel. Go forward, Faustus, in that famous art
    Wherein all nature's treasury is contained.
    Be thou on earth as Jove is in the sky,
    Lord and commander of these elements.
                                      Exeunt [ANGELS].
Faustus. How am I glutted with conceit of this!   80

---

66 S.D. *Enter* WAGNER] *placed as in* Wagner, *conj. Dyce 1; printed after l. 65
in A1.*   79.1. S.D. ANGELS] *B1 (An.); not in A1.*

---

also the reading in Marlowe's translation of *Ovid's Elegies*, I.xi.23: 'What
need she try her hand to hold the quill'; here again, editors emend *try* to *tire*.
    gain a deity] obtain the godlike powers of a magician.
    66. S.D. Enter *WAGNER*] The quartos all print Wagner's entrance before
Faustus speaks to him, but this may be simply a reflection of the need in the
theatre to anticipate an entrance. The configuration is common even in plays
printed from authorial papers; compare, for example, Enobarbus's entrance
in *Ant.*, I.ii.137. Greg conjectures that the stage direction stood in the
manuscript margin and was tucked in by the compositor where he found
room. As Paul Werstine has pointed out to us privately, compositorial reluctance to split a verse line in order to include a stage direction is well attested.
    70. *conference*] conversation (*OED*, sb. 4).
    75. *That*] i.e., that damned book.
    78. *Jove*] This pagan name (sometimes confused with the Hebrew
'Jehovah') was often applied to the Christian God in Renaissance writings. It
recurs at I.iii.91 and III.Chorus.3.
    79. *these elements*] the elements, as also at II.i.122. Two ('earth' and 'sky'
or air) are mentioned in the previous line, but God (Jove) is of course
commander of all four (including fire and water).
    80. *glutted with conceit*] i.e., filled with greedy longing by the
very thought, the notion (*OED*, 'glut', v.¹ 2b).

Shall I make spirits fetch me what I please,
Resolve me of all ambiguities,
Perform what desperate enterprise I will?
I'll have them fly to India for gold,
Ransack the ocean for orient pearl,   85
And search all corners of the new-found world
For pleasant fruits and princely delicates.
I'll have them read me strange philosophy
And tell the secrets of all foreign kings.
I'll have them wall all Germany with brass   90
And make swift Rhine circle fair Wittenberg.
I'll have them fill the public schools with silk,

92. silk] *Dyce 1;* skill *A1.*

---

82. *Resolve me of*] dispel, clear away for me, satisfy me as to (*OED*, 'resolve', v. 12).
83. *desperate*] outrageous, extravagant (*OED*, 6).
84. *India*] The word can refer indiscriminately to the East Indies and to the 'new-found world' of l. 86.
85. *orient pearl*] 'a pearl from the Indian seas, as distinguished from those of less beauty found in European mussels; hence a brilliant or precious pearl' (*OED*, sb. and adj. 2b).
87. *delicates*] delicacies.
90.] Friar Bacon, in Greene's *Friar Bacon and Friar Bungay,* similarly hopes to 'circle England round with brass' (ii.171). On the likelihood that Greene is copying Marlowe as he often did, rather than the reverse, see Introduction, pp. 1–2. Compare also Merlin's aspiration to build a brazen wall around Cairmardin, in Spenser's *The Faerie Queene,* III.iii.10 (Keefer).
91.] Wittenberg is south-west of Berlin, on the Elbe, perhaps 200 miles from the Rhine at its closest. The Duchy of Württemberg, on the other hand, borders the southern Rhine—an interesting fact in view of A1's spelling '*Wertenberge*' ('*Wertenberg*' at Prologue.13). Heidelberg, with which the historical John Faustus is associated, is on the Neckar near its juncture with the Rhine.
92. *public schools*] universities.
silk] Faustus apparently intends to defy the university dress codes, such as those in effect at Cambridge: 'no man, unless he were a doctor, should wear any hood lined with silk upon his gown . . . [nor] wear any stuff in the outward part of his gown but woollen cloth of black, puke, London brown, or other sad color' (Decree of Nov. 1578; Orders for apparel, 1585; *Cambridge University Transactions 16th and 17th centuries,* ed. J. Heywood, 2 vols., London, 1854, 1.220, 1.397). See Introduction, p. 17. Dyce's emendation has been accepted by most editors (Ormerod–Wortham being the only exception); as Greg notes, *bravely* in the next line 'disposes of the possibility that, by a rather forced metaphor, the students were meant to be attired in *skill*'.

Wherewith the students shall be bravely clad.
I'll levy soldiers with the coin they bring
And chase the Prince of Parma from our land,   95
And reign sole king of all our provinces;
Yea, stranger engines for the brunt of war
Than was the fiery keel at Antwerp's bridge
I'll make my servile spirits to invent.
Come, German Valdes and Cornelius,   100
And make me blest with your sage conference!

Enter VALDES *and* CORNELIUS.

Valdes, sweet Valdes, and Cornelius,
Know that your words have won me at the last
To practise magic and concealèd arts.
Yet not your words only, but mine own fantasy,   105

101.1. S.D.] *placed as in* B1; *printed after l. 102 in* A1.

---

93. *bravely*] splendidly, handsomely (*OED*, adv. 2).
94. *they*] i.e., the *spirits* of ll. 81 ff.
95. *Prince of Parma*] Spanish governor-general of the Netherlands from 1579 to 1592, much hated in England as a Catholic oppressor and commander of troops to have been landed in the Spanish Armada of 1588; hence, the model of the foreign tyrant whom Protestant patriots would wish to drive out.
97. *stranger engines*] more ingenious weapons.
brunt] assault, violent attack (*OED*, sb.¹ 2a), with a vivid pictorial anticipation of the 'fiery keel' in the next line.
98. *the fiery . . . bridge*] a fireship used by the Netherlands' forces on 4 April 1585 to destroy a bridge built by Parma over the Scheldt during his blockade of Antwerp. *Keel* is a metonymy for 'ship' (*OED*, sb.¹ 2) or possibly a flat-bottomed vessel used especially for coal (*OED*, sb.² 1). Perhaps (as John Cantrell has privately suggested to us) this allusion to Parma without mention of his role in the Armada invasion attempt in July 1588 lends support to a date of composition for *Doctor Faustus* in early 1588 rather than in 1592.
99. *servile*] subject to me as master (*OED*, 2), not 'cringing' or 'deferential'.
100. *Cornelius*] Probably we should not identify this character with Cornelius Agrippa, the Renaissance magician and friend of the historical Faustus, as Ward argues, for in ll. 119–20 Faustus talks with Cornelius and Valdes about Agrippa.
101. *blest*] prosperous, happy (with ironic allusion to the primary meaning, 'filled with heavenly grace').
104. *concealèd*] occult.
105. *fantasy*] (*a*) in scholastic psychology, the mental faculty used to perceive objects (*b*) imagination (*OED*, sb. 1 and 4).

That will receive no object, for my head
But ruminates on necromantic skill.
Philosophy is odious and obscure;
Both law and physic are for petty wits;
Divinity is basest of the three,   110
Unpleasant, harsh, contemptible, and vile.
'Tis magic, magic that hath ravished me.
Then, gentle friends, aid me in this attempt,
And I, that have with concise syllogisms
Gravelled the pastors of the German Church   115
And made the flow'ring pride of Wittenberg
Swarm to my problems as the infernal spirits
On sweet Musaeus when he came to hell,

106. no object, for my head] *Dyce 1*; no obiect for my head, *A1*.
111, I.iv.55, *and* v.i.42. vile] *A1* (vilde).   114. concise syllogisms] *Dyce 1*;
Consissylogismes *A1*.

---

106. *receive no object*] (*a*) perceive or think about nothing else, or (*b*) allow
no objection. Compare l. 137.
107. *But ruminates*] does nothing but ruminate.
110. *basest of the three*] 'even baser than the other three' (Greg), or else
Faustus is 'thinking only of the three learned professions, and tacitly
ignoring philosophy' (J. C. Maxwell, *N&Q*, n.s. XI (1964), 262).
113. *gentle*] (*a*) well-born, honourable (*b*) kind.
114–15.] Compare Luke ii.46–7: 'they found him in the Temple, sitting
in the midst of the doctors, both hearing them, and asking them questions.
And all that heard him were astonished at his understanding and answers'
(see Cornelius, p. 239, and Susan Snyder, 'Marlowe's *Doctor Faustus* as an
Inverted Saint's Life', *SP*, LXIII (1966), 573). As at l. 61, Faustus's implied
linking of his own intellectual achievements with those of Christ among the
doctors is blasphemous.
115. *Gravelled*] confounded, perplexed, amazed (*OED*, v. 4a). Compare
AYLI, IV.i.69–70: 'and when you were gravelled for lack of matter'.
116. *the . . . pride of Wittenberg*] the best in Wittenberg (*OED*, 'pride', sb.[1]
5a). A favourite construction of Marlowe's: compare 'the pride of Asia'
(*Dido*, II.i.187), 'the pride of Christendom' (*1Tamb.*, I.i.132), 'the pride of
Graecia' (*2Tamb.*, III.v.66).
flow'ring] flourishing, vigorous (*OED*, ppl. adj. 2).
117. *problems*] the questions proposed for academic discussion or scholastic
disputation (*OED*, 2). A technical scholastic term.
118. *Musaeus*] In Virgil's *Aeneid*, vi.666–7, the semi-mythical poet
Musaeus visits the underworld as Aeneas's guide and is thronged about by
spirits. Marlowe may conflate this account with the better-known legend of
Orpheus, Musaeus's teacher, who descended to the underworld in order to
rescue his wife, Eurydice, and charmed the spirits there with his music. (See
Virgil's *Georgics*, iv.453–84, and Ovid's *Metamorphoses*, x.1–68.)

Will be as cunning as Agrippa was,
Whose shadows made all Europe honour him.   120
Valdes. Faustus, these books, thy wit, and our experience
Shall make all nations to canonise us.
As Indian Moors obey their Spanish lords,
So shall the subjects of every element
Be always serviceable to us three.   125
Like lions shall they guard us when we please,
Like Almaine rutters with their horsemen's staves,
Or Lapland giants, trotting by our sides;
Sometimes like women, or unwedded maids,
Shadowing more beauty in their airy brows   130

122–5. us. . . . three.] *Kirschbaum (subst.)*; us, . . . three, *A1*.

119–20.] Henry Cornelius Agrippa von Nettesheim (1486–1535), the most famous Renaissance magician, was credited with the power to call up *shadows*, spectral forms or phantoms (*OED*, 'shadow', sb. 7), of the dead. As an indication of Agrippa's contemporary popularity, Boas aptly cites Lyly's *Campaspe* (1584), the Prologue at the Court (ed. Bond, ll. 13–14): 'Whatsoever we present, we wish it may be thought the dancing of Agrippa his shadows.' See Introduction, pp. 8–9.

122. *canonise*] treat as a saint or glorified person (*OED*, v. 4), but with a perhaps unintended and ironic connotation of 'place in the calendar of saints', 'consecrate'. Stressed on the middle syllable.

123. *Indian Moors*] Indians of the Americas. The word *moor* was commonly used of any dark-skinned people (*OED*, sb.[2] 1).

124. *subjects of every element*] bodily forms (taken here by the spirits) from the four elements; similar to the 'elemental shapes' discussed by the magicians in *Friar Bacon and Friar Bungay* (ix.41). Compare *2Tamb.*, v.iii.164–5, 168–70: 'Your soul gives essence to our wretched subjects / Whose matter is incorporate in your flesh . . . But sons, this subject, not of force enough / To hold the fiery spirit it contains, / Must part', cited by the *OED*, 'subject', sb. 5, as illustrating the definition 'the substance of which a thing consists'. The specific idea of bodily form, though not included in the *OED* definition, seems intended in *2Tamb.* and here in *Faustus*. Or *subjects* may mean 'those who are bound to obey'. The B1 reading, *spirits*, is easier to explain and is preferred by many editors.

127.] 'like German cavalrymen with their lances' (Jump).

128. *Lapland giants*] Compare *2Tamb.*, I.i.26–8: 'Vast Gruntland, compassed with the frozen sea, / Inhabited with tall and sturdy men, / Giants as big as hugy Polypheme' (Boas). Compare also Marlowe's grouping here (ll. 127–32) with *2Tamb.*, I.i.22–41: 'Almains, Rutters', Arctic 'Giants', and 'argosies'.

130. *Shadowing*] harbouring or imaging forth. Compare *1Tamb.*, v.i.513–14: 'Shadowing in her brows / Triumphs and trophies for my victories'.

airy] ethereal, heavenly (*OED*, adj. 3).

Than in the white breasts of the Queen of Love.
From Venice shall they drag huge argosies,
And from America the golden fleece
That yearly stuffs old Philip's treasury,
If learnèd Faustus will be resolute.   135
Faustus. Valdes, as resolute am I in this
As thou to live. Therefore object it not.
Cornelius. The miracles that magic will perform
Will make thee vow to study nothing else.
He that is grounded in astrology,   140
Enriched with tongues, well seen in minerals,
Hath all the principles magic doth require.
Then doubt not, Faustus, but to be renowned
And more frequented for this mystery
Than heretofore the Delphian oracle.   145

131. in the] *Greg;* in their *A1;* has the *B1.*   132. From] *B1;* For *A1.*
132. drag] *A2* (dragge); dregge *A1.*   141. seen in] *A2;* seene *A1.*   143.
renowned] *A1* (renowmd).   145. Delphian] *A2;* Dolphian *A1.*

132. *From*] B1 corrects A1's obvious error.
argosies] from the Italian *ragusea*, a vessel of Ragusa (*OED*)—rather than,
as Elizabethans mistakenly supposed, from the Medieval Latin *argis*, a vessel
of heavy burden, and (behind that word) from the Argo, Jason's famous
mythical ship (Ward).
133–4.] Marlowe's comparison of Jason's golden fleece with the incredible
wealth taken out of the New World by Philip II of Spain's soldiers may have
been prompted by historical misunderstanding of the word *argosies* as indicated in the previous note (Jump). The annual tribute carried aboard
Philip's plate fleet was an inviting target for English and Dutch raiders.
137. *object it not*] do not urge this as an objection to our going forward
(*OED*, 4), or, do not accuse me of irresolution (*OED*, 5).
141. *Enriched with tongues*] i.e., learned in Greek, Hebrew, and especially
Latin, the universal language for conversing with spirits. At l. 157 Faustus is
bidden to take along the Hebrew Psalter and the (Latin) New Testament to
his conjuring. He conjures in Latin. In the *Damnable Life*, ch. 1, Faustus's
companions also make use of Chaldean, Persian, and Arabic (Greg).
well seen in minerals] well versed in the properties of minerals (Keefer).
144. *frequented*] visited, resorted to.
mystery] secret art, skill (*OED*, sb.[1] 8 and sb.[2] 2c).
145. *Delphian oracle*] oracle of Apollo at Delphi.

The spirits tell me they can dry the sea
And fetch the treasure of all foreign wrecks—
Ay, all the wealth that our forefathers hid
Within the massy entrails of the earth.
Then tell me, Faustus, what shall we three want?   150
Faustus. Nothing, Cornelius. O, this cheers my soul!
Come, show me some demonstrations magical,
That I may conjure in some lusty grove
And have these joys in full possession.
Valdes. Then haste thee to some solitary grove,   155
And bear wise Bacon's and Albanus' works,
The Hebrew Psalter, and New Testament;
And whatsoever else is requisite
We will inform thee ere our conference cease.
Cornelius. Valdes, first let him know the words of art,   160
And then, all other ceremonies learned,
Faustus may try his cunning by himself.
Valdes. First I'll instruct thee in the rudiments,
And then wilt thou be perfecter than I.
Faustus. Then come and dine with me, and after meat   165

147. wrecks] *A1* (wrackes).

146–9.] The pecuniary advantages of raising a spirit are well attested to in Scot's *The Discovery of Witchcraft* (1584): 'if thou wilt command him to tell thee of hidden treasures that be in any place, he will tell it thee: or if thou wilt command him to bring thee gold or silver, he will bring it thee' (xv.xiii).
149. *massy*] massive, solid.
150. *want*] lack.
153. *lusty*] pleasant.
156.] Roger Bacon (c. 1212–92) was a Franciscan philosopher at Oxford and reputed magician, as he is portrayed in Greene's *Friar Bacon and Friar Bungay*. Pietro d'Abano (c. 1250–1316), Italian philosopher and physician, had a reputation as a conjurer and sorcerer. Cornelius Agrippa couples the names of 'Bachon and Apponus' in his writing (as Ward observes), but in view of the variations in spelling some editors have wondered if Faustus is referring instead to Albertus Magnus. See Introduction, pp. 8–9.
157.] The Psalms and the opening verses of St John's gospel were regularly used in conjuration (Ward).
160. *the words of art*] technical terms needed for incantation.
162. *cunning*] See note at Prologue.20, for the rich ambiguity of this word, including knowledge, specialised skill in magic, and deceitfulness.
164. *perfecter*] more trained, skilled, conversant (*OED*, 'perfect', adj. B 2).
165. *meat*] food.

We'll canvass every quiddity thereof,
For ere I sleep I'll try what I can do.
This night I'll conjure, though I die therefore.   *Exeunt.*

[I.ii]

Enter two SCHOLARS.

First Scholar. I wonder what's become of Faustus, that was
wont to make our schools ring with 'sic probo'.
Second Scholar. That shall we know, for see, here comes his
boy.

Enter WAGNER, [*carrying wine*].

First Scholar. How now, sirrah, where's thy master?   5
Wagner. God in heaven knows.
Second Scholar. Why, dost not thou know?
Wagner. Yes, I know, but that follows not.
First Scholar. Go to, sirrah! Leave your jesting, and tell us
where he is.   10
Wagner. That follows not necessary by force of argument
that you, being licentiate, should stand upon't. There-

I.ii.4.I.   S.D. *carrying wine*] *Kirschbaum (subst.); not in A1.*

---

166. *canvass every quiddity*] discuss and scrutinise each essential element.
The scholastic sense in which a *quiddity* is a quibble or captious nicety in
argument (*OED*, 2) gives ironic perspective to Faustus's zeal for 'cunning'.

I.ii.2. sic probo] I prove it thus. The currency of this phrase as an
expression of triumphant conclusion in scholastic debate continues the irony
of *quiddity* in the conclusion of the previous scene.
   5. *sirrah*] a conventional form of address to a social inferior or servant.
   8. *that follows not*] Wagner parodies his master's triumphs in disputation
by quibbling with an implied syllogism: 'God in heaven knows' ordinarily
means 'God alone knows', but since Wagner didn't say so precisely, it doesn't
necessarily follow that Wagner does not know. *Non sequitur* (it follows not),
like *sic probo* in l. 2, was a familiar formula in disputation that survives in
modern academic jargon.
   9. *Go to*] an expression of impatience or reproof.
   11-12. *That . . . upon't*] i.e., respectable scholars trained in logic like yourselves should know better than to assume it's been proven yet that I know
where Faustus is and that you therefore have a right to demand an answer.
(Wagner repeats and expands his chop-logic point in l. 8.)
   12. *licentiate*] technically, only those who have been licensed to ascend to a
Master's or Doctor's degree. Greg assumes that Faustus's students would

fore, acknowledge your error, and be attentive.
Second Scholar. Why, didst thou not say thou knew'st?
Wagner. Have you any witness on't?   15
First Scholar. Yes, sirrah, I heard you.
Wagner. Ask my fellow if I be a thief.
Second Scholar. Well, you will not tell us.
Wagner. Yes, sir, I will tell you. Yet if you were not dunces,
you would never ask me such a question. For is not he   20
corpus naturale? And is not that *mobile?* Then, wherefore
should you ask me such a question? But that I am by
nature phlegmatic, slow to wrath, and prone to lechery—
to love, I would say—it were not for you to come within

---

probably still be bachelors because 'Wagner would not be so familiar with
seniors', but Wagner's role as servant-clown in the tradition of the *zanni* in
the *commedia dell'arte* gives him a licence to mock virtually everything.
  stand upon't] insist upon, demand (*OED*, 'stand', v. 78m, giving a citation
from 1634 as the earliest usage).
  14.] The Second Scholar asks, 'What error are you talking about? Didn't
you just say in effect that you do know where Doctor Faustus is? And I've
asked you to tell us where he is.'
  15. *on't*] i.e., to prove that I said I knew where Doctor Faustus is.
  17.] Wagner proverbially suggests that 'the First Scholar's support for his
companion's statement is worth no more than one thief's testimony to
another's innocence' (Keefer). For other uses of this familiar phrase in the
drama of the early 1590s, see Dent F177.
  18.] The Second Scholar wearily recognises that he and his fellow are
unlikely to get much information in this mad game of chop-logic.
  19. *dunces*] (*a*) subtle, sophistical scholars; the name originally was applied
to followers of the Scottish scholastic theologian Duns Scotus (*c.* 1265–1308),
and later to 'hair-splitting reasoners' in general (*b*) blockheads, those whose
study of books has left them 'dull and stupid' (*OED*, sb. 3, 4, 5).
  21. *corpus naturale . . . mobile*] *Corpus naturale seu mobile* (a body that
is natural or liable to change) was a scholastic formulation, derived from
Aristotle, used to define in physics the capability of natural bodies for
movement or change (Ward). The signification here of this ridiculously
applied learning is that Doctor Faustus, being a human animal, is capable of
motion and hence of being wherever he wants to be.
  22–3. *But . . . lechery*] Compare James i.19: 'Wherefore my dear brethren,
let every man be swift to hear, slow to speak, slow to wrath' (Cornelius, p.
240). Wagner's insistence that he fulfils the behests of Paul to avoid wrath
and lust is comically undercut by his first saying *lechery* instead of *love*; see
I.i.61n. and I.i.114–15n.
  23. *prone*] (*a*) naturally inclined towards (*b*) horizontally positioned for.

forty foot of the place of execution, although I do not   25
doubt to see you both hanged the next sessions. Thus,
having triumphed over you, I will set my countenance
like a precisian and begin to speak thus: Truly, my dear
brethren, my master is within at dinner with Valdes and
Cornelius, as this wine, if it could speak, it would inform   30
your worships. And so the Lord bless you, preserve you,
and keep you, my dear brethren, my dear brethren.
                                                        Exit.

First Scholar. Nay, then, I fear he is fall'n into that damned
    art for which they two are infamous through the world.
Second Scholar. Were he a stranger, and not allied to me, yet   35
    should I grieve for him. But come, let us go and inform
    the Rector, and see if he, by his grave counsel, can
    reclaim him.
First Scholar. O, but I fear me nothing can reclaim him.
Second Scholar. Yet let us try what we can do.   *Exeunt.*   40

---

25. *the place of execution*] i.e., the room where Faustus, Valdes, and
Cornelius are attacking their victuals (see ll. 29–30); but Wagner applies the
phrase punningly to a jest about hanging. The point about not coming within
forty feet of the gallows is repeated in *Jew of Malta*, IV.ii.16–18 ('*Bella.* And
where didst meet him? / *Pilia.* Upon mine own freehold, within forty foot of
the gallows'), suggesting a legally prohibited space for public executions,
although 'forty foot' is also a conventional distance of separation (Dent F581).
See IV.i.131n.
    28. *precisian*] one who is rigidly precise in religious observance, a Puritan
(*OED*). Wagner apes the Puritan mannerism with a *set countenance* of sober
expression.
    31. *your worships*] i.e., your honours.
    31–2. *the Lord . . . keep you*] Compare the universally known Family
Prayer for evening in *The Book of Common Prayer*: 'The Lord bless us and
keep us. The Lord make his face to shine upon us, and be gracious unto us.
The Lord lift up his countenance upon us, and give us peace, this night and
evermore.' The prayer is based on a number of biblical passages, among
them Numbers vi.24 and Psalms xliv.2. Wagner's ending in a repetition of
'my dear brethren' continues his parody of Puritan affectation; compare
Falstaff's sanctimonious farewell to his companions at *1H4*, I.ii.148 ff., in the
mocking form of a collect at the close of a divine service.
    35. *allied to me*] i.e., bound to me in friendship.
    37. *Rector*] head of the university.
    39. *fear me*] fear. On *me* as an archaic dative, signifying 'with respect to
me', see Abbott 220.

[I.iii]

Enter FAUSTUS *to conjure,* [*holding a book*].

Faustus. Now that the gloomy shadow of the earth,
Longing to view Orion's drizzling look,
Leaps from th'Antarctic world unto the sky
And dims the welkin with her pitchy breath,

I.iii.0.1. S.D. *holding a book*] This ed.; not in A1.

I.iii.0.1. S.D.] At I.i.155–7, Valdes bids Faustus, 'haste thee to some solitary grove' with requisite books to do his conjuring, suggesting that Faustus enters in I.iii with a book or books. The B-text title-page illustration also visualises Faustus's conjuring in or in front of his study, with no suggestion of a grove—though whether this picture constitutes evidence as to theatrical practice, especially for the A-text, is a difficult question. Perhaps on the Elizabethan stage Faustus occupies the main stage in his robes, while his study, spatially identified at the start of I.i, is either curtained-off in the 'discovery' space or else is simply understood to be at a distant location. The text gives no indication that a grove is visually present.

1–4.] For the mood of this passage, and especially for two of its images, Marlowe may well have had in mind Spenser's *The Faerie Queene*, III.x.46: 'Now gan the humid vapour shed the grownd / With perly dew, and th'Earthes gloomy shade / Did dim the brightnesse of the welkin rownd.' Especially suggestive are 'th'Earthes gloomy shade' (compare 'the gloomy shadow of the earth') and 'Did dim the brightnesse of the welkin rownd' (compare 'dims the welkin with her pitchy breath'). For Marlowe's apparent borrowings from the *The Faerie Queene* elsewhere, see J. S. Cunningham's notes in his Revels edition of *1Tamb.*, V.i.259–62, 290–3, 302–3, and *2Tamb.*, IV.i.186–91. See also J. D. Jump, *N&Q*, n.s. XI (1964), 261–2.

1. *shadow of the earth*] Pierre de la Primaudaye, in *The French Academy*, III.xxxvii (trans. Richard Dolman, London: G. Bishop, 1601), similarly argues that night is 'no other thing but the shadow of the earth' (Gill 1). The *locus classicus* for this pre-Copernican belief may be Macrobius's *Commentum*, I.xx.18: 'the shadow of the earth which the sun, after setting and progressing into the lower hemisphere, sends out upwards, creating on earth the darkness which is called night' (John Norton-Smith, *N&Q*, n.s. XXV (1978), 436–7). This explanation seems to render unnecessary the speculation of Ormerod–Wortham that 'Faustus is evidently conjuring during an eclipse'; the darkness of the earth's shadow dims the whole 'welkin', not simply the moon.

2. *Orion's drizzling look*] 'the rainy constellation of Orion' (Gill 1). Orion is high in the sky in winter. Compare Virgil, *Aeneid*, 'nimbosus Orion' (i.535) and 'aquosus Orion' (iv.52; cited by Keefer).

3. *Leaps from th'Antarctic*] Compare *2Tamb.*, I.ii.51–2: 'When Phoebus leaping from his hemisphere / Descendeth downward to th'Antipodes'.

4. *welkin*] sky.
pitchy] (*a*) pitch black (*b*) viscous and stinking.

Faustus, begin thine incantations,   5
And try if devils will obey thy hest,
Seeing thou hast prayed and sacrificed to them.
                              [*He draws a circle.*]
Within this circle is Jehovah's name,
Forward and backward anagrammatised,
The breviated names of holy saints,   10
Figures of every adjunct to the heavens,
And characters of signs and erring stars,
By which the spirits are enforced to rise.
Then fear not, Faustus, but be resolute,
And try the uttermost magic can perform.   15
Sint mihi dei Acherontis propitii! Valeat numen triplex
Jehovae! Ignei, aerii, aquatici, terreni, spiritus, salvete!

7.1. S.D.] *This ed.; not in A1.*   9. anagrammatised] *B1 (Anagramatis'd); and*
Agramithist A1.   17. aquatici] *Tucker Brooke; Aquatani A1.*   17. terreni]
conj. Greg; not in A1.

---

6. *hest*] behest.
    8. *this circle*] Scot's *The Discovery of Witchcraft* dictates that the conjurer
'must make a circle . . . when that he has made, go into the circle, and close
again the place, there where thou wentest in' (xv.xiii). The circle both forced
the spirits to appear and protected the conjurer from them.
    9. *anagrammatised*] made into anagrams. B1 corrects A1's gibberish, *and*
Agramithist, which Greg considers to be owing to an actor or reporter or both,
but which could just as plausibly be a compositor's guess in dealing with an
unusual word. Possibly the compositor had the word *amethyst* in mind, as
Greg speculates about the actor or reporter.
    10. *breviated*] abbreviated.
    11–12.] charts of every heavenly body fixed in the firmament and astrol-
ogical symbols or diagrams of the constellations of the Zodiac and the
planets. (See 1.i.53n.) The planets are *erring* or wandering heavenly bodies in
contrast with the fixed stars.
    16–23.] May the gods of Acheron be propitious to me! Let the threefold
power of Jehovah be strong! Spirits of fire, air, water, and earth, all hail!
Lucifer, Prince of the East, Beelzebub, monarch of burning hell, and
Demogorgon, we ask your favour that Mephistopheles may appear and rise.
Why do you delay? By Jehovah, Gehenna, and the holy water I now sprinkle,
and by the sign of the cross I now make, and by our prayers, may
Mephistopheles himself arise at our command!
    16. Acherontis] Acheron is one of the rivers of Hades, here used to signify
the lower world.
    17. aquatici, terreni] A1 and B1 have only *Aquatani*, but the Latin is
generally corrupt. *Aquatani* is an easy error for *Aquatici*, and an appeal to the
spirits of all four elements seems likely.

Orientis princeps Lucifer, Beelzebub, inferni ardentis
monarcha, et Demogorgon, propitiamus vos, ut appareat
et surgat Mephistopheles! Quid tu moraris? Per Jehovam,   20
Gehennam, et consecratam aquam quam nunc spargo,
signumque crucis quod nunc facio, et per vota nostra, ipse
nunc surgat nobis dicatus Mephistopheles!
[*Faustus sprinkles holy water and makes a sign of the cross.*]

Enter a Devil [MEPHISTOPHELES].

I charge thee to return and change thy shape.
Thou art too ugly to attend on me.   25
Go, and return an old Franciscan friar;
That holy shape becomes a devil best.
                    Exit Devil [MEPHISTOPHELES].
I see there's virtue in my heavenly words.

---

18. *Lucifer*] *conj. Greg; not in A1.*   18, 58, II.i.5 *and* 12. *Beelzebub*] *A1*
(*Belsibub, or, as at II.i.5 and 12, Belsabub*).   19. *Demogorgon*] *A1*
(*demigorgon*).   19. *appareat*] *B1; apariat A1–3.*   20, *and throughout.*
Mephistopheles] *A1* (*Mephastophilis here and normally in A1, but Mephostophilis*
at I.iii.35.1 and III.ii.28.1 and Mephastophilus at III.i.0.1. S.D. and 1).
20. *Quid tu moraris*] *Ellis, conj. Bullen; quod tumeraris A1.*   23. *dicatus*] *B3;*
dicaetis A1; dicatis A2–3, B1.   23.1. S.D.] *This ed.; not in A1.*   23.2 *and*
27.1. S.D. MEPHISTOPHELES] *Ward; not in A1.*

---

18. Lucifer] The name is missing from A1 and B1, but Lucifer is the
Prince of the East in Isaiah xiv.12 and was widely known as such in medieval
tradition. Faustus uses this title in referring to Lucifer at II.i.107 below; see
note. Greg and others assume the name was dropped accidentally. The B-text
tends to support this reading by bringing on Lucifer. On the other hand, see
l. 58n. on Marlowe's confusing the names of Beelzebub and Lucifer.
    Beelzebub] A1's *Belsibub* or *Belsabub* and B1's *Belzebub* here and at II.i.5
and 12 indicate pronunciation in three syllables, as is metrically required. The
present edition uses the standard modernisation, as also with *Mephistopheles*.
    19. Demogorgon] Compare *1Tamb.*, IV.i.18: 'As monstrous as Gorgon,
prince of hell'.
    21. Gehennam] the Jewish hell.
    24–5.] In Scot's *The Discovery of Witchcraft*, the conjurer is instructed to
command that the spirit 'come unto us, in fair form of man . . . and not
terrible by any manner of way' (XV.xiii). Marlowe turns this instruction into
an anti-Catholic joke.
    28. virtue] supernatural power (*OED*, sb. 1).
    heavenly words] 'scriptural phrases used for conjuration' (Boas). But the
line suggests an ironic second meaning of moral goodness in divine utterance.
Compare I.i.52.

Who would not be proficient in this art?
How pliant is this Mephistopheles,   30
Full of obedience and humility!
Such is the force of magic and my spells.
Now, Faustus, thou art conjurer laureate,
That canst command great Mephistopheles.
Quin redis, Mephistopheles, fratris imagine!   35

    Enter MEPHISTOPHELES [*disguised as a friar*].

Mephistopheles. Now, Faustus, what wouldst thou have me do?
Faustus. I charge thee wait upon me whilst I live,
To do whatever Faustus shall command,
Be it to make the moon drop from her sphere
Or the ocean to overwhelm the world.   40
Mephistopheles. I am a servant to great Lucifer
And may not follow thee without his leave.
No more than he commands must we perform.
Faustus. Did not he charge thee to appear to me?
Mephistopheles. No, I came now hither of mine own accord.   45
Faustus. Did not my conjuring speeches raise thee? Speak.
Mephistopheles. That was the cause, but yet *per accidens.*
For when we hear one rack the name of God,

---

33. Now] *Wagner, conj. Albers;* No *A1.*   35. redis] *Boas, conj. Taylor; regis*
A1.   35.1. S.D. disguised as a friar] *Kirschbaum (subst.); not in A1.*   47.
accidens] *B4;* accident *A1.*

---

33. *laureate*] pre-eminent (*OED*, adj. 2), crowned with laurel.
35.] Why don't you return, Mephistopheles, in the guise of a friar!
39. *make . . . sphere*] a power traditionally ascribed to magicians. In Ovid's
Metamorphoses, Medea boasts that among the spells and arts of magicians
('*cantusque artisque magorum*'), she can draw the moon from the sky ('*te
quoque, Luna, traho*', 'I draw thee, O moon', vii.207). Compare Friar Bacon's
claim that he has the power to 'dim fair Luna to a dark eclipse' (*Friar Bacon
and Friar Bungay*, ii.48). Ward and Keefer cite Virgil, *Eclogues*, viii.69,
Horace, *Epodes*, v.45–6, and Apuleius, *Metamorphoseon* (*The Golden Ass*),
i.iii (trans. W. Adlington, Loeb Library (1915), pp. 6–7).
47.] i.e., your conjuration was the reason for my coming, all right, but
only because of what you happened to say, not because I was obliged to obey
your command. *Per accidens* is a scholastic term used to distinguish between
agents that produce their own effect (efficient cause) and happenings that
merely provide the occasion for the operation of some external agency (*per
accidens*).
48. *rack*] The metaphor of the torture rack suggests pulling or tearing
apart, as in anagrammatising or using God's name in vain.

Abjure the Scriptures and his Saviour Christ,
We fly in hope to get his glorious soul,   50
Nor will we come unless he use such means
Whereby he is in danger to be damned.
Therefore, the shortest cut for conjuring
Is stoutly to abjure the Trinity
And pray devoutly to the prince of hell.   55
Faustus. So Faustus hath
Already done, and holds this principle:
There is no chief but only Beelzebub,
To whom Faustus doth dedicate himself.
This word 'damnation' terrifies not him,   60
For he confounds hell in Elysium. —> *does not*
His ghost be with the old philosophers!   *believe in it*
                                             atheism.

56–7.] *divided as in Dyce 2; one line in A1.*

---

50. *glorious*] (*a*) radiant, beautiful (*b*) vainglorious (*OED*, adj. 1, 4).
54. *stoutly*] (*a*) resolutely, bravely (*b*) arrogantly.
58. *Beelzebub*] The confusion of Beelzebub with Lucifer as the names of Mephistopheles's lord (compare ll. 65 ff.) may be owing to the fact that, as Ormerod–Wortham observe, 'in Matthew xii.24–8, Mark iii.22–6, and Luke xi.15–20 the names Satan, Lucifer, and Beelzebub are all used for the chief devils'. Robert West notes that demonology generally ranks devils when they are tempting and overthrowing souls but dissolves such distinctions when the soul is taken off to damnation (*The Invisible World*, p. 83).
61. *confounds hell in Elysium*] (*a*) does not distinguish between the Christian hell and the pagan afterlife (*OED*, 'confound', 6, 7); or (*b*) 'destroys Hell, or brings it to ruin, by putting it in a bath of Elysium' (Empson, p. 125; *OED*, 1). Greg notes a similar (though reversed) combining of the two terms in Nashe's Preface to Greene's *Menaphon* (1589), where Nashe speaks of writers 'that thrust Elysium into hell' (ed. McKerrow, III.316). The two terms had already been coupled in *1Tamb.*, v.i.466, 'Hell and Elysium swarm with ghosts of men', a conception that may well be indebted to Homer's *Odyssey* (iv.563–9), where Menelaus is told that 'to the Elysian plain and the bounds of the earth will the immortals convey thee, where dwells the fair-haired Rhadamanthus', and to Virgil's *Aeneid* (vi.541–2), in which Elysium is placed not in the Western Ocean but in Hades (Bernhard Fabian, *ES*, XLI (1960), 365–8).
62. *ghost*] spirit.
the old philosophers] i.e., those pre-Christian philosophers who did not believe in an eternity of punishment and who, according to Christian theology, will spend eternity in Limbo, where they are neither tortured nor permitted to dwell with God. The original of this line, '*sit anima mea cum philosophis*', was attributed in the Renaissance to Averroes (1126–98), the Arab commentator on Aristotle who believed in corporate and un-

But leaving these vain trifles of men's souls,
Tell me what is that Lucifer thy lord?
Mephistopheles. Arch-regent and commander of all spirits.   65
Faustus. Was not that Lucifer an angel once?
Mephistopheles. Yes, Faustus, and most dearly loved of God.
Faustus. How comes it then that he is prince of devils?
Mephistopheles. O, by aspiring pride and insolence,
   For which God threw him from the face of heaven.   70
Faustus. And what are you that live with Lucifer?
Mephistopheles. Unhappy spirits that fell with Lucifer,
   Conspired against our God with Lucifer,
   And are for ever damned with Lucifer.
Faustus. Where are you damned?   75
Mephistopheles. In hell.
Faustus. How comes it then that thou art out of hell?
Mephistopheles. Why, this is hell, nor am I out of it.
   Think'st thou that I, who saw the face of God
   And tasted the eternal joys of heaven,   80
   Am not tormented with ten thousand hells
   In being deprived of everlasting bliss?
   O Faustus, leave these frivolous demands,
   Which strike a terror to my fainting soul!
Faustus. What, is great Mephistopheles so passionate   85
   For being deprivèd of the joys of heaven?
   Learn thou of Faustus manly fortitude,
   And scorn those joys thou never shalt possess.
   Go bear these tidings to great Lucifer:

89. *these*] *B1;* those *A1.*   89–91. Lucifer: . . . deity,] *Dilke (subst.*); *Lucifer,* . . . deitie: *A1.*

individuated eternity rather than an individual spiritual eternity. See J. C. Maxwell, *N&Q,* CXCIV (1949), 334–5, and John M. Steadman, *N&Q,* n.s. III (1956), 416 and n.s. IX (1962), 327–9.

79–82.] This picture of hell's torment is evidently derived from St John Chrysostom (AD 347–407): 'if one were to speak of ten thousand hells, they would be nothing compared with being excluded from the blessed vision of heaven', Homily in St Matthew, xxiii.9; see John Searle, *TLS,* 15 February 1936, p. 139, and Jump.

85. *passionate*] swayed by strong feeling (*OED,* adj. 3).

89. *these*] The B1 reading corrects A1's error, seemingly caused by a repetition of *those* from the previous line (Greg).

Seeing Faustus hath incurred eternal death   90
By desp'rate thoughts against Jove's deity,
Say he surrenders up to him his soul,
So he will spare him four-and-twenty years,
Letting him live in all voluptuousness,
Having thee ever to attend on me,   95
To give me whatsoever I shall ask,
To tell me whatsoever I demand,
To slay mine enemies and aid my friends,
And always be obedient to my will.
Go and return to mighty Lucifer,   100
And meet me in my study at midnight,
And then resolve me of thy master's mind.
Mephistopheles. I will, Faustus.   *Exit.*
Faustus. Had I as many souls as there be stars,
I'd give them all for Mephistopheles.   105
By him I'll be great emperor of the world
And make a bridge through the moving air
To pass the ocean with a band of men;
I'll join the hills that bind the Afric shore
And make that land continent to Spain,   110
And both contributory to my crown.
The Emp'ror shall not live but by my leave,
Nor any potentate of Germany.
Now that I have obtained what I desire,
I'll live in speculation of this art   115
Till Mephistopheles return again.   *Exit.*

---

93. four-and-twenty] *A1 (24.); also at II.i.109, II.iii.46–7, and V.ii.40.*

93. *So*] on condition that.
104. *as there be stars*] proverbial for an infinite amount (Dent s825.1).
108. *pass*] cross (*OED*, v. 30). Faustus may have in mind Xerxes's audacious undertaking to build a bridge of boats across the Hellespont en route to Greece in 481–480 BC. See Herodotus, *The Histories*, vii.54–6 (trans. A. D. Godley, Loeb Library, 1922), and Gill 3.
109. *bind*] gird (*OED*, v. 7).
110. *continent to*] connected to. Faustus proposes to close the straits of Gibraltar. *OED* cites this line as the first instance, but Marlowe had used it earlier in *1Tamb.*, I.i.127–8: 'Afric and Europe bordering on your land / And continent to your dominions'.
115. *speculation*] contemplation, profound study (*OED*, 4).

[I.iv]

Enter WAGNER *and* [ROBIN] *the* CLOWN.

Wagner. Sirrah boy, come hither.

Robin. How, 'boy'? 'Swounds, 'boy'! I hope you have seen
many boys with such pickedevants as I have. 'Boy',
quotha?

Wagner. Tell me, sirrah, hast thou any comings in?   5

Robin. Ay, and goings out too, you may see else.

Wagner. Alas, poor slave, see how poverty jesteth in his
nakedness! The villain is bare and out of service, and so
hungry that I know he would give his soul to the devil for
a shoulder of mutton, though it were blood raw.   10

Robin. How? My soul to the devil for a shoulder of mutton,
though 'twere blood raw? Not so, good friend. By'r
Lady, I had need have it well roasted, and good sauce to
it, if I pay so dear.

I.iv.0.1. S.D. ROBIN] *Greg; not in* A1.   2, 6, 11, *to* 75. S.H. *Robin*] *Jump;*
Clo. or Clow. throughout this scene in A1.   2. *'Swounds*] A1 (swowns).
12–13. *By'r Lady*] A1 (*burladie*).

I.iv.0.1. S.D. [*ROBIN*] *the* CLOWN] The B-text at II.ii.0 provides authority
for identifying Robin as the 'Clown' in that scene. The Clown, a kind of
rustic buffoon, is a highly identifiable stage character in the Elizabethan
theatre. In both texts, at II.ii.1–3, the Clown indicates that he has stolen one
of Faustus's conjuring books, further identifying him with the Clown of I.iv
who wants to learn from Wagner how to conjure with such books. This
'apprenticeship' to Wagner of an unemployed rascal ('bare and out of
service', l. 8) does not necessarily conflict with what we learn in II.ii, that
Robin is by then a stable-boy in an inn.
     2. *'Swounds*] by his (God's) wounds.
     3. *pickedevants*] short beards trimmed to a point (from French *pique* [or
?*pic*] *devant*, meant for 'peak in front', or *piqué devant*, 'peaked in front';
OED).
     4. *quotha*] i.e., forsooth (literally, quoth he, said he).
     5. *comings in*] income. (*OED*, 'coming', vbl. sb.¹ 7c, cites *H5*, IV.i.241:
'What are thy comings-in' as the first instance.) Actors sometimes exploit the
potential for bawdy wordplay in *comings in* and *goings out* (l. 6).
     6. *goings out*] (*a*) expenses (*b*) being out at elbow.
     else] if you don't believe me.
     8. *out of service*] unemployed.
     12–13. *By'r Lady*] by our Lady (the Virgin).

Wagner. Well, wilt thou serve me, and I'll make thee go like   15
Qui mihi discipulus?
Robin. How, in verse?
Wagner. No, sirrah, in beaten silk and stavesacre.
Robin. How, how, knave's acre? [*Aside.*] Aye, I thought that
was all the land his father left him. [*To Wagner.*] Do ye   20
hear? I would be sorry to rob you of your living.
Wagner. Sirrah, I say in stavesacre.
Robin. Oho, oho, 'stavesacre'! Why then, belike, if I were
your man, I should be full of vermin.
Wagner. So thou shalt, whether thou beest with me or no. But   25
sirrah, leave your jesting, and bind yourself presently

19, 20. S.D.] *This ed.; not in A1.*

16. Qui mihi discipulus] you who are my pupil. Wagner's search for a
Latin phrase with which to sound like Doctor Faustus and thereby awe a
social inferior takes him no further than the opening line of *Ad discipulos
carmen de moribus*, a didactic Latin poem by William Lyly (*c.* 1466–1522). It
was much read in the grammar schools, as was the Latin Grammar compiled
in part by this famous schoolmaster and grandfather of the dramatist John
Lyly.

18. in . . . silk] Compare Faustus's desire to dress university students 'with
silk' (I.i.92).

beaten] embroidered (*OED*, adj. 5c), but also with a punning suggestion of
'thrashed', since the silk is to be worn on the vulnerable body of a pupil.

stavesacre] the seeds of a species of delphinium used for killing vermin.
Wagner suggests wryly that Robin is louse-infected. As with *beaten*, Wagner
here puns on an 'ache' produced by a 'stave'.

18–19. *stavesacre . . . knave's acre*] In pretending to misunderstand what is
said to him, Robin resembles the *zanni* in the Italian *commedia dell'arte*.
Robin also intentionally mishears *Gridirons* for *guilders* and *Banio* for *Balioll*
in ll. 33, 60 and 71. Compare Shakespeare's *TGV*, III.i.277–80: '*Speed.*
What news with your mastership? / *Lance.* With my master's ship? Why
it is at sea. / *Speed.* Your old vice still: mistake the word.' *Knave's acre* is
'the old name of Poultney Street, formerly a poor neighbourhood' (Sleight).
'To go home to knave's acre' meant 'to be ruined'. Compare the following
from 1564: 'In the end they go home . . . by weeping cross, by beggar's barn,
and by knave's acre' (Eric Partridge, *A Dictionary of Slang and Unconventional English*, London: Routledge, 1937 and subsequent editions, s.v.
'beggar's bush').

23. *belike*] probably.

26. *leave your jesting*] Wagner apes the First Scholar's impatient response
to him at I.ii.9.

bind] apprentice. (Seven years was a standard apprenticeship.)
presently] at once.

unto me for seven years, or I'll turn all the lice about thee
into familiars, and they shall tear thee in pieces.
Robin. Do you hear, sir? You may save that labour. They are
     too familiar with me already. 'Swounds, they are as bold   30
     with my flesh as if they had paid for my meat and drink.
Wagner. Well, do you hear, sirrah? Hold, take these guilders.
                                             [*Offering money.*]
Robin. Gridirons? What be they?
Wagner. Why, French crowns.
Robin. Mass, but for the name of French crowns a man were   35
     as good have as many English counters. And what should
     I do with these?

---

30. 'Swounds] *A1* (swowns).   32.1. s.d.] *Dyce 1* (*subst.*); not in *A1*.

---

28. *familiars*] attendant evil spirits. *OED* (sb. 3) cites Scot's *The Discovery
of Witchcraft* (III.xv): 'A fly, otherwise called a devil or familiar'.
    30. *too familiar*] unduly intimate, taking liberties (*OED*, adj. 8), and with
a play upon *familiars* in l. 28.
    30–1. *they . . . drink*] 'they treat me with as little ceremony as if it was they
who kept and fatted me up for their own eating'. The B-text reading, 'as if
they paid for their meat and drink', yields the meaning 'as if they were guests
who had paid for their dinner and I the waiter whose business it was to
serve them (with my own flesh and blood)' (Greg).
    32. *guilders*] Dutch florins, though Wagner seems to have French crowns
instead. In either case, Wagner offers to confirm the hiring of Robin by
giving him wages.
    33. *Gridirons*] Robin's corruption of *guilders*. The hellish connotations of
gridirons, which were used as instruments of torture by fire (*OED*, sb. 1b),
coupled with *devil* in l. 39, proves to be too much for Robin, who tries to
give the coins back at ll. 40–1.
    34. *French crowns*] the English name for the French coins called *écus*.
Some editors (e.g., Ward, p. cxxxiv, note) have claimed that French crowns
would not have been commonly found in England before 1595—when
increased commerce between the two countries, coupled with the repayment
of the enormous sums that Queen Elizabeth had lent to Henry IV, brought a
large quantity of French money to England—and thus that this reference to
French crowns must be a 'post-Marlovian gag dating from about 1594–5'
(Bowers, II.125n.). However, William Harrison's *Description of England* in
Holinshed's *Chronicles* (London, 1577) lists among 'foreign coins we have . . .
the French and Flemish crowns, only current among us so long as they hold
weight' (ii.25).
    35. *Mass*] by the Mass.
    35–6. *but . . . counters*] i.e., if it were not for the impressive-sounding
name of 'French crowns', suggesting royalty, a man might just as soon have

Wagner. Why now, sirrah, thou art at an hour's warning
whensoever or wheresoever the devil shall fetch thee.
Robin. No, no, here, take your gridirons again.   40
    [*He attempts to return the money.*]
Wagner. Truly, I'll none of them.
Robin. Truly, but you shall.
Wagner. [*To the audience.*] Bear witness I gave them him.
Robin. Bear witness I give them you again.
Wagner. Well, I will cause two devils presently to fetch thee   45
away.—Balioll and Belcher!
Robin. Let your Balio and your Belcher come here and I'll
knock them. They were never so knocked since they were
devils. Say I should kill one of them, what would folks
say? 'Do ye see yonder tall fellow in the round slop? He   50
has killed the devil.' So I should be called 'Kill devil' all
the parish over.

40.1, 43. S.D.] *This ed.; not in A1.*

an equal number of English tokens used in counting money (*OED*, 'counter',
sb.¹ 2), which have no intrinsic value at all. *Counter* may also suggest 'the
Counter', the common name for debtors' prison (compare *Err.*, IV.ii.39). The
coins known as French crowns were often debased and counterfeited.
Shakespeare's clowns frequently pun on 'French crowns' as 'heads made bald
by venereal disease' (*OED*, 'French crown', sb. 1b; see *MND*, I.ii.86–9,
AWW, II.ii.21, and *MM*, I.ii.50 for examples).

46. *Balioll and Belcher*] *Balioll* is a comic rendition of 'Belial'. Nashe's
punning on Belial and 'Belly-all' in *Piers Penniless* (ed. McKerrow, I.201)
suggests wordplay that applies as well here to *Belcher*; Wagner's mind is
on his belly (Kocher, 'Nashe's Authorship', pp. 17–40). A devil named
'Belchar' appears in Barnabe Barnes's *The Devil's Charter* (1607; ed. Pogue, l.
3250).

50. *tall*] 'valiant' in a general sense, but the term was also used more
specifically in the Renaissance for 'brave enough to kill someone'. *OED* (adj.
3) cites John Northbrook's *A Treatise wherein Dicing, Dancing, Vain Plays or
Interludes are Reproved* (1577; Shakespeare Society edition, London, 1843), p.
8: 'If he can kill a man . . . he is called a tall man.' Compare Barabas's
remarks after Mathias and Lodowick have killed each other: 'now they have
showed themselves to be tall fellows' (*Jew of Malta*, III.ii.7).

round slop] wide baggy breeches.

51. *Kill devil*] a recklessly daring fellow. *OED* cites this line as the only
instance in this sense (sb. 1). Later (by 1651) the word was a West Indian
name for rum (*OED*, 2), and some such colloquialism may be intended here.

Enter two Devils, *and [Robin] the Clown runs up and down crying.*

Wagner. Balioll and Belcher! Spirits, away!

Exeunt [Devils].

Robin. What, are they gone? A vengeance on them! They have
vile long nails. There was a he devil and a she devil. I'll   55
tell you how you shall know them: all he devils has horns,
and all she devils has clefts and cloven feet.

Wagner. Well, sirrah, follow me.

Robin. But do you hear? If I should serve you, would you
teach me to raise up Banios and Belcheos?   60

Wagner. I will teach thee to turn thyself to anything, to a dog,
or a cat, or a mouse, or a rat, or anything.

Robin. How? A Christian fellow to a dog or a cat, a mouse or a
rat? No, no, sir. If you turn me into anything, let it be in
the likeness of a little, pretty, frisking flea, that I may be   65
here and there and everywhere. O, I'll tickle the pretty
wenches' plackets! I'll be amongst them, i'faith!

Wagner. Well, sirrah, come.

Robin. But do you hear, Wagner?

Wagner. How?—Balioll and Belcher!   70

Robin. O Lord, I pray sir, let Banio and Belcher go sleep.

52.2. S.D. *crying] A1; the Stage A2-3.*   53.1. S.D. Devils] *Dyce 1; not in A1.*

---

56. *has]* This acceptable plural (Abbott 333) is not necessarily colloquial here.

horns] (*a*) devils' horns (*b*) cuckolds' horns (*c*) by analogy, phalluses.

57. *clefts]* (*a*) cleft feet (*b*) vulvas. Thersites makes a similar pun in *Tro.*,
v.ii.10-11: 'And any man may sing her, if he can take her clef.'

60. *Banios]* probably nothing more than the Clown's comic perversion of
Balioll. Banio, however, was a common Elizabethan spelling of *Bagnio*—a
prison, and (later) a brothel (*OED*, 2 and 3)—and there may be some play on
these meanings.

64-7.] Compare II.iii.111-12 and Greene's *Friar Bacon and Friar Bungay*,
i.103-7: 'if thou beest a silken purse full of gold, then on Sundays she'll
hang thee by her side, and you must not say a word. Now, sir, when she
comes into a great press of people, for fear of the cutpurse, on a sudden she'll
swap thee into her plackerd; then, sirrah, being there, you may plead for
yourself.'

67. *plackets]* (*a*) slits in the skirt or petticoat (*b*) by analogy, vaginas.
Compare *Lear*, III.iv.95-6: 'Keep thy foot out of brothels, thy hand out of
plackets.'

Wagner. Villain, call me Master Wagner, and let thy left eye
be diametarily fixed upon my right heel, with *quasi*
vestigiis nostris insistere.   *Exit.*
Robin. God forgive me, he speaks Dutch fustian. Well, I'll   75
follow him, I'll serve him, that's flat.   *Exit.*

---

74. *vestigiis nostris*] Dyce 2; *vestigias nostras* A1.

73. *diametarily*] Compare *OED*, 'diameterly', used in John Florio's translation of Montaigne's *Essays* (1603) to mean 'diametrically' (2b), 'oppositely,
completely'. B1 reads *diametrally*, for which *OED* provides a separate entry
and citations from 1486 and 1589 meaning 'in the way of a diameter; in a
line passing through the centre'. Wagner is here using one of his master's
astrological terms for grand affect with no very precise meaning.
73–4. quasi . . . insistere] as if to follow in our footsteps. The Latin is here
regularised, as by most modern editors (such as Bowers; although Ribner and
Ormerod–Wortham prefer the faulty Latin of A1), on the grounds that an
audience would scarcely be able to hear the joke in the bad Latin or get the
point, whereas errors of this sort are common in transcription.
75. *fustian*] bombast, rant, gibberish (*OED*, sb. and adj. 2, citing this as
its earliest example). Literally, a cheap cloth. Compare *Oth.*, II.iii.274–5:
'discourse fustian with one's own shadow'. M. R. Ridley (New Arden ed.,
1958) notes that in Randall Cotgrave's *A Dictionary of the French and English
Tongues* (London: A. Islip, 1611), *Barragouin* is defined as 'Pedlar's French,
fustian language; any rude gibble-gabble'.
76. *I'll serve him*] (*a*) I'll enter his service (*b*) I'll give him what he's got
coming to him.
that's flat] that's certain; a common expression (Dent F345).

Act II

Enter FAUSTUS *in his study.*

Faustus. Now, Faustus, must thou needs be damned,
And canst thou not be saved.
What boots it then to think of God or heaven?
Away with such vain fancies and despair!
Despair in God and trust in Beelzebub.   5
Now go not backward. No, Faustus, be resolute.
Why waverest thou? O, something soundeth in mine ears:
'Abjure this magic, turn to God again!'
Ay, and Faustus will turn to God again.
To God? He loves thee not.   10
The god thou servest is thine own appetite,
Wherein is fixed the love of Beelzebub.
To him I'll build an altar and a church,
And offer lukewarm blood of new-born babes.

Enter GOOD ANGEL *and* EVIL [ANGEL].

Good Angel. Sweet Faustus, leave that execrable art.   15
Faustus. Contrition, prayer, repentance—what of them?
Good Angel. O, they are means to bring thee unto heaven.
Evil Angel. Rather illusions, fruits of lunacy,

II.i.2. saved.] *Dyce 1 (subst.);* saved? *A1.*   14.1. S.D. ANGEL] *Dyce 1; not in
A1.*   18. illusions, fruits] *A1* (illusious fruites).

II.i.2.] Both A1 and B1 end this line with a question mark; B1 also
introduces a question mark at the end of l. 1, and omits the *And* in l. 2.
Question marks are often intended as exclamation points in early texts
(though generally they mark questions in A1); the question mark here probably should be regarded as an accidental anticipation of that in l. 3.
  3. *boots*] avails (*OED,* v. 3a).
  7–8. *something ... again*] Compare Isaiah xxx.21: 'And thine ears shall
hear a word behind thee, saying, this is the way, walk ye in it' (Cornelius,
p. 245).

That makes men foolish that do trust them most.
Good Angel.
Sweet Faustus, think of heaven and heavenly things.   20
Evil Angel. No, Faustus, think of honour and wealth.
                                        Exeunt [ANGELS].
Faustus. Of wealth?
    Why, the seigniory of Emden shall be mine.
    When Mephistopheles shall stand by me,
    What god can hurt thee, Faustus? Thou art safe;   25
    Cast no more doubts. Come, Mephistopheles,
    And bring glad tidings from great Lucifer.
    Is't not midnight? Come, Mephistopheles!
    Veni, veni, Mephistophile!

                Enter MEPHISTOPHELES.

Now tell, what says Lucifer thy lord?   30
Mephistopheles. That I shall wait on Faustus whilst he lives,
    So he will buy my service with his soul.
Faustus. Already Faustus hath hazarded that for thee.

21.1. S.D.] *placed as in B1; printed after l. 22 in A1.*   21.1. S.D. ANGELS]
Dilke; not in A1.   31. he lives] B1; I liue A1.

21.] The B-text version of this line, 'No, Faustus, think of honour and of
wealth', suggests that the omission of the second *of* in the A1 line is
inadvertent and that l. 22 is intended as a new verse line, not as a completion
of l. 21.
    23. *the seigniory of Emden*] the governorship of Emden, a port on
Germany's North Sea coast and an active centre of trade with England and
other countries.
    24–5.] Compare, with ironic inversion, Romans viii.31: 'If God be on our
side, who can be against us?' (Cornelius, p. 247).
    26. *Cast*] emit, give birth to (*OED*, v. 8, 20), or ponder (*OED*, 42).
    27. *glad tidings*] The ironic echo of the angelic announcement of Christ's
birth, 'I bring you good tidings of great joy' (Luke ii.10), is related to other
passages in which Faustus blasphemously compares himself to Christ (as at
I.i.24 and II.i.74). Such parodic inversion is in the tradition of the Antichrist,
and continues at l. 29 in '*Veni, veni, Mephistophile!*' Compare the hymn, 'O
come, O come, Emmanuel.'
    31. *he lives*] B1 corrects an obvious error in A1.
    32. *So*] on condition that.

Mephistopheles. But, Faustus, thou must bequeath it solemnly
  And write a deed of gift with thine own blood,   35
  For that security craves great Lucifer.
  If thou deny it, I will back to hell.
Faustus. Stay, Mephistopheles, and tell me, what good will my
  soul do thy lord?
Mephistopheles. Enlarge his kingdom.   40
Faustus. Is that the reason he tempts us thus?
Mephistopheles. *Solamen miseris socios habuisse doloris.*
Faustus. Have you any pain, that tortures others?
Mephistopheles. As great as have the human souls of men.
  But tell me, Faustus, shall I have thy soul?   45
  And I will be thy slave, and wait on thee,
  And give thee more than thou hast wit to ask.
Faustus. Ay, Mephistopheles, I give it thee.
Mephistopheles. Then stab thine arm courageously,
  And bind thy soul that at some certain day   50
  Great Lucifer may claim it as his own,
  And then be thou as great as Lucifer.
Faustus. [*Cutting his arm.*]
  Lo, Mephistopheles, for love of thee
  I cut mine arm, and with my proper blood

53. S.D.] *Dyce 1 (subst.); not in A1.*

34-6. *bequeath . . . deed of gift . . . security*] Mephistopheles here speaks in
the mercenary language of 'paltry legacies' (I.i.30).
  40.] Compare James Mason's *The Anatomy of Sorcery* (London: J. Legatte,
1612), p. 55: 'Satan's chiefest drift and main point that he aimeth at is the
enlargement of his own kingdom by the eternal destruction of man in the life
to come' (Gill 1).
  42.] It is a comfort to the wretched to have had companions in misery.
(Or, more popularly, 'Misery loves company.') The Latin form of the
proverb was used widely in the medieval and Renaissance periods (see Dent
C571). Although a version of the line appears in Seneca's *De Consolatione ad
Polybium*, xii.2 (*Moral Essays*, trans. John W. Basore, Loeb Library, 1932),
no classical source for the hexameter has been found (Wagner).
  43.] Do you devils who torture others feel any pain?
  50. *certain*] (*a*) specified in the contract (*b*) unavoidable.
  52.] (*a*) and after you've signed you'll be as powerful as Lucifer (*b*) and
when your day of reckoning comes you'll be in the same boat as Lucifer.
Great in l. 51 means 'mighty', but also 'proud', 'arrogant', and hence
'damned' (*OED*, 4; compare Latin *magnus*).
  54. *proper*] own. (But with an ironic suggestion of a *blood* or passion that is
anything but proper.)

Assure my soul to be great Lucifer's,   55
Chief lord and regent of perpetual night.
View here the blood that trickles from mine arm,
And let it be propitious for my wish.
Mephistopheles. But Faustus, thou must write it in manner of a
     deed of gift.   60
Faustus. Ay, so I will. [*He writes.*] But Mephistopheles,
My blood congeals, and I can write no more.
Mephistopheles. I'll fetch thee fire to dissolve it straight. *Exit.*
Faustus. What might the staying of my blood portend?
     Is it unwilling I should write this bill?   65
     Why streams it not, that I may write afresh?
     'Faustus gives to thee his soul'—ah, there it stayed!
     Why shouldst thou not? Is not thy soul thine own?
     Then write again: 'Faustus gives to thee his soul.'

     Enter MEPHISTOPHELES *with a chafer of coals.*

Mephistopheles. Here's fire. Come Faustus, set it on.   70
Faustus. So; now the blood begins to clear again,
     Now will I make an end immediately. [*He writes.*]
Mephistopheles. [*Aside.*]
     O, what will not I do to obtain his soul?
Faustus. Consummatum est. This bill is ended,
     And Faustus hath bequeathed his soul to Lucifer.   75
     But what is this inscription on mine arm?

(handwritten marginal notes): why would claiming his own soul be blasphemous? because they may be believed their souls were in the hands of God

---

61, 72. S.D.] *Dyce 1 (subst.); not in A1.*   61–2.] *verse as in B1; as prose in*
A1.   73, 82. S.D.] *Dyce 1; not in A1.*

---

65. *bill*] deed (*OED*, sb.³ 1d).
68. *Is . . . own?*] Faustus gives an unconsciously ironic twist to the common expression 'May we not do with our own what we list?' (Dent 099).
69.1. *chafer*] portable grate.
70. *set it on*] The *Damnable Life*'s description of 'How Doctor Faustus set his blood in a saucer on warm ashes' (ch. 6) evidently suggests the stage action that Marlowe has in mind, though that source says nothing about Mephistopheles bringing the fire and only implies that the blood coagulates.
70–1.] This is 'certainly no earthly fire, that will liquify coagulated blood' (Greg, p. 404).
71. *now*] now that.
74. Consummatum est] 'It is finished'—the last words of Christ on the cross (John xix.30).

'*Homo, fuge!*' Whither should I fly?
If unto God, he'll throw thee down to hell.—
My senses are deceived; here's nothing writ.—
I see it plain. Here in this place is writ   80
'*Homo, fuge!*' Yet shall not Faustus fly.
Mephistopheles. [*Aside.*]
    I'll fetch him somewhat to delight his mind.   *Exit.*

Enter [MEPHISTOPHELES] *with* Devils, *giving crowns and
rich apparel to Faustus, and dance and then depart.*

Faustus. Speak, Mephistopheles. What means this show?
Mephistopheles.
    Nothing, Faustus, but to delight thy mind withal
    And to show thee what magic can perform.   85
Faustus. But may I raise up spirits when I please?
Mephistopheles. Ay, Faustus, and do greater things than these.
Faustus. Then there's enough for a thousand souls.
    Here, Mephistopheles, receive this scroll,
    A deed of gift of body and of soul—   90
    But yet conditionally that thou perform
    All articles prescribed between us both.
Mephistopheles. Faustus, I swear by hell and Lucifer
    To effect all promises between us made.
Faustus. Then hear me read them.   95
    'On these conditions following:
    First, that Faustus may be a spirit in form and substance.

82.1. S.D. MEPHISTOPHELES] *B1; not in A1.*   96.] *treated as a line of
dialogue in A1 rather than as part of the contract.*

---

77. Homo, fuge!] 'Fly, O man!' (1 Timothy vi.11).
77–8.] Compare Psalms cxxxix.7–8: 'Whither shall I go from thy spirit?
or whither shall I flee from thy presence? If I ascend into heaven, thou art
there: if I lie down in hell, thou art there.'
82.1–2. S.D.] Presumably Mephistopheles enters with the devils and then
re-enters after they depart. Compare the B-text's stage direction.
84. *withal*] with.
88. *for*] to compensate for the surrender of.
97. *spirit*] The word often connotes 'devil' in this play, and so the question
arises as to whether Faustus can be saved after he becomes a 'spirit', but the
word has other meanings as well. See Introduction, pp. 19–20.

Secondly, that Mephistopheles shall be his servant, and at
his command.
Thirdly, that Mephistopheles shall do for him and bring   100
him whatsoever.
Fourthly, that he shall be in his chamber or house
invisible.
Lastly, that he shall appear to the said John Faustus at all
times in what form or shape soever he please.   105
I, John Faustus of Wittenberg, Doctor, by these presents,
do give both body and soul to Lucifer, Prince of the East,
and his minister Mephistopheles; and furthermore grant
unto them that four-and-twenty years being expired, the
articles above written inviolate, full power to fetch or   110
carry the said John Faustus, body and soul, flesh, blood,
or goods, into their habitation wheresoever.
                            By me, John Faustus.'
Mephistopheles. Speak, Faustus. Do you deliver this as your
deed?   115
Faustus. [*Giving the deed.*] Ay. Take it, and the devil give thee
good on't.
Mephistopheles. Now, Faustus, ask what thou wilt.
Faustus. First will I question with thee about hell.
Tell me, where is the place that men call hell?   120
Mephistopheles. Under the heavens.

---

109. four-and-twenty] A1 (24).   116. S D.] This ed ; not in A1

106–7. *Faustus . . . body and soul*] The final version of this phrase differs
slightly from Faustus's initial attempts to write the bond at ll. 67 and 69; but
this minor inconsistency certainly does not justify Greg's conclusion that the
bond must therefore not have been written by either Marlowe or his collaborator, but instead 'was entrusted to someone with experience of legal
phraseology'.
106. *by these presents*] by this present document (*OED*, sb.¹ 2b). A legal
phrase.
107. *Prince of the East*] Faustus may use this title because Lucifer
(i.e., 'light-bearer') was widely identified with the morning star, Venus. The
source of this conflation was Isaiah xiv.12: 'How art thou fallen from heaven,
O Lucifer, son of the morning!'
110. *inviolate*] not having been violated.
116–17. *the devil . . . on't*] a common profanity (Dent D234.11), with
ironically literal application here.

[Handwritten annotations in top margin: "talking to a devil from hell and saying he doesn't believe in hell after signing his soul to the devil"]

[Handwritten annotation in left margin: "Mephistopheles suggesting that Faustus might be damned from the start"]

Faustus.   Ay, but whereabout?

Mephistopheles. Within the bowels of these elements,
     Where we are tortured and remain for ever.
     Hell hath no limits, nor is circumscribed
     In one self place, for where we are is hell,   125
     And where hell is must we ever be.
     And, to conclude, when all the world dissolves,
     And every creature shall be purified,
     All places shall be hell that is not heaven.

Faustus. Come, I think hell's a fable.   130

Mephistopheles.
     Ay, think so still, till experience change thy mind.

Faustus.
     Why, think'st thou then that Faustus shall be damned?

Mephistopheles. Ay, of necessity, for here's the scroll
     Wherein thou hast given thy soul to Lucifer.

Faustus. Ay, and body too. But what of that?   135
     Think'st thou that Faustus is so fond
     To imagine that after this life there is any pain?
     Tush, these are trifles and mere old wives' tales.

Mephistopheles.
     But, Faustus, I am an instance to prove the contrary,
     For I am damned and am now in hell.   140

Faustus. How? Now in hell? Nay, an this be hell,
     I'll willingly be damned here. What? Walking, disputing,

---

141.] *verse as in B1 (subst.); as prose in A1.*   141. an] *A1* (and).

122. *these elements*] the four elements comprising all that exists beneath the moon. See 1.i.79n.

125. *one self place*] 'one and the same place' (Ward).

127–8.] Mephistopheles's description draws on 2 Peter iii.10–11: 'the elements shall melt with heat . . . all these things must be dissolved', and Daniel xii.9–10: '. . . till the end of the time. Many shall be purified, made white, and tried.'

129.] Compare the proverb: 'Hell is wherever heaven is not' (Dent H406).

130.] On the paradoxical fatuousness and sceptical daring of this reply to a devil who says he has come directly from hell, see Introduction, pp. 26–7.

136. *fond*] foolish.

138. *old wives' tales*] a common expression (Dent W388).

141–3. *Nay . . . etc.*] B1 arranges this passage in two lines of somewhat hypermetric verse, specifying what *etc.* means, but the verse original of A1, if it ever existed, is past recovery. Both texts follow with prose.

etc.? But leaving off this, let me have a wife, the fairest *lustful*
maid in Germany, for I am wanton and lascivious and
cannot live without a wife.   145
Mephistopheles. How, a wife? I prithee, Faustus, talk not of a
wife.
Faustus. Nay, sweet Mephistopheles, fetch me one, for I will
have one.
Mephistopheles. Well, thou wilt have one. Sit there till I come. 150
I'll fetch thee a wife, in the devil's name.   [*Exit.*]

    Enter [MEPHISTOPHELES] *with a* Devil *dressed like
    a woman, with fireworks.*

Mephistopheles. Tell, Faustus, how dost thou like thy wife?
Faustus. A plague on her for a hot whore!
Mephistopheles. Tut, Faustus, marriage is but a ceremonial
toy. If thou lovest me, think no more of it.   155
                          [*Exit* Devil.]
I'll cull thee out the fairest courtesans
And bring them ev'ry morning to thy bed.
She whom thine eye shall like, thy heart shall have,

---

151. S.D. *Exit*] Dyce 1; not in A1.   151.1. S.D. MEPHISTOPHELES] *Dyce 1;
not in A1.*   155. no] B1; not in A1.   155.1. S.D.] *This ed.; not in A1.*

---

151. *in the devil's name*] another common profanity, like that at ll. 116–17,
and with similar ironic application.
    151.2. S.D.] The fireworks may have been squibs, in which the burning of
the fireworks terminates in a slight explosion. The Vice in John Heywood's
The Play of Love, c. 1533, 'cometh in running suddenly about the place
among the audience with a high copintank [i.e., copataine, a high-crowned
hat] on his head full of squibs fired' (l. 1294), and in the staging diagram for
The Castle of Perseverance Belial is directed to go to battle with 'gunpowder
burning in pipes in his hands and in his ears and in his arse'. The device is
common: in the Digby *Conversion of St Paul* (late fifteenth century), a devil
enters 'with thunder and fire', followed soon after by 'another devil called
Mercury, with a firing'—i.e., an explosion of powder (*Medieval Drama*, ed.
Bevington, ll. 411–32). C. R. Baskervill, *The Elizabethan Jig and Related
Song Drama* (University of Chicago Press, 1929; rpt. New York: Dover,
1965), pp. 315–16 and notes, provides other citations.
    155. *no*] B1 supplies a necessary word inadvertently omitted from A1.
    155.1. S.D. *Exit Devil*] No exit is provided in A1 or by other editors, but
exits of this sort are often omitted, and it seems unlikely that this devil
remains on stage to the end of the scene. He might leave at l. 153 or 161.
    156. *cull*] select.

Be she as chaste as was Penelope,
As wise as Saba, or as beautiful   160
As was bright Lucifer before his fall.
                              [*Presenting a book.*]
Hold, take this book. Peruse it thoroughly.
The iterating of these lines brings gold;
The framing of this circle on the ground
Brings whirlwinds, tempests, thunder, and lightning.   165
Pronounce this thrice devoutly to thyself,
And men in armour shall appear to thee,
Ready to execute what thou desir'st.
Faustus. Thanks, Mephistopheles. Yet fain would I have a
  book wherein I might behold all spells and incantations, 170
  that I might raise up spirits when I please.
Mephistopheles. Here they are in this book.
                              There turn to them.
Faustus. Now would I have a book where I might see all
  characters and planets of the heavens, that I might know
  their motions and dispositions.   175
Mephistopheles. Here they are too.   *Turn to them.*
Faustus. Nay, let me have one book more—and then I have
  done—wherein I might see all plants, herbs, and trees
  that grow upon the earth.

161.1. S.D.] *Dyce 1 (subst.); not in A1.*

159. *Penelope*] Odysseus's faithful wife in the *Odyssey.*
160. *Saba*] the Vulgate spelling of 'Sheba', that survived into the Bishops'
Bible and into the heading, though not the text, of the Geneva Bible (Greg).
See 1 Kings x.1: 'And the Queen of Sheba, hearing of the fame of Solomon
. . . came to prove him with hard questions.'
163. *iterating*] (*a*) repetition; or perhaps (*b*) making double or twofold,
duplication (*OED*, vbl. sb. 3). The *lines* may be occult symbols as at 1.i.53
above, to be inscribed by the conjurer.
169–82.] These lines may echo the apocryphal Wisdom of Solomon,
vii.17–22, in which the prophet thanks God for a true understanding of the
heavens, the changing seasons, and all living creatures and planets (Keefer).
169. *fain*] gladly.
172.1. S.D.] Mephistopheles turns to the pages Faustus desires to see, in
the book already given to him at l. 162.
174. *characters*] cabbalistic symbols, as at 1.i.53.
175. *dispositions*] situations of planets in a horoscope (*OED*, 5a). An
astrological term.

Mephistopheles. Here they be.   *Turn to them.*   180
Faustus. O, thou art deceived.
Mephistopheles. Tut, I warrant thee.   [*Exeunt.*]

[II.ii]

    Enter ROBIN *the ostler with a book in his hand.*

Robin. O, this is admirable! Here I ha' stol'n one of Doctor
    Faustus' conjuring books, and, i'faith, I mean to search
    some circles for my own use. Now will I make all the
    maidens in our parish dance at my pleasure stark naked
    before me, and so by that means I shall see more than e'er   5
    I felt or saw yet.

180. S.D.] *placed here this ed.; printed after l. 182 in A1.*   182. S.D.] *Bullen;
not in A1.*   II.ii.] *placed here Keefer and this ed.; printed in A1 after III.i and
a misplaced Chorus to Act IV, and before the comic scene labelled III.ii in this
edition.*

181–2.] Faustus perhaps expresses doubt as to the efficacy of the books
Mephistopheles is showing him, and is answered with an assurance that he
need not worry. Faustus is still testing the worth of his bargain.
   182. S.D.] B1 provides a choric speech at this point by Wagner, and so
most editors provide a scene break here in both texts (Ormerod–Wortham
and Gill 2 and 3 being the exceptions), even when (as in Bowers's B-text
edition) they leave out the chorus. Probably indeed a scene has been lost or
misplaced; see Appendix and Keefer, pp. lxxii–lxxvii.

   II.ii.] On the placement of this scene, printed in A1 after Faustus's visit to
Rome (III.i), see Appendix.
   0.1. S.D. ostler] stableman, groom. Robin, who was 'out of service' at
I.iv.8, when he took up with Wagner to learn how to conjure from Faustus's
books (one of which he has now stolen), seems to have apprenticed himself as
a stable-boy in an inn.
   3. *some circles*] magic circles drawn by the conjurer; but with suggestion of
the female sexual anatomy as well, as the rest of Robin's speech indicates.
Compare *Rom.*, II.i.24–7: ''Twould anger him / To raise a spirit in his
mistress' circle / Of some strange nature, letting it there stand / Till she had
laid it and conjured it down.'

Enter RAFE, *calling Robin.*

Rafe. Robin, prithee, come away. There's a gentleman tarries
to have his horse, and he would have his things rubbed
and made clean; he keeps such a chafing with my mistress
about it, and she has sent me to look thee out. Prithee,   10
come away.

Robin. Keep out, keep out, or else you are blown up, you are
dismembered, Rafe! Keep out, for I am about a roaring
piece of work.

Rafe. Come, what dost thou with that same book? Thou canst   15
not read.

Robin. Yes, my master and mistress shall find that I can
read—he for his forehead, she for her private study.
She's born to bear with me, or else my art fails.

Rafe. Why, Robin, what book is that?   20

Robin. What book? Why the most intolerable book for conjur-

15–16. book? Thou . . . read.] *Keefer;* booke thou canst not reade? *A1.*

6.1. S.D. RAFE] Most modernising editors prefer *Ralph* as the more
formal spelling today, but since *Rafe* is still common as a nickname there is
no real need to change it. Rafe is another horse-keeper, like Robin, as we
learn from III.ii.3.

8. *his things rubbed*] his leather saddle and other equipment polished;
but with a suggestion too of an erotic massage.

9. *chafing with*] (*a*) fretting at, railing at (*b*) rubbing, pressing against.
For the importance of 'chafing' in the Renaissance theatre, see Stephen
Greenblatt's essay 'Fiction and Friction' in *Shakespearean Negotiations: the
Circulation of Social Energy in Renaissance England* (Berkeley: University of
California Press, 1988), pp. 66–93.

12–13. *blown up . . . dismembered*] For the sexual suggestiveness of such
language of military violence, compare *AWW*, I.i.120–8.

13. *roaring*] noisy, riotous, befitting a 'roarer' (*OED*, ppl. adj. 2b).

15–16.] A1's punctuation (see collation) is possible, but the following
reply and B1's version of this dialogue at II.ii.11–12 both tend to support
emendation here.

19. *bear*] (*a*) endure, tolerate (*b*) support my weight during sexual intercourse (*c*) bear a child. The sexual joking follows from the allusion in
l. 18 to cuckold's horns on the master's *forehead* and to the mistress's *private
study*—what she thinks about in private or reads in her study (with suggestion of the study of her 'private parts').

21. *intolerable*] Even though the word can mean 'irresistible' (*OED*, adj.
2), as Ormerod–Wortham point out, that usage is so rare and the common
meaning so splendidly inappropriate here that we may be right to suspect a
malapropism for something like 'incomparable'.

ing that e'er was invented by any brimstone devil.
Rafe. Canst thou conjure with it?
Robin. I can do all these things easily with it: first, I can make
thee drunk with hippocras at any tavern in Europe for   25
nothing. That's one of my conjuring works.
Rafe. Our Master Parson says that's nothing.
Robin. True, Rafe; and more, Rafe, if thou hast any mind to
Nan Spit, our kitchen maid, then turn her and wind her
to thy own use as often as thou wilt, and at midnight.   30
Rafe. O brave, Robin! Shall I have Nan Spit, and to mine own
use? On that condition I'll feed thy devil with horse-bread
as long as he lives, of free cost.
Robin. No more, sweet Rafe. Let's go and make clean our
boots, which lie foul upon our hands, and then to our   35
conjuring, in the devil's name.   *Exeunt.*

[II.iii]

[*Enter* FAUSTUS *in his study, and* MEPHISTOPHELES.]

Faustus. When I behold the heavens, then I repent
And curse thee, wicked Mephistopheles,

---

31. brave, Robin] *This ed.;* braue *Robin A1.*   II.iii.0.1. s.d.] *B1; not in A1.*

22. *brimstone*] Once a common vernacular name for sulphur, the word here
suggests divine punishment and the fires of hell, as in Genesis xix.24 and
Revelation xix.20. Compare Sir Toby's 'Fire and brimstone!' in *TN*, II.v.49
(*OED*, 1 and 1b).
25. *hippocras*] a wine drink flavoured with spices, named *vinum
Hippocraticum* because it was filtered through a conical cloth bag known as
Hippocrates's sleeve (*OED*).
27. *nothing*] worthless, wrong (punning on *nothing*, 'no cost', in l. 26),
suggesting also that Rafe is easily made drunk and that anyone can conjure
the devil.
29–30. *Nan Spit . . . midnight*] The demeaning name suggests one who is
easily turned and wound about as a sexual object. Midnight is appropriate to
both conjuring and sex.
32. *horse-bread*] bread made of beans, bran, etc. for the food of horses
(*OED*), and fittingly ignoble as something with which a horse-keeper might
try to bribe the devil.
36. *in the devil's name*] a commonplace oath (compare Dent D286.11), with
ironic literal application here, as at II.i.151.

II.iii.1. *When . . . heavens*] Faustus quotes Psalms viii.3.

Because thou hast deprived me of those joys.
Mephistopheles. Why Faustus,
  Think'st thou heaven is such a glorious thing?   5
  I tell thee, 'tis not half so fair as thou
  Or any man that breathes on earth.
Faustus. How provest thou that?
Mephistopheles.
  It was made for man; therefore is man more excellent.
Faustus. If it were made for man, 'twas made for me.   10
  I will renounce this magic and repent.

     Enter GOOD ANGEL *and* EVIL ANGEL.

Good Angel. Faustus, repent yet, God will pity thee.
Evil Angel. Thou art a spirit. God cannot pity thee.
Faustus. Who buzzeth in mine ears I am a spirit?
  Be I a devil, yet God may pity me;   15
  Ay, God will pity me if I repent.
Evil Angel. Ay, but Faustus never shall repent.
               Exeunt [ANGELS].
Faustus. My heart's so hardened I cannot repent.
  Scarce can I name salvation, faith, or heaven
  But fearful echoes thunder in mine ears: 20
  'Faustus, thou art damned!' Then swords and knives,
  Poison, guns, halters, and envenomed steel
  Are laid before me to dispatch myself;

17.1. S.D. ANGELS] *Dilke; not in A1.*   20. thunder] *Dyce 1;* thunders *A1.*

9.] The sophistry of Mephistopheles's proof depends on the fallacious
assumption that anything 'made for man' must be inferior to and dependent
on humankind in the hierarchy of things.
  12.] This A1 punctuation is perhaps less plausible than B1's *repent, yet
God* but may be defensible. A1's version could mean, 'Faustus, repent while
there is time; God will pity thee', while B1's version suggests, 'Faustus,
repent! Even now, God will pity thee.'
  13. *spirit*] devil. See II.i.97n.
  15. *Be I*] (*a*) even if I am, or (*b*) even though I were (Ward).
  20. *thunder*] The A1 reading, *thunders*, is defensible as an Elizabethan third
person singular for the plural, but it may well represent contamination from
'echoes' and 'ears' in the same line.
  22. *halters*] nooses.
  steel] steel swords.

[Marginalia: could suggest Calvinism — the belief that God is rather than hardened man himself — his script]

[Marginalia: implication → not truth]

And long ere this I should have slain myself
Had not sweet pleasure conquered deep despair.   25
Have not I made blind Homer sing to me
Of Alexander's love and Oenone's death?
And hath not he that built the walls of Thebes
With ravishing sound of his melodious harp
Made music with my Mephistopheles?   30
Why should I die, then, or basely despair?
I am resolved Faustus shall ne'er repent.
Come, Mephistopheles, let us dispute again
And argue of divine astrology.
Tell me, are there many heavens above the moon?   35

27.] The story of Oenone and 'Alexandros', as Paris is usually called in the
Iliad, is found in post-Homeric continuations of the Troy story, especially in
the *Cypria* (surviving only in fragments), in Ovid's *Heroides* v, and in book x
of Quintus Smyrnaeus's *The Fall of Troy*, fourth century AD (trans. Arthur
S. Way, Loeb Library, 1913; see Keefer). A composite story emerges as
follows. Paris deserts Oenone, a nymph of Mount Ida, for the lovely Helen
as his prize for awarding the golden apple to Aphrodite, thus setting in
motion the abduction of Helen from her Grecian husband and the resulting
Trojan War. Subsequently wounded by a poisoned arrow for which Oenone
alone can provide the cure, Paris is carried to her but dies when she refuses
to treat him. She kills herself out of remorse. Marlowe here imagines in an
Ovidian vein the death of the heartbroken woman. *Oenone* is here pronounced
in two syllables, with the stress on the first.
    28-9.] Amphion, ruler of Thebes, excelled so as a harper that his music
drew the stones into their places for a wall around the city (see Ovid, *Metamorphoses*, vi.176-9, and Apollonius Rhodius, *Argonautica*, i.735-41, trans.
R. C. Seaton, Loeb Library, 1912; see Keefer). Homer alludes to Amphion
as the builder of Thebes in the *Odyssey*, xi.260-5, but the story of the harp is
of later date. It became a favourite Renaissance illustration of the power of
music.
    30.] The line suggests that Mephistopheles has fetched the most famous
musicians from antiquity to entertain Faustus and then played in a consort
with them, though we are not shown this in the theatre.
    32. *resolved*] resolved that; but compare the B-text, where a comma after
'resolved' persuasively divides the line into two declarative statements.
    34. *astrology*] practical astronomy applied to human uses (*OED*, 1).
    35-61.] The universe that Mephistopheles describes is a modified form of
the Ptolemaic system, featuring a 'centric earth' surrounded by nine concentric spheres, eight of them in motion. From the earth outward, the
spheres are of the seven 'planets' or 'erring stars' (the moon, Mercury,
Venus, the sun, Mars, Jupiter, and Saturn); then the 'firmament' of the
fixed stars; then the 'empyreal heaven' (l. 61). See Introduction, pp. 27-9.

Are all celestial bodies but one globe,
As is the substance of this centric earth?
Mephistopheles. As are the elements, such are the spheres,
Mutually folded in each others' orb;
And, Faustus, all jointly move upon one axletree,   40
Whose terminine is termed the world's wide pole.
Nor are the names of Saturn, Mars, or Jupiter
Feigned, but are erring stars.
Faustus. But tell me, have they all one motion, both *situ et*
tempore?   45
Mephistopheles. All jointly move from east to west in four-and-
twenty hours upon the poles of the world, but differ in
their motion upon the poles of the zodiac.
Faustus. Tush, these slender trifles Wagner can decide.
Hath Mephistopheles no greater skill?   50
Who knows not the double motion of the planets?
The first is finished in a natural day,

---

39. others'] *Boas; others A1; other's Dyce 1.*   46–7. four-and-twenty] *A1*
(24.); foure and twenty B1. (Numbers are silently expanded in this edition when
no ambiguity is present such as 30., 12., *and* 4. *at ll.* 53–4 *below, but see note to*
ll. 53–5.)

36–7.] Do the heavenly spheres form a single globe, as does the earth
itself at the centre?
38–9.] i.e., just as the four elements are contained in concentric spheres,
with the heavier elements of earth and water at the centre, surrounded by air,
which in turn is surrounded by fire (the most upwardly aspiring of the
elements), even so the heavenly spheres are arranged concentrically, one
inside the next.
40. *axletree*] Marlowe refers to 'the axletree of heaven' in *1Tamb.*, IV.ii.50
and *2Tamb.*, I.i.90.
41. *terminine*] boundary, extremity. The poles of the universe and of the
earth are coextensive. The *OED* lists 'terminine' as a separate entry (giving
this instance as its only citation), conjecturally defining it as an 'error for
termining, or extended form of TERMINE *sb.*'. B1's *termine (terminè)* may be
authoritative.
44–5. *both* situ et tempore] 'as to both the direction of, and the time
occupied by, their revolutions' (Ward).
48. *the poles of the zodiac*] the 'axletree' on which the planets appear to
move through the constellations of the zodiac, as do the sun and moon. Its
difference from the pole of the earth itself provided some explanation for the
planets' 'erring' course (l. 43).

The second thus, as Saturn in thirty years,
Jupiter in twelve, Mars in four, the sun, Venus, and
Mercury in a year, the moon in twenty-eight days. Tush,   55
these are freshmen's suppositions. But tell me, hath every
sphere a dominion or *intelligentia*?
Mephistopheles. Ay.
Faustus. How many heavens or spheres are there?
Mephistopheles. Nine: the seven planets, the firmament, and   60
the empyreal heaven.

53.] *verse as in B1; as prose in A1.*   55. twenty-eight] *A1 (28.);* twenty eight
B1.   57. *intelligentia*] *B1; Intelligentij A1.*   61. empyreal] *A1 (imperiall);*
Emperiall *B1.*

53–5. *Saturn . . . days*] Saturn appears to revolve around the earth each
day, of course, but it also moves through the Zodiac over a much longer
period of time; and so, in varying periods, with the other planets. Greg cites
the periods of revolution listed in a popular Elizabethan handbook, Robert
Recorde's *The Castle of Knowledge* (London, 1556), pp. 572–9: Saturn
twenty-eight years, Jupiter twelve years, Mars two years, the sun, Venus,
and Mercury one year, and the moon one month. These figures are approxi-
mately correct except for Venus, which completes its cycle in seven and a half
months, and Mercury, which completes a revolution every eighty-eight days.
The play's indication of four years for Mars instead of two is probably just an
error.

56. *freshmen's suppositions*] 'the sort of elementary facts we give freshmen
to argue about' (Greg). The *OED*, as Ormerod–Wortham observe, gives
1596 as the earliest date for *Freshmen* in the sense of a first-year university
student (at Cambridge, in this case), but in the sense of 'novice' it dates back
to *c.* 1550, and Marlowe's use here almost surely points to his university
experience. *Supposition* is a term in scholastic logic for something held to be
true and taken as the basis of an argument (*OED*, 1).

57 *dominion or* intelligentia] Faustus asks if each sphere is under a particular controlling influence, often regarded as that of the angels. *OED*,
'intelligence', sb. 4, cites Puttenham, *Art of English Poesie* (ed. Willcock and
Walker, I.iii): 'The divine intelligences or good angels', and Robert Boyle, *A
Free Enquiry into the Vulgarly Received Notion of Nature* (London: J. Taylor,
1685), p. 53: 'The school philosophers . . . teach the celestial orbs to be
moved or guided by intelligences or angels.' Mephistopheles's dry mono-
syllabic answer ('Ay') may indicate his lack of enthusiasm for the direction
the conversation here takes.

61. *empyreal*] of or pertaining to the sky or visible heaven (*OED*, adj. 1,
giving this as its second citation). The word derived from the Greek *empyros*,
'fiery', though, as Francis Johnson observes, it was often confused with
imperiall (the A1 spelling) or *Emperiall* (the B1 spelling) in the sense of
'pertaining to an empire' ('Marlowe's "Imperial Heaven"', *ELH*, XII (1945),
35–44; see *OED*, 'imperial', adj. and sb.). The modernised form in this

Faustus. Well, resolve me in this question: why have we not
  conjunctions, oppositions, aspects, eclipses all at one
  time, but in some years we have more, in some less?
Mephistopheles. Per inaequalem motum respectu totius.   65
Faustus. Well, I am answered. Tell me who made the world.
Mephistopheles. I will not.
Faustus. Sweet Mephistopheles, tell me.
Mephistopheles. Move me not, for I will not tell thee.
Faustus. Villain, have I not bound thee to tell me anything? 70
Mephistopheles. Ay, that is not against our kingdom, but this
  is. Think thou on hell, Faustus, for thou art damned.
Faustus. Think, Faustus, upon God, that made the world.
Mephistopheles. Remember this.   *Exit.*
Faustus. Ay, go, accursèd spirit, to ugly hell!   75
  'Tis thou hast damned distressèd Faustus' soul.
  Is't not too late?

     Enter GOOD ANGEL *and* EVIL [ANGEL].

Evil Angel. Too late.

---

63. eclipses] *A1* (eclipsis). 71–2.] *prose as in Dyce 1; as verse divided at*
this is, / Thinke *in A1.*   77.1. S.D. ANGEL] *Dyce 1; not in A1.*

edition, as in other modern spelling editions, loses some resonance of the
spoken original.
  63.] *Conjunctions* occur when two heavenly bodies appear nearly together,
as seen from the earth's surface; *oppositions*, when they appear exactly
opposite to each other. *Aspects* describe their relative positions, as seen by an
earthbound observer. All these configurations, and *eclipses*, are important in
astrology.
  63–4. *all at one time*] 'all during the same stretch of time (and all recurring
during each subsequent period of the same length). In other words, at regular
intervals' (Jump).
  65.] on account of their unequal motion with respect to the whole. As
Faustus sardonically suggests in his reply, this 'explanation' is a masterpiece
of saying nothing, obfuscating as it does the central inadequacy of the
Ptolemaic system. How to account for unequal motion of the planets was the
problem that inspired the revisionist theories of Tycho Brahe and others. See
Introduction, pp. 27–9.
  69. *Move*] (*a*) anger, vex (*b*) urge (*OED*, v. 9b, 12).
  74.] (*a*) remember that you said this (when you're called to account for it
later) or (*b*) remember that you're damned.

Good Angel. Never too late, if Faustus can repent.
Evil Angel. If thou repent, devils shall tear thee in pieces.   80
Good Angel. Repent, and they shall never raze thy skin.
                                        Exeunt [ANGELS].
Faustus. Ah, Christ, my Saviour,
    Seek to save distressèd Faustus' soul!

        Enter LUCIFER, BEELZEBUB, *and* MEPHISTOPHELES.

Lucifer. Christ cannot save thy soul, for he is just.
    There's none but I have int'rest in the same.   85
Faustus. O, who art thou that look'st so terrible?
Lucifer. I am Lucifer,
    And this is my companion prince in hell.
Faustus. O Faustus, they are come to fetch away thy soul!
Lucifer. We come to tell thee thou dost injure us.   90
    Thou talk'st of Christ, contrary to thy promise.
    Thou shouldst not think of God. Think of the devil,
    And of his dame, too.
Faustus. Nor will I henceforth. Pardon me in this,
    And Faustus vows never to look to heaven,   95

---

81. raze] *A1* (race).   81.1. s.d. ANGELS] *Dilke; not in A1.*   82–3.] *verse as in B1 (subst.); as prose in A1.*   87–8.] *verse as in Dilke; as prose in A1.*

79.] The Good Angel varies the proverb 'repentance never comes too late' (Dent R80). On the possible theological implications of the contrast between the A-text's *can repent* and the B-text's *will repent* (II.iii.80), see Introduction, p. 29, and Keefer, pp. lxv–lxvi.
    81. *raze*] scratch, wound, tear, scrape (*OED*, v.1–2). A1's *race* and B1's *raise* are both variants of *rase* or *raze*.
    83. *Seek*] On the possible theological significance of B1's *Helpe*, see Introduction, p. 30, Warren, p. 124, and Keefer, pp. lxiv–lxv.
    85. *int'rest*] The financial and legal senses are clearly present here, all the more so since Christ has offered a 'ransom' for the sinner's soul (see V.ii.100 below).
    91. *contrary to thy promise*] Nothing in the bond at II.i.97–113 directly justifies Lucifer's complaint. However, the bond in the *Damnable Life* does include the conditions that Faustus 'would be an enemy to all Christian people' and 'would deny his Christian belief' (ch. 4).
    92–3. *devil . . . his dame*] Lucifer cracks a common anti-feminist joke (see Dent D225). It appears to undercut the seriousness of the exchange here about damnation, but evil is never far from obscene mirth in this play. The A1 spelling, *dame*, is interchangeable with *dam*.

Never to name God or to pray to him,
To burn his Scriptures, slay his ministers,
And make my spirits pull his churches down.
Lucifer. Do so, and we will highly gratify thee.
  Faustus, we are come from hell to show thee some pas-   100
time. Sit down, and thou shalt see all the Seven Deadly
Sins appear in their proper shapes.
Faustus. That sight will be as pleasing unto me as paradise was
to Adam the first day of his creation.
Lucifer. Talk not of paradise nor creation, but mark this show.   105
Talk of the devil, and nothing else.—[*Calling offstage.*]
Come away!   [*Faustus sits.*]

      Enter the SEVEN DEADLY SINS.

Now, Faustus, examine them of their several names and
dispositions.
Faustus. What art thou, the first?   110
Pride. I am Pride. I disdain to have any parents. I am like to
Ovid's flea: I can creep into every corner of a wench.
Sometimes like a periwig I sit upon her brow, or like a
fan of feathers I kiss her lips. Indeed I do—what do I
not? But fie, what a scent is here! I'll not speak another   115
word, except the ground were perfumed and covered with
cloth of arras.

106, 107. S.D.] *This ed.; bracketed material not in A1.*   110. S.H. *Faustus*]
A1 (Eau:).

97–8.] Compare *Jew of Malta*, v.i.64–5: 'I'll help to slay their children
and their wives, / To fire the churches, pull their houses down', and *Edw.II*,
I.iv.100–1: 'I'll fire thy crazed buildings, and enforce / The papal towers to
kiss the lowly ground.'
  102. *proper*] own.
  108. *several*] various.
  112. *Ovid's flea*] A poem of uncertain date, possibly medieval, called
Elegia de Pulice and wrongly attributed to Ovid, contains a line in which the
envying poet complains to the flea, '*Is quocumque placet; nil tibi, saeve, latet*',
'You go wherever you want. Nothing is hidden from you, you savage!'
Compare Robin's longing to be a flea in some pretty wench's placket,
I.iv.64–7.
  113. *periwig*] wig.
  116. *except*] unless.
  117. *cloth of arras*] rich tapestry fabric, originally from Arras in Artois,
into which scenes are woven in colours—a luxurious cloth used for the best
wall tapestries and too rich for floor covering. *2Tamb.*, I.ii.44–5, speaks of
'cloth of arras' as 'Fit objects for thy princely eye to pierce'.

Faustus. What art thou, the second?

Covetousness. I am Covetousness, begotten of an old churl in
an old leathern bag; and might I have my wish, I would   120
desire that this house and all the people in it were turned
to gold, that I might lock you up in my good chest. O my
sweet gold!

Faustus. What art thou, the third?

Wrath. I am Wrath. I had neither father nor mother. I leaped   125
out of a lion's mouth when I was scarce half an hour old,
and ever since I have run up and down the world with
this case of rapiers, wounding myself when I had nobody
to fight withal. I was born in hell, and look to it, for some
of you shall be my father.   130

Faustus. What art thou, the fourth?

Envy. I am Envy, begotten of a chimney-sweeper and an
oyster-wife. I cannot read, and therefore wish all books
were burnt. I am lean with seeing others eat. O, that
there would come a famine through all the world, that all   135
might die, and I live alone! Then thou shouldst see how
fat I would be. But must thou sit and I stand? Come
down, with a vengeance!

Faustus. Away, envious rascal!—What are thou, the fifth?

Gluttony. Who, I, sir? I am Gluttony. My parents are all dead,   140
and the devil a penny they have left me but a bare
pension, and that is thirty meals a day, and ten bevers—
a small trifle to suffice nature. O, I come of a royal
parentage. My grandfather was a gammon of bacon, my

---

120. *le*a*thern bag*] miser's money-bag, common in medieval and
Renaissance depictions of covetousness.

128. *case*] pair.

129. *look to it*] look sharp, watch out.

130. *shall be*] will prove to be.

132–3. *chimney-sweeper . . . oyster-wife*] With such a parentage, Envy is
sooty and malodorous; filth and poverty engender enviousness in him.

137–8. *Come down*] i.e., come down off that chair. Envy speaks as though
Faustus were enthroned, and possibly Faustus's chair is raised.

138. *with a vengeance*] i.e., God's curse on you. The tag was common
(Dent M1003).

142. *pension*] 'payment for board and lodging, or for the board and education of a child' (*OED*, sb. 6, incorrectly giving 1611 as the earliest citation).
In the broader sense of an annuity, the term is earlier.

bevers] drink or between-meal snacks.

grandmother a hogshead of claret wine. My godfathers   145
were these: Peter Pickle-herring and Martin Martlemas-
beef. O, but my godmother, she was a jolly gentlewoman,
and well beloved in every good town and city; her name
was Mistress Margery March-beer. Now, Faustus, thou
hast heard all my progeny, wilt thou bid me to supper?   150
Faustus. No, I'll see thee hanged. Thou wilt eat up all my
victuals.
Gluttony. Then the devil choke thee!
Faustus. Choke thyself, glutton!—What art thou, the sixth?
Sloth. I am Sloth. I was begotten on a sunny bank, where I   155
have lain ever since, and you have done me great injury
to bring me from thence. Let me be carried thither again
by Gluttony and Lechery. I'll not speak another word for
a king's ransom.
Faustus. What are you, Mistress Minx, the seventh and last?   160
Lechery. Who, I, sir? I am one that loves an inch of raw

---

145. *hogshead*] sixty-three-gallon liquor cask.

claret wine] originally a light red, rosé wine, distinguished from both 'red'
and 'white' wine. By 1600, the term came to be applied to red wines
generally (*OED*).

146. *Pickle-herring*] (*a*) a pickled herring (*b*) a buffoon (*OED*, 2, citing
a humorous character in a German collection of English plays, *Englische
Comedien und Tragedien . . . sampt dem Pickelhering*, 1620, and later English
usages).

146–7. *Martin Martlemas-beef*] Cattle were commonly slaughtered at
Martinmas, the Feast of St Martin (11 November), and salted for winter
provision (*OED*, 'Martinmas', 1). Poins refers to Falstaff as 'the martlemas'
in *2H4*, II.ii.96. There may be a dig at Martin Marprelate and the gluttony of
the Puritans (Kocher, 'Nashe's Authorship', p. 29).

149. *March-beer*] a strong beer brewed in March (*OED*, 'March', sb.² 2b).
thou] that thou.

150. *progeny*] lineage, parentage (*OED*, 5).

159. *a king's ransom*] a commonplace phrase for a huge amount, though
not listed in Dent or *OED*, 'king', sb. 14.

160. *Mistress Minx*] a lewd or wanton woman. *OED* cites this line as the
first instance ('minx', 2b–c), but Kocher ('Nashe's Authorship', p. 30)
observes that this is the name of a prostitute in Lodge's *Alarum against
Usurers* (1584) and that a 'Mistress Minx, a Merchant's wife . . . that looks
simperingly as if she were besmeared', also appears in Nashe's *Piers
Penniless*, 1592 (ed. McKerrow, I.173).

161–2. *I am . . . stockfish*] Lechery combines two proverbs and exploits
their potential for sexual meaning: 'he loves raw mutton' (Dent M1338) and
'he prefers an inch of his pleasure before an ell of his profit' (Dent 150). *Raw*

mutton better than an ell of fried stockfish, and the first
letter of my name begins with lechery.

Lucifer. Away, to hell, to hell!

> *Exeunt the* SINS.

Now, Faustus, how dost thou like this?   165

Faustus. O, this feeds my soul!

Lucifer. Tut, Faustus, in hell is all manner of delight.

Faustus. O, might I see hell and return again, how happy were
I then!

Lucifer. Thou shalt. I will send for thee at midnight.   170
[*Presenting a book.*] In meantime, take this book. Peruse
it throughly, and thou shalt turn thyself into what shape
thou wilt.

Faustus. [*Taking the book.*] Great thanks, mighty Lucifer.
This will I keep as chary as my life.   175

Lucifer. Farewell, Faustus, and think on the devil.

Faustus. Farewell, great Lucifer. Come, Mephistopheles.

> *Exeunt omnes,* [*different ways*].

---

163. lechery] *A1; L Dyce 2.*   164. S.H. *Lucifer] B1; printed at l. 165 in A1;
Faustus Dyce 1.*   171, 174. S.D.] *This ed.; not in A1.*   174–5.] *verse as in
B1; as prose in A1.*   177.1. *different ways] B1 (seuerall waies); not in A1.*

---

mutton is common slang for lust or for prostitutes (*OED*, 'mutton', 4);
stockfish or dried cod is a slang term of contempt suggesting emaciation and
sexual insufficiency (as in *1H4*, II.iv.243, and *MM*, III.ii.106). By choosing
an *inch* of one over an *ell* (a measure of 45 inches) of the other, Lechery
expresses her preference for quality rather than inferior quantity.

162–3 *the first . . . lechery*] For the humorousness of this remark, which
baffled early editors, compare 'They call them rewards, but bribes is the first
letter of their Christian name' (Hugh Latimer's *Seven Sermons before Edward
VI*, 1552, ed. Edward Arber, London: A. Murray, 1869, p. 139), 'a
gentlewoman . . . the first letter of whose name . . . is Camilla' (Lyly's
Euphues, ed. Bond, II.110–11), and 'Her name begins with Mistress Purge,
does it not?' (Thomas Middleton's *Family of Love*, 1608, *Works*, ed. A. H.
Bullen, London: Nimmo, 1885, vol. III, II.iii.53–4, cited by Ward). In the
American ballad of 'Peter Gray', the hero falls in love with 'a nice young girl'
and learns that 'The first three letters of her name were Lucy Annie Pearl'.

171–2. *take . . . throughly*] a repetition of II.i.162 (substituting *throughly* for
thoroughly).

172. *throughly*] thoroughly.

175. *chary*] carefully. Compare *Sonn.*, xxii.11–12: 'Bearing thy heart,
which I will keep so chary / As tender nurse her babe from faring ill'.

Act III

[III.Chorus]

Enter WAGNER *solus.*

Wagner. Learnèd Faustus,
  To know the secrets of astronomy
  Graven in the book of Jove's high firmament,
  Did mount himself to scale Olympus' top,
  Being seated in a chariot burning bright   5
  Drawn by the strength of yoky dragons' necks.
  He now is gone to prove cosmography,
  And, as I guess, will first arrive at Rome
  To see the Pope and manner of his court
  And take some part of holy Peter's feast   10
  That to this day is highly solemnised.   *Exit* WAGNER.

[III.i]

Enter FAUSTUS *and* MEPHISTOPHELES.

Faustus. Having now, my good Mephistopheles,

III.Chorus.0.1. S.D. Enter *WAGNER* solus] Wagner's name may suggest
that Wagner and the Chorus double. Since, in any case, this speech is a short
version of the Chorus marked as such at the beginning of Act III in B1, the
identification of this speech as a 'Chorus' seems likely.
  3. *Graven*] engraved, carved on a surface (*OED*, ppl. adj. 2).
  4. *mount himself*] i.e., ascend to the seat of the chariot.
  6. *yoky*] coupled by a yoke (*OED*, first instance).
  7. *prove*] make trial of, put to the test (*OED*, v. 1).
  10. *take some part of*] take part in (*OED*, 'part', sb. 23).
  holy Peter's feast] 29 June.
  11. *That to this day*] A1's reading yields a kind of sense—'that even
today'—but its irrelevance to the scene at hand makes it suspect in comparison with B1's 'The which this day'.

  III.i.0.1. S.D.] The stage direction at 59.1–2, *Enter . . . to the banquet*, raises
the possibility that a banquet and chairs are set out at the start of this scene.
Wagner has already prepared us to expect to see action at 'holy Peter's feast',
and Mephistopheles assures Faustus at ll. 24–5 that he has secured the

Passed with delight the stately town of Trier,
Environed round with airy mountain-tops,
With walls of flint and deep intrenchèd lakes,
Not to be won by any conquering prince;   5
From Paris next, coasting the realm of France,
We saw the river Maine fall into Rhine,
Whose banks are set with groves of fruitful vines.
Then up to Naples, rich Campania,
Whose buildings, fair and gorgeous to the eye,   10
The streets straight forth and paved with finest brick,
Quarters the town in four equivalents.
There saw we learnèd Maro's golden tomb,

III.i.12. equivalents] *Dyce 1;* equiuolence *A1.*

Pope's private chambers for their use. On the unlocalised Elizabethan stage, on the other hand, we should be wary of restricting the imaginative sense in which Mephistopheles is showing Faustus the sights of Rome, perhaps from some high vantage point, in ll. 29–43.

   2. *Trier*] a town on the Mosel river, on the western edge of Germany, near modern-day Luxembourg.

   3. *Environèd round*] surrounded.

   4. *intrenchèd lakes*] moats. Compare the *Damnable Life*'s description of Trier: 'a mighty large castle . . . with three walls and three great trenches, so strong that it was impossible for any prince's power to win it' (ch. 22). Faustus's whole speech here is indebted in detail to ch. 22 of the *Damnable Life*.

   6. *coasting*] making the rounds of, exploring (*OED*, 'coast', v. 5a), or perhaps 'skirting' (*OED*, 2). Faustus's itinerary, as in the *Damnable Life*, seems to take him from Paris through the Rhineland, where the Main or Maine River joins the Rhine, and so southward, skirting France to the west. Compare *Jew of Malta*, 1.i.91: 'Belike they coasted round by Candy shore.'

   9. *Naples, rich Campania*] The *Damnable Life*'s 'Campania in the kingdom of Neapolis' (ch. 22) mistranslates the German original of which the sense is that Faustus 'came, in Campania, to the city of Naples' (Greg). The playwright's ambivalent phrasing avoids the mistranslating error, but does not suggest that he consulted the German version instead. Campania is today the large province in which Naples is located; in Elizabethan times Campania was limited to the district of Capua, while Naples was known as a kingdom.

   11. *straight forth*] in straight lines.

   12. *Quarters*] an acceptable plural form in *-s* (Abbott 333).

   13. *Maro's*] Virgil, or Publius Vergilius Maro (70–19 BC), was often referred to by his cognomen in the Middle Ages and Renaissance. He enjoyed a reputation both as a great epic poet and as a magician. For the story of his reputed magical feat of carving a tunnel through rock in a single night, see Introduction, p. 4. The tunnel ascribed to Virgil is, in fact, an ancient passageway between Naples and Pozuoli.

The way he cut an English mile in length
Thorough a rock of stone in one night's space.   15
From thence to Venice, Padua, and the rest,
In midst of which a sumptuous temple stands
That threats the stars with her aspiring top.
Thus hitherto hath Faustus spent his time.
But tell me now, what resting place is this?   20
Hast thou, as erst I did command,
Conducted me within the walls of Rome?
Mephistopheles. Faustus, I have. And because we will not
be unprovided, I have taken up his Holiness' privy
chamber for our use.   25
Faustus. I hope his Holiness will bid us welcome.
Mephistopheles. Tut, 'tis no matter, man. We'll be bold with
his good cheer.
And now, my Faustus, that thou mayst perceive
What Rome containeth to delight thee with,   30
Know that this city stands upon seven hills
That underprops the groundwork of the same.
Just through the midst runs flowing Tiber's stream,
With winding banks that cut it in two parts,

---

24. Holiness'] *A1* (holinesse).   33–4.] *B1; not in A1.*

14. *way*] road, path (*OED*, 1a).
16–18.] Faustus refers to St Mark's in Venice, which, though it lacks a
steeple or tower, is nearby to a campanile and is itself a monument of
architecture deserving of any superlatives. Perhaps the playwright had in
mind the description from the *Damnable Life* of how 'all the roof or loft of
the church' was 'double gilded over'. The lines in B1 at III.i.18–19 about the
roof with its 'curious work in gold', not found in A1, are explicitly taken
from the prose source.
17. *of which*] i.e., of Venice.
21. *erst*] earlier, a little while since.
23. *because*] in order that (*OED*, conj. 2).
24. *taken up*] taken possession of, commandeered (*OED*, 'take', v. 93d).
24–5. *privy chamber*] private apartment in a royal residence (*OED*, 2).
31–43.] An inventory of the Admiral's Men in 1598, listing 'the sittie of
Rome' as one of its properties, suggests the possibility of a back-cloth for this
scene (Henslowe's *Diary*, p. 319).
32. *underprops*] The singular verb is perhaps attracted to 'city' in the
previous line.
33–4.] B1 supplies two lines necessary to make sense of the bridges in l.
35.

Over the which four stately bridges lean,   35
That makes safe passage to each part of Rome.
Upon the bridge called Ponte Angelo
Erected is a castle passing strong,
Within whose walls such store of ordnance are,
And double cannons, framed of carvèd brass,   40
As match the days within one complete year—
Besides the gates and high pyramides
Which Julius Caesar brought from Africa.
Faustus. Now, by the kingdoms of infernal rule,

---

37. Ponte] *Dyce 1; Ponto A1.*   39. ordnance] *A1 (ordonance).*

36. *makes*] For the singular ending, compare *underprops* in l. 32 above and *Quarters* in l. 12.

37–8.] *Ponte Angelo*, formerly the *Pons Aelius*, was built across the Tiber by Hadrian in AD 135 to connect his mausoleum (now the Castello di S. Angelo) with the Campus Martius. As C. B. Wheeler points out (*Marlowe's 'Doctor Faustus', with an Introduction by Sir Adolphus William Ward and Notes by C. B. Wheeler*, Oxford University Press, 1915), the castle 'directly faces the bridge, but is not, and never was, built upon it'. The playwright seems to have relied on the wording of the *Damnable Life*, where it is reported that 'upon one bridge called Ponte S. Angelo is the castle of S. Angelo' (ch. 22).

38. *passing*] surpassingly.

40. *double cannons*] 'probably cannons of a very large calibre' (Jump, giving persuasive citations). The *Damnable Life* reports that the impressive cannon in the castle of S. Angelo 'will shoot seven bullets off with one fire'.

41.] This unusual detail is simply a rendition of the *Damnable Life*'s 'wherein are so many great cast pieces [i.e., brass cannon] as there are days in a year'.

42–3. *pyramides . . . Africa*] The playwright read in the *Damnable Life* that Faustus 'visited the churchyard of S. Peter's, where he saw the pyramid that Julius Caesar brought out of Africa' (ch. 22). In fact the obelisk still standing before St Peter's was brought back from Egyptian Thebes in AD 353 by Constantius. Jump notes that a similar obelisk brought back by Caligula in the first century AD from Heliopolis was moved to the Piazza San Pietro in 1586 and is still standing there. The Roman emperors were often referred to as 'Caesar'. As Boas notes, the plural form of 'pyramides' is used by Marlowe for the singular in *Massacre at Paris*, ii.40–2: 'Set me to scale the high Pyramides . . . I'll either rend it with my nails'. One wonders if Cleopatra's vow to 'make / My country's high pyramides my gibbet' in *Ant.*, v.ii.59–60, must not refer also to a single structure. Both Marlowe and Shakespeare are thinking of an obelisk; Cleopatra is not about to try to hang herself from one of the great pyramids. The word *pyramides* is here pronounced with the stress on the second and fourth of four syllables.

Of Styx, Acheron, and the fiery lake   45
Of ever-burning Phlegethon, I swear
That I do long to see the monuments
And situation of bright splendent Rome.
Come, therefore, let's away!
Mephistopheles.
    Nay, Faustus, stay. I know you'd fain see the Pope   50
And take some part of holy Peter's feast,
Where thou shalt see a troupe of bald-pate friars
Whose *summum bonum* is in belly cheer.
Faustus. Well, I am content to compass then some sport,
And by their folly make us merriment.   55
Then charm me that I may be invisible, to do what I
please unseen of any whilst I stay in Rome.
Mephistopheles. [*Placing a robe on Faustus.*] So, Faustus, now
do what thou wilt, thou shalt not be discerned.

    Sound a sennet. Enter the POPE *and the* CARDINAL OF
    LORRAINE *to the banquet, with* FRIARS *attending.*

Pope. My lord of Lorraine, will't please you draw near?   60

---

58. S.D. *Placing a robe on Faustus*] This ed.; *not in* A1; *Mephistopheles charms*
him Dyce 1.   59.1. S.D. *sennet*] A1 (*Sonnet*).

45–6. *Styx . . . Phlegethon*] Faustus's oath takes the form of a Virgilian
journey through the underworld, no doubt inspired by Mephistopheles's
account of the wonders of Rome. The Styx separates the under from the
upper world; Acheron is the river of woe; Phlegethon (here called a 'lake') is
the river of liquid fire. Faustus does not mention the fourth river, Cocytus
(lamentation).
    48. *bright splendent*] Printed here without hyphenation as in both A1
and B1, the phrase means 'shining brightly and resplendent'. Plausibly
hyphenated by some modern editors (such as Jump), the phrase takes on the
single meaning of 'brilliantly magnificent'.
    51. *of*] in.
    53. *summum bonum*] greatest good—a scholastic term that defines the
infinite goodness of God, but is here put to profane use by Mephistopheles
and by the friars.
    54. *compass*] devise, contrive, usually in a bad sense (*OED*, v.[1] 1–2).
    58. S.D. *robe*] The Admiral's Men owned a 'robe for to go invisible'
(Henslowe's *Diary*, p. 325); it is likely that such a prop was used here, or else
a girdle, as in the B-text.
    59.1. S.D. *sennet*] 'set of notes on the trumpet or cornet . . . as a signal for
the ceremonial entrance or exit of a body of players' (*OED*, giving this as its
first citation).

Faustus. Fall to, and the devil choke you an you spare.
Pope. How now, who's that which spake? Friars, look about.
Friar. Here's nobody, if it like your Holiness.
Pope. My lord, here is a dainty dish was sent me from the
    Bishop of Milan.   [*He presents a dish.*]   65
Faustus. I thank you, sir.   *Snatch it.*
Pope. How now, who's that which snatched the meat from
    me? Will no man look?—My lord, this dish was sent me
    from the Cardinal of Florence.
Faustus. [*Snatching the dish.*] You say true. I'll ha't.   70
Pope. What again?—My lord, I'll drink to your Grace.
Faustus. [*Snatching the cup.*] I'll pledge your Grace.
Lorraine. My lord, it may be some ghost, newly crept out of
    purgatory, come to beg a pardon of your Holiness.
Pope. It may be so. Friars, prepare a dirge to lay the fury of   75
    this ghost. Once again, my lord, fall to.
                    The Pope crosseth himself.
Faustus. What, are you crossing of yourself? Well, use that
    trick no more, I would advise you.
               [*The Pope*] *cross*[*es himself*] *again.*
    Well, there's a second time. Aware the third, I give you
    fair warning.   80
           [*The Pope*] *cross*[*es himself*] *again, and Faustus*
          hits him a box of the ear, and they all run away.
    Come on, Mephistopheles. What shall we do?

---

61. an] *A1* (*and*); *similarly at IV.i.65 and 166, etc.*   62, 67. who's] *A1*
(*whose*).   63. S.H. *Friar*] *A1* (*Fri*).   65. S.D.] *This ed.; not in A1.*
70. S.D.] *Dyce 1* (*subst.*); *not in A1.*   70. ha't] *A1* (*hate*).   72. S.D.] *Dyce 1*
(*subst.*); *not in A1.*   77–8.] *prose, this ed.; divided at selfe? / Well in A1.*
78.1., 80.1. S.D.] *bracketed material, Dyce 1; not in A1.*   79. Well] *A1* (*Fau.*
Well).   79–80.] *prose as in Gill 2; as verse divided at third, / I in A1.*
81. Come] *A1* (*Fau: Come*).

---

   61. *an you spare*] if you eat only sparingly.
   63. *like*] please.
   74. *pardon*] indulgence.
   75. *dirge*] technically, from *dirige*, 'the first word of the antiphon at Matins
in the Office of the Dead' (*OED*, sb. 1), applied here to the text sung at the
burial of one who is dead. See l. 87.1n for the comic inappropriateness of
what is actually sung.
   79. *Aware*] beware (*OED*, 3).
   79–80. *I . . . warning*] a common expression (Dent w73).
   80.2. S.D. of] on.

Mephistopheles. Nay, I know not. We shall be cursed with bell,
    book, and candle.
Faustus. How? Bell, book, and candle, candle, book, and bell,
    Forward and backward, to curse Faustus to hell.   85
    Anon you shall hear a hog grunt, a calf bleat, and an ass
        bray,
    Because it is Saint Peter's holy day.

    Enter all the FRIARS *to sing the dirge.*

Friar. Come, brethren, let's about our business with good
    devotion.
            [*The Friars*] *sing this:*
    Cursèd be he that stole away his Holiness' meat from the
        table.   90
    Maledicat Dominus!
    Cursèd be he that struck his Holiness a blow on the face.
    Maledicat Dominus!
    Cursèd be he that took Friar Sandelo a blow on the pate.
    Maledicat Dominus!   95
    Cursèd be he that disturbeth our holy dirge.
    Maledicat Dominus!

86–7.] *verse as in Dyce 1; as prose in A1.*   89.1. S.D. *The Friars*] *This ed.;*
not in A1.   95, 97. *Maledicat Dominus!*] *A1* (*male, &c.*).

82–3. *cursed . . . candle*] excommunicated by means of a ritual in which
the bell is tolled, the book (Bible) is closed, and the candle is extinguished.
The phrase is proverbial (Dent B276). The office of excommunication is
confused, here and in the *Damnable Life* (ch. 22), with that of exorcism.
    85. *Forward and backward*] Compare I.iii.9. As Harry Levin notes in *The
Overreacher*, p. 120, the dirge of malediction serves as the religious counter-
part to the sacrilegious rite Faustus performed in anagrammatising the name
of God.
    87.1. S.D. dirge] 'a wholly inappropriate term for the cursing that follows'
(Greg).
    91. Maledicat Dominus] may the Lord curse (him). From the ceremony of
excommunication (Logeman).
    94. *took*] gave. Compare *MM*, II.i.181: 'If he took you a box o' th' ear'.
Evidently Faustus has just taken a swipe at one of the friars. The name
Sandelo may suggest 'sandal', often spelled *sandell* in the sixteenth century;
the Franciscans were the only order permitted to wear sandals, and were
often criticised (especially by Protestants) for their allegedly lavish style of
living, in violation of their strict rule of poverty (Ormerod–Wortham).

Cursèd be he that took away his Holiness' wine.
Maledicat Dominus!
Et omnes sancti. Amen.   100
   [FAUSTUS *and* MEPHISTOPHELES] *beat the* FRIARS,
   and fling fireworks among them, and so exeunt.

[III.ii]

Enter ROBIN [*with a conjuring book*] *and* RAFE
with a silver goblet.

Robin. Come, Rafe, did not I tell thee we were for ever made
by this Doctor Faustus' book? *Ecce signum!* Here's a
simple purchase for horse-keepers. Our horses shall eat
no hay as long as this lasts.

Enter the VINTNER.

Rafe. But Robin, here comes the Vintner.   5
Robin. Hush, I'll gull him supernaturally.—Drawer, I hope

100.1. S.D. FAUSTUS *and* MEPHISTOPHELES] *Dyce 1 (subst.); not in A1.*
III.ii.0.] *A1 here provides the Chorus printed in the present edition (and in other
modern editions) as the Chorus to Act IV, followed by the comic scene printed in
this edition (and in Keefer) as II.ii, and followed then by the present comic scene.*
0.1. S.D. *with a conjuring book*] *This ed.; not in A1.*

100. *Et omnes sancti* and may all the saints (curse him). From the Litany
of Saints (N. C. Carpenter, *N&Q*, cxcv (1950), 180–1).
100.1. S.D. beat the FRIARS] The action indicated in this original stage
direction must begin during the chanting of the excommunication ceremony;
see l. 94.

III.ii.1. *for ever made*] assured for ever of success. Compare 'made man' at
IV.i.130.
2. *Ecce signum*] Behold the sign. The phrase—a favourite of Elizabethan
clowns, and of Falstaff in *1H4*, II.iv.166–7—echoes the language of the Mass
(see Dent s443).
2–3. *Here's . . . horse-keepers*] i.e., here's quite a haul for two simple stable-
boys! *Purchase* means 'pillage, plunder' (*OED*, sb. 1).
3–4. *eat no hay*] i.e., eat like kings.
4.1. S.D. VINTNER] innkeeper selling wine.
6. *gull*] cheat, dupe.
Drawer] tapster, one who draws beer, etc. Robin puts on airs by assuming
the innkeeper to be a mere tapster. He repeats this insult at l. 19, and so the
word here in l. 6 cannot be explained as Robin's calling offstage, pretending
to settle his drinking score with a tapster before leaving the tavern. On
the other hand, in the B-text version of this scene Robin thinks that 'the

all is paid. God be with you. Come, Rafe.
                                        [*They start to go.*]
Vintner. [*To Robin.*] Soft, sir, a word with you. I must yet
   have a goblet paid from you ere you go.
Robin. I, a goblet? Rafe, I, a goblet? I scorn you, and you are   10
   but a etc. I, a goblet? Search me.
Vintner. I mean so, sir, with your favour.
                              [*The Vintner searches Robin.*]
Robin. How say you now?
Vintner. I must say somewhat to your fellow—you, sir.
Rafe. Me, sir? Me, sir? Search your fill. [*He gives the goblet to*   15
   Robin; then the Vintner searches Rafe.] Now, sir, you may
   be ashamed to burden honest men with a matter of truth.
Vintner. Well, t'one of you hath this goblet about you.
Robin. You lie, drawer, 'tis afore me. Sirrah, you, I'll teach ye
   to impeach honest men. Stand by. I'll scour you for a   20
   goblet. Stand aside, you had best, I charge you in the
   name of Beelzebub. [*Tossing the goblet to Rafe.*] Look to
   the goblet, Rafe.
Vintner. What mean you, sirrah?
Robin. I'll tell you what I mean.   *He reads.*   25

7.1, 8. S.D.] *This ed.; not in A1.*   12.1. S.D.] *Dyce 1 (subst.); not in A1.*
15–16. S.D.] *This ed.; not in A1; Vintner searches him Dyce 1.*   22. S.D.]
This ed.; not in A1.

Vintner's boy' is following them hard at heels, suggesting that the Vintner
may have been substituted for the Vintner's boy as some point.
   8. *Soft*] i.e., wait a minute.
   10–11. *you are but a etc.*] either (*a*) a direction for the actor to improvise
(Boas), or (*b*) a euphemistic insult that the actor is to speak with withering
suggestion as to what it implies (*OED*, 2b).
   12. *with your favour*] by your leave.
   14. *somewhat*] something.
   19. *afore me*] Robin quibbles: the goblet is not on his person or on Rafe's
('about you', l. 18) but is being held by Robin in front of him in plain sight.
Or perhaps, as Kirschbaum suggests, Robin tosses the goblet into the
audience.
   20. *impeach*] call in question, accuse.
   scour] beat, scourge, punish (*OED*, v.^{2} 9), with some play on the primary
meaning of *scour* (v.^{2} 1), 'to cleanse or polish', which would apply to the
goblet.

Sanctobulorum Periphrasticon! Nay, I'll tickle you,
Vintner. Look to the goblet, Rafe. *Polypragmos
Belseborams framanto pacostiphos tostu Mephistopheles!* etc.

Enter to them MEPHISTOPHELES.

[*Exit the* VINTNER, *running.*]
Mephistopheles. Monarch of hell, under whose black survey
   Great potentates do kneel with awful fear,   30
   Upon whose altars thousand souls do lie,

28.1. S.D. *Enter to them* MEPHISTOPHELES] *This ed.; Enter Mephostophilis: sets squibs at their backes: / they runne about. / Vintner. O nomine Domine, what meanst thou Robin? thou / hast no goblet. / Rafe. Peccatum peccatorum, heeres thy goblet, good Vint- / ner. / Robin. Misericordia pro nobis what shal I doe? good diuel / forgiue me now, and Ile neuer rob thy Library more. / Enter to them Meph. / Meph. Vanish vilaines, th one like an Ape, an other like / a Beare, the third an Asse, for doing this enterprise. A1.* 28.2. S.D. *Exit the* VINTNER, *running*] *This ed.; not in A1; placed after the fourth line of the original ending of the scene (see commentary note to 28.2) in Dyce 1.* 29. S.H. *Mephistopheles*] *not in A1 at this line; see collation note for 28.1.*

26–8. Sanctobulorum . . . Mephistopheles] Gibberish, partly Latin and Greek, in parody of Faustus's conjuring at 1.iii.16–23. Both times, as Ormerod–Wortham observe, Mephistopheles appears when he is named. *Polypragmos* may be a corruption of the Greek *polypragmon*, meaning 'busybody' (Kocher, 'Nashe's Authorship', p. 21).

26. *tickle*] (ironically) beat, chastise (*OED*, v. 6b, giving as its earliest citation Warner's *Albion's England*, London: J. Broome, 1592, p. 207; in fact, the word also appears in Warner's 1586 edition, London: T. Cadman, 1586).

28.1. S.D. Enter to them *MEPHISTOPHELES*] The A-text includes at this point what appears to be a first shot for the remainder of the scene. one that the dramatist (presumably not Marlowe) cancelled in favour of what follows; see collation and p. 67 for textual analysis. The Latin scraps in the original ending, 'O nomine Domine', 'Peccatum peccatorum', 'Misericordia pro nobis', are probably a garbled recollection of the familar 'Benedictus qui venit in nomine Domini', 'Blessed is he who comes in the name of the Lord' (assuming that *Domine* is only an accidental variant of *Domini*), together with 'in remissionem peccatorum' ('for the remission of sins') and 'miserere nobis' ('have mercy on us') from the Mass.

28.2. S.D. Exit the *VINTNER*, running] The timing of the Vintner's exit is uncertain. He has no part in the remainder of the scene, although in the first-shot version (see previous note) he too is presumably transformed into an animal by Mephistopheles.

30. *awful*] dreadful.

How am I vexèd with these villains' charms!
From Constantinople am I hither come
Only for pleasure of these damnèd slaves.
Robin. How, from Constantinople? You have had a great   35
journey. Will you take sixpence in your purse to pay for
your supper and be gone?
Mephistopheles. Well, villains, for your presumption I trans-
form thee [*To Robin.*] into an ape and thee [*To Rafe.*]
into a dog. And so, begone!   *Exit.*   40
Robin. How, into an ape? That's brave. I'll have fine sport
with the boys; I'll get nuts and apples enough.
Rafe. And I must be a dog.
Robin. I'faith, thy head will never be out of the pottage pot.
                                            Exeunt.

---

39. S.D.] *This ed.; not in A1.*   42. enough] *A1* (enow).   44.1. S.D.
Exeunt] placed as in Dyce 1; printed after l. 43 in A1.

32–4.] These lines seem at first to contradict Mephistopheles's explanation
of conjuring at I.iii.41–55, where he informs Faustus that he was not necessarily raised by Faustus's conjuring speeches, but comes of his own accord
when he hears someone 'rack' the name of God. Greg is probably right to
assert that we should not 'expect the philosophical outlook of the serious
scenes to be maintained in farce', but the inconsistency is less great than it
might seem: Mephistopheles has heard someone conjuring and swearing in
the name of Beelzebub (ll. 21–2), and comes only to discover that the prey is
not worth collecting.
    33. *Constantinople*] In the B-text version of this scene, we learn that
Faustus and Mephistopheles visit the great Turk's court (III.iii.55), as in the
Damnable Life, ch. 22.
    39–40.] Presumably some comic physical transformation takes place
on stage. The Admiral's Men possessed 'j black dogge' in their inventory of
1598; see B-text commentary at III.iii.44–9 (Henslowe's *Diary*, p. 321).
    41. *brave*] fine, excellent.
    43–4.] Dogs' heads proverbially always get into porridge (pottage) pots
(Dent H491).

Act IV

Enter CHORUS.

Chorus. When Faustus had with pleasure ta'en the view
Of rarest things and royal courts of kings,
He stayed his course and so returnèd home,
Where such as bear his absence but with grief—
I mean his friends and nearest companions—   5
Did gratulate his safety with kind words.
And in their conference of what befell,
Touching his journey through the world and air,
They put forth questions of astrology,
Which Faustus answered with such learnèd skill   10
As they admired and wondered at his wit.
Now is his fame spread forth in every land.
Amongst the rest the Emperor is one,
Carolus the Fifth, at whose palace now
Faustus is feasted 'mongst his noblemen.   15
What there he did in trial of his art
I leave untold, your eyes shall see performed.   *Exit.*

IV.Chorus.] *placed as in Boas; printed after III.i. in A1.*   1. S.H. *Chorus]*
Oxberry; not in A1.

IV.Chorus.] This Chorus appears in A1 after III.i, where it is plainly out of
place. Since the Choruses may been written on separate slips of paper in the
manuscript behind A1 such misplacement would have been easy. See Introduction, pp. 69, 71, and Appendix.
   3. *stayed his course*] ceased his journey.
   6. *gratulate*] express joy at, salute, welcome (*OED*, v. 1).
   11. *As*] that.
   14. *Carolus the Fifth*] Charles V of Spain, Holy Roman Emperor from
1519 to 1556.
   16–17. *What . . . untold*] whatever I leave untold as to what he did there in
putting his skill to the test.

[IV.i]

Enter EMPEROR, FAUSTUS, [MEPHISTOPHELES,]
and a KNIGHT, *with* Attendants.

Emperor. Master Doctor Faustus, I have heard strange report
of thy knowledge in the black art—how that none in my
empire, nor in the whole world, can compare with thee
for the rare effects of magic. They say thou hast a familiar
spirit by whom thou canst accomplish what thou list.   5
This, therefore, is my request: that thou let me see some
proof of thy skill, that mine eyes may be witnesses to
confirm what mine ears have heard reported. And here I
swear to thee, by the honour of mine imperial crown, that
whatever thou dost, thou shalt be no ways prejudiced or   10
endamaged.
Knight. (*Aside.*) I'faith, he looks much like a conjurer.
Faustus. My gracious sovereign, though I must confess myself far inferior to the report men have published, and
nothing answerable to the honour of your Imperial   15
Majesty, yet, for that love and duty binds me thereunto, I
am content to do whatsoever your Majesty shall command
me.
Emperor. Then, Doctor Faustus, mark what I shall say.
As I was sometime solitary set   20

IV.i.0.1. S.D. MEPHISTOPHELES] *Boas; not in A1; Attendants among whom*
Mephistophilis. Wagner.   10. dost] *A1* (doest).   19–30.] *verse as in Dyce*
1; as prose in A1.

IV.i.1. *strange*] exciting wonder (*OED*, adj. 10).
4. *rare*] splendid, excellent (*OED*, adj. 6b).
5. *list*] desire.
12.] The Knight speaks ironically.
15. *nothing answerable*] not at all suitable or correspondent.
16. *for that*] because.
19–30.] Dyce's verse arrangement of this passage, printed as prose in A1,
is generally persuasive, but results in excessive metrical irregularity in l. 26;
l. 27, too, would be improved if *never* were emended to *ne'er*. Quite possibly
A1's transcription is attempting to deal with a corrupted or partly illegible
passage of something intended for verse.
20. *sometime*] at one time, recently (*OED*, adv. 2). Compare the *Damnable*
Life: 'Being once solitary in my house', etc. (ch. 29). The Emperor's speech
and Faustus's replies up to l. 57 are closely modelled on ch. 29 of the
Damnable Life.

Within my closet, sundry thoughts arose
About the honour of mine ancestors—
How they had won by prowess such exploits,
Got such riches, subdued so many kingdoms
As we that do succeed or they that shall   25
Hereafter possess our throne shall,
I fear me, never attain to that degree
Of high renown and great authority.
Amongst which kings is Alexander the Great,
Chief spectacle of the world's pre-eminence,   30
The bright shining of whose glorious acts
Lightens the world with his reflecting beams—
As when I hear but motion made of him,
It grieves my soul I never saw the man.
If, therefore, thou by cunning of thine art   35
Canst raise this man from hollow vaults below
Where lies entombed this famous conqueror,
And bring with him his beauteous paramour,

---

29. Amongst] *A1* (amongest).   33. motion] *A1*; mention *Wagner*.

21. *closet*] private room.
23. *won . . . exploits*] attained such military success by force of arms (*OED*, 'win', v. 11, 'exploit', sb. 1).
25. *succeed*] follow as successors.
30.] the greatest marvel of all those who have been pre-eminent in the world.
32. *reflecting*] shining (*OED*, 'reflect', v. 9b). Compare *Tit.*, 1.i.226-7: 'whose virtues will, I hope, / Reflect on Rome as Titan's rays on earth'.
33. *As*] to such an extent that (*OED*, adv. 21, citing this instance).
motion] a proposal or suggestion (*OED*, sb. 2), or, mention. Wagner's emendation to *mention* is attractive in view of the *Damnable Life* reading: 'as the Chronicles makes mention' (ch. 29). Such *e:o* misreadings are common in Renaissance texts. The emendation is probably unnecessary, however, since 'motion' evidently could mean 'mention'. J. C. Maxwell cites (inaccurately) *Antonio's Revenge* (ed. W. Reavley Gair, The Revels Plays, Manchester University Press, 1978), IV.i.62-3: '*Antonio.* Asked he for Julio yet? / *Lucio.* No motion of him' (*N&Q*, n.s. XI (1964), 262).
38. *paramour*] Alexander married the beautiful captive princess Roxana in 329 BC, but was reputed to have had many mistresses, including Thais. *Paramour*, the *Damnable Life*'s translation of the German *Gemahlin* (ch. 29), can mean 'beloved' or 'consort', though the dominant meaning in the Renaissance was probably 'mistress'.

Both in their right shapes, gesture, and attire
They used to wear during their time of life,   40
Thou shalt both satisfy my just desire
And give me cause to praise thee whilst I live.
Faustus. My gracious lord, I am ready to accomplish your
request, so far forth as by art and power of my spirit I am
able to perform.   45
Knight. (*Aside.*) I'faith, that's just nothing at all.
Faustus. But if it like your Grace, it is not in my ability to
present before your eyes the true substantial bodies of
those two deceased princes, which long since are consumed to dust.   50
Knight. (*Aside.*) Ay, marry, Master Doctor, now there's a sign
of grace in you, when you will confess the truth.
Faustus. But such spirits as can lively resemble Alexander and
his paramour shall appear before your Grace in that
manner that they best lived in, in their most flourishing   55
estate—which I doubt not shall sufficiently content your
Imperial Majesty.
Emperor. Go to, Master Doctor. Let me see them presently.
Knight. Do you hear, Master Doctor? You bring Alexander

---

55. best] *A1;* both *Dyce 2.*

39–40.] The Emperor's eagerness to see Alexander and his paramour in the attire they wore during their lifetimes may suggest that we be cautious about accepting too readily the commonplace view that the Elizabethans didn't much bother with such details in their historical plays.

49–50. *consumed to dust*] Compare *Ham.*, v.i.209–10: 'Alexander returneth to dust.' Harold Jenkins (New Arden ed., 1982) notes that Alexander was regularly cited in meditations on death, and footnotes Lucian's *Dialogues of the Dead* (xii–xiv in traditional arrangement; xiv, xiii, and xxv in the Loeb Library).

51. *marry*] a mild oath. Originally, 'by the Virgin Mary'.

53. *lively*] vividly, 'to the life' (*OED*, adv. 4).

55. *best*] Dyce's emendation to *both* finds some support in the corresponding line in the *Damnable Life*: 'in manner and form as they both lived in their most flourishing time' (ch. 29). As at l. 33 above, however, we cannot be sure that the dramatist did not intentionally diverge from the source.

58. *Go to*] an exclamation of derisive incredulity, remonstrance, etc. (*OED*, 'go', v. 91b). Here the Emperor merely demurs at Faustus's apologetics and tells him to get on with it.

presently] at once.

59. *You bring*] i.e., you mean to say you're going to bring.

and his paramour before the Emperor?   60
Faustus. How then, sir?
Knight. I'faith, that's as true as Diana turned me to a stag.
Faustus. No, sir, but when Actaeon died, he left the horns for
  you. [*Aside to Mephistopheles.*] Mephistopheles, begone!
                                                Exit MEPHISTOPHELES.
Knight. Nay, an you go to conjuring, I'll be gone.   65
                                                Exit KNIGHT.
Faustus. [*Aside.*] I'll meet with you anon for interrupting me
  so.—Here they are, my gracious lord.

Enter MEPHISTOPHELES *with* ALEXANDER *and his* PARAMOUR.

Emperor. Master Doctor, I heard this lady while she lived had
  a wart or mole in her neck. How shall I know whether it
  be so or no?   70
Faustus. Your Highness may boldly go and see.
            [*The Emperor makes an inspection, and then*]
            Exeunt ALEXANDER [*and his* PARAMOUR].
Emperor. Sure these are no spirits, but the true substantial
  bodies of those two deceased princes.
Faustus. Will't please your Highness now to send for the
  knight that was so pleasant with me here of late?   75

---

64. S.D. *Aside to Mephistopheles*] *This ed.; not in* A1.   66. S.D. *Aside*] *This
ed.; not in* A1.   71.1. S.D. *The Emperor makes an inspection, and then*] *This
ed.; not in* A1.   71 2. S.D.] *placed as in* A1; *placed after l.* 73 *in Boas.*
71.2. S.D. *Exeunt*] A1 *(exit).*   71.2. S.D. *and his* PARAMOUR] *Boas; not
in* A1.

---

62. *as true as*] as true as that.
62–3. *Diana . . . Actaeon*] This myth of a huntsman, who was turned into
a stag and torn apart by his own hounds for daring to boast of his superiority
to Artemis or Diana and for intruding on her private bathing, was widely
known through Ovid's *Metamorphoses* (iii.138–252) and Golding's English
translation. The application here of this often-moralised tale centres upon the
Knight's presumption in daring to challenge Faustus, for which the Knight is
to receive the horns associated with cuckoldry. At the same time, the myth
also offers ironic comment on Faustus's pride and enslavement to ungovern-
able desires that will prove his undoing.
65. *an*] if.
66. *meet with*] be even with (*OED*, 'meet', v.11.i, citing this passage as its
earliest example). Compare l. 87.
75. *pleasant*] jocular, facetious (*OED*, adj. 3).

Emperor. One of you call him forth.

[*An* Attendant *goes to summon the Knight.*]

Enter the KNIGHT *with a pair of horns on his head.*

How now, sir knight? Why, I had thought thou hadst
been a bachelor, but now I see thou hast a wife, that not
only gives thee horns but makes thee wear them. Feel on
thy head.   cuckily   80

Knight. [*To Faustus.*] Thou damnèd wretch and execrable dog,
Bred in the concave of some monstrous rock,
How dar'st thou thus abuse a gentleman?
Villain, I say, undo what thou hast done.

Faustus. O, not so fast, sir. There's no haste but good.   85
Are you remembered how you crossed me in my conference
with the Emperor? I think I have met with you for it.

Emperor. Good Master Doctor, at my entreaty release him. He
hath done penance sufficient.

Faustus. My gracious lord, not so much for the injury he   90
offered me here in your presence as to delight you with
some mirth hath Faustus worthily requited this injurious
knight; which being all I desire, I am content to release
him of his horns.—And, sir knight, hereafter speak well
of scholars. [*Aside to Mephistopheles.*] Mephistopheles,   95
transform him straight. [*The horns are removed.*] Now, my

76.1. S.D. *An* Attendant *goes to summon the Knight*] *Dyce 1 (subst.); not in A1.*
77. How] *A1 (emp. How).*   81. S.D.] *This ed.; not in A1.*   85.] *as verse
this ed.; as prose in A1.*   95. S.D.] *This ed.; not in A1.*   96. S.D.] *Dyce 1
(subst.); not in A1.*

---

78. *bachelor*] with biting irony: (*a*) knight (*b*) unmarried man.
79.] On the cuckoldry theme implicit in the horns, see Kay Stockholder,
'"Within the massy entrailes of the earth": Faustus's Relation to Women', in
Friedenreich et al., pp. 203–19.
82. *concave*] hollow, cavity. An echo of *2Tamb.*, III.ii.89: 'Fenced with the
concave of a monstrous rock'.
85. *There's . . . good*] a proverb (Dent H199) that suggests the foolishness
of ill-considered haste, as do several other proverbs about haste (Dent H189,
H197–8).
86. *Are you remembered*] do you remember.
87. *have met with*] am even with. Compare l. 66.
88. *release him*] release him from the spell that has provided him with
horns.
90. *injury*] insult (*OED*, 2).
96. *straight*] at once.

good lord, having done my duty, I humbly take my leave.
Emperor. Farewell, Master Doctor. Yet, ere you go,
  Expect from me a bounteous reward.

     Exeunt EMPEROR, [KNIGHT, *and* Attendants].

Faustus. Now, Mephistopheles, the restless course   100
  That time doth run with calm and silent foot,
  Short'ning my days and thread of vital life,
  Calls for the payment of my latest years.
  Therefore, sweet Mephistopheles, let us make haste
  To Wittenberg.   105
Mephistopheles. What, will you go on horseback or on foot?
Faustus. Nay, till I am past this fair and pleasant green,
  I'll walk on foot.

     Enter a HORSE-COURSER.

Horse-courser. I have been all this day seeking one Master
  Fustian. Mass, see where he is.—God save you, Master 110
  Doctor.
Faustus. What, Horse-courser! You are well met.
Horse-courser. [*Offering money.*] Do you hear, sir? I have
  brought you forty dollars for your horse.

98–9.] *verse as in Dyce 1; as prose in A1.* 99.1. S.D. *Exeunt*] *A1 (exit).*
99.1. S.D. KNIGHT, *and* Attendants] *Dyce 1; not in A1.* 100–1.] *verse as in*
Dyce 1; as prose in A1. 104–5.] *as verse this ed.; as prose in A1.* 107–8.]
verse as in Dyce 1; as prose in A1. 113. S.D.] *This ed.; not in A1.*

 102. *thread*] the thread that is spun, measured, and cut by the three Fates.
 103.] my last years must shortly pay the inevitable debt to time's passing.
 104–8.] Following the exit of the Emperor and his entourage, Faustus and
Mephistopheles are imagined to have begun their journey back to Germany.
The scene is altered not by scenic devices, in all probability, but by this
dialogue. By the time Faustus sleeps in his chair, at l. 144, he is in his study
at Wittenberg.
 108.1. S.D. a *HORSE-COURSER*] a horse-dealer (*OED*).
 109–10. *Master Fustian*] The Horse-courser's ignorant approximation of
Faustus's name has ironic appropriateness; *fustian* is bombast (see I.iv.75n).
The word is used in Nashe's *The Terrors of the Night* (ed. McKerrow,
I.363–5), along with talk of horse-leeches, urine analysis, conjuring, and
other suggestive parallels to the present passage (Kocher, 'Nashe's Authorship', p. 24).
 112. *You are well met*] I am glad to see you.
 114. *dollars*] large silver coins of varying value, used especially in the
German states: the *thaler.*

Faustus. I cannot sell him so. If thou lik'st him for fifty, take   115
    him.
Horse-courser. Alas, sir, I have no more. [*To Mephistopheles.*]
    I pray you, speak for me.
Mephistopheles. [*To Faustus.*] I pray you, let him have him.
    He is an honest fellow, and he has a great charge, neither   120
    wife nor child.
Faustus. Well, come, give me your money. [*He takes the
    money.*] My boy will deliver him to you. But I must tell
    you one thing before you have him: ride him not into the
    water, at any hand.   125
Horse-courser. Why, sir, will he not drink of all waters?
Faustus. O, yes, he will drink of all waters, but ride him not
    into the water. Ride him over hedge, or ditch, or where
    thou wilt, but not into the water.

---

117. S.D.] *Boas; not in A1.*   119. S.D.] *This ed.; not in A1.*   122–3. S.D.]
Dyce 1 (subst.); not in A1.

---

117. S.D. To Mephistopheles] Evidently the Horse-courser can see
Mephistopheles, taking him to be Faustus's servant, even though
Mephistopheles was probably understood to be invisible earlier in the scene
as he carried out Faustus's commands to fetch Alexander and his paramour.
Perhaps Mephistopheles has changed costume accordingly, as Greg specu-
lates. Spirits on the Renaissance stage did have the ability to be seen or not as
they wished, as when the Ghost appears to Hamlet but not to his mother, or
Banquo appears to Macbeth but not to his guests.

120–1. *he has . . . child*] Mephistopheles wryly turns the proverb 'wife and
children are bills of charges' (Dent W379) to ironic use in describing the
Horse-courser as one who has huge expenses—having no family at all.

123. *My boy*] probably Mephistopheles. Even though Faustus has at least
one other servant (Wagner) as well, the Horse-courser makes it plain at
ll. 157–8 that he takes Mephistopheles for a menial. The term was used for
a manservant of any age.

124–5. *ride him . . . water*] Dryden's *An Evening's Love*, III.i.182–3, offers
an explanatory statement: 'A witch's horse, you know, when he enters into
water, returns into a bottle of hay again' (*The Works of John Dryden*, gen. ed.
H. T. Swedenberg, Berkeley: University of California Press, 1970, vol. x;
compare l. 154 below and Jump's note). Dryden may have had this episode
in mind, but it may also reflect a broader legend.

125. *at any hand*] on any account (*OED*, 'hand', sb. 25g).

126. *will he . . . waters?*] 'will he not be ready for anything?' (Boas, com-
paring *TN*, IV.ii.63: 'I am for all waters'), or, will he not go anywhere (Greg).
In either case, the phrase was proverbial (Dent W131.11).

127. *he will . . . waters*] Faustus puns on the literal meaning: O, he'll drink
from any water he comes to. But don't ride him into it.

Horse-courser. Well, sir. [*Aside.*] Now am I made man for   130
ever. I'll not leave my horse for forty. If he had but the
quality of hey, ding, ding, hey, ding, ding, I'd make a
brave living on him; he has a buttock as slick as an eel.
[*To Faustus.*] Well, goodbye, sir. Your boy will deliver
him me? But hark ye, sir: if my horse be sick or ill at   135
ease, if I bring his water to you, you'll tell me what it is?
Faustus. Away, you villain! What, dost think I am a horse-
doctor?

                                        Exit HORSE-COURSER.

What art thou, Faustus, but a man condemned to die?
Thy fatal time doth draw to final end.   140
Despair doth drive distrust unto my thoughts.
Confound these passions with a quiet sleep.
Tush! Christ did call the thief upon the cross;
Then rest thee, Faustus, quiet in conceit.

                                        Sleep in his chair.

---

130. s.d.] *Dyce 1; not in A1.*   134. s.d.] *Jump; not in A1.*   134. goodbye]
A1 (god buy).   138.1. s.d.] *placed as in Dyce 1; printed after l. 136 in
A1.*   139.] *verse as in Dyce 1; as prose in A1.*

---

130. *made man*] See note to III.ii.1. *OED* gives this as the first instance
('made', ppl. adj. 7), but Dent (MM1) cites some earlier examples.
    131. *I'll . . . forty*] Forty is frequently used as an indefinite large number,
as in *Cor.*, III.i.248: 'I could beat forty of them', and *Wiv.*, I.i.182: 'I had
rather than forty shillings.' But here the joke is in the anticlimax: 'I wouldn't
sell this horse for—exactly what I paid for it.'
    131–3. *If he . . . eel*] i.e., if the horse is virile, I can make a fine living by
charging stud fees. The refrain *hey, ding, ding, hey, ding, ding,* often found in
Elizabethan popular songs (e.g., *AYLI*, v.iii.19: 'When birds do sing, hey
ding a ding, ding'), could have vulgar connotations, as it does in Nashe's
Have With You to Saffron Walden, 1596: 'Yea, Madam Gabriela, are you such
an old jerker? Then hey ding a ding, up with your petticoat, have at your
plum-tree' (ed. McKerrow, III.113). The slick buttock and the eel suggest
virility. 'Slick as an eel' is a common comparison (Dent E60).
    136. *water*] urine, regularly used in medical diagnosis.
    140. *fatal time*] (*a*) time allotted by fate (Ward) (*b*) time of death.
    142. *Confound*] silence, allay, disperse. (Said to himself.)
    143.] Faustus alludes to Luke xxiii.43: 'Then Jesus said unto him [the
repentant thief], "Verily I say unto thee, today shalt thou be with me in
Paradise."'
    144. *in conceit*] in mind (*OED*, sb. 1).

Enter HORSE-COURSER *all wet, crying.*

Horse-courser. Alas, alas! 'Doctor' Fustian, quotha! Mass,   145
Doctor Lopus was never such a doctor. H'as given me a
purgation, h'as purged me of forty dollars. I shall never
see them more. But yet, like an ass as I was, I would not
be ruled by him, for he bade me I should ride him into no
water. Now I, thinking my horse had had some rare   150
quality that he would not have had me known of, I, like a
venturous youth, rid him into the deep pond at the
town's end. I was no sooner in the middle of the pond but
my horse vanished away and I sat upon a bottle of hay,
never so near drowning in my life. But I'll seek out my   155
doctor and have my forty dollars again, or I'll make it the
dearest horse! O, yonder is his snipper-snapper.—Do you
hear? You, hey-pass, where's your master?
Mephistopheles. Why, sir, what would you? You cannot speak
with him.   160
Horse-courser. But I will speak with him.
Mephistopheles. Why, he's fast asleep. Come some other time.

---

158. hey-pass] *A1* (hey, passe).

146. *Doctor Lopus*] Dr Lopez, the Portuguese Jewish physician who was
hanged in 1594 for his purported role in a plot to poison Queen Elizabeth,
was evidently well known as Elizabeth's physician from the time of his
appointment in 1586. Greg (p. 32) argues that the A-text contains revision
from 1594 or later, but see note at I.iv.34.
146–7.] 'To give one's purse a purgation' is proverbial (Dent P663), and
particularly applicable to a medical doctor; see l. 136n. This purgation or
purge would have been an emetic—one that, in the unhappy patient's view,
has cleaned him out.
151. *known of*] aware of. Compare *Oth.* (Q1), III.iii.335: 'Be not you
known on't.'
154. *bottle*] bundle (*OED*, sb.³).
157. *dearest*] most expensive. The Horse-courser implies revenge.
snipper-snapper] 'a young insignificant or conceited fellow' (*OED*, giving
this as its first citation). Compare 'whipper-snapper'. The Horse-courser
plainly views Mephistopheles as a manservant of Faustus, his 'master'
(l. 158).
158. *hey-pass*] 'an exclamation of jugglers commanding an article to move:
often joined with *repass*. Hence a name for the command, and an appellation
of a juggler' (*OED*, 'Hey', int. 3c, giving this as its first citation). The phrase
appears also in Nashe's *Piers Penniless* and *The Unfortunate Traveller*, 1594
(ed. McKerrow, I.184 and II.259).

Horse-courser. I'll speak with him now, or I'll break his glass
windows about his ears.
Mephistopheles. I tell thee he has not slept this eight nights.   165
Horse-courser. An he have not slept this eight weeks, I'll speak
with him.
Mephistopheles. See where he is, fast asleep.
Horse-courser. Ay, this is he.—God save ye, Master Doctor.
Master Doctor, Master Doctor Fustian! Forty dollars,   170
forty dollars for a bottle of hay!
Mephistopheles. Why, thou seest he hears thee not.
Horse-courser. (*Holler in his ear.*) So-ho, ho! So-ho, ho!
No, will you not wake? I'll make you wake ere I go.
                    Pull him by the leg, and pull it away.
Alas, I am undone! What shall I do?   175
Faustus. O my leg, my leg! Help, Mephistopheles! Call the
officers! My leg, my leg!
Mephistopheles. [*Seizing the Horse-courser.*] Come, villain, to
the constable.
Horse-courser. O Lord, sir, let me go, and I'll give you forty   180
dollars more.
Mephistopheles. Where be they?
Horse-courser. I have none about me. Come to my hostry, and
I'll give them you.
Mephistopheles. Begone, quickly.   185
                    HORSE-COURSER *runs away.*
Faustus. What, is he gone? Farewell, he! Faustus has his leg
again, and the Horse-courser, I take it, a bottle of hay for
his labour. Well, this trick shall cost him forty dollars
more.

173. S.D. *Holler*] A1 (*Hallow*).   178. S.D.] *This ed.; not in* A1.   183.
hostry] A1 (*Oastrie*).

163–4. *break . . . about his ears*] The wording seems to derive from an
unrelated episode in the *Damnable Life* in which the Knight hits his new-
found horns 'against the glass that the panes thereof flew about his ears'
(ch. 30).
    glass windows] spectacles.
    165. *this eight nights*] for a week now.
    173. *So-ho*] a call of huntsmen directing the dog or other hunters to the
hare or to encourage them in the chase (*OED*).
    183. *hostry*] hostelry, inn.
    186. *Farewell, he*] i.e., good riddance.
    187. *again*] as before (*OED*, adv. 3b).

Enter WAGNER.

How now, Wagner, what's the news with thee?   190
Wagner. Sir, the Duke of Vanholt doth earnestly entreat your
     company.
Faustus. The Duke of Vanholt! An honourable gentleman, to
     whom I must be no niggard of my cunning. Come,
     Mephistopheles, let's away to him.   *Exeunt.*   195

[IV.ii]

[*Enter* FAUSTUS *with* MEPHISTOPHELES.] *Enter to them
the* DUKE [OF VANHOLT] *and the* [*pregnant*] DUCHESS.
The DUKE *speaks.*

Duke. Believe me, Master Doctor, this merriment hath much
     pleaoed me.
Faustus. My gracious lord, I am glad it contents you so
     well.—But it may be, madam, you take no delight in
     this. I have heard that great-bellied women do long for   5
     some dainties or other. What is it, madam? Tell me, and
     you shall have it.

IV.ii.0.1. S.D. *Enter* FAUSTUS *with* MEPHISTOPHELES] B1 *(subst.); not in* A1.
0.2. S.D. OF VANHOLT] B1; *not in* A1; OF ANHOLT *Boas.*   0.2. S.D.
pregnant] *Kirschbaum; not in* A1.

---

191. *Vanholt*] The spelling is *Anholt* in the *Damnable Life* and *Anhalt* in
the German original. Anhalt 'is a duchy of central Germany, almost on the
eastern borders of which lies Wittenberg (in Prussian Saxony)' (Greg).

IV.ii.0.1. S.D. Enter to them] The awkward presence of Faustus and
Mephistopheles in this scene immediately after their having exited from the
previous one (something that occurs only rarely in Elizabethan drama; see
Appendix), together with the fact that B1 provides a comic scene at this
point, suggests some sort of textual rearrangement in A1 or perhaps a
lost scene (especially since the A-text overall is so short; see Introduction,
pp. 69–71). Moreover, no entrance is provided in A1 for Faustus and
Mephistopheles; the Duke and Duchess *Enter to them* as though they are
already on stage. Yet they cannot have remained on stage from the previous
scene, for Faustus there announces his intention of going to the Duke of
Vanholt's court in answer to the invitation. As the text imperfectly stands,
Faustus and Mephistopheles must exit and re-enter, thereby establishing a
shift in time and place. The dialogue resumes in mid conversation; during
the interim, evidently, Faustus has demonstrated his skill.
5. *great-bellied*] pregnant.

Duchess. Thanks, good Master Doctor. And, for I see your
courteous intent to pleasure me, I will not hide from you
the thing my heart desires. And were it now summer, as   10
it is January and the dead time of the winter, I would
desire no better meat than a dish of ripe grapes.
Faustus.   Alas,   madam,   that's   nothing.   [*Aside   to*
Mephistopheles.] Mephistopheles, begone!
                                    Exit MEPHISTOPHELES.
Were it a greater thing than this, so it would content you,   15
you should have it.

          Enter MEPHISTOPHELES *with the grapes.*

Here they be, madam. Will't please you taste on them?
                              [*The Duchess tastes the grapes.*]
Duke. Believe me, Master Doctor, this makes me wonder
above the rest, that, being in the dead time of winter and
in the month of January, how you should come by these   20
grapes.
Faustus. If it like your Grace, the year is divided into two
circles over the whole world, that when it is here winter
with us, in the contrary circle it is summer with them, as
in India, Saba, and farther countries in the East; and by   25
means of a swift spirit that I have, I had them brought
hither, as ye see.—How do you like them, madam? Be
they good?
Duchess. Believe me, Master Doctor, they be the best grapes
that e'er I tasted in my life before.   30
Faustus. I am glad they content you so, madam.

8.] *prose as in Dyce 1; as verse divided at* doctor, / And *in A1.*   13–14. S.D.]
This ed.; not in A1.   17.1. S.D.] *This ed.; not in A1.*

9. *pleasure*] please.
12. *meat*] food.
13–14. S.D. Aside to Mephistopheles] Mephistopheles is assumed to be
invisible in this scene, as in several previous scenes.
24. *in the contrary circle*] The notion that the East enjoys summer during
Europe's winter season is understandable in view of the warmer climate in
countries like India and Saba (i.e., Sheba, mentioned at II.i.160). Factually,
of course, the *contrary circle* should be in the southern hemisphere. In the B-
text version, Faustus clearly refers to a climate that bears fruit twice a year
rather than, as the present passage suggests, to the inverse seasons of the
northern and southern hemispheres.

Duke. Come, madam, let us in,
   Where you must well reward this learnèd man
   For the great kindness he hath showed to you.
Duchess. And so I will, my lord, and whilst I live   35
   Rest beholding for this courtesy.
Faustus. I humbly thank your Grace.
Duke. Come, Master Doctor, follow us and receive your reward.
                                        Exeunt.

32–4.] *as verse this ed.; as prose in A1.*

------

36. *Rest beholding*] remain indebted.

Act V

[v.i]

Enter WAGNER *solus.*

Wagner. I think my master means to die shortly,
For he hath given to me all his goods.
And yet methinks if that death were near
He would not banquet and carouse and swill
Amongst the students, as even now he doth,   5
Who are at supper with such belly-cheer
As Wagner ne'er beheld in all his life.
See where they come. Belike the feast is ended.   [*Exit.*]

Enter FAUSTUS *with two or three* SCHOLARS
[*and* MEPHISTOPHELES].

First Scholar. Master Doctor Faustus, since our conference

---

v.i.8. s.d. *Exit*] B1; *not in* A1.   8.2. s.d. *and* MEPHISTOPHELES] B1 *lists
'Mephostophilis' after 'Faustus'; not in* A1.

---

v.i.o.1. s.d. Enter WAGNER solus] In the B-text, devils carry a banquet
over the stage '*into Faustus's study*'. The opening monologue of the present
scene, ll 4–8, plainly indicates that a banquet is in progress behind the
scenes, but the devils are not necessary to the staging and are the kind of
elaboration found elsewhere in the B-text version.

1–8.] Wagner's speech bears some resemblance to his choric speech at
III.Chorus, especially in setting the stage for what follows ('See where they
come', l. 8). In this case, however, because Wagner plainly speaks 'in
character' as the servant of Faustus, the speech is treated textually as part of
v.i, rather than as a formal chorus. Compare B v.i.1–9.

4. *swill*] drink heavily (*OED*, v. 3b).

8. *Belike*] in all likelihood.

8. s.d. *Exit*] B1's indication of an exit here suggests that the omission in
A1 is inadvertent, though Wagner could conceivably remain on stage (Greg).

8.1. s.d. with two or three] On the likelihood that an authorial manuscript
stands behind such imprecise stage directions, see Introduction, p. 67.

8.2. s.d. *and* MEPHISTOPHELES] A1 makes no mention of Mephostophiles
at this point. His entry here in B1 might be viewed as the kind of elaboration
we find elsewhere in the B-text, except that Mephostophiles has to be on
stage at ll. 51 ff. He could conceivably enter at ll. 25 or 51.

9. *our conference*] The First Scholar refers to an ongoing conversation
among the scholars on a familiar topic, one that hearkens back to Paris's

about fair ladies—which was the beautifull'st in all the   10
world—we have determined with ourselves that Helen of
Greece was the admirablest lady that ever lived. There-
fore, Master Doctor, if you will do us that favour as to let
us see that peerless dame of Greece, whom all the world
admires for majesty, we should think ourselves much   15
beholding unto you.
Faustus. Gentlemen,
For that I know your friendship is unfeigned,
And Faustus' custom is not to deny
The just requests of those that wish him well,   20
You shall behold that peerless dame of Greece
No otherways for pomp and majesty
Than when Sir Paris crossed the seas with her
And brought the spoils to rich Dardania.
Be silent then, for danger is in words.   25
        [MEPHISTOPHELES *goes to the door.*]

17-18.] *divided as in Dilke; as prose in A1; as one line in B1.*   19-25.]
verse as in B1; as prose in A1.   25.1. S.D. MEPHISTOPHELES *goes to the door*]
This ed.; not in A1.

---

decision to award the golden apple inscribed 'For the fairest' to Aphrodite—a
judgement that resulted in the abduction of Helen and the Trojan War.
   11. *determined with*] settled among (*OED*, v. 4).
   14-15. *that peerless . . . majesty*] These phrases anticipate ll. 21 and 27.
   18. *For that*] because.
   22. *otherways*] otherwise.
   for] as regards, with respect to (*OED*, prep. 26).
   23. *Sir*] 'the chivalrous prefix of mediaeval romance' (Ward).
   24. *spoils*] booty, including Helen.
   Dardania] Troy, so named for the city built on the Hellespont reputedly by
Dardanus, ancestor of the kings of Troy.
   25. *Be silent then*] Silence was necessary during magical performances.
Frank Kermode notes that in the third book of his *Occult Philosophy*,
Agrippa explains that a talkative companion can ruin an experiment (New
Arden *Temp.*, 1954, p. 97). Compare Prospero's warning to Ferdinand and
Miranda as the masque begins in *Temp.*, IV.i.59: 'No tongue! All eyes! Be
silent.' Such language is also a good way of getting a theatre audience to pay
attention to an important moment.
   25.1. S.D. *MEPHISTOPHELES* goes to the door] Although Faustus here
works his magic without explicitly calling on Mephistopheles, as he has
invariably done previously, the B-text's stage direction in the parallel scene,
Mephistopheles brings in HELEN (implying a prior exit for that purpose), offers
a compelling parallel.

Music sounds. [MEPHISTOPHELES *returns,*]
and HELEN *passeth over the stage.*

Second Scholar. Too simple is my wit to tell her praise,
    Whom all the world admires for majesty.
Third Scholar. No marvel though the angry Greeks pursued
    With ten years' war the rape of such a queen,
    Whose heavenly beauty passeth all compare.   30
First Scholar. Since we have seen the pride of nature's works
    And only paragon of excellence,

Enter an OLD MAN.

Let us depart; and for this glorious deed
Happy and blest be Faustus evermore.
Faustus. Gentlemen, farewell. The same I wish to you.   35
                    Exeunt SCHOLARS.
Old Man. Ah, Doctor Faustus, that I might prevail
    To guide thy steps unto the way of life,
    By which sweet path thou mayst attain the goal
    That shall conduct thee to celestial rest!
    Break heart, drop blood, and mingle it with tears—   40
    Tears falling from repentant heaviness
    Of thy most vile and loathsome filthiness,
    The stench whereof corrupts the inward soul
    With such flagitious crimes of heinous sins
    As no commiseration may expel   45
    But mercy, Faustus, of thy Saviour sweet,
    Whose blood alone must wash away thy guilt.

25.2. S.D. MEPHISTOPHELES *returns*] B1 (*Mephosto brings in Hellen*); not
in A1.

25.3. S.D. passeth over the stage] a common stage direction in Renaissance
dramatic texts for entry by one door and exit by another. Allardyce Nicoll's
theory of entry through the yard and out again through the yard on the other
side of the stage is probably unnecessarily elaborate; see 'Passing Over the
Stage', *SSur. XII* (1959), 47–55.
    28. *pursued*] avenged (*OED*, v. 1b).
    29. *rape*] carrying away by force (*OED*, sb.² 2).
    30. *compare*] comparison (*OED*, sb.²).
    34. *Happy and blest*] blessed with good fortune (but with ironic application
to the state of spiritual grace).
    44. *flagitious*] extremely wicked, heinous.

Faustus.
Where art thou, Faustus? Wretch, what hast thou done?
Damned art thou, Faustus, damned! Despair and die!
Hell calls for right, and with a roaring voice   50
Says, 'Faustus, come! Thine hour is come.'
                    Mephistopheles gives him a dagger.
And Faustus will come to do thee right.
                    [*Faustus prepares to stab himself.*]
Old Man. Ah, stay, good Faustus, stay thy desperate steps!
I see an angel hovers o'er thy head,
And with a vial full of precious grace   55
Offers to pour the same into thy soul.
Then call for mercy and avoid despair.
Faustus. Ah, my sweet friend, I feel thy words
To comfort my distressèd soul.
Leave me a while to ponder on my sins   60
Old Man. I go, sweet Faustus, but with heavy cheer,
Fearing the ruin of thy hopeless soul.   [*Exit.*]
Faustus. Accursèd Faustus, where is mercy now?
I do repent, and yet I do despair.
Hell strives with grace for conquest in my breast.   65
What shall I do to shun the snares of death?
Mephistopheles. Thou traitor, Faustus, I arrest thy soul
For disobedience to my sovereign lord.

52.1. S.D.] *Jump (subst.); not in A1.*   55. vial] *A1* (violl).   62. S.D.] *B1;
not in A1.*

48. *Where art thou, Faustus?*] Compare Genesis iii.9: 'But the Lord God
called to the man, and said unto him, "Where art thou?" '
    50. *roaring*] Compare 1 Peter v.8: 'the devil, as a roaring lion'.
    51.] Compare John xiii.1: 'Jesus knew that his hour was come, that he
should depart out of this world' (Cornelius, p. 268).
    52. *do thee right*] pay you what is due, pay the 'right' that is called for in l.
50.
    54–6.] Although Revelation v.8 speaks of 'golden vials full of odours,
which are the prayers of saints', most images of vials in that apocalyptic book
are instruments of divine vengeance, as at xvi.1: 'And I heard a great voice
out of the temple, saying to the seven angels, "Go your ways, and pour out
the vials of the wrath of God upon the earth." ' See also Revelation xv.7,
xvi.4, 8, 10, 12, 17, xvii.1, and xxi.9 (Ormerod–Wortham, Cornelius, p.
268). The biblical echo sets up an ironically ominous contrast between vials
of wrath and vials of grace (especially Extreme Unction).
    61. *heavy cheer*] downcast mood and countenance (*OED*, 'cheer', sb. 2–3).

Revolt, or I'll in piecemeal tear thy flesh.

Faustus. Sweet Mephistopheles, entreat thy lord   70
To pardon my unjust presumption,
And with my blood again I will confirm
My former vow I made to Lucifer.

Mephistopheles. Do it then quickly, with unfeignèd heart,
Lest greater danger do attend thy drift.   75

[*Faustus cuts his arm and writes with his blood.*]

Faustus. Torment, sweet friend, that base and crooked age
That durst dissuade me from thy Lucifer,
With greatest torments that our hell affords.

Mephistopheles. His faith is great. I cannot touch his soul.
But what I may afflict his body with
I will attempt, which is but little worth.   80

Faustus. One thing, good servant, let me crave of thee
To glut the longing of my heart's desire:
That I might have unto my paramour
That heavenly Helen which I saw of late,
Whose sweet embracings may extinguish clean   85
These thoughts that do dissuade me from my vow,
And keep mine oath I made to Lucifer.

Mephistopheles. Faustus, this, or what else thou shalt desire,
Shall be performed in twinkling of an eye.   90

75.1. S.D.] *Boas (subst.), conj. Dyce 1; not in A1.*

69. *Revolt*] return to your allegiance to Lucifer (*OED*, 2b).

74. *unfeignèd heart*] Mephistopheles's language ironically recalls 1 Timothy i.5: 'For the end of the commandment is love out of a pure heart, and of a good conscience, and of faith unfeigned.'

75. *thy drift*] the direction you're drifting in.

76. *sweet friend*] with ironic repetition of Faustus's way of addressing the Old Man in l. 58.

crooked age] old man. Although the *OED* quotes no instance of *age* being used for an old man, Autolycus calls the Shepherd 'Age' in *WT*, IV.iv.764 (Ward). The figure of speech is a familiar one, and readily available to Marlowe.

84. *unto*] as.

86. *clean*] wholly (*OED*, 'clean', adv. 5). The A-text reading is supported by *2Tamb.*, v.iii.89: 'Is almost clean extinguishèd'.

90. *in . . . eye*] a familiar expression (Dent T635).

Enter HELEN [*brought in by* MEPHISTOPHELES].

Faustus. Was this the face that launched a thousand ships
And burnt the topless towers of Ilium?
Sweet Helen, make me immortal with a kiss.
                                    [*They kiss.*]
Her lips sucks forth my soul. See where it flies!
Come, Helen, come, give me my soul again.   95
                                    [*They kiss again.*]
Here will I dwell, for heaven be in these lips,
And all is dross that is not Helena.

Enter OLD MAN.

I will be Paris, and for love of thee
Instead of Troy shall Wittenberg be sacked,
And I will combat with weak Menelaus,   100
And wear thy colours on my plumèd crest.
Yea, I will wound Achilles in the heel

90.1. S.D. *brought in by* MEPHISTOPHELES] *This ed.; not in* A1.   93.1. S.D.
They kiss] B7 *(Kisses her); not in* A1.   95.1. S.D.] *This ed.; not in* A1.

91.] This famous line almost certainly derives from Lucian's *Dialogues of
the Dead* (xviii in traditional arrangement; v in the Loeb Library), where
Hermes shows Menippus the skull of Helen and he responds: 'Was it then
for this that the thousand ships were manned from all of Greece?' (see W. H.
Williams, 'Marlowe and Lucian', *MLR*, X (1915), 222, and W. S.
Heckscher, 'Was this the face . . . ?' *Journal of the Warburg and Courtauld
Institutes*, II (1937–8), 295–7). Compare *2Tamb.*, II.iv.87–8: 'Helen, whose
beauty summoned Greece to arms / And drew a thousand ships to Tenedos'.
    92. *topless*] immeasurably high, so high as to be invisible. Compare *Dido*,
IV.iii.12: 'topless hills'.
    Ilium] i.e., Troy.
    93. *make . . . kiss*] Marlowe uses the same phrase in *Dido*, IV.4.123.
    94. *sucks*] For singular ending, see Abbott 333 and III.i.12, 32, and 36
above.
    100. *Menelaus*] Helen's husband, often presented in demeaning terms as
the ineffectual cuckold; hence, described here as 'weak'.
    101.] The image recalls medieval versions of the tale of Troy (Ward).
    102.] The infant Achilles was plunged by his mother into the River Styx
and was thus invulnerable except for the heel by which he was held. Eventually he was shot in the heel by Paris (as in this account) or by Apollo. The
story gives a name to the Achilles's heel or tendon as a vulnerable spot.

And then return to Helen for a kiss.
O, thou art fairer than the evening air,
Clad in the beauty of a thousand stars.   105
Brighter art thou than flaming Jupiter
When he appeared to hapless Semele,
More lovely than the monarch of the sky
In wanton Arethusa's azured arms;
And none but thou shalt be my paramour.   110

           Exeunt [FAUSTUS *and* HELEN].

Old Man. Accursèd Faustus, miserable man,
That from thy soul exclud'st the grace of heaven
And fliest the throne of His tribunal seat!

      Enter the Devils. [*They menace the Old Man.*]

Satan begins to sift me with his pride.
As in this furnace God shall try my faith,   115
My faith, vile hell, shall triumph over thee.

110.1. S.D. FAUSTUS *and* HELEN] *Boas (subst.); not in A1.*   113.1. S.D.
They menace the Old Man] This ed.; not in A1.

107. *Semele*] Semele urged her lover, Zeus or Jupiter, to appear to her in
his full splendour as a god. When he did so she was consumed by lightning,
thereby becoming (for some Renaissance mythographers at least) an emblem
of presumptuousness punished by divine fury. See Ovid, *Metamorphoses*,
iii.259–315.
    109.] The nymph Arethusa fled from the river god Alpheus, whose lust
she had awakened by bathing in his stream, and was transformed by Artemis
into a fountain. The story was sometimes allegorised into the soul's pursuit of
truth (Ormerod–Wortham), but Faustus speaks of Arethusa more as if she
were one of Jupiter's conquests, or perhaps of the sun god ('the monarch of
the sky', l. 108); George Sandys, in his commentary on book v of the
Metamorphoses, states that the river god Alpheus 'drew his pedigree from the
sun' (*Ovid's Metamorphoses Englished*, London: W. Barret, 1621; cited by Gill
3). Arethusa's arms are spoken of here as 'azured' by the blue reflection in
the water of the sky (Bowers).
    113.1. S.D.] Presumably the Devils, armed with pitchforks, menace the
Old Man but are repulsed through the strength of his faith (ll. 116–18).
    114.] Compare Luke xxii.31: 'Satan hath earnestly desired to have you,
that he may sift you as wheat.' Since, as Ormerod–Wortham observe, the
Geneva Bible reads 'winnow' for 'sift', Marlowe must have remembered the
Bishops' Bible here.
    115. *furnace*] alluding to the fiery furnace of Daniel iii.

Ambitious fiends, see how the heavens smiles
At your repulse and laughs your state to scorn!
Hence, hell! For hence I fly unto my God.

                                        Exeunt [different ways].

[v.ii]

                    Enter FAUSTUS *with the* SCHOLARS.

Faustus. Ah, gentlemen!
First Scholar. What ails Faustus?
Faustus. Ah, my sweet chamber-fellow! Had I lived with thee,
    then had I lived still, but now I die eternally. Look,
    comes he not? Comes he not?   referring to Lucifer   5
Second Scholar. What means Faustus?
Third Scholar. Belike he is grown into some sickness by being
    over-solitary.
First Scholar. If it be so, we'll have physicians to cure him.
    [*To Faustus.*] 'Tis but a surfeit. Never fear, man.   10
Faustus. A surfeit of deadly sin that hath damned both body
    and soul.
Second Scholar. Yet, Faustus, look up to heaven. Remember
    God's mercies are infinite.
Faustus. But Faustus' offence can ne'er be pardoned. The   15
    serpent that tempted Eve may be saved, but not Faustus.
    Ah, gentlemen, hear me with patience, and tremble not at
    my speeches. Though my heart pants and quivers to
    remember that I have been a student here these thirty
    years, O, would I had never seen Wittenberg, never read   20
    book! And what wonders I have done, all Germany

119.1. S.D. *different ways*] Dyce 1 *(subst.); not in A1.*   V.ii.10. S.D.] *This ed.;
not in A1.*   15–16. But . . . saved] *prose as in Dilke; as verse divided at*
pardoned, / The *in A1.*   18. speeches. Though] *Dyce 1 (subst.);* speeches,
though *A1.*

117–18.] The Old Man uses the language of Psalms ii.4: 'He that dwelleth
in heaven will laugh them to scorn' (Bishops' Bible; see Cornelius, p. 271).
Compare *1Tamb.*, I.i.117: 'laughs our regiment to scorn'. For the singular
endings of *smiles* and *laughs*, see Abbott 333.

v.ii.16. *but not*] i.e., sooner than.
18. *pants*] throbs, palpitates (*OED*, v. 3).

can witness, yea, all the world, for which Faustus hath
lost both Germany and the world, yea, heaven itself—
heaven, the seat of God, the throne of the blessed, the
kingdom of joy—and must remain in hell for ever. Hell,   25
ah, hell for ever! Sweet friends, what shall become of
Faustus, being in hell for ever?
Third Scholar. Yet, Faustus, call on God.
Faustus. On God, whom Faustus hath abjured? On God,
whom Faustus hath blasphemed? Ah, my God, I would   30
weep, but the devil draws in my tears. Gush forth blood
instead of tears, yea, life and soul. O, he stays my tongue!
I would lift up my hands, but see, they hold them, they
hold them.
All. Who, Faustus?   35
Faustus. Lucifer and Mephistopheles. Ah, gentlemen! I gave
them my soul for my cunning.
All. God forbid!
Faustus. God forbade it indeed, but Faustus hath done it. For
vain pleasure of four-and-twenty years hath Faustus lost   40
eternal joy and felicity. I writ them a bill with mine own
blood. The date is expired, the time will come, and he
will fetch me.
First Scholar. Why did not Faustus tell us of this before, that
divines might have prayed for thee?   45
Faustus. Oft have I thought to have done so, but the devil
threatened to tear me in pieces if I named God, to fetch

36–7.] *prose as in B1; divided at* Mephastophilis. / Ah Gentlemen! *in A1.*
40. four-and-twenty] *A1* (24.); foure and twenty *B1.*

22–3. *all the world . . . lost*] The language recalls Mark viii.36: 'For what
shall it profit a man, if he shall win all the world, and lose his own soul?'
(Bishops' Bible; see Cornelius, p. 273).
  31. *the devil . . . tears*] a common sign of spiritual reprobation, as in James
VI and I's *Daemonology* (Edinburgh: R. Waldengrave, 1597), p. 81 (Gill 3).
  39. *God forbade*] Faustus plays mordantly on the strict meaning of the
scholars' 'God forbid', a conventional mild expostulation that has the flavour
of 'We pray to God it isn't so'.
  40. *vain*] fruitless, worthless (*OED*, adj. 1).
  four-and-twenty] The A1 reading, '24', could be expanded to *twenty-four*,
especially in a prose line, but the B1 reading of *foure and twenty* offers useful
authority here; compare I.iii.93.
  41. *bill*] deed, as at II.i.65.
  46–7. *the devil . . . in pieces*] Bajazeth makes the same threat in *1Tamb.*,
IV.iv.38: 'legions of devils shall tear thee in pieces'.

both body and soul if I once gave ear to divinity. And
now 'tis too late. Gentlemen, away, lest you perish
with me.   50
Second Scholar. O, what shall we do to save Faustus?
Faustus. Talk not of me, but save yourselves and depart.
Third Scholar. God will strengthen me. I will stay with
Faustus.
First Scholar. [*To the Third Scholar.*] Tempt not God, sweet   55
friend, but let us into the next room and there pray
for him.
Faustus. Ay, pray for me, pray for me! And what noise soever
ye hear, come not unto me, for nothing can rescue me.
Second Scholar. Pray thou, and we will pray that God may   60
have mercy upon thee.
Faustus. Gentlemen, farewell. If I live till morning, I'll visit
you; if not, Faustus is gone to hell.
All. Faustus, farewell.   *Exeunt* SCHOLARS.
                                         The clock strikes eleven.
Faustus. Ah, Faustus,   65
Now hast thou but one bare hour to live,
And then thou must be damned perpetually.
Stand still, you ever-moving spheres of heaven,
That time may cease and midnight never come!
Fair nature's eye, rise, rise again, and make   70
Perpetual day; or let this hour be but
A year, a month, a week, a natural day,

51. save] *B1; not in A1.*   55. S.D.] *This ed.; not in A1.*   71–2.] *divided as
in Oxberry; divided at* but a yeere, / A moneth *in A1.*

51. *save*] This word, absent in A1 and supplied from B1, seems necessary
to Greg but intrusive to Warren (p. 123), who sees the differences in the texts
as possibly meaningful. To the present editors, as to Greg, the A1 version
does not make sense; colloquial usage would allow 'what shall we do with
Faustus', but to 'do' something 'to' him is to act upon him in some way that
is hard to imagine in the context, whereas the B-text reading is centrally
appropriate. The repetition of the word in the next line takes its force from
what the Second Scholar says. 'Don't worry about saving *me*', Faustus
replies: 'Save *yourselves.*'
55. *Tempt not God*] i.e., don't court God's anger by presumptuously
testing how far one can go with him (*OED*, 'tempt', v. 2a). Compare Christ's
answer to the first temptation in the wilderness: 'Thou shalt not tempt the
Lord thy God' (Matthew iv.7).
70. *Fair nature's eye*] the sun.

That Faustus may repent and save his soul!
O lente, lente currite noctis equi!
The stars move still; time runs; the clock will strike;   75
The devil will come, and Faustus must be damned.
O, I'll leap up to my God! Who pulls me down?
See, see where Christ's blood streams in the firmament!
One drop would save my soul, half a drop. Ah, my Christ!
Ah, rend not my heart for naming of my Christ!   80
Yet will I call on him. O, spare me, Lucifer!
Where is it now? 'Tis gone; and see where God
Stretcheth out his arm and bends his ireful brows!
Mountains and hills, come, come and fall on me,
And hide me from the heavy wrath of God!   85
No, no!
Then will I headlong run into the earth.
Earth, gape! O, no, it will not harbour me.

82–3.] *divided as in Dyce 1; divided at* gone: / And see . . . arme, / And bends
in *A1*.   86–7.] *divided as in Dyce 1; as one line in A1.*

74.] O, run slowly, slowly, ye horses of the night! Quoted, with effective
variation, from Ovid's *Amores*, I.xiii.40, where the speaker, as he embraces
Corinna, is imploring Aurora, goddess of the dawn, to imagine her own
reluctance to leave the arms of her lover. Marlowe translated this passage in
his *Ovid's Elegies*, and alludes to it also in *Dido*, I.i.26. The erotic undertone
in Faustus's cry of terror bespeaks his attachment to sensual and aesthetic
pleasure (Donald C. Baker, *Classical Journal*, LV (1959), 126–8).
    77.] The image of this line may have been suggested by a familiar
Renaissance emblem showing a man with one arm winged and raised toward
heaven, the other weighted down towards hell. One version of this emblem is
printed on the title-page of *A1* (1604). See also Geoffrey Whitney's *A Choice
of Emblems* (Leyden: F. Raphelengius, 1586), p. 152 (Ormerod–Wortham).
    82. *'Tis gone*] 'The vision of Christ's blood has faded because Faustus in
his terror has called on Lucifer' (Jump).
    84–5.] Compare Revelation vi.16: 'And said to the mountains and rocks,
"Fall on us, and hide us from the presence of him that sitteth on the throne,
and from the wrath of the Lamb," ' and Hosea x.8: 'and they shall say to the
mountains, "Cover us," and to the hills, "Fall on us." ' Luke xxiii.30 is
similar to Hosea.
    88. *Earth, gape!*] In *1Tamb.*, Zabina issues the same imperative, 'Gape,
earth' (V.i.242), not to escape the devil, but to allow the fiends to view the
hell on earth that Tamburlaine has created.

his fate was pre-determined.

You stars that reigned at my nativity, *birth*
Whose influence hath allotted death and hell,   90
Now draw up Faustus like a foggy mist
Into the entrails of yon labouring cloud, → *reborn*
That when you vomit forth into the air, *through me*
My limbs may issue from your smoky mouths, *clouds*
So that my soul may but ascend to heaven.   95

                   The watch strikes.

   Ah, half the hour is past!
'Twill all be past anon.
O God,
If thou wilt not have mercy on my soul,
Yet for Christ's sake, whose blood hath ransomed me,
Impose some end to my incessant pain.   100
Let Faustus live in hell a thousand years,
A hundred thousand, and at last be saved.
O, no end is limited to damnèd souls.
Why wert thou not a creature wanting soul?
Or why is this immortal that thou hast?   105
Ah, Pythagoras' *metempsychosis*, were that true,

his body will go to hell / his soul will ascend

asking for some and to the torment

95.1. S.D.] *placed as in* B1; *printed after* l. 96 *in* A1.   98–9.] *divided as in*
Dyce 2; *as one line in* A1.

89–95.] Faustus prays that the planets of his horoscope (whose positions
at the time of his birth determined his fate) may now suck him up into a
cloud, much as moisture is exhaled from the earth by the sun, where his
earthly body may be violently expelled in a thunderbolt and his soul thereby
freed to ascend to heaven.
    89.] Compare *1Tamb.*, IV.ii.33: 'Smile, stars that reigned at my nativity.'
    90. *influence*] 'the supposed flowing or streaming from the stars or heavens
of an ethereal fluid acting upon the character and destiny of men' (*OED*, sb.
2).
    92–4. *labouring cloud . . . mouths*] The Renaissance belief that lightning
resulted from a conflict between a compacted exhalation and an enclosing
cloud derived from Aristotle's *Metaphysics*, ii.369a. Compare *1Tamb.*,
IV.ii.43–4: 'As when a fiery exhalation / Wrapt in the bowels of a freezing
cloud'. 'You' and 'your' in ll. 93–4 must refer to the cloud, by attraction to
that nearby substantive (as Boas argues), even though grammatically they
seem to refer back to 'You stars' (l. 89).
    95.1. S.D. watch] clock.
    104. *limited*] appointed, fixed definitely (*OED*, v. 1).
    105. *wanting*] lacking.
    107. *Pythagoras' metempsychosis*] The doctrine of the transmigration of
souls, attributed to the sixth–century (BC) Greek philosopher Pythagoras of
Samos, was a favourite topic of the Elizabethans. Compare *TN*, IV.ii.50–60.

This soul should fly from me and I be changed
Unto some brutish beast.
All beasts are happy, for, when they die,   110
Their souls are soon dissolved in elements;
But mine must live still to be plagued in hell.
Curst be the parents that engendered me!
No, Faustus, curse thyself. Curse Lucifer,
That hath deprived thee of the joys of heaven.   115

[handwritten margin note: hoping for a new religion taking responsibility and cursing Lucifer]

                    The clock striketh twelve.
O, it strikes, it strikes! Now, body, turn to air,
Or Lucifer will bear thee quick to hell.
                    Thunder and lightning.
O soul, be changed into little waterdrops,
And fall into the ocean, ne'er be found!
My God, my God, look not so fierce on me!   120

    Enter [LUCIFER, MEPHISTOPHELES, *and other*] Devils.

Adders and serpents, let me breathe a while!
Ugly hell, gape not. Come not, Lucifer!
I'll burn my books. Ah, Mephistopheles!
               [*The* Devils] *exeunt with him.*

109-10.] *divided as in B1; as one line in A1.*   120.1. S.D. LUCIFER,
MEPHISTOPHELES, *and other*] This ed.; *not in A1.*   123.1. S.D. *The* Devils]
Dyce 1 (subst.); *not in A1.*

---

112. *still*] ever (*OED*, adv. 4).
117. *quick*] alive.
118-19.] Compare Andrew Marvell's 'On a Drop of Dew' (1681) for a
later expression of this metaphor of the soul's return to an undifferentiating
universal nature. The idea is traceable to medieval non-Christian Arab
philosophers (Ormerod–Wortham).
120.] Compare Psalms xxii.1-2: 'My God, my God, why hast thou
forsaken me?' and Mark xv.34.
123. *I'll burn my books*] A conventional form of abjuring magic (compare
drowning in *Temp.*, v.i.57), but here manifestly too late for Faustus. Roger
Bacon burned his books and John Dee claimed to have done so; Albertus
Magnus drowned his (David Woodman, *White Magic and English Renaissance
Drama*, p. 40). See also Andrew V. Ettin, 'Magic Into Art: the Magician's
Renunciation of Magic in English Renaissance Drama', *TSLL*, XIX (1977),
268-93.

[Epilogue]

Enter CHORUS.

Chorus. Cut is the branch that might have grown full straight,
And burnèd is Apollo's laurel bough
That sometime grew within this learnèd man.
Faustus is gone. Regard his hellish fall,
Whose fiendful fortune may exhort the wise   5
Only to wonder at unlawful things,
Whose deepness doth entice such forward wits
To practise more than heavenly power permits.   [*Exit.*]

Terminat hora diem; terminat author opus.

Epilogue.1. s.h. *Chorus*] *Dyce 1; not in A1.*   8. s.d.] *Dyce 2; not in A1.*

Epilogue.2. *Apollo's laurel bough*] Apollo, god of light, oracles, and
prophecy, was also invoked as the patron of poetry and music (as in Virgil's
Eclogues), and was thus often portrayed wearing a laurel bough as emblem of
distinction in poetry.
    3. *sometime*] formerly.
    9.] The hour ends the day; the author ends his work. A conventional
motto, found also at the end of the manuscript play *Charlemagne* (1584–c.
1605). It may have been added here by the printer.

DOCTOR FAUSTUS
B-text (1616)

The Tragicall History of the Life and Death

of *Doctor Faustus*.

With new Additions.

VVritten by *Ch. Mar.*

LONDON,
Printed for *John Wright*, and are to be fold at his fhop without
Newgate, at the figne of the Bible. 1619.

Title-page of the Quarto (B2) of 1619. This is the first edition of the B-text to be advertised 'With new Additions'. Courtesy of the Princeton University Library.

[DRAMATIS PERSONAE

THE CHORUS.
DOCTOR JOHN FAUSTUS.
WAGNER.
GOOD ANGEL.
BAD ANGEL.   5
VALDES.
CORNELIUS.
THREE SCHOLARS.
LUCIFER.
DEVILS.   10
MEPHISTOPHELES.
ROBIN, *the Clown.*
A WOMAN DEVIL.
DICK.
BEELZEBUB.   15
PRIDE.
COVETOUSNESS.
ENVY.
WRATH.   } *The Seven Deadly Sins*
GLUTTONY.   20
SLOTH.
LECHERY.
POPE ADRIAN.
RAYMOND, KING OF HUNGARY.
BRUNO, *the rival Pope.*   25
THE CARDINAL OF FRANCE.
THE CARDINAL OF PADUA.
THE ARCHBISHOP OF RHEIMS.
THE BISHOP OF LORRAINE.
MONKS.   30
FRIARS.
A VINTNER.
MARTINO.
FREDERICK.
OFFICERS.   35

DRAMATIS PERSONAE.1–54] *Oxberry (in hierarchical order); not in B1.*

GENTLEMEN.
BENVOLIO.
THE EMPEROR OF GERMANY, CHARLES V.
THE DUKE OF SAXONY.
ALEXANDER THE GREAT. ⎫   40
HIS PARAMOUR.   ⎬ *Spirits*
DARIUS.   ⎭
BELIMOTH.   ⎫ *Devils*
ASHTAROTH. ⎭
SOLDIERS.   45
A HORSE-COURSER.
A CARTER.
A HOSTESS.
THE DUKE OF VANHOLT.
THE DUCHESS OF VANHOLT.   50
A SERVANT.
HELEN OF TROY, *a spirit.*
AN OLD MAN.
TWO CUPIDS.]

The Tragedy of Doctor Faustus
(B-text)

[Prologue]

Enter CHORUS.

Chorus. Not marching in the fields of Trasimene
    Where Mars did mate the warlike Carthagens,
    Nor sporting in the dalliance of love
    In courts of kings where state is overturned,
    Nor in the pomp of proud audacious deeds,   5
    Intends our muse to vaunt his heavenly verse.
    Only this, gentles: we must now perform
    The form of Faustus' fortunes, good or bad.
    And now to patient judgements we appeal,
    And speak for Faustus in his infancy.   10
    Now is he born, of parents base of stock,
    In Germany, within a town called Rhode.
    At riper years to Wittenberg he went,
    Whereas his kinsmen chiefly brought him up.
    So much he profits in divinity   15
    That shortly he was graced with doctor's name,
    Excelling all, and sweetly can dispute
    In th'heavenly matters of theology;
    Till, swoll'n with cunning of a self-conceit,
    His waxen wings did mount above his reach,   20
    And melting, heavens conspired his overthrow.
    For, falling to a devilish exercise,
    And glutted now with learning's golden gifts,
    He surfeits upon cursèd necromancy;
    Nothing so sweet as magic is to him,   25
    Which he prefers before his chiefest bliss.
    And this the man that in his study sits.   [*Exit.*]

---

1. S.H. *Chorus*] Oxberry; *not in* B1.   12. Rhode] *Boas; Rhodes* B1.
27. S.D. *Exit*] A1; *not in* B1.

Prologue.6. *vaunt*] display proudly.

Act I

FAUSTUS *in his study.*

Faustus. Settle thy studies, Faustus, and begin
To sound the depth of that thou wilt profess.
Having commenced, be a divine in show,
Yet level at the end of every art,
And live and die in Aristotle's works.   5
Sweet *Analytics,* 'tis thou hast ravished me!
[*He reads.*] *Bene disserere est finis logices.*
Is to dispute well logic's chiefest end?
Affords this art no greater miracle?
Then read no more; thou hast attained that end.   10
A greater subject fitteth Faustus' wit.
Bid *Oeconomy* farewell, and Galen, come!
Be a physician, Faustus. Heap up gold,
And be eternised for some wondrous cure.
[*He reads.*] *Summum bonum medicinae sanitas*:   15
The end of physic is our body's health.
Why Faustus, hast thou not attained that end?
Are not thy bills hung up as monuments,

I.i.7, 15. S.D. *He reads*] Kirschbaum *(subst.); not in* B1.   7. logices] B4;
Logicis B1.   12. Oeconomy] A2–3, B1; Oncaymaeon A1; On kai me on
Bullen.

1.i.12. Oeconomy] This reading was defended by some early editors
(including Ward) as being Aristotle's term for the science of domestic
management; Aristotle was reputed to have written two books entitled
Oeconomonia. Ward cites R. Adamson's suggestion that Marlowe may have
had in mind a passage from the *Politics* where, shortly after giving a definition of the goal of medicine similar to that in l. 16, Aristotle declares that 'the
art of getting wealth is a part of the management of a household [i.e.,
oeconomics] and the art of medicine not' (bk. 1, ch. 10, 1258.a.28). *Oeconomy*
is unanimously rejected by modern editors in favour of '*On kai me on*'—
Bullen's persuasive emendation of A1's *Oncaymaeon. Oeconomy* is printed
here to preserve a distinction between A1 and B1 over which scholars have
differed, even though B1's indebtedness to the reading of A2–3 further
weakens its authority.

Whereby whole cities have escaped the plague
And thousand desperate maladies been cured?   20
Yet art thou still but Faustus, and a man.
Couldst thou make men to live eternally,
Or, being dead, raise them to life again,
Then this profession were to be esteemed.
Physic, farewell! Where is Justinian?   25
[*He reads.*] *Si una eademque res legatur duobus,*
Alter rem, alter valorem rei, etc.
A petty case of paltry legacies!
[*He reads.*] *Exhaereditare filium non potest pater nisi—*
Such is the subject of the Institute   30
And universal body of the law.
This study fits a mercenary drudge
Who aims at nothing but external trash—
Too servile and illiberal for me.
When all is done, divinity is best.   35
Jerome's Bible, Faustus, view it well.
[*He reads.*] *Stipendium peccati mors est.* Ha!
Stipendium, etc.
The reward of sin is death? That's hard.
[*He reads.*] *Si peccasse negamus, fallimur*   40
Et nulla est in nobis veritas.
If we say that we have no sin,
We deceive ourselves, and there is no truth in us.
Why then belike we must sin,
And so consequently die.   45
Ay, we must die an everlasting death.
What doctrine call you this? *Che serà, serà:*
What will be, shall be. Divinity, adieu!
                              [*He picks up a book of magic.*]
These metaphysics of magicians
And necromantic books are heavenly,   50
Lines, circles, letters, characters—
Ay, these are those that Faustus most desires.

26, 29, 37, 40. S.D. *He reads*] *Dyce 1 (subst.); not in B1.*   26. *legatur*] *Dilke;*
legatus B1.   29. *Exhaereditare*] *Dyce 1; Exhereditari B1.*   37–8. *Stipendium*
. . . etc.] *divided here this ed.; one line in B1.*   37. *Ha*] *treated typographically*
in B1 as though part of the quotation.   40–1.] *divided as in Boas; one*
line in B1.   48.1. S.D.] *Kirschbaum (subst.); not in B1.*   50. *necromantic*]
B1 (Negromantick).

O, what a world of profit and delight,
Of power, of honour, and omnipotence,
Is promised to the studious artisan!   55
All things that move between the quiet poles
Shall be at my command. Emperors and kings
Are but obeyed in their several provinces,
But his dominion that exceeds in this
Stretcheth as far as doth the mind of man.   60
A sound magician is a demigod.
Here, tire my brains to get a deity.
Wagner!

Enter WAGNER.

    Commend me to my dearest friends,
The German Valdes and Cornelius.
Request them earnestly to visit me.   65
Wagner. I will, sir.   *Exit.*
Faustus. Their conference will be a greater help to me
    Than all my labours, plod I ne'er so fast.

Enter the [GOOD] ANGEL *and* SPIRIT, [*the* BAD ANGEL].

Good Angel. O Faustus, lay that damnèd book aside
    And gaze not on it, lest it tempt thy soul   70
    And heap God's heavy wrath upon thy head!
    Read, read the Scriptures That is blasphemy.
Bad Angel. Go forward, Faustus, in that famous art
    Wherein all nature's treasure is contained.
    Be thou on earth as Jove is in the sky,   75
    Lord and commander of these elements.
                    Exeunt ANGELS.
Faustus. How am I glutted with conceit of this!
    Shall I make spirits fetch me what I please?
    Resolve me of all ambiguities?
    Perform what desperate enterprise I will?   80
    I'll have them fly to India for gold,
    Ransack the ocean for orient pearl,

---

63. S.D.] *placed as in Wagner, conj. Dyce 1; after l. 62 in B1.*   68.1. S.D.]
bracketed material this ed.; not in B1.   81. India] *A1; Indian B1.*

---

81. *India*] A1's reading replaces the obvious error of B1's *Indian*.

And search all corners of the new-found world
For pleasant fruits and princely delicates.
I'll have them read me strange philosophy   85
And tell the secrets of all foreign kings.
I'll have them wall all Germany with brass
And make swift Rhine circle fair Wittenberg.
I'll have them fill the public schools with silk,
Wherewith the students shall be bravely clad.   90
I'll levy soldiers with the coin they bring
And chase the Prince of Parma from our land,
And reign sole king of all the provinces;
Yea, stranger engines for the brunt of war
Than was the fiery keel at Antwerp bridge   95
I'll make my servile spirits to invent.
Come, German Valdes and Cornelius,
And make me blest with your sage conference!

Enter VALDES *and* CORNELIUS.

Valdes, sweet Valdes, and Cornelius,
Know that your words have won me at the last   100
To practise magic and concealèd arts.
Philosophy is odious and obscure;
Both law and physic are for petty wits;
'Tis magic, magic that hath ravished me.
Then, gentle friends, aid me in this attempt,   105
And I, that have with subtle syllogisms
Gravelled the pastors of the German Church
And made the flow'ring pride of Wittenberg
Swarm to my problems as th'infernal spirits
On sweet Musaeus when he came to hell,   110
Will be as cunning as Agrippa was,
Whose shadows made all Europe honour him.
Valdes. Faustus, these books, thy wit, and our experience
Shall make all nations to canonise us.

89. silk] *Dyce 1;* skill *B1.*   109. Swarm] *A1;* Sworne *B1.*   112. shadows]
A1; shadow *B1.*

109. *Swarm*] A1 supplies the reading needed to replace B1's erroneous
Sworne.

112. *shadows*] A1's reading is clearly superior; B1's *shadow* is an easy
compositorial error.

As Indian Moors obey their Spanish lords,   115
So shall the spirits of every element
Be always serviceable to us three.
Like lions shall they guard us when we please,
Like Almaine rutters with their horsemen's staves,
Or Lapland giants, trotting by our sides;   120
Sometimes like women, or unwedded maids,
Shadowing more beauty in their airy brows
Than has the white breasts of the Queen of Love.
From Venice shall they drag huge argosies,
And from America the golden fleece   125
That yearly stuffed old Philip's treasury,
If learnèd Faustus will be resolute.
Faustus. Valdes, as resolute am I in this
As thou to live. Therefore object it not.
Cornelius. The miracles that magic will perform   130
Will make thee vow to study nothing else.
He that is grounded in astrology,
Enriched with tongues, well seen in minerals,
Hath all the principles magic doth require.
Then doubt not, Faustus, but to be renowned   135
And more frequented for this mystery
Than heretofore the Delphian oracle.
The spirits tell me they can dry the sea
And fetch the treasure of all foreign wrecks—
Yea, all the wealth that our forefathers hid   140
Within the massy entrails of the earth.
Then tell me, Faustus, what shall we three want?
Faustus. Nothing, Cornelius. O, this cheers my soul!
Come, show me some demonstrations magical,
That I may conjure in some bushy grove   145
And have these joys in full possession.
Valdes. Then haste thee to some solitary grove,
And bear wise Bacon's and Albanus' works,

120. Lapland] *B1* (Lopland); Lapland *A1*.   123. has the] *B1;* have the *B2;*
in their *A1;* in the *Greg.*   135. renowned] *B1* (renowm'd).   139. wrecks]
B1 (wrackes).

126. *stuffed*] On the possible dating significance of the shift from the
A-text's *stuffs* (1.i.134) see Introduction, p. 73. The use of the past tense here
presumably reflects the death of Philip II of Spain in 1598.

The Hebrew Psalter, and New Testament;
And whatsoever else is requisite   150
We will inform thee ere our conference cease.
Cornelius. Valdes, first let him know the words of art,
And then, all other ceremonies learned,
Faustus may try his cunning by himself.
Valdes. First I'll instruct thee in the rudiments,   155
And then wilt thou be perfecter than I.
Faustus. Then come and dine with me, and after meat
We'll canvass every quiddity thereof,
For ere I sleep I'll try what I can do.
This night I'll conjure, though I die therefore.   160
                                   Exeunt omnes.

[1.ii]

Enter two SCHOLARS.

First Scholar. I wonder what's become of Faustus, that was
    wont to make our schools ring with '*sic probo*'.

Enter WAGNER, [*carrying wine*].

Second Scholar. That shall we presently know. Here comes
    his boy.
First Scholar. How now, sirrah, where's thy master?   5
Wagner. God in heaven knows.
Second Scholar. Why, dost not thou know, then?
Wagner. Yes, I know, but that follows not.
First Scholar. Go to, sirrah! Leave your jesting, and tell us
    where he is.   10
Wagner. That follows not by force of argument, which you,
    being licentiates, should stand upon. Therefore, acknowl-
    edge your error, and be attentive.
Second Scholar. Then you will not tell us?
Wagner. You are deceived, for I will tell you. Yet if you were 15
    not dunces, you would never ask me such a question. For
    is he not *corpus naturale*? And is not that *mobile*? Then,
    wherefore should you ask me such a question? But that I

1.ii.1–2.] *prose as in* A1; *divided at* wont / To *with capital 'T' as though
dividing for verse, in* B1.   2.1. S.D. *carrying wine*] Kirschbaum (subst.); *not
in* B1.

am by nature phlegmatic, slow to wrath, and prone to
lechery—to love, I would say—it were not for you to   20
come within forty foot of the place of execution, although
I do not doubt but to see you both hanged the next
sessions. Thus, having triumphed over you, I will set my
countenance like a precisian and begin to speak thus:
Truly, my dear brethren, my master is within at dinner   25
with Valdes and Cornelius, as this wine, if it could speak,
would inform your worships. And so the Lord bless you,
preserve you, and keep you, my dear brethren.   *Exit.*
First Scholar. O Faustus,
Then I fear that which I have long suspected,   30
That thou art fall'n into that damnèd art
For which they two are infamous through the world.
Second Scholar. Were he a stranger, not allied to me,
The danger of his soul would make me mourn.
But come, let us go and inform the Rector.   35
It may be his grave counsel may reclaim him.
First Scholar. I fear me nothing will reclaim him now.
Second Scholar. Yet let us see what we can do.   *Exeunt.*

[I.iii]

    Thunder. Enter LUCIFER *and four* Devils [*above*], FAUSTUS
    to them with this speech. [*He holds a book.*]

Faustus. Now that the gloomy shadow of the night,
    Longing to view Orion's drizzling look,
    Leaps from th'Antarctic world unto the sky
    And dims the welkin with her pitchy breath,
    Faustus, begin thine incantations,   5

25. master] *B1* (*Mr.*).   29–30.] *divided as in Dyce 1; one line in B1.*
I.iii.0.1. S.D. *above*] *Greg; not in B1.*   0.2. S.D. *He holds a book*] *This ed.;
not in B1.*

_____

I.iii.0.1–2. S.D.] Faustus enters after the devils (*to them*), but is unaware
of their presence and does not speak to them. This stage business would be
facilitated by their entry *above*, as also appears likely in v.ii. The four devils
might well include Beelzebub, who later appears in the company of Lucifer
and Mephistopheles at II.iii.84.1 and v.ii.0.1. Faustus also implores the aid
of Demogorgon at l. 19 in the present scene; Demogorgon therefore may
be understood to be on stage here with Lucifer as one of the four devils, but
he does not appear elsewhere.

And try if devils will obey thy hest,
Seeing thou hast prayed and sacrificed to them.
                                    [*He draws a circle.*]
Within this circle is Jehovah's name
Forward and backward anagrammatised,
Th'abbreviated names of holy saints,   10
Figures of every adjunct to the heavens,
And characters of signs and erring stars,
By which the spirits are enforced to rise.
Then fear not, Faustus, to be resolute,
And try the utmost magic can perform.   *Thunder.*   15
Sint mihi dei Acherontis propitii! Valeat numen triplex
Jehovae! Ignei, aerii, aquatici, terreni, spiritus, salvete!
Orientis princeps Lucifer, Beelzebub, inferni ardentis
monarcha, et Demogorgon, propitiamus vos, ut appareat et
surgat, Mephistopheles! Quid tu moraris? Per Jehovam,   20
Gehennam, et consecratam aquam quam nunc spargo,
signumque crucis quod nunc facio, et per vota nostra, ipse
nunc surgat nobis dicatus Mephistopheles!

[*Faustus sprinkles holy water and makes a sign of the cross.*]

Enter a Devil [MEPHISTOPHELES, *in the shape of a*] dragon.

I charge thee to return and change thy shape.

7.1. s.d.] *This ed.; not in* B1.   12. erring] A1; euening B1.   16. dei] A1;
Dij B1.   17. aquatici] Tucker Brooke; Aquatani B1.   17. terreni] conj.
Greg; not in B1.   18. Lucifer] conj. Greg; not in B1.   18, II.i.5 and 11, etc.
Beelzebub] B1 (Belzebub).   19. Demogorgon] B1 (demigorgon).   20, and
throughout. Mephistopheles] B1 (Mephostophilis here and normally in B1, but
Mephastophilis at II.i.107, III.ii.o.3, IV.i.161).   20. Quid tu moraris] Ellis,
conj. Bullen; quod tumeraris B1.   21. Gehennam] B1 (gehennan).   23.
dicatus] B3; dicatis B1.   23.1. s.d.] This ed.; not in B1.   23.2 and 27.1.
s.d. MEPHISTOPHELES] Ward; not in B1.   23.2. s.d. in the shape of a] This
ed.; not in B1.   23.2. s.d. dragon] placed here this ed.; placed at l. 20 Boas;
as part of the spoken text ('Mephostophilis Dragon, quod') at l. 20 in B1.

---

12. *erring*] A1's reading; B1's *euening* is an error probably derived from the
common phrase, 'evening star'.
    23.2. s.d.] The word *dragon*, not found in the A-text, appears in the B-text
at l. 20 after *Mephostophilis* and unseparated from it by punctuation:
'Mephostophilis Dragon'. Some editors, following Robert K. Root's explanation (pp. 144–9) that the word is a stage direction placed disconcertingly in

Thou art too ugly to attend on me.   25
Go, and return an old Franciscan friar;
That holy shape becomes a devil best.
                              Exit Devil [MEPHISTOPHELES].
I see there's virtue in my heavenly words.
Who would not be proficient in this art?
How pliant is this Mephistopheles,   30
Full of obedience and humility!
Such is the force of magic and my spells.

                    Enter MEPHISTOPHELES [*disguised as a friar*].

Mephistopheles. Now, Faustus, what wouldst thou have me do?
Faustus. I charge thee wait upon me whilst I live,
          To do whatever Faustus shall command,   35
          Be it to make the moon drop from her sphere
          Or the ocean to overwhelm the world.
Mephistopheles. I am a servant to great Lucifer
          And may not follow thee without his leave.
          No more than he commands must we perform.   40
Faustus. Did not he charge thee to appear to me?
Mephistopheles. No, I came now hither of mine own accord.
Faustus. Did not my conjuring raise thee? Speak.

32.1. S.D. *disguised as a friar*] Kirschbaum (*subst.*); *not in B1.*   42. hither]
B1 (hether); hither *B2*.

---

the midst of Faustus's invocation, treat it as a direction for a dragon to
appear briefly at l. 20 hovering in the air above Faustus, as is reported in the
Damnable Life, ch. 2 (Boas). The present editors agree that *dragon* is a
misplaced stage direction, but reason that its position need not then carry
much authority—especially since, under the best of circumstances, the
precise location of stage directions (often written in the margins of manuscripts) is generally hard to determine. If a dragon were to appear at l. 20,
Faustus's expostulation, 'Why do you delay?', would seem an odd response.
On the other hand, the word is immediately connected with the name of
Mephistopheles. Since the title-page woodcut of the 1616 B1 text shows a
dragon appearing in front of the conjuring Faustus, we suggest that *dragon*
indicates the 'too ugly' shape (l. 25) in which Mephistopheles appears and to
which Faustus objects, and that the dragon should enter on the main stage
rather than above. The Admiral's Men possessed in their inventory of 1598 'j
dragon in fostes' (Henslowe's *Diary*, p. 320); see Introduction, p. 50.
Kirschbaum suggests that a dragon-head rises from the open trap and then
sinks into it at l. 27.1.

Mephistopheles. That was the cause, but yet *per accidens.*
    For when we hear one rack the name of God,   45
    Abjure the Scriptures and his Saviour Christ,
    We fly in hope to get his glorious soul,
    Nor will we come unless he use such means
    Whereby he is in danger to be damned.
    Therefore, the shortest cut for conjuring   50
    Is stoutly to abjure all godliness
    And pray devoutly to the prince of hell.
Faustus. So Faustus hath
    Already done, and holds this principle:
    There is no chief but only Beelzebub,   55
    To whom Faustus doth dedicate himself.
    This word 'damnation' terrifies not me,
    For I confound hell in Elysium.
    My ghost be with the old philosophers!
    But leaving these vain trifles of men's souls,   60
    Tell me, what is that Lucifer, thy lord?
Mephistopheles. Arch-regent and commander of all spirits.
Faustus. Was not that Lucifer an angel once?
Mephistopheles. Yes, Faustus, and most dearly loved of God.
Faustus. How comes it then that he is prince of devils?   65
Mephistopheles. O, by aspiring pride and insolence,
    For which God threw him from the face of heaven.
Faustus. And what are you that live with Lucifer?
Mephistopheles. Unhappy spirits that fell with Lucifer,
    Conspired against our God with Lucifer,   70
    And are for ever damned with Lucifer.
Faustus. Where are you damned?
Mephistopheles. In hell.
Faustus. How comes it then that thou art out of hell?
Mephistopheles. Why, this is hell, nor am I out of it.   75
    Think'st thou that I, that saw the face of God
    And tasted the eternal joys of heaven,
    Am not tormented with ten thousand hells

---

44. *accidens*] *B4; accident B1.*   53–4.] *divided as in Dyce 2; one line in B1.*
69. fell] *A1; liue B1.*

---

69. *fell*] the A1 reading; B1's *liue*, though possible as to sense, is almost
certainly an erroneous repetition of 'live' in the previous line.

In being deprived of everlasting bliss?
O Faustus, leave these frivolous demands,   80
Which strikes a terror to my fainting soul!
Faustus. What, is great Mephistopheles so passionate
For being deprivèd of the joys of heaven?
Learn thou of Faustus manly fortitude,
And scorn those joys thou never shalt possess.   85
Go bear these tidings to great Lucifer:
Seeing Faustus hath incurred eternal death
By desperate thoughts against Jove's deity,
Say he surrenders up to him his soul,
So he will spare him four-and-twenty years,   90
Letting him live in all voluptuousness,
Having thee ever to attend on me,
To give me whatsoever I shall ask,
To tell me whatsoever I demand,
To slay mine enemies and to aid my friends,   95
And always be obedient to my will.
Go and return to mighty Lucifer,
And meet me in my study at midnight,
And then resolve me of thy master's mind.
Mephistopheles. I will, Faustus.   *Exit.*   100
Faustus. Had I as many souls as there be stars,
I'd give them all for Mephistopheles.
By him I'll be great emperor of the world
And make a bridge through the moving air
To pass the ocean; with a band of men   105
I'll join the hills that bind the Afric shore
And make that country continent to Spain,
And both contributory to my crown.
The Emperor shall not live but by my leave,
Nor any potentate of Germany.   110
Now that I have obtained what I desired,
I'll live in speculation of this art
Till Mephistopheles return again.
                    Exit [FAUSTUS *below;*
            exeunt LUCIFER *and other* Devils *above*].

113.1–2. S.D. FAUSTUS . . . *above*] *Jump (subst.); not in B1.*

[I.iv]

Enter WAGNER *and* [ROBIN] *the* CLOWN.

Wagner. Come hither, sirrah boy.
Robin. 'Boy'? O, disgrace to my person! Zounds, 'boy' in
   your face! You have seen many boys with beards, I am
   sure.
Wagner. Sirrah, hast thou no comings in?   5
Robin. Yes, and goings out too, you may see, sir.
Wagner. Alas, poor slave, see how poverty jests in his naked-
   ness! I know the villain's out of service, and so hungry
   that I know he would give his soul to the devil for a
   shoulder of mutton, though it were blood raw.   10
Robin. Not so, neither. I had need to have it well roasted, and
   good sauce to it, if I pay so dear, I can tell you.
Wagner. Sirrah, wilt thou be my man and wait on me? And I
   will make thee go like *Qui mihi discipulus.*
Robin. What, in verse?   15
Wagner. No, slave, in beaten silk and stavesacre.
Robin. Stavesacre? That's good to kill vermin. Then belike if I
   serve you, I shall be lousy.
Wagner. Why, so thou shalt be, whether thou dost it or no;
   for, sirrah, if thou dost not presently bind thyself to me   20
   for seven years, I'll turn all the lice about thee into
   familiars and make them tear thee in pieces.
Robin. Nay, sir, you may save yourself a labour, for they are
   as familiar with me as if they paid for their meat and
   drink, I can tell you.   25
Wagner. Well, sirrah, leave your jesting, and take these
   guilders. [*Offering money.*]
Robin. Yes, marry, sir, and I thank you, too.
Wagner. So, now thou art to be at an hour's warning whensoever and wheresoever the devil shall fetch thee.   30
Robin. Here, take your guilders. I'll none of 'em.
                    [*He attempts to return the money.*]

I.iv.0.1. S.D. ROBIN] *Greg; not in B1.*   2, 6, 11 *to* 50. S.H. Robin] *Jump;*
Clow. or Clo. throughout this scene in B1.   27. S.D.] *Dyce 1 (subst.); not in*
B1.   31.1, 37. S.D.] *This ed.; not in B1.*

I.iv.18. *lousy*] (*a*) full of vermin (*b*) contemptible.

Wagner. Not I. Thou art pressed. Prepare thyself, for I will presently raise up two devils to carry thee away.—Banio! Belcher!
Robin. Belcher? An Belcher come here, I'll belch him. I am   35
not afraid of a devil.

Enter two Devils.

Wagner. [*To Robin.*] How now, sir, will you serve me now?
Robin. Ay, good Wagner. Take away the devil, then.
Wagner. Spirits, away!
[*Exeunt* Devils.]
Now, sirrah, follow me.   40
Robin. I will, sir. But hark you, master, will you teach me this conjuring occupation?
Wagner. Ay, sirrah, I'll teach thee to turn thyself to a dog, or a cat, or a mouse, or a rat, or anything.
Robin. A dog, or a cat, or a mouse, or a rat? O brave Wagner!   45
Wagner. Villain, call me Master Wagner, and see that you walk attentively, and let your right eye be always diametrally fixed upon my left heel, that thou mayst *quasi vestigiis nostris insistere.*
Robin. Well, sir, I warrant you.   *Exeunt.*   50

35. An] *B1 (and); also at II.i.141 and 151, II.ii.7.*   39.1. S.D.] *Oxberry; not in B1; Exeunt A1.*   49. *vestigiis nostris*] *Dyce 2; vestigias nostras B1.*

32. *pressed*] (*a*) drafted into military service, by virtue of this impressment money (*b*) hired. The B1 spelling, *Prest*, also suggests 'ready', anticipating 'Prepare thyself' in the next sentence.
48. *diametrally*] The difference between the B1 spelling and A1's *diametarily* may well be non-authorial; see A-text commentary note at i.iv.73.

Act II

[II.i]

Enter FAUSTUS *in his study.*

Faustus. Now, Faustus, must thou needs be damned?
    Canst thou not be saved?
    What boots it then to think on God or heaven?
    Away with such vain fancies, and despair!
    Despair in God and trust in Beelzebub.   5
    Now go not backward, Faustus, be resolute.
    Why waver'st thou? O, something soundeth in mine ear:
    'Abjure this magic, turn to God again!'
    Why, he loves thee not.
    The god thou serv'st is thine own appetite,   10
    Wherein is fixed the love of Beelzebub.
    To him I'll build an altar and a church,
    And offer lukewarm blood of new-born babes.

Enter the two ANGELS.

Bad Angel. Go forward, Faustus, in that famous art.
Good Angel. Sweet Faustus, leave that execrable art.   15
Faustus. Contrition, prayer, repentance—what of these?

II.i.6. backward, Faustus,] *B1* (backward *Faustus); backeward: no Faustus, A1.*   9–10.] *divided as in A1; one line in B1.*   14. S.H. *Bad Angel]* *Cunningham; Euill An. B1.*

II.i.1–2.] The question marks may be only accidental variants, in a compositor's attempt to rationalise the A-text with its single (and apparently erroneous) question mark at the end of l. 2; but the B1 question marks are defensible here as they stand, and l. 2 would seem awkward with a period. Compare the A-text and commentary note at II.i.2.

4.] Both the B-text's comma after 'fancies' and the A-text's absence of punctuation provide intelligible readings. In B, 'despair' looks forward to l. 5, 'Despair in God'. The line in A suggests 'brush aside idle fancies and desperate thoughts'.

14. S.H. Bad Angel] B1 prints '*Euill An.*' here, though '*Bad A.*' thereafter, suggesting the influence of the A-text reading here.

Good Angel. O, they are means to bring thee unto heaven.
Bad Angel. Rather illusions, fruits of lunacy,
   That make them foolish that do use them most.
Good Angel.
   Sweet Faustus, think of heaven and heavenly things.   20
Bad Angel. No, Faustus, think of honour and of wealth.
                              Exeunt ANGELS.
Faustus. Wealth?
   Why, the seigniory of Emden shall be mine.
   When Mephistopheles shall stand by me,
   What power can hurt me? Faustus, thou art safe;   25
   Cast no more doubts. Mephistopheles, come,
   And bring glad tidings from great Lucifer.
   Is't not midnight? Come, Mephistopheles!
   Veni, veni, Mephistophile!

               Enter MEPHISTOPHELES.

   Now tell me what saith Lucifer thy lord.   30
Mephistopheles. That I shall wait on Faustus whilst he lives,
   So he will buy my service with his soul.
Faustus. Already Faustus hath hazarded that for thee.
Mephistopheles. But now thou must bequeath it solemnly
   And write a deed of gift with thine own blood,   35
   For that security craves Lucifer.
   If thou deny it, I must back to hell.
Faustus. Stay, Mephistopheles, and tell me,
   What good will my soul do thy lord?
Mephistopheles. Enlarge his kingdom.   40
Faustus. Is that the reason why he tempts us thus?
Mephistopheles. Solamen miseris socios habuisse doloris.
Faustus. Why, have you any pain, that torture other?
Mephistopheles. As great as have the human souls of men.
   But tell me, Faustus, shall I have thy soul?   45

22-3.] *divided as in A1; one line in B1.*   26. Mephistopheles] *B1 (Mepho:).*
31. S.H. *Mephistopheles] A1; not in B1.*   38, 53, *also at* III.i.57, 160.1, 162,
196, IV.i.80. Mephistopheles] *B1 (Mephosto.); also Mephasto. at* III.ii.11, 26,
V.i.73.

19. *make them*] i.e., make men (as in the A-text).

And I will be thy slave, and wait on thee,
And give thee more than thou hast wit to ask.
Faustus. Ay, Mephistopheles, I'll give it him.
Mephistopheles. Then, Faustus, stab thy arm courageously,
   And bind thy soul that at some certain day   50
   Great Lucifer may claim it as his own,
   And then be thou as great as Lucifer.
Faustus. [*Cutting his arm.*]
   Lo, Mephistopheles, for love of thee
   Faustus hath cut his arm, and with his proper blood
   Assures his soul to be great Lucifer's,   55
   Chief lord and regent of perpetual night.
   View here this blood that trickles from mine arm,
   And let it be propitious for my wish.
Mephistopheles. But Faustus,
   Write it in manner of a deed of gift.   60
Faustus. Ay, so I do. [*He writes.*] But Mephistopheles,
   My blood congeals, and I can write no more.
Mephistopheles. I'll fetch thee fire to dissolve it straight. *Exit.*
Faustus. What might the staying of my blood portend?
   Is it unwilling I should write this bill?   65
   Why streams it not, that I may write afresh?
   'Faustus gives to thee his soul'—O, there it stayed!
   Why shouldst thou not? Is not thy soul thine own?
   Then write again: 'Faustus gives to thee his soul.'

       Enter MEPHISTOPHELES *with the chafer of fire.*

Mephistopheles. See, Faustus, here is fire. Set it on.   70
Faustus. So. Now the blood begins to clear again.
   Now will I make an end immediately. [*He writes.*]
Mephistopheles. [*Aside.*]
   What will not I do to obtain his soul?
Faustus. Consummatum est. This bill is ended,
   And Faustus hath bequeathed his soul to Lucifer.   75
   But what is this inscription on mine arm?

---

53. S.D.] *Dyce 1 (subst.); not in B1.*   53–5.] *divided as in A1; as two lines
divided at* arme, / And *in B1.*   61, 72. S.D. *He writes*] *Dyce 1 (subst.); not in
B1.*   73, 82. S.D. *Aside*] *Dyce 1; not in B1.*

'*Homo, fuge!*' Whither should I fly?
If unto heaven, he'll throw me down to hell.—
My senses are deceived; here's nothing writ.—
O, yes, I see it plain. Even here is writ   80
'*Homo, fuge!*' Yet shall not Faustus fly.
Mephistopheles. [*Aside.*]
    I'll fetch him somewhat to delight his mind.   *Exit.*

Enter Devils, *giving crowns and rich apparel to Faustus.*
            They dance, and then depart.

                Enter MEPHISTOPHELES.

Faustus. What means this show? Speak, Mephistopheles.
Mephistopheles. Nothing, Faustus, but to delight thy mind
    And let thee see what magic can perform.   85
Faustus. But may I raise such spirits when I please?
Mephistopheles. Ay, Faustus, and do greater things than these.
Faustus. Then Mephistopheles, receive this scroll,
    A deed of gift of body and of soul—
    But yet conditionally that thou perform   90
    All covenants and articles between us both.
Mephistopheles. Faustus, I swear by hell and Lucifer
    To effect all promises between us both.
Faustus. Then hear me read it, Mephistopheles.
    'On these conditions following: 95
    First, that Faustus may be a spirit in form and substance.
    Secondly, that Mephistopheles shall be his servant, and
    be by him commanded.
    Thirdly, that Mephistopheles shall do for him and bring
    him whatsoever.   100
    Fourthly, that he shall be in his chamber or house
    invisible.
    Lastly, that he shall appear to the said John Faustus at all
    times in what shape and form soever he please.

77. Whither] *B1* (*whether*).   95.] *treated as a line of dialogue in B1 rather
than as part of the contract.*
_____

77. *Whither*] B1's *whether* might seem to mean 'whether to fly or not', but
whether is a common Elizabethan spelling of *whither*, and the following lines
make clear the choice of 'whither' to fly. 'Whether should I fly' would be
idiomatically anomalous. The spelling should probably be regarded as an
accidental variant.

I, John Faustus of Wittenberg, Doctor, by these presents,   105
do give both body and soul to Lucifer, Prince of the East,
and his minister Mephistopheles; and furthermore grant
unto them that four-and-twenty years being expired, and
these articles above written being inviolate, full power to
fetch or carry the said John Faustus, body and soul, flesh,   110
blood, into their habitation wheresoever.
                              By me, John Faustus.'
Mephistopheles. Speak, Faustus. Do you deliver this as your
    deed?
Faustus. [*Giving the deed.*] Ay. Take it, and the devil give thee   115
    good of it.
Mephistopheles. So. Now, Faustus, ask me what thou wilt.
Faustus. First I will question thee about hell.
    Tell me, where is the place that men call hell?
Mephistopheles. Under the heavens.   120
Faustus. Ay, so are all things else. But whereabouts?
Mephistopheles. Within the bowels of these elements,
    Where we are tortured and remain for ever.
    Hell hath no limits, nor is circumscribed
    In one self place, but where we are is hell,   125
    And where hell is there must we ever be.
    And, to be short, when all the world dissolves,
    And every creature shall be purified,
    All places shall be hell that is not heaven.
Faustus. I think hell's a fable.   130
Mephistopheles.
    Ay, think so still, till experience change thy mind.
Faustus.
    Why, dost thou think that Faustus shall be damned?
Mephistopheles. Ay, of necessity, for here's the scroll
    In which thou hast given thy soul to Lucifer.
Faustus. Ay, and body too. But what of that?   135
    Think'st thou that Faustus is so fond to imagine
    That after this life there is any pain?
    No, these are trifles and mere old wives' tales.
Mephistopheles. But I am an instance to prove the contrary,
    For I tell thee I am damned and now in hell.   140
Faustus. Nay, an this be hell, I'll willingly be damned.

115. S.D.] *This ed.; not in B1.*

What? Sleeping, eating, walking, and disputing?
But leaving this, let me have a wife, the fairest maid
in Germany, for I am wanton and lascivious and cannot
live without a wife.   145
Mephistopheles. Well, Faustus, thou shalt have a wife.

He fetches in a woman Devil.

Faustus. What sight is this?
Mephistopheles. Now, Faustus, wilt thou have a wife?
Faustus. Here's a hot whore indeed! No, I'll no wife.
Mephistopheles. Marriage is but a ceremonial toy.   150
    An if thou lovest me, think no more of it.
                                                     [*Exit* Devil.]
    I'll cull thee out the fairest courtesans
    And bring them every morning to thy bed.
    She whom thine eye shall like, thy heart shall have,
    Were she as chaste as was Penelope,   155
    As wise as Saba, or as beautiful
    As was bright Lucifer before his fall.
                                                [*Presenting a book.*]
    Here, take this book and peruse it well.
    The iterating of these lines brings gold;
    The framing of this circle on the ground   160
    Brings thunder, whirlwinds, storm, and lightning.
    Pronounce this thrice devoutly to thyself,
    And men in harness shall appear to thee,
    Ready to execute what thou command'st.
Faustus. Thanks, Mephistopheles, for this sweet book.   165
    This will I keep as chary as my life.   *Exeunt.*

151.1. S.D. *Exit* Devil] *This ed.; not in* B1.   157.1. S.D.] *Dyce 1* (A-*text,*
subst.); *not in* B1.

146.1. S.D. a *woman* Devil] The A-text specifies '*a Devil dressed like a*
woman', laying more emphasis perhaps on diabolical illusion, whereas the B-
text takes the more anti-feminist line of woman as devil.
    151. An *if*] if. B1's *And if* could be retained in a modernised text as 'And
if', but the A-text reading, *If*, perhaps encourages the reading here of *And* as
a common spelling of *An*.
    165–6.] The repetition in substance of these lines in II.iii.171–2,
addressed there to Lucifer instead of Mephistopheles as here, is suggestive of
revision in the B-text. Evidently the reviser or revisers of the later version,
wishing to shorten the end of II.i, took a passage from the original (A
II.iii.174–5; essentially the same as the lines at B II.iii.171–2) and used it to
bring II.i to a quick close.

[II.ii]

Enter [ROBIN] *the* CLOWN [*with a conjuring book*].

Robin. [*Calling offstage.*] What, Dick, look to the horses there
till I come again.—I have gotten one of Doctor Faustus'
conjuring books, and now we'll have such knavery as't
passes.

Enter DICK.

Dick. What, Robin, you must come away and walk the horses.   5
Robin. I walk the horses? I scorn't, 'faith. I have other matters
in hand. Let the horses walk themselves an they will. [*He
reads.*] 'A' *per se* 'a'; 't', 'h', 'e', 'the'; 'o' *per se* 'o'; 'deny
orgon, gorgon'.—Keep further from me, O thou illiterate
and unlearned ostler.   10
Dick. 'Snails, what hast thou got there, a book? Why, thou
canst not tell ne'er a word on't.
Robin. That thou shalt see presently. [*He draws a circle.*] Keep
out of the circle, I say, lest I send you into the hostry,
with a vengeance.   15
Dick. That's like, 'faith! You had best leave your foolery, for

---

II.ii.] *placed here this ed.; printed after II.iii in B1. At the end of II.i, B1 prints
(in place of the present comic scene) a speech by Wagner that is essentially identical
to the Chorus of Act III in A1.* 0.1. S.D. ROBIN] *Dyce 1; not in B1.*
0.1. S.D. *with a conjuring book*] *A1 (with a booke in his hand); not in B1.*
1. S.H. *Robin*] *Dyce 1; not in B1.* 1. S.D. *Calling offstage*] *Kirschbaum
(subst.); not in B1.* 7–8. S.D.] *Dyce 1 (subst.); not in B1.* 13. S.D.] *placed
here this ed.; placed at l. 8 (Chants, making a circle) Kirschbaum; not in B1.*

II.ii.1–35.] Compare II.ii in the A-text, where the clownish stable-boys are
called Robin and Rafe.
3–4. *as't passes*] as beats everything.
8. 'A' . . . 'o'] 'A' by itself is 'a', 't, h, e' spells 'the', 'o' by itself is 'o'.
Robin is struggling with some word, possibly *Theos*, Greek for 'God'. In the
next line he takes a stab at *Demogorgon*, a word Faustus used in his conjuring
in I.iii.
11. *'Snails*] by his (God's) nails (on the cross).
12. *tell*] make out, understand (*OED*, v. 7b).
14. *hostry*] hostelry, inn (where they are stable-boys).
15. *with a vengeance*] i.e., God's curse on you (a strong oath). Compare
A-text II.iii.138 and Dent M1003.
16. *That's like*] i.e., a likely chance.

an my master come he'll conjure you, 'faith.
Robin. My master conjure me? I'll tell thee what: an my
master come here, I'll clap as fair a pair of horns on's
head as e'er thou sawest in thy life.   20
Dick. Thou need'st not do that, for my mistress hath done it.
Robin. Ay, there be of us here that have waded as deep into
matters as other men, if they were disposed to talk.
Dick. A plague take you! I thought you did not sneak up and
down after her for nothing. But I prithee tell me in good   25
sadness, Robin, is that a conjuring book?
Robin. Do but speak what thou'lt have me to do, and I'll do't.
If thou'lt dance naked, put off thy clothes, and I'll conjure thee about presently. Or if thou'lt go but to the
tavern with me, I'll give thee white wine, red wine, claret   30
wine, sack, muscadine, malmsey, and whippincrust, hold
belly hold, and we'll not pay one penny for it.
Dick. O brave! Prithee let's to it presently, for I am as dry as
a dog.
Robin. Come, then, let's away.   *Exeunt.*   35

[II.iii]

Enter FAUSTUS *in his study, and* MEPHISTOPHELES.

Faustus. When I behold the heavens, then I repent
And curse thee, wicked Mephistopheles,
Because thou hast deprived me of those joys.

---

17. *my master*] probably the innkeeper.
conjure] i.e., constrain you to obey; or, perhaps, spirit away. (With jesting
reference to the idea of invoking the devil.)
19. *horns*] cuckold's horns.
22–3.] Robin hints boastfully at his own and others' success with their
mistress, if he were free to tell all.
of us] some of us.
waded . . . deep . . . matters] The sexual suggestion is apparent also in *JC*,
I.i.21–3: 'I meddle with no tradesman's matters nor women's matters'
(Boas).
25–6. *in good sadness*] in earnest.
31. *sack, muscadine, malmsey*] various strong wines.
whippincrust] i.e., hippocras, a spiced wine drink, with perhaps a suggestion of 'whipping cheer' (Greg). See A II.ii.25n. on *hippocras*.
31–2. *hold belly hold*] as much as the belly will hold.

Mephistopheles.
    'Twas thine own seeking, Faustus. Thank thyself.
    But think'st thou heaven is such a glorious thing?   5
    I tell thee, Faustus, it is not half so fair
    As thou or any man that breathe on earth.
Faustus. How prov'st thou that?
Mephistopheles. 'Twas made for man; then he's more excellent.
Faustus. If heaven was made for man, 'twas made for me.   10
    I will renounce this magic and repent.

        Enter the two ANGELS.

Good Angel. Faustus, repent! Yet God will pity thee.
Bad Angel. Thou art a spirit. God cannot pity thee.
Faustus. Who buzzeth in mine ears I am a spirit?
    Be I a devil, yet God may pity me;   15
    Yea, God will pity me if I repent.
Bad Angel. Ay, but Faustus never shall repent.
                          Exeunt ANGELS.
Faustus. My heart is hardened; I cannot repent.
    Scarce can I name salvation, faith, or heaven.
    Swords, poison, halters, and envenomed steel   20
    Are laid before me to dispatch myself;
    And long ere this I should have done the deed,
    Had not sweet pleasure conquered deep despair.
    Have not I made blind Homer sing to me
    Of Alexander's love and Oenone's death?   25
    And hath not he that built the walls of Thebes
    With ravishing sound of his melodious harp
    Made music with my Mephistopheles?
    Why should I die, then, or basely despair?
    I am resolved, Faustus shall not repent.   30
    Come, Mephistopheles, let us dispute again
    And reason of divine astrology.

II.iii.17. S.H. *Bad Angel*] Boas; *Euill An. B1.*   17.1. S.D. *Exeunt*] *B1 (Exit)*

    II.iii.7. *breathe*] A1's *breathes* is the better reading, at least to our ears, but *breathe* is perhaps justifiable as reflecting a collective sense of 'any of us that breathe on earth'. Elizabethan rules for singular-plural agreement are relaxed by modern standards, though more commonly with singular verb endings and plural subjects (Abbott 332–7).

Speak. Are there many spheres above the moon?
Are all celestial bodies but one globe,
As is the substance of this centric earth?   35
Mephistopheles. As are the elements, such are the heavens,
Even from the moon unto the empyreal orb,
Mutually folded in each others' spheres,
And jointly move upon one axletree,
Whose terminè is termed the world's wide pole.   40
Nor are the names of Saturn, Mars, or Jupiter
Feigned, but are erring stars.
Faustus. But have they all one motion, both *situ et tempore*?
Mephistopheles. All move from east to west in four-and-twenty
hours upon the poles of the world, but differ in their   45
motions upon the poles of the zodiac.
Faustus. These slender questions Wagner can decide.
Hath Mephistopheles no greater skill?
Who knows not the double motion of the planets?
That the first is finished in a natural day,   50
The second thus: Saturn in thirty years,
Jupiter in twelve, Mars in four, the sun, Venus, and
Mercury in a year, the moon in twenty-eight days. These
are freshmen's questions. But tell me, hath every sphere a
dominion or *intelligentia*?   55
Mephistopheles. Ay.
Faustus. How many heavens or spheres are there?
Mephistopheles. Nine: the seven planets, the firmament, and
the empyreal heaven.
Faustus. But is there not *coelum igneum et crystallinum*?   60

37, 59. empyreal] *B1* (Emperiall).   38. others'] *Boas; others B1;* other's
Dyce 1.   42. erring] *A1;* euening *B1.*   52–5. Jupiter . . . *intelligentia*] *as
prose Boas; as verse divided at* and / *Mercury* . . . daies. / These . . . euery /
Spheare *in B1; as prose from l. 51 in A1.*

---

37. *empyreal orb*] the outermost sphere of the universe. See A II.iii.61n.
42. *erring*] Compare B1's identical error at I.iii.12.
60. coelum igneum et crystallinum] the fiery sphere and the crystalline
sphere—the latter introduced by some Renaissance astronomers to account
for the precession of the equinoxes. Mephistopheles describes a universe of
eight moving spheres inside the empyrean, thus rejecting the *coelum igneum*
and the *coelum crystallinum* as did a number of Renaissance astronomers also.
See Introduction, pp. 27–9. Lines 60–1 are not in the A-text.

Mephistopheles. No, Faustus, they be but fables.

Faustus. Resolve me then in this one question: why are not conjunctions, oppositions, aspects, eclipses all at one time, but in some years we have more, in some less?

Mephistopheles. Per inaequalem motum respectu totius.   65

Faustus. Well, I am answered. Now tell me who made the world.

Mephistopheles. I will not.

Faustus. Sweet Mephistopheles, tell me.

Mephistopheles. Move me not, Faustus.   70

Faustus. Villain, have not I bound thee to tell me anything?

Mephistopheles. Ay, that is not against our kingdom.
This is. Thou art damned. Think thou of hell.

Faustus. Think, Faustus, upon God, that made the world.

Mephistopheles. Remember this.   *Exit.*   75

Faustus. Ay, go, accursèd spirit, to ugly hell!
'Tis thou hast damned distressèd Faustus' soul.
Is't not too late?

Enter the two ANGELS.

Bad Angel. Too late.

Good Angel. Never too late, if Faustus will repent.   80

Bad Angel. If thou repent, devils will tear thee in pieces.

Good Angel. Repent, and they shall never raze thy skin.

Exeunt ANGELS.

Faustus. O Christ, my Saviour, my Saviour,
Help to save distressèd Faustus' soul!

Enter LUCIFER, BEELZEBUB, *and* MEPHISTOPHELES.

Lucifer. Christ cannot save thy soul, for he is just.   85
There's none but I have interest in the same.

Faustus. O, what art thou that look'st so terribly?

Lucifer. I am Lucifer,
And this is my companion prince in hell.

62.] *prose as in Dyce 1; divided at* question: / Why *in B1.*   77–8.] *divided as in A1; one line in B1.*   82. raze] *B1* (raise).   88–9.] *divided as in Dilke; one line in B1.*

---

80. *will*] On the possible theological implications of this change of the A-text's *can*, see Introduction, pp. 29–30, and similarly with *Help* at l. 84 in place of the A-text's *Seek.*

Faustus. O, Faustus, they are come to fetch thy soul!   90
Beelzebub. We are come to tell thee thou dost injure us.
Lucifer. Thou call'st on Christ, contrary to thy promise.
Beelzebub. Thou shouldst not think on God.
Lucifer. Think on the devil.
Beelzebub. And his dam, too.   95
Faustus. Nor will Faustus henceforth. Pardon him for this,
    and Faustus vows never to look to heaven.
Lucifer. So shalt thou show thyself an obedient servant,
    and we will highly gratify thee for it.
Beelzebub. Faustus, we are come from hell in person to show   100
    thee some pastime. Sit down, and thou shalt behold the
    Seven Deadly Sins appear to thee in their own proper
    shapes and likeness.
Faustus. That sight will be as pleasant to me as paradise was to
    Adam the first day of his creation.   105
Lucifer. Talk not of paradise or creation, but mark the show.
    Go, Mephistopheles, fetch them in.   [*Faustus sits.*]

[MEPHISTOPHELES *fetches the* SINS.]
Enter the SEVEN DEADLY SINS.

Beelzebub. Now, Faustus, question them of their names and
    dispositions.
Faustus. That shall I soon.—What art thou, the first?   110
Pride. I am Pride. I disdain to have any parents. I am like to
    Ovid's flea: I can creep into every corner of a wench.
    Sometimes like a periwig I sit upon her brow; next, like a
    necklace I hang about her neck; then, like a fan of
    feathers I kiss her, and then, turning myself to a wrought   115

96–7.] *prose, this ed.; as verse divided at* this, / And *in* B1.   98–9.] *prose as in Kirschbaum; as verse divided at* seruant / And *in* B1.   107. S.D. *Faustus sits*] *This ed.; not in* B1.   107.1. S.D. MEPHISTOPHELES *fetches the* SINS] *Dyce 1 (subst.); not in* B1; *led by a* Piper *Greg.*

91–5.] Beelzebub is silent in the A-text. The division of lines here between two speakers is characteristic of a pattern of redundancy in the B-text; see Introduction, pp. 44–5.
    107.1–2. S.D.] Mephistopheles may simply go to the door, or may exit and re-enter. Some editors specify that the Seven Deadly Sins are led in by a piper, in view of the phrase 'On, piper!' at l. 162 below (not in the A-text). The phrase 'Go, Mephistopheles, fetch them in' may require only that Mephistopheles go to the door.
    115. *wrought*] embroidered (*OED*, adj. 2b).

smock, do what I list. But fie, what a smell is here! I'll
not speak a word more for a king's ransom, unless the
ground be perfumed and covered with cloth of arras.

Faustus. Thou art a proud knave, indeed.—What art thou,
the second?   120

Covetousness. I am Covetousness, begotten of an old churl in a
leather bag; and might I now obtain my wish, this house,
you, and all should turn to gold, that I might lock you
safe into my chest. O my sweet gold!

Faustus. And what art thou, the third?   125

Envy. I am Envy, begotten of a chimney-sweeper and an
oyster-wife. I cannot read, and therefore wish all books
burnt. I am lean with seeing others eat. O, that there
would come a famine over all the world, that all might die
and I live alone! Then thou shouldst see how fat I'd be.   130
But must thou sit and I stand? Come down, with a
vengeance!

Faustus. Out, envious wretch!—But what art thou, the
fourth?

Wrath. I am Wrath. I had neither father nor mother. I leaped   135
out of a lion's mouth when I was scarce an hour old, and
ever since have run up and down the world with these
case of rapiers, wounding myself when I could get none
to fight withal. I was born in hell, and look to it, for some
of you shall be my father.   140

Faustus. And what art thou, the fifth?

Gluttony. I am Gluttony. My parents are all dead, and the
devil a penny they have left me but a small pension, and
that buys me thirty meals a day, and ten bevers—a small
trifle to suffice nature. I come of a royal pedigree. My   145
father was a gammon of bacon, and my mother was a
hogshead of claret wine. My godfathers were these: Peter
Pickled-herring and Martin Martlemas-beef. But my

126–40.] The B-text reverses A's order of speaking for Wrath and Envy.
Various rankings of the Deadly Sins were possible. Both texts accept the
traditional grouping of spiritual sins first and fleshly sins last. Covetousness,
representing the World in the traditional triad of World, Flesh, and Devil, is
sometimes placed centrally in fourth position.

137. *these*] The plural is acceptable because a 'case' or pair of rapiers is a
plural concept. A1's *this* is also acceptable.

godmother, O, she was an ancient gentlewoman; her
name was Margery March-beer. Now, Faustus, thou hast   150
heard all my progeny, wilt thou bid me to supper?
Faustus. Not I.
Gluttony. Then the devil choke thee!
Faustus. Choke thyself, glutton!—What art thou, the sixth?
Sloth. Heigh-ho. I am Sloth. I was begotten on a sunny bank.   155
   Heigh-ho. I'll not speak a word more for a king's ransom.
Faustus. And what are you, Mistress Minx, the seventh and
   last?
Lechery. Who, I? I, sir? I am one that loves an inch of raw
   mutton better than an ell of fried stockfish, and the first   160
   letter of my name begins with lechery.
Lucifer. Away, to hell, away! On, piper!
                              Exeunt the SEVEN SINS.
Faustus. O, how this sight doth delight my soul!
Lucifer. But Faustus, in hell is all manner of delight.
Faustus. O, might I see hell and return again safe, how happy   165
   were I then!
Lucifer. Faustus, thou shalt. At midnight I will send for thee.
   [*Presenting a book.*] Meanwhile, peruse this book, and
   view it throughly, and thou shalt turn thyself into what
   shape thou wilt.   170
Faustus. [*Taking the book.*] Thanks, mighty Lucifer.
   This will I keep as chary as my life.
Lucifer. Now, Faustus, farewell.
Faustus. Farewell, great Lucifer. Come, Mephistopheles.
                         Exeunt omnes, several ways.

167–70. Faustus . . . wilt] *prose as in A1; as verse divided at* thee; / Meane
while . . . throughly, / And *in B1.*   168. S.D.] *This ed.; not in B1.*   171.
S.D.] *This ed.; not in B1.*

162. *On, piper*] See note at 107.1–2. S.D. above. Possibly one of the Sins
plays the pipe instead of an onstage musician as piper, or Lucifer may be
speaking metaphorically.

Act III

Enter the CHORUS.

Chorus. Learnèd Faustus,
   To find the secrets of astronomy
   Graven in the book of Jove's high firmament,
   Did mount him up to scale Olympus' top,
   Where, sitting in a chariot burning bright   5
   Drawn by the strength of yokèd dragons' necks,
   He views the clouds, the planets, and the stars,
   The tropics, zones, and quarters of the sky,
   From the bright circle of the hornèd moon
   Even to the height of *Primum Mobile*;   10
   And, whirling round with this circumference
   Within the concave compass of the pole,
   From east to west his dragons swiftly glide
   And in eight days did bring him home again.
   Not long he stayed within his quiet house   15

III.Chorus.1. S.H. *Chorus*] *Dyce 1; not in B1.*   1–2.] *divided as in A1; one line in B1.*   8. tropics] *Greg;* Tropick *B1.*

III.Chorus.8.] The *tropics* of Cancer and Capricorn divide the sky into the tropical zone at the equator, the two temperate zones on either side of it, and the polar zones at the poles — five zones, as defined in Robert Recorde's *The Castle of Knowledge*, 1556. On the other hand, the *OED* (sb. 1) cites from about 1500 a tripartite scheme of one hot and two cold zones, suggesting that various numbers of zones were possible. The sky was also divided into *quarters* corresponding with the four seasons of the year: a solstitial circle passing through the north and south poles intersected the two tropics at points corresponding to winter and summer solstices (shortest and longest days), while an equinoctial circle intersected the equator at two points corresponding to the start of spring and fall when days and nights are of equal length (see Manilius's *Astronomica*, i.561–630, trans. G. P. Goold, Loeb Library, 1977; cited by Keefer). B1's *Tropick* seems an error for *tropics*.
   9–10.] i.e., 'from the lowest to the highest of the moving spheres' (Jump).
   11. *with this circumference*] on this circuitous course (*OED*, 5).
   12.] All that is within the compass or limit of the *pole* or axle on which the universe revolves is, from the perspective of the earth at its centre, *concave* in shape.

To rest his bones after his weary toil,
But new exploits do hale him out again,
And, mounted then upon a dragon's back,
That with his wings did part the subtle air,
He now is gone to prove cosmography,   20
That measures coasts and kingdoms of the earth,
And, as I guess, will first arrive at Rome
To see the Pope and manner of his court
And take some part of holy Peter's feast,
The which this day is highly solemnised.   *Exit.*   25

[III.i]

Enter FAUSTUS *and* MEPHISTOPHELES.

Faustus. Having now, my good Mephistopheles,
Passed with delight the stately town of Trier,
Environed round with airy mountain-tops,
With walls of flint and deep intrenchèd lakes,
Not to be won by any conquering prince;   5
From Paris next, coasting the realm of France,
We saw the river Maine fall into Rhine,
Whose banks are set with groves of fruitful vines.
Then up to Naples, rich Campania,
Whose buildings, fair and gorgeous to the eye,   10
The streets straight forth and paved with finest brick.
There saw we learnèd Maro's golden tomb,
The way he cut an English mile in length
Through a rock of stone in one night's space.
From thence to Venice, Padua, and the east,   15
In one of which a sumptuous temple stands

21. coasts] *B1* (costs).   III.i.6. coasting] *B1* (costing).   7. Rhine] *A1;*
Rhines B1.

---

19. *subtle*] of thin consistency.

III.i.0.1. S.D.] A papal throne is possibly brought on stage at this point in
anticipation of the big entry at l. 88; see A III.i.o.1. S.D.n.

7. *Rhine*] B1's *Rhines* appears to be an error for the A-text reading *Rhine.*

15. *east*] The B-text's reading may be an error for A's *rest,* but is not
manifestly wrong if Faustus refers to places in the east of Italy, including
Padua and Venice.

16. *one*] This B1 reading makes a kind of minimal sense, but it very likely
represents 'editorial tinkering' (Greg).

That threats the stars with her aspiring top,
Whose frame is paved with sundry coloured stones,
And roofed aloft with curious work in gold.
Thus hitherto hath Faustus spent his time.   20
But tell me now, what resting place is this?
Hast thou, as erst I did command,
Conducted me within the walls of Rome?
Mephistopheles. I have, my Faustus, and for proof thereof
    This is the goodly palace of the Pope;   25
    And 'cause we are no common guests
    I choose his privy chamber for our use.
Faustus. I hope his Holiness will bid us welcome.
Mephistopheles. All's one, for we'll be bold with his venison.
    But now, my Faustus, that thou mayst perceive   30
    What Rome contains for to delight thine eyes,
    Know that this city stands upon seven hills
    That underprop the groundwork of the same.
    Just through the midst runs flowing Tiber's stream,
    With winding banks that cut it in two parts,   35
    Over the which two stately bridges lean,
    That make safe passage to each part of Rome.
    Upon the bridge called Ponte Angelo
    Erected is a castle passing strong,
    Where thou shalt see such store of ordnance   40
    As that the double cannons, forged of brass,
    Do match the number of the days contained
    Within the compass of one complete year—
    Beside the gates and high pyramides

---

31. eyes,] *Dyce 1*; eyes. *B1.*   38, 186. Ponte] *Dyce 1*; *Ponto B1.*   40.
ordnance] *B1* (Ordinance).   42. match] *A1*; watch *B1.*

---

27. *choose*] B1's *chuse* is a common spelling of *choose*, but may instead be a
misreading of *chose* in the manuscript; in the comparable passage in the A-
text, Mephistopheles uses the perfect tense to describe what he has done.

36. *two*] an error; the *Damnable Life* supports A1's *four*. See Introduction,
p. 65.

40. *ordnance*] The B1 spelling, *Ordinance*, encourages trisyllabic pronunciation. We modernise in order to acknowledge today's distinction between
ordnance, artillery, and *ordinance*, decree. The metre at A III.i.39 calls for
disyllabic pronunciation.

42. *match*] B1's *watch* is clearly a misprint.

44. *Beside*] besides (the A1 spelling).

That Julius Caesar brought from Africa.   45
Faustus. Now, by the kingdoms of infernal rule,
    Of Styx, of Acheron, and the fiery lake
    Of ever-burning Phlegethon, I swear
    That I do long to see the monuments
    And situation of bright splendent Rome.   50
    Come, therefore, let's away!
Mephistopheles.
    Nay stay, my Faustus. I know you'd see the Pope
    And take some part of holy Peter's feast,
    The which this day with high solemnity
    This day is held through Rome and Italy   55
    In honour of the Pope's triumphant victory.
Faustus. Sweet Mephistopheles, thou pleasest me.
    Whilst I am here on earth, let me be cloyed
    With all things that delight the heart of man.
    My four-and-twenty years of liberty   60
    I'll spend in pleasure and in dalliance,
    That Faustus' name, whilst this bright frame doth stand,
    May be admirèd through the furthest land.
Mephistopheles.
    'Tis well said, Faustus. Come, then, stand by me,
    And thou shalt see them come immediately.   65
Faustus. Nay, stay, my gentle Mephistopheles,
    And grant me my request, and then I go.
    Thou know'st within the compass of eight days
    We viewed the face of heaven, of earth, and hell.
    So high our dragons soared into the air   70
    That, looking down, the earth appeared to me
    No bigger than my hand in quantity.

54. this day with] *B1;* in state and *B2.*   57–8. pleasest me. / Whilst . . .
earth,] *Dyce 1;* pleaseth me / Whilst . . . earth: *B1.*

53–5.] Compare III.Chorus.24–5. Perhaps, as Bowers suggests, the writer
of the addition here 'envisaged the excision of the Chorus and was awkwardly
providing within the scene itself the same information' ('Marlowe's *Doctor
Faustus*: the 1602 Additions', *SB*, XXVI (1973), 6). The repetition of 'this
day . . . This day' suggests awkwardness in revision; the B2 'improvement'
(see collation) is inviting though without authority.
    56. *victory*] i.e., victory in defeating the German emperor and in capturing
Bruno, the rival pope elected by the Emperor. See ll. 89 ff.
    60. *liberty*] (*a*) free opportunity to act without restraint; license to overstep
bounds (*OED*, sb. 4–5) (*b*) freedom from durance in hell.
    62. *this bright frame*] i.e., this resplendent body.

There did we view the kingdoms of the world,
And what might please mine eye I there beheld.
Then in this show let me an actor be,   75
That this proud Pope may Faustus' cunning see.
Mephistopheles. Let it be so, my Faustus. But first stay
And view their triumphs as they pass this way,
And then devise what best contents thy mind,
By cunning in thine art, to cross the Pope   80
Or dash the pride of this solemnity—
To make his monks and abbots stand like apes
And point like antics at his triple crown,
To beat the beads about the friars' pates
Or clap huge horns upon the cardinals' heads,   85
Or any villainy thou canst devise,
And I'll perform it, Faustus. Hark, they come.
This day shall make thee be admired in Rome.
                                        [*They stand aside.*]

Enter the CARDINALS [*of France and Padua*] *and* BISHOPS
[*of Lorraine and Rheims*], *some bearing crosiers, some the pillars;*
MONKS *and* FRIARS *singing their procession. Then the* POPE
[ADRIAN] *and* RAYMOND, KING OF HUNGARY, *with* BRUNO [*the
rival Pope*] *led in chains.* [*Bruno's papal crown is borne in.*]

76, 80. cunning] *B4;* comming *B1.*   83. antics] *B1* (Antiques).   88.1–6.
S.D.] *bracketed material this ed.; not in B1.*

---

78. *triumphs*] victory celebrations, including processions and shows.
80. *cunning*] The B-text's *comming* is an obvious error.
83. *antics*] grotesques, clowns.
triple crown] diadem of the papacy, the three crowns of which symbolised
perhaps the Church militant, suffering, and triumphant.
84. *beads*] prayer beads.
88. *admired*] wondered at.
88.1. S.D. They stand aside] Faustus and Mephistopheles have not yet
assumed invisibility, as they will do at III.ii.15 ff. Their present prank
depends on their disguise as cardinals.
88.2. S.D. *BISHOPS*] One of them is addressed as 'Lord Archbishop of
Rheims' at III.ii.57.
88.3. S.D. crosiers] crooks or hooked staffs of pastoral office for cardinals
and bishops. The Admiral's Men had 'j crosers stafe' in their inventory of
props in 1598; see Henslowe's *Diary,* p. 320.
pillars] portable pillars. Historically, Cardinal Wolsey and Cardinal Pole
had such pillars carried before them, replacing the silver mace to which a
cardinal was entitled. No use is recorded elsewhere (*OED,* sb. 5).
88.4. S.D. procession] litany, prayer, or office sung in a religious procession (*OED,* sb. 3).

Pope. Cast down our footstool.
Raymond.   Saxon Bruno, stoop,
Whilst on thy back his Holiness ascends   90
Saint Peter's chair and state pontifical.
Bruno. Proud Lucifer, that state belongs to me!
But thus I fall to Peter, not to thee.
                              [*He kneels in front of the throne.*]
Pope. To me and Peter shalt thou grovelling lie
And crouch before the papal dignity.   95
Sound trumpets, then, for thus Saint Peter's heir
From Bruno's back ascends Saint Peter's chair.
                              A flourish while he ascends.
Thus, as the gods creep on with feet of wool
Long ere with iron hands they punish men,
So shall our sleeping vengeance now arise   100
And smite with death thy hated enterprise.
Lord Cardinals of France and Padua,
Go forthwith to our holy consistory

93.1. s.d.] *Kirschbaum (subst.); not in B1.*

89–160.] This dramatisation of Pope Adrian's humiliation of Bruno, the
rival pope elected by the Emperor, is loosely based on John Foxe's *Acts and
Monuments*, II.195–6. Foxe tells of a confrontation between Pope Alexander
III (1159–81) and the Emperor Frederick Barbarossa, in which Frederick set
up a rival pope, Victor IV, but was forced to submit and place his neck under
the papal foot. Adrian (or Hadrian) IV, Alexander's predecessor as pope
(1154–9), took no part in this particular episode, but was in open conflict
with the Emperor. Raymond, King of Hungary, is an invented character,
neither historical nor in the *Damnable Life.*
   89. *Saxon*] The word enlists sympathy in Anglo-Saxon Britain for this
German pope supported by the Holy Roman Empire. Compare 'Saxon
Bruno, stoop' with *1Tamb.*, IV.ii.1–22, where Tamburlaine uses Bajazeth as
his footstool to ascend his throne, saying, 'Stoop, villain, stoop, stoop!'
   92. *state*] throne (*OED*, sb. 20). The elaborate throne must be brought on
stage either at the start of the scene (see 0.1. s.d.n.) or as the procession
begins at l. 88.
   93–4.] According to Foxe (II.196), when Alexander placed his foot on the
Emperor's neck, Frederick replied defiantly, '*Non tibi sed Petro*', 'Not to
thee, but to Saint Peter', accepting the authority of the papacy in principle
but not of this particular pope. The Pope replied, '*Et mihi et Petro*', 'Both to
me and Peter' (Greg).
   98–9.] Compare the proverb, 'God comes with leaden (woolen) feet but
strikes with iron hands' (Dent G182).
   103. *consistory*] ecclesiastical senate in which the Pope and cardinals debate
on Church affairs (*OED*, 6).

And read amongst the statutes decretal
What, by the holy council held at Trent,   105
The sacred synod hath decreed for him
That doth assume the papal government
Without election and a true consent.
Away, and bring us word with speed.
First Cardinal. We go, my lord.   *Exeunt* CARDINALS.   110
Pope. Lord Raymond—
                [*Pope Adrian and Raymond converse apart.*]
Faustus. [*Aside.*] Go haste thee, gentle Mephistopheles.
Follow the cardinals to the consistory,
And as they turn their supersti..ous books
Strike them with sloth and drowsy idleness,   115
And make them sleep so sound that in their shapes
Thyself and I may parley with this Pope,
This proud confronter of the Emperor,
And in despite of all his holiness
Restore this Bruno to his liberty   120
And bear him to the states of Germany.
Mephistopheles. Faustus, I go.
Faustus. Dispatch it soon.
The Pope shall curse that Faustus came to Rome.
                Exeunt FAUSTUS *and* MEPHISTOPHELES.
Bruno. Pope Adrian, let me have some right of law.   125
I was elected by the Emperor.

111.1. S.D.] *Ribner (subst.); not in B1.*   112. S.D. *Aside] This ed.; not in B1.*   123. Dispatch] *B1 (Dispath).*   124.1. S.D. *Exeunt] B1 (Exit).*

104. *statutes decretal*] i.e., papal decrees.
105. *council held at Trent*] The Council of Trent, established to reform the Catholic Church, sat at intervals from 1545 to 1563, centuries after the episode Foxe narrates but with timely relevance to a Reformation audience.
106. *synod*] church assembly.
108. *election*] formal choosing for office, by election in the College of Cardinals or (at l. 126) by Imperial appointment.
119. *his holiness*] (a) his pretensions to saintliness (b) his honorific title of 'his Holiness'.
125. *Adrian*] The dramatist seems to have had in mind Adrian (or Hadrian) IV, the predecessor of Alexander III (see ll. 89–160n.), but may also have been thinking of Adrian VI (1522–3) as a more contemporary name (Jump).
126. *elected*] formally appointed. See l. 108n.

Pope. We will depose the Emperor for that deed
And curse the people that submit to him.
Both he and thou shalt stand excommunicate
And interdict from Church's privilege   130
And all society of holy men.
He grows too proud in his authority,
Lifting his lofty head above the clouds,
And like a steeple overpeers the Church.
But we'll pull down his haughty insolence.   135
And as Pope Alexander, our progenitor,
Trod on the neck of German Frederick,
Adding this golden sentence to our praise,
'That Peter's heirs should tread on emperors
And walk upon the dreadful adder's back,   140
Treading the lion and the dragon down,
And fearless spurn the killing basilisk',
So will we quell that haughty schismatic
And by authority apostolical
Depose him from his regal government.   145
Bruno. Pope Julius swore to princely Sigismund,
For him and the succeeding popes of Rome,
To hold the emperors their lawful lords.
Pope. Pope Julius did abuse the Church's rights,

149. rights] *Dyce 1;* Rites *B1.*

___

128. *curse*] excommunicate.
129.] Pope Alexander III excommunicated Frederick in 1165. More
recently, Pope Pius V had excommunicated Queen Elizabeth in 1570.
130. *interdict*] debarred.
134. *overpeers*] (a) peers down upon, towers above (b) domineers over his
peers.
136. *progenitor*] Adrian IV was in fact predecessor of Alexander III.
138. *to our praise*] to the praise of the papacy.
139–45.] According to Foxe (II.196), Alexander III recited this verse as he
placed his foot on Frederick's neck: '*Super aspidem et basiliscum ambulabis, et
conculcabis leonem et draconem*', 'Thou shalt walk upon the adder and on the
basilisk, and shalt tread down the lion and the dragon.' The present scene
conflates Adrian IV and Alexander III.
142. *basilisk*] a fabulous reptile, the breath and gaze of which were thought
to be fatal.
146–8.] This confrontation is unhistorical, but the Emperor Sigismund did
do battle with the papacy in the early fifteenth century, and Julius III was a
familiar name to Renaissance audiences as pope from 1550 to 1559.
149. *rights*] The B-text's *Rites* can be modernised as 'rights' or 'rites'. Both
meanings are available in the theatre, since pronunciation is identical.

And therefore none of his decrees can stand.   150
Is not all power on earth bestowed on us?
And therefore, though we would, we cannot err.
Behold this silver belt, whereto is fixed
Seven golden keys fast sealed with seven seals
In token of our sevenfold power from heaven,   155
To bind or loose, lock fast, condemn, or judge,
Resign, or seal, or whatso pleaseth us.
Then he and thou and all the world shall stoop,
Or be assurèd of our dreadful curse
To light as heavy as the pains of hell.   160

Enter FAUSTUS *and* MEPHISTOPHELES,
[*dressed*] *like the cardinals.*

Mephistopheles. [*Aside.*]
Now tell me, Faustus, are we not fitted well?
Faustus. [*Aside.*]
Yes, Mephistopheles, and two such cardinals
Ne'er served a holy pope as we shall do.
But whilst they sleep within the consistory,
Let us salute his reverend Fatherhood.   165
Raymond. [*To the Pope.*]
Behold, my lord, the cardinals are returned.
Pope. Welcome, grave fathers. Answer presently:
What have our holy council there decreed
Concerning Bruno and the Emperor,
In quittance of their late conspiracy   170

154. keys] *Oxberry;* seales *B1.*   160.2. s.d. *dressed*] *Dyce 1 (subst.); not in
B1.*   161, 162. s.d. *Aside*] *Kirschbaum; not in B1.*   166. s.d.] *This ed.; not
in B1.*

152. *though we would*] even if we wished to. The recently promulgated
notion of papal infallibility was much jeered at in Protestant England.
154. *keys*] i.e., keys of St Peter. B1's *seales* appears to be an anticipation of
the word at the end of this line.
157. *Resign*] Latin *resignare*, unseal (Boas).
160. *light*] alight; but with wordplay on the antithesis of 'light' and
'heavy'.
163. *served*] (*a*) performed official duties for (*b*) waited on at a banquet (*c*)
played a trick on, delivered blows to.
170. *quittance of*] requital for (*OED*, 'quittance', sb. 3, citing IV.ii.55
below as its earliest instance).

Against our state and papal dignity?
Faustus. Most sacred patron of the Church of Rome,
By full consent of all the synod
Of priests and prelates, it is thus decreed:
That Bruno and the German Emperor   175
Be held as Lollards and bold schismatics
And proud disturbers of the Church's peace.
And if that Bruno by his own assent,
Without enforcement of the German peers,
Did seek to wear the triple diadem   180
And by your death to climb Saint Peter's chair,
The statutes decretal have thus decreed:
He shall be straight condemned of heresy
And on a pile of faggots burnt to death.
Pope. It is enough. Here, take him to your charge, 185
And bear him straight to Ponte Angelo,
And in the strongest tower enclose him fast.
Tomorrow, sitting in our consistory
With all our college of grave cardinals,
We will determine of his life or death.   190
Here, take his triple crown along with you
And leave it in the Church's treasury.
[*Bruno's papal crown is given to Faustus and Mephistopheles.*]
Make haste again, my good lord cardinals,
And take our blessing apostolical.
Mephistopheles. [*Aside.*]
So, so, was never devil thus blest before!   195
Faustus. [*Aside.*] Away, sweet Mephistopheles, begone.
The cardinals will be plagued for this anon.

192.1. S.D.] *Kirschbaum (subst.); not in B1*.   195, 196. S.D. *Aside*] *Kirschbaum*
(*subst.*); *not in B1*.

---

176. *Lollards*] i.e., heretics, schismatics. Literally, followers of the English
radical reformer John Wycliff (1320–84).
179. *enforcement of*] being compelled by.
189. *college . . . cardinals*] the cardinals of the Church, who constitute the
Pope's council (*OED*, sb. 1). See l. 108n.
191. *his triple crown*] the papal tiara that Bruno had assumed. The
Admiral's Men had a 'poopes miter' among their properties (Henslowe's
Diary, p. 320).
193. *again*] back here again.

Exeunt FAUSTUS *and* MEPHISTOPHELES [*with* BRUNO].

Pope. Go presently and bring a banquet forth,
   That we may solemnise Saint Peter's feast
   And with Lord Raymond, King of Hungary,   200
   Drink to our late and happy victory.   *Exeunt.*

[III.ii]

*A sennet while the banquet is brought in. [Seats are provided
at the banquet. Exeunt* Attendants,] *and then enter* FAUSTUS
and MEPHISTOPHELES *in their own shapes.*

Mephistopheles. Now, Faustus, come prepare thyself for mirth.
   The sleepy cardinals are hard at hand
   To censure Bruno, that is posted hence
   And on a proud-paced steed, as swift as thought,
   Flies o'er the Alps to fruitful Germany,   5
   There to salute the woeful Emperor.
Faustus. The Pope will curse them for their sloth today,
   That slept both Bruno and his crown away.
   But now, that Faustus may delight his mind
   And by their folly make some merriment,   10
   Sweet Mephistopheles, so charm me here
   That I may walk invisible to all
   And do whate'er I please, unseen of any.
Mephistopheles.
   Faustus, thou shalt. Then kneel down presently,
                                      [*Faustus kneels.*]
   Whilst on thy head I lay my hand   15
   And charm thee with this magic wand.
                           [*Presenting a magic girdle.*]

197.1. S.D. *with* BRUNO] *Dyce 1; not in B1.*   III.ii.0.1. S.D. *sennet*] *B1*
(*Senit*).   0.1–2. S.D. *Seats* . . . Attendants] *This ed.; not in B1.*   14.1,
16.1, 23. S.D.] *This ed.; not in B1.*   15–23.] *Printed in roman in B1, as
distinguished from the black-letter type used for normal speech.*

III.ii.0.1. S.D. A sennet] This trumpet flourish probably belongs at l. 28,
as in the comparable scene in the A-text, though the carrying on of the
banquet may well occur here. A sennet may also have been sounded for the
Pope's departure at the end of the previous scene.
   6. *woeful*] i.e., concerned about Bruno's captivity.
   8. *slept*] lost though inattentiveness.
   16. *wand*] an acceptable rhyme with *hand* in l. 15.

First wear this girdle; then appear
Invisible to all are here.
The planets seven, the gloomy air,
Hell, and the Furies' forkèd hair,   20
Pluto's blue fire, and Hecate's tree
With magic spells so compass thee
That no eye may thy body see.   [*Faustus rises.*]
So, Faustus, now, for all their holiness,
Do what thou wilt, thou shalt not be discerned.   25
Faustus. Thanks, Mephistopheles. Now, friars, take heed
Lest Faustus make your shaven crowns to bleed.
Mephistopheles.
Faustus, no more. See where the cardinals come.

Enter POPE *and all the lords:* [RAYMOND, KING OF HUNGARY,
the ARCHBISHOP OF RHEIMS, *etc.*, Friars *and* Attendants.]
Enter the [*two*] CARDINALS [*of France and Padua*]
with a book.

Pope. Welcome, lord cardinals. Come sit down.   [*They sit.*]
Lord Raymond, take your seat. Friars, attend,   30
And see that all things be in readiness,
As best beseems this solemn festival.
First Cardinal. First, may it please your sacred Holiness
To view the sentence of the reverend synod
Concerning Bruno and the Emperor?   35
Pope. What needs this question? Did I not tell you
Tomorrow we would sit i'th'consistory

28.1–2. S.D. RAYMOND . . . Attendants] *D*y*ce 1 (subst.); not in B1.*   28.3.
S.D. *two . . . of France and Padua*] *Dyce 1 (subst.); not in B1.*   29. S.D. *They
sit*] *This ed.; not in B1.*

---

17. *girdle*] a belt worn round the waist, often used to carry a weapon or
purse.
18. *all are*] all that are.
20. *Furies' forkèd hair*] The Furies were dread goddesses with forked-
tongued snakes twined in the hair (Greg).
21.] i.e., the sulphurous flames of Pluto's underworld, and the gallows tree
associated with Hecate, or Trivia, as goddess of cross-ways, where gallows
were set up (Greg). Or perhaps *tree* is an error for *three*, alluding to Hecate's
triform divinity (Boas).
22. *compass*] encompass.
32. *solemn*] ceremonious, sacred.

And there determine of his punishment?
You brought us word even now, it was decreed
That Bruno and the cursèd Emperor   40
Were by the holy council both condemned
For loathèd Lollards and base schismatics.
Then wherefore would you have me view that book?
First Cardinal.
Your Grace mistakes. You gave us no such charge.
Raymond. Deny it not. We all are witnesses   45
That Bruno here was late delivered you,
With his rich triple crown to be reserved
And put into the Church's treasury.
Both Cardinals. By holy Paul, we saw them not.
Pope. By Peter, you shall die   50
Unless you bring them forth immediately.—
Hale them to prison. Lade their limbs with gyves!—
False prelates, for this hateful treachery
Curst be your souls to hellish misery.
       [*Exeunt* Attendants *with the two* CARDINALS.]
Faustus. [*Aside.*]
So, they are safe. Now, Faustus, to the feast.   55
The Pope had never such a frolic guest.
Pope. Lord Archbishop of Rheims, sit down with us.
Archbishop. [*Sitting.*] I thank your Holiness.
Faustus. Fall to. The devil choke you an you spare.
Pope. Who's that spoke? Friars, look about.   60
Lord Raymond, pray fall to. I am beholding
To the Bishop of Milan for this so rare a present.
Faustus. [*Snatching the meat.*] I thank you, sir.
Pope. How now? Who snatched the meat from me?
Villains, why speak you not?—   65
My good Lord Archbishop, here's a most dainty dish

49. S.H. *Both Cardinals*] *B1* (*Amb. Card*).   54.1. S.D.] *Dyce 1; not in B1.*
55. S.D. *Aside*] *Kirschbaum; not in B1.*   58, 80. S.H. *Archbishop*] *Dyce 1;*
Bish. B1.   58. S.D. *Sitting*] *This ed.; not in B1.*   63. S.D.] *A1 (subst.); not*
in B1.

47. *reserved*] stored, set aside.
52. *Lade . . . gyves*] load . . . shackles.
55. *safe*] safely out of the way.
56. *frolic*] full of pranks.

Was sent me from a Cardinal in France.   .

Faustus. [*Snatching the dish.*] I'll have that, too.

Pope. What Lollards do attend our Holiness,

    That we receive such great indignity?   70

    Fetch me some wine.   [*Wine is brought.*]

Faustus. [*Aside.*] Ay, pray do, for Faustus is adry.

Pope. Lord Raymond, I drink unto your Grace.

Faustus. [*Snatching the cup.*] I pledge your Grace.

Pope. My wine gone, too? Ye lubbers, look about   75

    And find the man that doth this villainy,

    Or by our sanctitude you all shall die!—

    I pray, my lords, have patience at this troublesome ban-

    quet.

Archbishop. Please it your Holiness, I think it be some ghost   80

    crept out of purgatory and now is come unto your

    Holiness for his pardon.

Pope. It may be so.

    Go, then, command our priests to sing a dirge

    To lay the fury of this same troublesome ghost.   85

                       [*Exit one.*]

                 [*The Pope crosses himself.*]

Faustus. How now? Must every bit be spicèd with a cross?

             [*The Pope crosses himself again.*]

    Nay, then, take that!

          [*Faustus gives the Pope a blow on the head.*]

Pope. O, I am slain! Help me, my lords.

    O, come and help to bear my body hence.

    Damned be this soul for ever for this deed!   90

              Exeunt the POPE *and his train.*

---

68. s.d.] *Dyce 1 (subst.); not in B1.*   70–1.] *divided as in Oxberry; one line
in B1.*   71. s.d.] *Kirschbaum (subst.); not in B1.*   72. s.d. Aside]
Kirschbaum; not in B1.   74. s.d.] *Dyce 1 (subst.); not in B1.*   78–9.] *prose
as in Gill 1; as verse divided at* this / Troublesome *in B1.*   85.1. s.d. *Exit
one*] *Dyce 1 (subst.); not in B1.*   85.2, 86.1, 87.1. s.d.] *A1 (subst.); not in
B1.*

---

67. *Was*] that was.
72. *adry*] dry, thirsty.
75. *lubbers*] clumsy louts.
82. *pardon*] indulgence.

Mephistopheles. Now, Faustus, what will you do now? For I
    can tell you you'll be cursed with bell, book, and candle.
Faustus. Bell, book, and candle; candle, book, and bell,
    Forward and backward, to curse Faustus to hell.

Enter the FRIARS *with bell, book, and candle, for the dirge.*

First Friar. Come, brethren, let's about our business with   95
    good devotion.
                    [*The Friars chant.*]
Cursèd be he that stole his Holiness' meat from the table.
    Maledicat Dominus!
Cursèd be he that struck his Holiness a blow on the face.
    Maledicat Dominus!   100
Cursèd be he that struck Friar Sandelo a blow on the pate.
    Maledicat Dominus!
Cursèd be he that disturbeth our holy dirge.
    Maledicat Dominus!
Cursèd be he that took away his Holiness' wine.   105
    Maledicat Dominus!
        [FAUSTUS *and* MEPHISTOPHELES] *beat the* FRIARS,
            fling firework among them, and exeunt.

[III.iii]

        Enter CLOWN [ROBIN], *and* DICK *with a cup.*

Dick. Sirrah Robin, we were best look that your devil can
    answer the stealing of this same cup, for the Vintner's
    boy follows us at the hard heels.

91–2.] *prose as in Dyce 1; as verse divided at* you / You'le *in* B1.   96.1. S.D.]
Ribner (subst.); not in B1; *Sing this* A1.   99. on] A1; *not in* B1.   102, 104,
106. Dominus] B1 *(Dom.).*   106.1. S.D. FAUSTUS *and* MEPHISTOPHELES]
Dyce 1 (subst.); not in B1.   106.1–2. S.D. beat . . . and] *printed in black letter
in* B1, *as distinguished from the roman type usually used for stage directions.*
106.2. S.D. exeunt] A1; *Exeunt. Exeunt.* B1.   III.iii.0.1. S.D. ROBIN] *Dyce 1;
not in* B1.

99. *on*] A1 supplies this word omitted in error from B1.

III.iii.2. *answer*] answer charges in regard to.
2–3. *the Vintner's boy*] The one who chases them is instead the Vintner
(see l. 27), but see A III.ii.6.n on the possibility that the character was
originally the Vintner's boy.
3. *at the hard heels*] hard on our heels.

Robin. 'Tis no matter. Let him come. An he follow us, I'll
so conjure him as he was never conjured in his life, I   5
warrant him. Let me see the cup.

Enter VINTNER.

Dick. [*Giving the cup to Robin.*] Here 'tis. Yonder he comes.
Now, Robin, now or never show thy cunning.
Vintner. O, are you here? I am glad I have found you. You are
a couple of fine companions! Pray, where's the cup you   10
stole from the tavern?
Robin. How, how? We steal a cup? Take heed what you say.
We look not like cup-stealers, I can tell you.
Vintner. Never deny't, for I know you have it, and I'll search
you.   15
Robin. Search me? Ay, and spare not. [*Aside to Dick, giving
him the cup.*] Hold the cup, Dick. [*To the Vintner.*] Come,
come, search me, search me.

[*The Vintner searches Robin.*]

Vintner. [*To Dick.*] Come on, sirrah, let me search you now.
Dick. Ay, ay, do, do. [*Aside to Robin, giving him the cup.*]   20
Hold the cup, Robin. [*To the Vintner.*] I fear not your
searching. We scorn to steal your cups, I can tell you.

[*The Vintner searches Dick.*]

Vintner. Never outface me for the matter, for sure the cup is
between you two.
Robin. [*Brandishing the cup.*] Nay, there you lie. 'Tis beyond   25
us both.

7. S.D. *Giving the cup to Robin*] Wagner (subst.); not in *B1*.   16. S.D. *Aside to
Dick*] Oxberry; not in *B1*.   16–17, 20. S.D. *giving him the cup*] Dyce *1*; not in
B1.   17, 21. S.D. *To the Vintner*] Jump; not in *B1*.   18.1. S.D. *The Vintner
searches Robin*] Dyce *1* (subst.); not in *B1*.   19. S.D. *To Dick*] Boas; not in
B1.   20. S.D. *Aside to Robin*] Oxberry; not in *B1*.   22.1. S.D. *The Vintner
searches Dick*] Dyce *1* (subst.); not in *B1*.   25. S.D. *Brandishing the cup*] This
ed.; not in *B1*.

10. *companions*] fellows.
23. *Never . . . matter*] don't impudently deny it to me.
23–4. *is between you two*] is on one of you. But Robin quibbles on the
sense of 'physically in between'.
25–6. *'Tis beyond us both*] Compare the A-text version, where Robin holds
out the goblet and says it is right there in front of him, not 'about' him or on
his person. *Beyond* here is a similar quibble: 'The cup isn't in *between* the two
of us, it's out *here*.'

Vintner. A plague take you! I thought 'twas your knavery to
take it away. Come, give it me again.
Robin. Ay, much! When, can you tell? Dick, make me a
circle, and stand close at my back, and stir not for   30
thy life. [*Dick makes a circle.*] Vintner, you shall have
your cup anon. Say nothing, Dick. 'O' *per se* 'O',
Demogorgon, Belcher, and Mephistopheles!

    Enter MEPHISTOPHELES.

                              [*Exit the* VINTNER, *running.*]
Mephistopheles. You princely legions of infernal rule,
How am I vexèd by these villains' charms!   35
From Constantinople have they brought me now
Only for pleasure of these damnèd slaves.
Robin. By Lady, sir, you have had a shrewd journey of it. Will
it please you to take a shoulder of mutton to supper and a
tester in your purse, and go back again?   40
Dick. Ay, I pray you heartily, sir, for we called you but in
jest, I promise you.
Mephistopheles. To purge the rashness of this cursèd deed,
[*To Dick.*] First, be thou turnèd to this ugly shape,
For apish deeds transformèd to an ape.   45
Robin. O brave, an ape! I pray, sir, let me have the carrying
of him about to show some tricks.

---

31. S.D.] *Kirschbaum; not in B1.*   33.2. S.D. *Exit the* VINTNER, *running*]
Kirschbaum (subst.); not in B1; placed after l. 35 in Dyce 1.   38. shrewd] *B1*
(shroud).   44. S.D. *To Dick*] *Kirschbaum (subst.); not in B1.*

29. *Ay* ... *tell*] i.e., (jeeringly) sure, right away.
29–30. *make . . . circle*] draw a circle for me on the ground.
32. *Say nothing*] Speech is dangerous in conjuring; compare IV.i.92–6,
V.i.26.
33.2. S.D.] The timing of the Vintner's exit is uncertain, as in the A-text
version.
38. *By Lady*] by our Lady.
shrewd] vexatious (*OED*, adj. 4).
40. *tester*] sixpence.
42. *promise*] assure.
44–9.] As in the A-text version, some comic transformations presumably
occur for the audience to see. Later, at IV.v.55–6, Robin recalls that one of
Faustus's devils 'turned me into the likeness of an ape's face', perhaps
suggesting (despite the confusion as to which of the clowns is turned into an
ape) that the transformations here in III.iii are to be achieved by means of

Mephistopheles. And so thou shalt. Be thou transformed to a
dog, and carry him upon thy back. Away, begone!

Robin. A dog? That's excellent. Let the maids look well to   50
their porridge pots, for I'll into the kitchen presently.
Come, Dick, come.

   Exeunt the two CLOWNS [*with Dick on Robin's back*].

Mephistopheles. Now with the flames of ever-burning fire
 I'll wing myself and forthwith fly amain
 Unto my Faustus, to the Great Turk's court.   *Exit.*   55

52.1. S.D. *with Dick on Robin's back*] *Kirschbaum (subst.); not in B1.*

---

masks. The actors' ludicrous apelike and doglike gestures would also help
create the illusion, of course. The Admiral's Men had 'j black dogge' in their
inventory of props in 1598; see Henslowe's *Diary*, p. 321.

 54. *amain*] at full speed, in all haste.

 55. *the Great Turk's court*] This points to an adventure recorded in the
Damnable Life (ch. 22) but not in either text of the play as we have them.

Act IV

Enter MARTINO *and* FREDERICK [*with other* Officers
and Gentlemen] *at several doors.*

Martino. What ho, officers, gentlemen!
　Hie to the presence to attend the Emperor.
　Good Frederick, see the rooms be voided straight;
　His Majesty is coming to the hall.
　Go back, and see the state in readiness. 　　　　　5

　　　　　　　　　　　　　　[Exeunt some.]
Frederick. But where is Bruno, our elected pope,
　That on a Fury's back came post from Rome?
　Will not his Grace consort the Emperor?
Martino. O, yes, and with him comes the German conjurer,
　The learnèd Faustus, fame of Wittenberg, 　　　　10
　The wonder of the world for magic art;
　And he intends to show great Carolus
　The race of all his stout progenitors,
　And bring in presence of his Majesty
　The royal shapes and warlike semblances 　　　　15
　Of Alexander and his beauteous paramour.
Frederick. Where is Benvolio?
Martino. Fast asleep, I warrant you.
　He took his rouse with stoups of Rhenish wine

IV.i.0.1–2. S.D. *with other* Officers *and* Gentlemen] *This ed.; not in* B1.
5.1. S.D.] *This ed.; not in* B1.

IV.i.2. *presence*] presence chamber, room for ceremonial attendance.
3. *voided straight*] cleared at once.
5. *state*] throne.
7. *post*] at full speed (as though with post-horses).
8.] i.e., is Bruno expected to be here shortly, attending the Emperor?
12. *Carolus*] the Emperor Charles V.
13. *stout progenitors*] brave ancestors and predecessors.
19. *took his rouse*] went on a binge. The whole line seems to be borrowed from *Ham.*, I.iv.8–10, 'The King doth wake tonight and takes his rouse . . . drains his draughts of Rhenish down', written here as part of an addition

249

So kindly yesternight to Bruno's health   20
That all this day the sluggard keeps his bed.
Frederick. See, see, his window's ope. We'll call to him.
Martino. What ho, Benvolio!

Enter BENVOLIO *above at a window, in his nightcap, buttoning.*

Benvolio. What a devil ail you two?
Martino. Speak softly, sir, lest the devil hear you;   25
    For Faustus at the court is late arrived,
    And at his heels a thousand Furies wait
    To accomplish whatsoever the doctor please.
Benvolio. What of this?
Martino. Come, leave thy chamber first, and thou shalt see   30
    This conjurer perform such rare exploits
    Before the Pope and royal Emperor
    As never yet was seen in Germany.
Benvolio. Has not the Pope enough of conjuring yet?
    He was upon the devil's back late enough;   35
    An if he be so far in love with him,
    I would he would post with him to Rome again.
Frederick. Speak, wilt thou come and see this sport?
Benvolio.   Not I.
Martino. Wilt thou stand in thy window and see it, then?
Benvolio. Ay, an I fall not asleep i'th'meantime.   40
Martino. The Emperor is at hand, who comes to see
    What wonders by black spells may compassed be.
Benvolio. Well, go you attend the Emperor. I am content for
    this once to thrust my head out at a window, for they say
    if a man be drunk overnight the devil cannot hurt him in   45

---

36. An] *B1* (And); *also at* ll. *40, 98, 133, 164.*

---

after 1601 (Bowers, II.137–8). These are the *OED*'s first two citations
('rouse', sb.³ 3).
    stoups] tankards-full.
    20. *kindly*] fittingly, readily, properly, agreeably. (Said ironically.)
    32. *the Pope*] i.e., Bruno. (In ll. 34–7, Benvolio refers to Bruno's magical
ride 'as swift as thought', III.ii.4, from Rome to Germany.)
    42. *compassed*] encompassed.

the morning. If that be true, I have a charm in my head
shall control him as well as the conjurer, I warrant you.

    Exeunt [FREDERICK *and* MARTINO.
    BENVOLIO *remains at his window*].

A sennet. [*Enter*] CHARLES THE GERMAN EMPEROR, BRUNO,
[THE DUKE OF] SAXONY, FAUSTUS, MEPHISTOPHELES,
FREDERICK, MARTINO, *and* Attendants. [*The Emperor
sits in his throne.*]

Emperor. Wonder of men, renowned magician,
 Thrice-learnèd Faustus, welcome to our court.
 This deed of thine, in setting Bruno free   50
 From his and our professèd enemy,
 Shall add more excellence unto thine art
 Than if by powerful necromantic spells
 Thou couldst command the world's obedience.
 For ever be beloved of Carolus.   55
 And if this Bruno thou hast late redeemed
 In peace possess the triple diadem
 And sit in Peter's chair, despite of chance,

47.1. S.D. *Exeunt*] B1 (*Exit*). 47.1. S.D. FREDERICK *and* MARTINO] Dyce
1; *not in* B1. 47.2. S.D. BENVOLIO *remains at his window*] Greg (*but placed
at* 47.6), *conj.* Dyce 1; *not in* B1. 47.3, 102.2. S.D. *sennet*] B1 (*Senit*).
47.3. S.D. *Enter*] B4; *not in* B1. 47.4. S.D. THE DUKE OF] *Oxberry*; *not in*
B1. 47.5–6. S.D. *The Emperor sits in his throne*] Kirschbaum (subst.); *not
in* B1.

46–7. *I have . . . conjurer*] i.e., my hangover should do as well at coping
with the devil as Doctor Faustus's conjuring would.
 47.1–2. S.D.] B1's *Exit* clearly cannot apply to Benvolio, who remains at
his window. It may well apply to Frederick and Martino, who have been
ordered to go 'attend the Emperor' at l. 43 and who re-enter at l. 47.5. Since
the Emperor and his entourage now enter, however, Frederick and Martino
may simply join in the entering throng; compare *AWW* at the transition from
v.ii. to v.iii. Another possibility is that they exit at l. 43 and that Benvolio
then speaks in soliloquy to the audience. In any case, the continued presence
of Benvolio militates against the marking of a new scene, as most editors do.
Compare *H8*, v.ii.35, where editorial tradition usually marks a new scene
even though King Henry remains at a window (behind a curtain) and
Cranmer remains on stage.
 51. *professèd*] openly declared.
 56. *late redeemed*] lately rescued.
 58. *despite of chance*] in spite of fortune.

Thou shalt be famous through all Italy
And honoured of the German Emperor.   60
Faustus. These gracious words, most royal Carolus,
Shall make poor Faustus to his utmost power
Both love and serve the German Emperor
And lay his life at holy Bruno's feet.
For proof whereof, if so your Grace be pleased,   65
The doctor stands prepared by power of art
To cast his magic charms, that shall pierce through
The ebon gates of ever-burning hell
And hale the stubborn Furies from their caves
To compass whatsoe'er your Grace commands.   70
Benvolio. [*Aside, at the window.*] Blood, he speaks terribly.
But for all that, I do not greatly believe him. He looks as
like a conjurer as the Pope to a costermonger.
Emperor. Then, Faustus, as thou late didst promise us,
We would behold that famous conqueror   75
Great Alexander and his paramour
In their true shapes and state majestical,
That we may wonder at their excellence.
Faustus. Your Majesty shall see them presently.—
[*Aside to Mephistopheles.*] Mephistopheles, away,   80
And with a solemn noise of trumpet's sound
Present before this royal Emperor
Great Alexander and his beauteous paramour.
Mephistopheles. [*Aside to Faustus.*] Faustus, I will.   [*Exit.*]
Benvolio. [*At the window.*] Well, Master Doctor, an your   85
devils come not away quickly, you shall have me asleep
presently. Zounds, I could eat myself for anger to think I
have been such an ass all this while, to stand gaping after
the devil's governor and can see nothing.

71. S.D. *Aside*] *Dyce 1; not in B1.*   71, 85, 98. S.D. *at the window*] *This ed.;
not in B1; above Boas (at l. 71 only).*   73. like a] *B2;* like *B1.*   80. S.D.]
Kirschbaum (subst.); not in B1.   84. S.D. *Aside to Faustus*] *Kirschbaum
(subst.); not in B1.*   84. S.D. *Exit*] *A1; not in B1.*   85, 154. Master]
B1 (M.).

66. *The doctor*] i.e., Faustus himself.
68. *ebon*] ebony, black.
71. *Blood*] 'sblood, by his (Christ's) blood. (An oath.)
73. *costermonger*] fruit seller.
88–9. *after the devil's governor*] i.e., at one who claims to command the
devil.

Faustus. [*Aside.*] I'll make you feel something anon, if my art   90
    fail me not.—
    [*To Emperor.*] My lord, I must forewarn your Majesty
    That when my spirits present the royal shapes
    Of Alexander and his paramour,
    Your Grace demand no questions of the king,   95
    But in dumb silence let them come and go.
Emperor. Be it as Faustus please. We are content.
Benvolio. [*At the window.*] Ay, ay, and I am content too. An
    thou bring Alexander and his paramour before the Em-
    peror, I'll be Actaeon and turn myself to a stag.   100
Faustus. [*Aside.*] And I'll play Diana and send you the horns
    presently.

                [*Enter* MEPHISTOPHELES]

    A sennet. Enter at one [door] the Emperor ALEXANDER, *at the
other* DARIUS. *They meet; Darius is thrown down. Alexander kills
him, takes off his crown, and, offering to go out, his* PARAMOUR
*meets him. He embraceth her and sets Darius's crown upon her
head; and, coming back, both salute the [German] Emperor,
who, leaving his state, offers to embrace them, which Faustus
seeing suddenly stays him.
    Then trumpets cease and music sounds.*

    My gracious lord, you do forget yourself.
    These are but shadows, not substantial.
Emperor. O, pardon me. My thoughts are so ravishèd   105
    With sight of this renownèd emperor
    That in mine arms I would have compassed him.
    But Faustus, since I may not speak to them
    To satisfy my longing thoughts at full,
    Let me this tell thee: I have heard it said   110
    That this fair lady, whilst she lived on earth,

90, 101. S.D. *Aside*] *Wagner; not in* B1.   92. S.D.] *This ed.; not in* B1.
102.1. S.D. *Enter* MEPHISTOPHELES] *Bowers; not in* B1.   102.2. S.D. *A
sennet*] B1 (*Senit*); ('A' *is printed as the catchword on the previous page but
mistakenly omitted from the* S.D. *itself*).   102.2. S.D. *door*] B2; *not in* B1.
102.6. S.D. *German*] *This ed.; not in* B1.   111. *whilst*] B1 (*whilest*).

    102.3. S.D. *DARIUS*] Alexander defeated Darius III, King of Persia, in
333 BC.
    102.4. S.D. *offering to*] as he is about to.
    107. *compassed*] enfolded.

Had on her neck a little wart or mole.
How may I prove that saying to be true?
Faustus. Your Majesty may boldly go and see.
Emperor. [Making an inspection.] Faustus, I see it plain,   115
And in this sight thou better pleasest me
Than if I gained another monarchy.
Faustus. [To the spirits.] Away, begone!

                                        Exit Show.
See, see, my gracious lord, what strange beast is yon, that
thrusts his head out at window.   120
            [Benvolio is seen to have sprouted horns.]
Emperor. O wondrous sight! See, Duke of Saxony,
Two spreading horns most strangely fastenèd
Upon the head of young Benvolio.
Saxony. What, is he asleep, or dead?
Faustus. He sleeps, my lord, but dreams not of his horns.   125
Emperor. This sport is excellent. We'll call and wake him.—
What ho, Benvolio!
Benvolio. A plague upon you! Let me sleep a while.
Emperor. I blame thee not to sleep much, having such a head
of thine own.   130
Saxony. Look up, Benvolio. 'Tis the Emperor calls.
Benvolio. The Emperor? Where? O, zounds, my head!
Emperor. Nay, an thy horns hold, 'tis no matter for thy head,
for that's armed sufficiently.
Faustus. Why, how now, sir knight? What, hanged by the   135
horns? This is most horrible. Fie, fie, pull in your head,
for shame. Let not all the world wonder at you.
Benvolio. Zounds, doctor, is this your villainy?
Faustus. O, say not so, sir. The doctor has no skill,

115, 118. S.D.] *This ed.; bracketed material not in B1.*   120.1. S.D.] *This ed.;
not in B1; Enter the Knight with a paire of hornes on his head A1.*   136. is]
B2; not in B1.

---

129. *I blame . . . much*] I don't much blame you for sleeping.

132-4.] Benvolio, wakening with a jolt as he bangs his head on the
window frame, laments the shameful signs of cuckoldry he now wears. The
Emperor jests that Benvolio has no need to worry about his head ('O,
zounds, my head!'), since he's provided there with such magnificent horns to
defend himself.

139. *has no skill*] Faustus mockingly paraphrases Benvolio's insults.

No art, no cunning to present these lords   140
Or bring before this royal Emperor
The mighty monarch, warlike Alexander.
If Faustus do it, you are straight resolved
In bold Actaeon's shape to turn a stag.—
And therefore, my lord, so please your Majesty,   145
I'll raise a kennel of hounds shall hunt him so
As all his footmanship shall scarce prevail
To keep his carcass from their bloody fangs.
Ho, Belimoth, Argiron, Ashtaroth!

Benvolio. Hold, hold! Zounds, he'll raise up a kennel of   150
devils, I think, anon.—Good my lord, entreat for me.—
[*Benvolio is attacked by devils.*] 'Sblood, I am never able to
endure these torments.

Emperor. Then, good Master Doctor,
Let me entreat you to remove his horns.   155
He has done penance now sufficiently.

Faustus. My gracious lord, not so much for injury done to
me as to delight your Majesty with some mirth hath
Faustus justly requited this injurious knight; which
being all I desire, I am content to remove his horns.—   160
Mephistopheles, transform him. [*Mephistopheles removes
the horns.*] And hereafter, sir, look you speak well of
scholars.

Benvolio. [*Aside.*] Speak well of ye? 'Sblood, an scholars be
such cuckold-makers to clap horns of honest men's heads   165

---

149. Belimoth . . . Ashtaroth] *B1* (*Belimote . . . Asterote*).   152. S.D.] *This
ed.; not in B1.*   161–2, 164. S.D.] *Dyce 1; not in B1.*

---

146. *shall*] that shall.
147. *footmanship*] skill in running.
149.] Two of these devils turn up again at IV.ii.78. Ashtaroth or Astarte
(B1, *Asterote*) is a Phoenician deity. Greg, suggesting that *Belimoth* and
Argiron may be corruptions of Behemoth and Acheron, compares Barnabe
Barnes's *The Devil's Charter* (1607) where the chief devil Astaroth calls upon
Orcus, Erebus, and Acheron as among 'those ghosts which haunt . . .
Cimmerian shades' (ed. Pogue, ll. 3255–7).
152. *'Sblood*] by his (Christ's) blood.
never able] totally unable.
157. *injury*] insult.
165. *of*] on.

o' this order, I'll ne'er trust smooth faces and small ruffs
more. But, an I be not revenged for this, would I might
be turned to a gaping oyster and drink nothing but salt
water.   [*Exit from the window.*]

Emperor. Come, Faustus. While the Emperor lives,   170
In recompense of this thy high desert
Thou shalt command the state of Germany
And live beloved of mighty Carolus.   *Exeunt omnes.*

[IV.ii]

     Enter BENVOLIO, MARTINO, FREDERICK, *and* Soldiers.

Martino. Nay, sweet Benvolio, let us sway thy thoughts
From this attempt against the conjurer.
Benvolio. Away! You love me not, to urge me thus.
Shall I let slip so great an injury
When every servile groom jests at my wrongs   5
And in their rustic gambols proudly say,
'Benvolio's head was graced with horns today'?
O, may these eyelids never close again
Till with my sword I have that conjurer slain!
If you will aid me in this enterprise,   10
Then draw your weapons and be resolute.
If not, depart. Here will Benvolio die
But Faustus' death shall quit my infamy.
Frederick. Nay, we will stay with thee, betide what may,
And kill that doctor if he come this way.   15

---

169. S:D. *Exit*] Dyce 1; not in B1.   169. S.D. *from the window*] Kirchbaum
(*subst.*); not in B1.

166. *o' this order*] in this fashion.
    smooth . . . ruffs] 'beardless scholars in academical garb' (Boas). Benvolio's
remark, seemingly at odds with the discussion of Faustus's beard at IV.ii.59–
61, may simply reflect the conventional pejorative use of 'smooth-faced', i.e.,
'ingratiating'; compare 'That smooth-faced gentleman, tickling Commodity'
(*John*, II.i.574; *OED*'s first citation, adj. 1b).
    168–9. *and drink . . . water*] A fate worse than death for one like Benvolio
who loves his drink.

    IV.ii.5. *groom*] low fellow.
    13. *But*] unless.
    quit] repay.

Benvolio. Then, gentle Frederick, hie thee to the grove,
And place our servants and our followers
Close in an ambush there behind the trees.
By this, I know, the conjurer is near;
I saw him kneel and kiss the Emperor's hand   20
And take his leave, laden with rich rewards.
Then, soldiers, boldly fight. If Faustus die,
Take you the wealth; leave us the victory.
Frederick. Come, soldiers, follow me unto the grove.
Who kills him shall have gold and endless love.   25
                    Exit FREDERICK *with the* Soldiers.
Benvolio. My head is lighter than it was by th'horns,
But yet my heart's more ponderous than my head
And pants until I see that conjurer dead.
Martino. Where shall we place ourselves, Benvolio?
Benvolio. Here will we stay to bide the first assault.   30
O, were that damnèd hellhound but in place,
Thou soon shouldst see me quit my foul disgrace.

                    Enter FREDERICK.

Frederick. Close, close! The conjurer is at hand
And all alone comes walking in his gown.
Be ready, then, and strike the peasant down.   35
Benvolio.
Mine be that honour, then. Now, sword, strike home!
For horns he gave, I'll have his head anon.

                    Enter FAUSTUS, *with the false head.*

IV.ii.27. heart's] *B2;* heart *B1.*

_____

16.] a seeming echo of I.i.147.
18. *Close*] closely hidden.
19. *By this*] by this time.
25. *Who*] whoever.
26. *lighter*] (*a*) less heavy (*b*) in better spirits.
27.] On the resemblance of this line to Folio *Lear,* I.i.77–8, 'And yet not so, since I am sure my love's / More ponderous than my tongue', see Introduction, pp. 73–4. The correction of B1's *heart* to *heart's* seems necessary.
31. *in place*] here.
37.1. S.D. *the false head*] The phrase points to a recognisable stage property, the only one of its kind owned by the acting company. Compare *MND,* III.i.97.1, where, according to the Folio text, Bottom enters '*with the Asse head*'.

Martino. See, see, he comes.
Benvolio.   No words. This blow ends all.
   Hell take his soul! His body thus must fall.
                              [*He strikes Faustus.*]
Faustus. [*Falling.*] O!   40
Frederick. Groan you, Master Doctor?
Benvolio.
   Break may his heart with groans! Dear Frederick, see,
   Thus will I end his griefs immediately.
Martino. Strike with a willing hand.
                    [*Benvolio strikes off Faustus's false head.*]
                              His head is off!
Benvolio. The devil's dead. The Furies now may laugh.   45
Frederick. Was this that stern aspect, that awful frown,
   Made the grim monarch of infernal spirits
   Tremble and quake at his commanding charms?
Martino. Was this that damnèd head whose heart conspired
   Benvolio's shame before the Emperor?   50
Benvolio. Ay, that's the head, and here the body lies,
   Justly rewarded for his villainies.
Frederick. Come, let's devise how we may add more shame
   To the black scandal of his hated name.
Benvolio. First, on his head, in quittance of my wrongs,   55
   I'll nail huge forkèd horns and let them hang
   Within the window where he yoked me first,
   That all the world may see my just revenge.
Martino. What use shall we put his beard to?
Benvolio. We'll sell it to a chimney-sweeper. It will wear out   60
   ten birchen brooms, I warrant you.

39.1. S.D. *He strikes Faustus*] Dyce 1 (*Stabs Faustus*); *not in B1*.   40. S.D.
Falling] Dyce 1; *not in B1*.   44. S.D.] Robinson; *not in B1*.

---

43. *end his griefs*] put him out of his misery. (Said mockingly.)
45. *laugh*] i.e., laugh with revengeful glee.
46. *awful*] awe-inspiring.
47. *Made*] that made.
49. *heart*] Some editors emend, unnecessarily, to *art*.
57. *yoked me*] i.e., imprisoned me with my horned head stuck out of the
window, as in a yoke or pillory.
60. *wear out*] outlast.
61. *birchen*] made of birch twigs.

Frederick. What shall his eyes do?

Benvolio. We'll put out his eyes, and they shall serve for
    buttons to his lips to keep his tongue from catching cold.

Martino. An excellent policy. And now, sirs, having divided   65
    him, what shall the body do?

                                        [*Faustus rises.*]

Benvolio. Zounds, the devil's alive again!

Frederick. Give him his head, for God's sake!

Faustus. Nay, keep it. Faustus will have heads and hands,
    Ay, all your hearts, to recompense this deed.   70
    Knew you not, traitors, I was limited
    For four-and-twenty years to breathe on earth?
    And had you cut my body with your swords,
    Or hewed this flesh and bones as small as sand,
    Yet in a minute had my spirit returned,   75
    And I had breathed a man made free from harm.
    But wherefore do I dally my revenge?
    Ashtaroth, Belimoth, Mephistopheles!

    Enter MEPHISTOPHELES *and other* Devils [BELIMOTH
                and ASHTAROTH].

    Go horse these traitors on your fiery backs,
    And mount aloft with them as high as heaven;   80
    Thence pitch them headlong to the lowest hell.
    Yet stay. The world shall see their misery,
    And hell shall after plague their treachery.
    Go, Belimoth, and take this caitiff hence,

---

62. his] *B2; not in B1.*   66.1. S.D.] *Robinson (subst.); not in B1.*   70. Ay,
all] *Oxberry;* I call *B1.*   78.1-2. S.D. BELIMOTH *and* ASHTAROTH] *This ed.;
not in B1.*

---

65. *policy*] stratagem.

71-2.] Although Faustus here implies that his twenty-four-year contract is
common knowledge, it will later come as a complete surprise to the scholars
(see B v.ii.65-74). The inconsistency suggests that the revisers in 1602 were
anticipating what was no doubt by that time common knowledge in England.

71. *limited*] appointed to a specific term.

77. *dally*] trifle with, put off.

79. *horse*] mount. Devils often carry off their victims to hell in cycle and
morality plays.

84. *this caitiff*] i.e., Martino. (See IV.iii.4-5.)

And hurl him in some lake of mud and dirt.   85
[*To Ashtaroth.*]
Take thou this other; drag him through the woods
Amongst the pricking thorns and sharpest briers,
Whilst with my gentle Mephistopheles
This traitor flies unto some steepy rock
That, rolling down, may break the villain's bones   90
As he intended to dismember me.
Fly hence. Dispatch my charge immediately.
Frederick. Pity us, gentle Faustus. Save our lives!
Faustus. Away!
Frederick.   He must needs go that the devil drives.
        Exeunt Spirits *with the* KNIGHTS [*on their backs*].

        Enter the ambushed SOLDIERS.

First Soldier.
    Come, sirs. Prepare yourselves in readiness;   95
    Make haste to help these noble gentlemen.
    I heard them parley with the conjurer.
Second Soldier.
    See where he comes. Dispatch, and kill the slave.
Faustus. What's here? An ambush to betray my life?
    Then, Faustus, try thy skill. Base peasants, stand!   100
        [*Trees come between Faustus and the Soldiers.*]
    For lo, these trees remove at my command
    And stand as bulwarks 'twixt yourselves and me
    To shield me from your hated treachery.

85.1 S.D.] *This ed.; not in* B1.   94.1. S.D. *on their backs*] *This ed.; not in* B1.
100.1. S.D.] *placed here this ed.; placed after l. 103* Kirschbaum (subst.); *not
in* B1.

86. *this other*] i.e., Frederick.
89. *This traitor*] i.e., Benvolio.
94. *He ... drives*] proverbial; see Dent D278.
94.2. S.D. ambushed] placed in ambush (*OED*, 'ambush', v. 1). See
ll. 16–25.
100.1. S.D.] Faustus's language in ll. 101–3 suggests that some spectacular stage device is actually used. See also ll. 16–18. The *Damnable Life* may
well give a hint as to what happened in its report that 'suddenly all the
bushes were turned into horsemen, which also ran to encounter with the
Knight and his company' (ch. 31). See Introduction, pp. 46–7.
101. *remove*] change location.

Yet to encounter this your weak attempt,
Behold an army comes incontinent.   105

FAUSTUS *strikes the door, and enter a* Devil *playing on a drum,*
after him another bearing an ensign, and divers with weapons;
MEPHISTOPHELES *with fireworks. They set upon the* SOLDIERS
and drive them out.

[*Exit* FAUSTUS.]

[IV.iii]

Enter at several doors BENVOLIO, FREDERICK, *and* MARTINO,
their heads and faces bloody and besmeared with mud and dirt,
all having horns on their heads.

Martino. What ho, Benvolio!
Benvolio.   Here. What, Frederick, ho!
Frederick. O, help me, gentle friend. Where is Martino?
Martino. Dear Frederick, here,
    Half smothered in a lake of mud and dirt
    Through which the Furies dragged me by the heels.   5
Frederick. Martino, see! Benvolio's horns again.
Martino. O misery! How now, Benvolio?
Benvolio. Defend me, heaven. Shall I be haunted still?
Martino. Nay, fear not, man. We have no power to kill.
Benvolio. My friends transformèd thus! O hellish spite!   10
    Your heads are all set with horns.
Frederick.   You hit it right.
    It is your own you mean. Feel on your head.

105.5. S.D. *Exit* FAUSTUS] *Boas; not in B1.*   IV.iii.6.] *one line as in Oxberry;*
two lines divided at see, / *Benuolio's in B1.*   12. mean. Feel] *Dilke (subst.);*
meane feel *B1.*

---

105. *incontinent*] on the instant.
105.1. S.D. strikes the door] Faustus evidently summons his devils by
loudly striking the stage door (conceivably a trap door) through which they
are to appear.

IV.iii.8–9.] Benvolio, seeing horns on his fellows, fears they have come to
haunt him like devils. Martino replies soothingly, not realising how frightening he looks to Benvolio. (Boas suggests a pun on 'haunted' and 'hunted'.)
11–12.] The joke here, of Benvolio's seeing horns on his friends' heads
and only belatedly discovering that he too has horns, is a variation on the
classic puzzle of the three philosophers who, awakening from a nap under a

Benvolio. [*Feeling his head.*] Zounds, horns again!
Martino. Nay, chafe not, man, we all are sped.
Benvolio. What devil attends this damned magician,   15
    That, spite of spite, our wrongs are doublèd?
Frederick. What may we do, that we may hide our shames?
Benvolio. If we should follow him to work revenge,
    He'd join long asses' ears to these huge horns
    And make us laughing-stocks to all the world.   20
Martino. What shall we then do, dear Benvolio?
Benvolio. I have a castle joining near these woods,
    And thither we'll repair and live obscure
    Till time shall alter this our brutish shapes.
    Sith black disgrace hath thus eclipsed our fame,   25
    We'll rather die with grief than live with shame.

                                                Exeunt omnes.

[IV.iv]

        Enter FAUSTUS, *and the* HORSE-COURSER, *and*
                    MEPHISTOPHELES.

Horse-courser. [*Offering money.*] I beseech your worship, accept
    of these forty dollars.
Faustus. Friend, thou canst not buy so good a horse for so

---

13. S.D.] *Kirschbaum (subst.); not in B1.*   13. Zounds] *B1* ('Zons).
IV.iv.1. S.D.] *Kirschbaum (subst.); not in B1.*

---

tree, laugh to see what appear to be owl droppings on the others' foreheads;
one of them stops laughing when he realises he too must look like that.
    14. *sped*] done for. By now, they all realise they are horned.
    16. *spite of spite*] in spite of all we can do (*OED*, 'spite', sb. 5c).
    our wrongs] the harms done us.
    24. *this*] these.
    25. *Sith*] since.
    26.] proverbial: 'It is better to die with honour (grief, silence) than to live
with shame' (Dent H576).

    IV.iv.0.1–2. S.D. and *MEPHISTOPHELES*] Many editors, including
Bowers, delete Mephistopheles from this scene, and it is true that as it stands
in B1 this is the only scene in which Mephistopheles is present without
taking part or being addressed by Faustus; indeed, the B-text specifically cuts
the exchanges between Mephistopheles and the Horse-courser in the A-text
version of this same scene. Still, it seems preferable to follow B1's authority
in view of Faustus's express wish to have Mephistopheles 'ever to attend on'
him.

small a price. I have no great need to sell him, but if thou
likest him for ten dollars more, take him, because I see   5
thou hast a good mind to him.
Horse-courser. I beseech you, sir, accept of this. I am a very
poor man and have lost very much of late by horseflesh,
and this bargain will set me up again.
Faustus. Well, I will not stand with thee. Give me the money.   10
[*He takes the money.*] Now, sirrah, I must tell you that
you may ride him o'er hedge and ditch, and spare him
not. But do you hear? In any case ride him not into the
water.
Horse-courser. How, sir, not into the water? Why, will he not   15
drink of all waters?
Faustus. Yes, he will drink of all waters. But ride him not into
the water. O'er hedge and ditch, or where thou wilt, but
not into the water. Go bid the ostler deliver him unto
you, and remember what I say.   20
Horse-courser. I warrant you, sir.—O, joyful day! Now am I
a made man for ever.   *Exit.*
Faustus. What art thou, Faustus, but a man condemned to die?
Thy fatal time draws to a final end.
Despair doth drive distrust into my thoughts.   25
Confound these passions with a quiet sleep.
Tush! Christ did call the thief upon the cross;
Then rest thee, Faustus, quiet in conceit.
                                    He sits to sleep.

Enter the HORSE-COURSER, *wet.*

Horse-courser. O, what a cozening doctor was this! I, riding my
horse into the water, thinking some hidden mystery had   30
been in the horse, I had nothing under me but a little
straw and had much ado to escape drowning. Well, I'll
go rouse him and make him give me my forty dollars
again.—Ho, sirrah doctor, you cozening scab! Master

11. S.D.] *Dyce 1 (subst.); not in B1.*

---

10. *stand*] strive, haggle (*OED*, v. 79).
19. *the ostler*] Could this be Robin, the vagrant 'Clown' of I.iv and stable-
boy of II.ii and III.iii? He is called 'Robin the ostler' in the A-text at
II.ii.0.1. S.D.
34. *cozening scab*] cheating scoundrel.

Doctor, awake, and rise, and give me my money again,   35
for your horse is turned to a bottle of hay. Master
Doctor! (*He pulls off his leg.*) Alas, I am undone! What
shall I do? I have pulled off his leg.

Faustus. O, help, help! The villain hath murdered me.

Horse-courser. Murder or not murder, now he has but one leg   40
I'll outrun him and cast this leg into some ditch or
other.   [*Exit with the leg.*]

Faustus. Stop him, stop him, stop him!—Ha, ha, ha! Faustus
hath his leg again, and the Horse-courser a bundle of hay
for his forty dollars.   45

Enter WAGNER.

How now, Wagner, what news with thee?

Wagner. If it please you, the Duke of Vanholt doth earnestly
entreat your company and hath sent some of his men to
attend you with provision fit for your journey.

Faustus. The Duke of Vanholt's an honourable gentleman,   50
and one to whom I must be no niggard of my cunning.
Come away.   *Exeunt.*

[IV.v]

Enter CLOWN [ROBIN], DICK, HORSE-COURSER, *and a*
CARTER.

Carter. Come, my masters, I'll bring you to the best beer in
Europe.—What ho, Hostess!—Where be these whores?

Enter HOSTESS.

Hostess. How now, what lack you? What, my old guests,
welcome!

42. S.D. *Exit*] Oxberry; not in B1; Horsecourser runnes away A1.   42. S.D.
with the leg] Kirschbaum; not in B1.   IV.V.0.1. S.D. ROBIN] Dyce 1; not in
B1.   3. guests] B2; Guesse B1.

44. *again*] still. Faustus exults that he has not lost his real leg.
52. *Come away*] This could be said to Mephistopheles as well as to
Wagner. Indeed, Mephistopheles is the one who accompanies Faustus to the
Duke's court. Compare the A-text's 'Come, Mephistopheles, let's away to
him.'

IV.V.3–4.] The Hostess's welcome makes clear that the setting is a tavern.

Robin. [*Aside to Dick.*] Sirrah Dick, dost thou know why I   5
stand so mute?
Dick. [*Aside to Robin.*] No, Robin, why is't?
Robin. [*Aside to Dick.*] I am eighteen pence on the score. But
say nothing. See if she have forgotten me.
Hostess. [*Seeing Robin.*] Who's this that stands so solemnly by   10
himself? [*To Robin.*] What, my old guest?
Robin. O, Hostess, how do you? I hope my score stands still.
Hostess. Ay, there's no doubt of that, for methinks you make
no haste to wipe it out.
Dick. Why, Hostess, I say, fetch us some beer.   15
Hostess. You shall, presently.—Look up into th' hall there,
ho!   *Exit.*
Dick. Come, sirs, what shall we do now till mine Hostess
comes?
Carter. Marry, sir, I'll tell you the bravest tale how a conjurer   20
served me. You know Doctor Fauster?
Horse-courser. Ay, a plague take him! Here's some on's have
cause to know him. Did he conjure thee, too?
Carter. I'll tell you how he served me. As I was going to
Wittenberg t'other day with a load of hay, he met me and   25
asked me what he should give me for as much hay as he
could eat. Now, sir, I thinking that a little would serve
his turn, bade him take as much as he would for three
farthings. So he presently gave me my money and fell to
eating; and, as I am a cursen man, he never left eating till   30

5, 8, 12, 33, 54, 58, *and* IV.vi.60, 115.S.H. *Robin*] Dyce *1; Clow. or Clo.*
throughout IV.v and IV.vi in B1.   5, 7, 8. S.D.] *Kirschbaum (subst.); not in*
B1.   10, 11. S.D.] *This ed.; not in B1.*

8. *on the score*] in debt. (From the custom of marking notches or scores in
a tally stick.)
12-13. *I hope . . . of that*] Robin either means 'I hope my credit as a
customer is still good' or 'I hope my debt isn't growing.' The Hostess
answers, 'Your debt is still there, all right.'
16. *You shall, presently*] i.e., coming, right away. (The Hostess then calls
out to her tapsters, telling them to take care of the customers in another
room.)
20. *bravest*] finest.
22. *on's*] of us.
30. *cursen*] christen, i.e., Christian (dialectical form), but perhaps with
ironic suggestion of 'cursed' or 'cursing'.

he had eat up all my load of hay.

All. O monstrous! Eat a whole load of hay!

Robin. Yes, yes, that may be, for I have heard of one that has eat a load of logs.

Horse-courser. Now, sirs, you shall hear how villainously he   35
served me. I went to him yesterday to buy a horse of him,
and he would by no means sell him under forty dollars.
So, sir, because I knew him to be such a horse as would
run over hedge and ditch and never tire, I gave him his
money. So when I had my horse, Doctor Fauster bade me   40
ride him night and day and spare him no time. 'But',
quoth he, 'in any case ride him not into the water.' Now,
sir, I, thinking the horse had had some quality that he
would not have me know of, what did I but rid him into a
great river? And when I came just in the midst, my horse   45
vanished away, and I sat straddling upon a bottle of hay.

All. O brave doctor!

Horse-courser. But you shall hear how bravely I served him for
it. I went me home to his house, and there I found him
asleep. I kept a halloing and whooping in his ears, but all   50
could not wake him. I, seeing that, took him by the leg
and never rested pulling till I had pulled me his leg quite
off, and now 'tis at home in mine hostry.

Robin. And has the doctor but one leg, then? That's excellent,
for one of his devils turned me into the likeness of an   55
ape's face.

Carter. Some more drink, Hostess!

Robin. Hark you, we'll into another room and drink a while,
and then we'll go seek out the doctor.

Exeunt omnes.

31, 34. *eat*] eaten.

33-4.] Robin's observation is either an obscure joke or, more likely, a
demonstration of gullible faith in tall tales.

49. *went me*] went. (*Me* is the ethic dative.)

55-6. *into . . . ape's face*] At III.iii.44-5 and IV.vi.112 it is Dick who is
transformed into an ape; Robin is turned into a dog. The confusion may be
the result of revision. In the A-text version, Robin is turned into an ape and
Rafe into a dog.

[IV.vi]

Enter the DUKE OF VANHOLT, *his* [*pregnant*] DUCHESS,
FAUSTUS, *and* MEPHISTOPHELES [*and* Servants].

Duke. Thanks, Master Doctor, for these pleasant sights. Nor
know I how sufficiently to recompense your great deserts
in erecting that enchanted castle in the air, the sight
whereof so delighted me as nothing in the world could
please me more.   5

Faustus. I do think myself, my good lord, highly recompensed
in that it pleaseth your Grace to think but well of that
which Faustus hath performed.—But, gracious lady, it
may be that you have taken no pleasure in those sights.
Therefore, I pray you tell me what is the thing you most   10
desire to have; be it in the world, it shall be yours. I have
heard that great-bellied women do long for things are rare
and dainty.

Duchess. True, Master Doctor, and, since I find you so kind, I
will make known unto you what my heart desires to have.   15
And were it now summer, as it is January, a dead time of
the winter, I would request no better meat than a dish of
ripe grapes.

Faustus. This is but a small matter. [*Aside to Mephistopheles.*]
Go, Mephistopheles, away!   20

                                    Exit MEPHISTOPHELES.

Madam, I will do more than this for your content.

IV.vi.0.1. S.D. *pregnant*] *Kirschbaum; not in* B1.   0.2. S.D. *and* Servants]
Kirschbaum; not in B1.   1.] *prose as in Kirschbaum; as verse divided at*
sights, / Nor *in* B1.   3–5. sight . . . more] *prose as in Greg; as verse divided*
at me, / As nothing *in* B1.   14, 34, 121. S.H. Duchess] A1; Lady B1.   19,
23.1. S.D.] *Kirschbaum (subst.); not in* B1.

IV.vi.1–5.] The B-text's imperfect attempt at verse lineation does show
that 'Thanks . . . sights' (l. 1) and 'as nothing . . . me more' (ll. 4–5) are
metrically regular. If emended, 'the sight whereof [hath] so delighted me' is
also regular. Conceivably, parts of this scene were once in verse.

   12. *are*] that are.

Enter MEPHISTOPHELES *again with the grapes.*

Here. Now taste ye these. They should be good, for
they come from a far country, I can tell you.

[*The Duchess tastes the grapes.*]

Duke. This makes me wonder more than all the rest, that at
this time of the year, when every tree is barren of his   25
fruit, from whence you had these ripe grapes.

Faustus. Please it your Grace, the year is divided into two
circles over the whole world, so that, when it is winter
with us, in the contrary circle it is likewise summer with
them, as in India, Saba, and such countries that lie far   30
east, where they have fruit twice a year. From whence,
by means of a swift spirit that I have, I had these grapes
brought, as you see.

Duchess. And, trust me, they are the sweetest grapes that e'er I
tasted.   35

The CLOWN[S] *bounce at the gate, within.*

Duke. What rude disturbers have we at the gate?
Go pacify their fury. Set it ope,
And then demand of them what they would have.

They knock again and call out to talk with Faustus.

[*A Servant goes to the gate.*]

Servant. Why, how now, masters, what a coil is there!
What is the reason you disturb the duke?   40

Dick. [*Offstage.*] We have no reason for it. Therefore, a fig
for him!

Servant. Why, saucy varlets, dare you be so bold?

22–3.] *prose as in Dilke; as verse divided at* be good / For they *in* B1.
35.1. S.D. CLOWNS] *Dyce 1; Clowne* B1.   38.2. S.D. *A Servant goes to the
gate*] *Kirschbaum (subst.); not in* B1.   39. S.H. *Servant*] B1 (A Seruant).
41, 44, 50, 52. S.D. *Offstage*] *Kirschbaum; Within Wagner; not in* B1.

---

31. *where . . . year*] This B-text addition is perhaps the revisers' attempt to
clarify a point about seasonal differences between East and West that is
ambiguous in the A-text; see note at A-text IV.ii.24.

35.1. S.D. *bounce*] knock (*OED*, v. 2). Compare *The Faerie Queene*,
v.ii.21: 'Yet still he bet, and bounst uppon the dore'.

39. *masters*] sirs. Said to social inferiors.

coil] noisy disturbance, row.

41. *a fig*] a contemptuous and vulgar gesture of thrusting the thumb
between two closed fingers. (The word may be suggested by a common pun
on 'reason'/'raisin'; see J. C. Maxwell, *N&Q.*, n.s. XI (1964), 262.)

Horse-courser. [*Offstage.*] I hope, sir, we have wit enough to be
  more bold than welcome.   45
Servant. It appears so. Pray be bold elsewhere, and trouble
  not the duke.
Duke. [*To the Servant.*] What would they have?
Servant. They all cry out to speak with Doctor Faustus.
Carter. [*Offstage.*] Ay, and we will speak with him.   50
Duke. Will you, sir?—Commit the rascals.
Dick. [*Offstage.*] Commit with us? He were as good commit
  with his father as commit with us.
Faustus. I do beseech your Grace, let them come in.
  They are good subject for a merriment.   55
Duke. Do as thou wilt, Faustus. I give thee leave.
Faustus. I thank your Grace.

                        [*The Servant opens the gate.*]

            Enter the CLOWN [ROBIN], DICK, CARTER,
                and HORSE-COURSER.

                    Why, how now, my good friends?
  'Faith, you are too outrageous. But come near;
  I have procured your pardons. Welcome all!
Robin. Nay, sir, we will be welcome for our money, and we   60

46–7. It appears . . . duke] *prose as in Dyce 1; as verse divided at* else-where, /
And trouble *in B1.*   48. S.D. *To the Servant*] *This ed.; not in B1.*
57.1. S.D. *The Servant opens the gate*] *This ed.; not in B1.*   57.2. S.D.
ROBIN] *Dyce 1; not in B1.*   60, 115. S.H. *Robin*] *Dyce 1; Clow. B1.*

---

51. *Commit*] commit to prison. But Dick replies in the sense of 'fornicate'.
58. *outrageous*] unrestrained, bold.
60–8.] In their drunkenness, the clowns appear to think they have found
Faustus in some tavern, but which one is not clear. At the end of the
previous scene, their plan was to drink a while and then go seek out Faustus
(IV.v.58–9). In this present scene they knock loudly at the door and call for
beer, as though certain they have found him in some public house (see ll.
67–8). Evidently, Faustus has charmed their senses and wafted them here to
amuse by their not knowing their 'place', and to be given the comeuppance
they deserve for trying to cheat him. He even arranges for them to have beer
(l. 74). The arrival of the Hostess at l. 99.1 with drink might seem to confuse
matters, for she speaks of her guests as though in her own tavern, but
probably she is to be understood also as labouring under the delusion that
Faustus has devised. The lack of clarity may be the result of adding comic
business to an already existing scene at the Duke of Vanholt's court. See
Introduction, pp. 43–4.

will pay for what we take.—What ho! Give's half a dozen
of beer here, and be hanged.
Faustus. Nay, hark you, can you tell me where you are?
Carter. Ay, marry, can I. We are under heaven.
Servant. Ay, but, sir saucebox, know you in what place?   65
Horse-courser. Ay, ay, the house is good enough to drink in.
    Zounds, fill us some beer, or we'll break all the barrels in
    the house and dash out all your brains with your bottles.
Faustus. Be not so furious. Come, you shall have beer.—
    My lord, beseech you give me leave a while.   70
    I'll gage my credit 'twill content your Grace.
Duke. With all my heart, kind doctor. Please thyself.
    Our servants and our court's at thy command.
Faustus. I humbly thank your Grace.—Then fetch some beer.
Horse-courser. Ay, marry, there spake a doctor indeed, and,   75
    'faith, I'll drink a health to thy wooden leg for that word.
Faustus. My wooden leg? What dost thou mean by that?
Carter. Ha, ha, ha! Dost hear him, Dick? He has forgot his
    leg.
Horse-courser. Ay, ay. He does not stand much upon that.   80
Faustus. No, 'faith, not much upon a wooden leg.
Carter. Good Lord, that flesh and blood should be so frail with
    your worship! Do not you remember a horse-courser you
    sold a horse to?
Faustus. Yes, I remember I sold one a horse.   85
Carter. And do you remember you bid he should not ride into
    the water?
Faustus. Yes, I do very well remember that.

---

67. Zounds] *B1* (Zons).

62. *and be hanged*] i.e., and to hell with you. A common tag; compare
Dent H130.1.
64. *under heaven*] There may be an ironic echo of II.i.120, 'Under the
heavens'. Compare a similarly wry joke in *Cor.*, IV.v.40–1: 'Where dwell'st
thou?' 'Under the canopy.'
71. *gage*] pledge, stake.
74. *Then fetch some beer*] This could be said to a servant or to
Mephistopheles. Faustus is clearly orchestrating a comic plot; see ll. 60–8n.
80. *stand much upon that*] (*a*) attach much importance to that (*OED*,
'stand', 78j) (*b*) stand on ceremony (*c*) have a leg to stand on (literally).
Faustus replies in the same punning sense.
82–3. *that . . . worship*] i.e., that your memory should be so weak.

Carter. And do you remember nothing of your leg?

Faustus. No, in good sooth.   90

Carter. Then, I pray, remember your curtsy.

Faustus. [*Making a curtsy.*] I thank you, sir.

Carter. 'Tis not so much worth. I pray you tell me one thing.

Faustus. What's that?

Carter. Be both your legs bedfellows every night together?   95

Faustus. Wouldst thou make a Colossus of me, that thou
    askest me such questions?

Carter. No, truly, sir, I would make nothing of you. But I
    would fain know that.

Enter HOSTESS *with drink.*

Faustus. Then, I assure thee, certainly they are.   100

Carter. I thank you. I am fully satisfied.

Faustus. But wherefore dost thou ask?

Carter. For nothing, sir. But methinks you should have a
    wooden bedfellow of one of 'em.

Horse-courser. Why, do you hear, sir? Did not I pull off one of   105
    your legs when you were asleep?

Faustus. But I have it again now I am awake. Look you
    here, sir.   [*He shows them his legs.*]

All. O, horrible! Had the doctor three legs?

Carter. Do you remember, sir, how you cozened me and eat   110
    up my load of—   *Faustus charms him dumb.*

---

92. S.D.] *Kirschbaum (subst.); not in B1.*   99.1. S.D. *Enter* HOSTESS *with
drink] B1; Enter* Hostesse *brought hither by magic with drink Bowers.*
108. S.D.] *Kirschbaum (subst.); not in B1.*

---

91. *remember your curtsy*] (*a*) remember to make a 'leg', or obeisance—
something hard for a one-legged person to do (*b*) remember the need for
courtesy. (The B1 spelling, *curtesie*, captures the duality of meaning.)

93. *'Tis . . . worth*] i.e., that's a pretty mediocre curtsy. (In curtsying, a
man draws one leg back, bent at the knee, and bows low over the extended
front leg.)

96. *Colossus*] i.e., colossal statue, with huge legs like those that bestrid the
harbour of Rhodes.

98. *make nothing of*] make light of, or have nothing to do with (with pun
on *make* in l. 96).

108. S.D.] Faustus's academic gown presumably covered his legs when he
curtsied at l. 92.

110. *eat*] ate.

Dick. Do you remember how you made me wear an ape's—
                    [*Faustus charms him dumb.*]
Horse-courser. You whoreson conjuring scab, do you remember
     how you cozened me with a ho—
                    [*Faustus charms him dumb.*]
Robin. Ha' you forgotten me? You think to carry it away with   115
     your 'hey-pass' and 'repass'. Do you remember the
     dog's fa—   [*Faustus charms him dumb.*]
                                Exeunt CLOWNS.
Hostess. Who pays for the ale? Hear you, Master Doctor, now
     you have sent away my guests, I pray, who shall pay me
     for my a—   [*Faustus charms her dumb.*]   120
                                Exit HOSTESS.
Duchess. [*To the Duke.*] My lord,
     We are much beholding to this learnèd man.
Duke. So are we, madam, which we will recompense
     With all the love and kindness that we may.
     His artful sport drives all sad thoughts away.   125
                                Exeunt.

112.1, 114.1, 117, 120. S.D. *Faustus . . . dumb*] *Dyce 1 (subst.); not in B1.*
114. you] *B1* (yo).   119. guests] *B2;* guesse *B1.*   121. S.D. *To the Duke*]
This ed.; not in B1.

---

115. *carry it away*] carry the day (*OED*, 'carry', v. 46e).
116. *'hey-pass' and 'repass'*] 'abracadabra' (Gill 1). Compare the A-text,
IV.i.158.

Act V

Thunder and lightning. Enter Devils *with covered dishes.*
MEPHISTOPHELES *leads them into Faustus's study.*
Then enter WAGNER.

Wagner. I think my master means to die shortly.
He has made his will and given me his wealth:
His house, his goods, and store of golden plate,
Besides two thousand ducats ready coined.
I wonder what he means. If death were nigh,   5
He would not frolic thus. He's now at supper
With the scholars, where there's such belly-cheer
As Wagner in his life ne'er saw the like.
And see where they come. Belike the feast is done. *Exit.*

Enter FAUSTUS, MEPHISTOPHELES, *and two or three* SCHOLARS.

First Scholar. Master Doctor Faustus, since our conference   10
about fair ladies—which was the beautifullest in all the
world—we have determined with ourselves that Helen of
Greece was the admirablest lady that ever lived. There-
fore, Master Doctor, if you will do us so much favour as
to let us see that peerless dame of Greece, whom all the   15
world admires for majesty, we should think ourselves
much beholding unto you.
Faustus. Gentlemen,
For that I know your friendship is unfeigned,
It is not Faustus' custom to deny   20
The just request of those that wish him well:
You shall behold that peerless dame of Greece,
No otherwise for pomp or majesty
Than when Sir Paris crossed the seas with her
And brought the spoils to rich Dardania.   25
Be silent then, for danger is in words.

v.i.1–9.] *verse as in Boas, following in part a similar passage in A1; as prose in*
B1.   18–19.] *divided as in Dilke; one line in B1.*

273

[MEPHISTOPHELES *goes to the door.*]

Music sound. MEPHISTOPHELES *brings in* HELEN.
She passeth over the stage.

Second Scholar. Was this fair Helen, whose admirèd worth
  Made Greece with ten years' wars afflict poor Troy?
Third Scholar. Too simple is my wit to tell her worth,
  Whom all the world admires for majesty.   30
First Scholar. Now we have seen the pride of nature's work,
  We'll take our leaves, and for this blessèd sight
  Happy and blest be Faustus evermore.
Faustus. Gentlemen, farewell. The same wish I to you.

                                        Exeunt SCHOLARS.

Enter an OLD MAN.

Old Man. O gentle Faustus, leave this damnèd art,   35
  This magic, that will charm thy soul to hell
  And quite bereave thee of salvation!
  Though thou hast now offended like a man,
  Do not persever in it like a devil.
  Yet, yet thou hast an amiable soul,   40
  If sin by custom grow not into nature.
  Then, Faustus, will repentance come too late;
  Then thou art banished from the sight of heaven.
  No mortal can express the pains of hell.
  It may be this my exhortation   45
  Seems harsh and all unpleasant. Let it not,
  For, gentle son, I speak it not in wrath

26.1. S.D. MEPHISTOPHELES *goes to the door*] This ed.; *not in* B1.   34.1.
S.D. *Exeunt* SCHOLARS] *placed as in* A1; *after l. 33 in* B1.

---

v.i.35–51.] The Old Man's speech to Faustus is extensively rewritten in
the B-text as an exhortation to restrain the corrosive effects of bad habits, in
place of the emphasis on contrite tears and faith in divine mercy obtained
through Christ's sacrifice in the A-text. See Warren's analysis of the two
versions, pp. 129–42.
  39. *persever*] This B1 spelling (*perseuer*) indicates the accent on the second
syllable.
  40. *amiable*] worthy to be loved (by God).
  41.] 'so long as sin does not through custom become your nature' (Greg).
  45. *exhortation*] pronounced in five syllables, ending in '-see-own' instead
of the '-shun' of modern English.

          Or envy of thee, but in tender love
          And pity of thy future misery;
          And so have hope that this my kind rebuke,   50
          Checking thy body, may amend thy soul.
Faustus.
          Where art thou, Faustus? Wretch, what hast thou done?
          Hell claims his right, and with a roaring voice
          Says, 'Faustus, come! Thine hour is almost come.'
                              Mephistopheles gives him a dagger.
          And Faustus now will come to do thee right.   55
                              [*Faustus prepares to stab himself.*]
Old Man. O, stay, good Faustus, stay thy desperate steps!
          I see an angel hover o'er thy head,
          And with a vial full of precious grace
          Offers to pour the same into thy soul.
          Then call for mercy and avoid despair.   60
Faustus.
          O friend, I feel thy words to comfort my distressèd soul.
          Leave me a while to ponder on my sins.
Old Man. Faustus, I leave thee, but with grief of heart,
          Fearing the enemy of thy hapless soul.   *Exit.*
Faustus. Accursèd Faustus, wretch, what hast thou done?   65
          I do repent, and yet I do despair.
          Hell strives with grace for conquest in my breast.
          What shall I do to shun the snares of death?
Mephistopheles. Thou traitor, Faustus, I arrest thy soul
          For disobedience to my sovereign lord.   70
          Revolt, or I'll in piecemeal tear thy flesh.
Faustus. I do repent I e'er offended him.
          Sweet Mephistopheles, entreat thy lord
          To pardon my unjust presumption,
          And with my blood again I will confirm   75
          The former vow I made to Lucifer.
Mephistopheles. Do it then, Faustus, with unfeignèd heart,
          Lest greater dangers do attend thy drift.
                    [*Faustus cuts his arm and writes with his blood.*]

55.1. S.D.] *Jump (subst.); not in B1.*   77. S.H. *Mephistopheles*] *A1; not in*
B1.   78.1. S.D.] *Boas, conj. Dyce 1 (in A-text); not in B1.*

          48. *envy of*] enmity towards.
          51. *Checking*] reproving, restraining.

Faustus. Torment, sweet friend, that base and agèd man
    That durst dissuade me from thy Lucifer,   80
    With greatest torment that our hell affords.
Mephistopheles. His faith is great. I cannot touch his soul.
    But what I may afflict his body with
    I will attempt, which is but little worth.
Faustus. One thing, good servant, let me crave of thee   85
    To glut the longing of my heart's desire:
    That I may have unto my paramour
    That heavenly Helen, which I saw of late,
    Whose sweet embraces may extinguish clear
    Those thoughts that do dissuade me from my vow,   90
    And keep my vow I made to Lucifer.
Mephistopheles. This, or what else my Faustus shall desire,
    Shall be performed in twinkling of an eye.

        Enter HELEN *again* [*brought in by* MEPHISTOPHELES],
                passing over between two Cupids.

Faustus. Was this the face that launched a thousand ships
    And burnt the topless towers of Ilium?   95
    Sweet Helen, make me immortal with a kiss.
                                        [*They kiss.*]
    Her lips suck forth my soul. See where it flies!
    Come, Helen, come, give me my soul again.
                                        [*They kiss again.*]
    Here will I dwell, for heaven is in these lips,
    And all is dross that is not Helena.   100
    I will be Paris, and for love of thee
    Instead of Troy shall Wittenberg be sacked,
    And I will combat with weak Menelaus,
    And wear thy colours on my plumèd crest.
    Yea, I will wound Achilles in the heel   105
    And then return to Helen for a kiss.
    O, thou art fairer than the evening's air,

79. S.H. *Faustus*] *A1; not in B1.*   93.1. S.D. *brought in by* MEPHISTOPHELES]
This ed.; not in B1.   96.1 S.D. *They kiss*] *B7 (Kisses her); not in B1.*
98.1 S.D. *They kiss again*] *This ed.; not in B1.*

89. *clear*] entirely. Compare A1, *clean.*
93.2. S.D. *passing over*] passing over the stage, entering at one door and
exiting by another, as at l. 26.3.

Clad in the beauty of a thousand stars.
Brighter art thou than flaming Jupiter
When he appeared to hapless Semele,   110
More lovely than the monarch of the sky
In wanton Arethusa's azure arms;
And none but thou shalt be my paramour.   *Exeunt.*

[v.ii]

> *Thunder. Enter* LUCIFER, BEELZEBUB, *and* MEPHISTOPHELES
> [*above*].

Lucifer. Thus from infernal Dis do we ascend
     To view the subjects of our monarchy,
     Those souls which sin seals the black sons of hell,
     'Mong which as chief, Faustus, we come to thee,
     Bringing with us lasting damnation   5
     To wait upon thy soul. The time is come
     Which makes it forfeit.
Mephistopheles.   And this gloomy night
     Here in this room will wretched Faustus be.
Beelzebub. And here we'll stay
     To mark him how he doth demean himself.   10
Mephistopheles. How should he, but in desperate lunacy?
     Fond worldling, now his heart-blood dries with grief;
     His conscience kills it, and his labouring brain
     Begets a world of idle fantasies

V.ii.0.2. S.D. *above*] Boas; *not in* B1.   3. sin seals] *B3 (subst.);* sinne, seales
B1.

---

112. *azure*] A1's *azurde* seems stronger than B1's *azure*, and B1 could
represent an easy error in transmission, but the B1 reading is defensible as it
stands.

V.ii.0.1–2. S.D.] The presence of these devils from the start of the final
scene lends a determinism to the tragedy not found in the A-text version.
Probably the devils are above, in the gallery over the stage. See Introduction,
p. 45.
     1. *Dis*] the kingdom of Dis Pater or Pluto, in the underworld.
     6. *wait upon*] (*a*) attend, like servants (*b*) lie in wait for.
     10. *demean*] conduct; but perhaps with a suggestion of 'lower reputation
and character' (a meaning the *OED* dates from 1601).
     12. *Fond*] foolish.

To overreach the devil. But all in vain.   15
His store of pleasures must be sauced with pain.
He and his servant Wagner are at hand,
Both come from drawing Faustus' latest will.
See where they come.

Enter FAUSTUS *and* WAGNER.

Faustus. Say, Wagner. Thou hast perused my will;   20
    How dost thou like it?
Wagner.   Sir, so wondrous well
    As in all humble duty I do yield
    My life and lasting service for your love.

Enter the SCHOLARS.

Faustus. Gramercies, Wagner.—Welcome, gentlemen.
                                [*Exit* WAGNER.]
First Scholar. Now, worthy Faustus, methinks your looks are   25
    changed.
Faustus. O gentlemen!
Second Scholar. What ails Faustus?
Faustus. Ah, my sweet chamber-fellow! Had I lived with thee,
    then had I lived still, but now must die eternally. Look,   30
    sirs, comes he not? Comes he not?
First Scholar. O my dear Faustus, what imports this fear?
Second Scholar. Is all our pleasure turned to melancholy?
Third Scholar. [*To the other Scholars.*] He is not well with
    being over-solitary.   35
Second Scholar. If it be so, we'll have physicians, and Faustus
    shall be cured.

24.1. S.D.] *Oxberry; not in* B1.   29–31.] *prose as in* A1*; as verse divided at*
thee, / Then . . . eternally. / Looke *in* B1.   34, 38. S.D.] *This ed.; not in* B1.

---

18. *come*] having come.

drawing . . . will] This detail seems to conflict with Wagner's knowing of
the will and its contents at v.i.2–4. The confusion is probably the result of
revision.

latest] (*a*) most recent (*b*) last.

24. *Gramercies*] thank you.

24.1. S.D. Exit WAGNER] The placement of this stage direction is uncertain, but the exit is necessary at some point.

32. *imports*] signifies.

Third Scholar. [To Faustus.] 'Tis but a surfeit, sir. Fear
nothing.

Faustus. A surfeit of deadly sin, that hath damned both body   40
and soul.

Second Scholar. Yet, Faustus, look up to heaven, and remember mercy is infinite.

Faustus. But Faustus' offence can ne'er be pardoned. The
serpent that tempted Eve may be saved, but not Faustus.   45
O gentlemen, hear with patience, and tremble not at my
speeches. Though my heart pant and quiver to remember
that I have been a student here these thirty years, O,
would I had never seen Wittenberg, never read book!
And what wonders I have done, all Germany can witness,   50
yea, all the world, for which Faustus hath lost both
Germany and the world, yea, heaven itself—heaven, the
seat of God, the throne of the blessed, the kingdom of
joy—and must remain in hell for ever. Hell, O, hell for
ever! Sweet friends, what shall become of Faustus, being   55
in hell for ever?

Second Scholar. Yet, Faustus, call on God.

Faustus. On God, whom Faustus hath abjured? On God,
whom Faustus hath blasphemed? O my God, I would
weep, but the devil draws in my tears. Gush forth blood   60
instead of tears, yea, life and soul. O, he stays my tongue!
I would lift up my hands, but see, they hold 'em, they
hold 'em.

All. Who, Faustus?

Faustus. Why, Lucifer and Mephistopheles. O gentlemen, I   65
gave them my soul for my cunning.

All. O, God forbid!

Faustus. God forbade it indeed, but Faustus hath done it. For
the vain pleasure of four-and-twenty years hath Faustus

44–5.] *prose as in Dilke; as verse divided at* pardoned, / The . . . saued, / But
in *B1.*   47–9. speeches. Though . . . years, O, would] *Dyce 1 (subst.);*
speeches, though . . . yeares. O would *B1.*

62–3. *they hold 'em*] Whether these words are accompanied by any stage
action (in which the devils would be understood to be 'invisible' to the
audience), or represent instead Faustus's fearful imaginings, depends on
whether the devils are near at hand or above. See v.ii.0.1–2. s.d.n. and 92n.
In the A-text version, the terrors of this idea are left to the imagination.

lost eternal joy and felicity. I writ them a bill with mine   70
own blood. The date is expired. This is the time, and he
will fetch me.

First Scholar. Why did not Faustus tell us of this before, that
divines might have prayed for thee?

Faustus. Oft have I thought to have done so, but the devil   75
threatened to tear me in pieces if I named God, to fetch
me body and soul if I once gave ear to divinity. And now
'tis too late. Gentlemen, away, lest you perish with me.

Second Scholar. O, what may we do to save Faustus?

Faustus. Talk not of me, but save yourselves and depart.   80

Third Scholar. God will strengthen me. I will stay with
Faustus.

First Scholar. [*To the Third Scholar.*] Tempt not God, sweet
friend, but let us into the next room and pray for him.

Faustus. Ay, pray for me, pray for me! And what noise soever   85
you hear, come not unto me, for nothing can rescue me.

Second Scholar. Pray thou, and we will pray that God may
have mercy upon thee.

Faustus. Gentlemen, farewell. If I live till morning, I'll visit
you; if not, Faustus is gone to hell.   90

All. Faustus, farewell.   *Exeunt* SCHOLARS.

Mephistopheles. Ay, Faustus, now thou hast no hope of heaven;
Therefore despair. Think only upon hell,
For that must be thy mansion, there to dwell.

Faustus. O thou bewitching fiend, 'twas thy temptation   95
Hath robbed me of eternal happiness.

Mephistopheles. I do confess it, Faustus, and rejoice.
'Twas I that, when thou wert i'the way to heaven,
Dammed up thy passage. When thou took'st the book

---

78. 'tis] *A1* (tis); 'ts *B1.*   83. s.d.] *This ed.; not in B1.*

92.] If Mephistopheles is above with Lucifer and Beelzebub at the start of
the scene, he probably descends by this point to the main stage. If he were to
speak above, Faustus would become aware of being overheard by a diabolical
audience, which seems unlikely. In either case, Mephistopheles's boasting at
ll. 97–101 of his success in tempting Faustus, a boast not found in the
A-text, increases the sense of the odds against Faustus. See Introduction,
pp. 45–8.

99. *Dammed*] with a play on the sense of *damned.* The B1 reading is
Damb'd.

To view the Scriptures, then I turned the leaves   100
And led thine eye.
What, weep'st thou? 'Tis too late. Despair, farewell!
Fools that will laugh on earth must weep in hell.   *Exit.*

Enter the GOOD ANGEL *and the* BAD ANGEL *at several doors.*

Good Angel. O Faustus, if thou hadst given ear to me,
   Innumerable joys had followed thee.   105
   But thou didst love the world.
Bad Angel.   Gave ear to me,
   And now must taste hell's pains perpetually.
Good Angel. O, what will all thy riches, pleasures, pomps
   Avail thee now?
Bad Angel.   Nothing but vex thee more,
   To want in hell, that had on earth such store.   110
               Music while the throne descends.
Good Angel. O, thou hast lost celestial happiness,
   Pleasures unspeakable, bliss without end.
   Hadst thou affected sweet divinity,
   Hell or the devil had had no power on thee.
   Hadst thou kept on that way, Faustus, behold   115
   In what resplendent glory thou hadst set
   In yonder throne, like those bright shining saints,
   And triumphed over hell. That hast thou lost.

---

102. What, weep'st] *B1* (What weep'st).   103. must] *B2;* most *B1.*
116. set] *B1;* sit *B2;* sat *Cunningham.*

---

102 *What, weep'st thou*] With no comma, as in B1, the phrase could mean
'Why do you weep?'
  103. *must weep*] The B1 reading, *most weepe,* is defensible, but the antithesis of 'will' and 'must' supports B2's emendation.
  103. S.D. Exit] Possibly Mephistopheles returns to the upper acting area
to rejoin Lucifer and Beelzebub, or possibly they all leave at this point. The
staging of the devils throughout the B-text version of the scene is uncertain.
  110.1. S.D. the throne descends] i.e., a throne is let down from the
'heavens' of the theatre by means of winch, cords, and pulleys. See Introduction, pp. 45–6.
  113. *affected*] aspired to, been drawn to.
  116. *set*] sat.
  117. *those . . . saints*] The pageant presented to Faustus with the descend-
ing throne includes some pictorial representation of the saints, or possibly
representation by mute actors.

282   DOCTOR FAUSTUS, B-TEXT (1616)   [ACT V

And now, poor soul, must thy good angel leave thee.
The jaws of hell are open to receive thee.   120
        [*The throne ascends.*] *Exit* [GOOD ANGEL].
                        Hell is discovered.
Bad Angel. Now, Faustus, let thine eyes with horror stare
Into that vast perpetual torture-house.
There are the Furies tossing damnèd souls
On burning forks; their bodies boil in lead.
There are live quarters broiling on the coals,   125
That ne'er can die. This ever-burning chair
Is for o'er-tortured souls to rest them in.
These that are fed with sops of flaming fire
Were gluttons, and loved only delicates,

120.1. S.D. *The throne ascends*] Dyce *1; not in B1.*   120.1. S.D. GOOD
ANGEL] This ed.; *not in B1.*   124. boil] B3 (boyle); broyle *B1.*

120.1 S.D. Exit GOOD ANGEL] Possibly the Good Angel exits by means
of the ascending throne.
    120.2. S.D. Hell is discovered] A backcloth is made visible by drawing
aside of a curtain, or a pictorial representation of hell is achieved in some
other way, that must include a burning 'chair' or throne. The Admiral's Men
included a 'Hell mought' in their inventory of props (Henslowe's *Diary*, p.
319). Use of a trap door is possible. Hellmouths, in medieval illustration and
theatrical practice, were often visualised as huge, scaly, sharp-toothed heads
of leviathans, within whose gaping jaws could be seen the devils of hell and
their victims in grotesque postures of torture; smoke billowed forth, and
violent noises were audible from within. See, for example, the manuscript
illustration of the Valenciennes Passion Play, reproduced in Bevington, ed.,
*Homo, Memento Finis: The Iconography of Just Judgment in Medieval Art and
Drama* (Kalamazoo, Mi.: Medieval Institute Publications, 1985). Hellmouth
motifs are also common in the apocalyptic paintings of Hieronimus Bosch
and Brueghel. See Introduction, pp. 45–6.
    124. boil] B1's *broyle* is probably an anticipation of 'broiling' in the next
line.
    125. quarters] quarters of carcasses, each with an arm or leg.
    126. That] refers ambiguously to the live quarters and to the coals.
    127. o'er-tortured] tortured beyond limits of endurance.
    rest them] with ironic play of meaning: (a) remain forever (b) sit down (c)
enjoy a respite from labour (d) have quiet of mind (?) be saved (as in 'God
rest his soul') (f) be arrested (g) wrest, twist, torture.
    128. sops of flaming fire] This deadly tidbit, impaled no doubt on a skewer,
ironically suggests the kind of delicacy a glutton might savour, consisting of a
wine-soaked morsel of bread served flambé.
    129. gluttons] Perhaps Gluttony from the show of the Seven Deadly Sins is
discovered in hell at this point.
    delicates] delicacies.

And laughed to see the poor starve at their gates.   130
But yet all these are nothing. Thou shalt see
Ten thousand tortures that more horrid be.
Faustus. O, I have seen enough to torture me!
Bad Angel. Nay, thou must feel them, taste the smart of all.
He that loves pleasure must for pleasure fall.   135
And so I leave thee, Faustus, till anon;
Then wilt thou tumble in confusion.   *Exit.*
                              The clock strikes eleven.
Faustus. O Faustus,
Now hast thou but one bare hour to live,
And then thou must be damned perpetually.   140
Stand still, you ever-moving spheres of heaven,
That time may cease and midnight never come!
Fair nature's eye, rise, rise again, and make
Perpetual day; or let this hour be but
A year, a month, a week, a natural day,   145
That Faustus may repent and save his soul!
O lente, lente currite noctis equi!
The stars move still; time runs; the clock will strike;
The devil will come, and Faustus must be damned.
O, I'll leap up to heaven! Who pulls me down?   150
One drop of blood will save me. O, my Christ!
Rend not my heart for naming of my Christ!
Yet will I call on him. O, spare me, Lucifer!
Where is it now? 'Tis gone;
And see, a threat'ning arm, an angry brow.   155
Mountains and hills, come, come and fall on me,

144–5.] *divided as in Oxberry; divided at* but a yeare, / A month *in B1.*
155. see, a] *B1 (see a).*

130.] In medieval descriptions of the Last Judgement, Christ as judge
rewards the virtuous for performing the seven so-called corporal works of
mercy—feeding and clothing the hungry and the poor, etc.—and punishes
the damned for turning away the poor and hungry from their gates. See, for
example, The Wakefield Master's pageant of 'The Last Judgement' in the
Towneley Corpus Christi cycle, ll. 442–511 (ed. Bevington).
137. *confusion*] destruction, perdition.
137. S.D. Exit] Possibly the Bad Angel exits into the hellmouth. The
pageant of hell may remain visible during Faustus's ensuing soliloquy; as
Greg points out, Faustus's anguished cry at l. 190, 'Ugly hell, gape not',
would be most effective if the hellmouth is seen to gape anew at that point.

And hide me from the heavy wrath of heaven!
No? Then will I headlong run into the earth.
Gape, earth! O, no, it will not harbour me.
You stars that reigned at my nativity,   160
Whose influence hath allotted death and hell,
Now draw up Faustus like a foggy mist
Into the entrails of yon labouring cloud,
That when you vomit forth into the air,
My limbs may issue from your smoky mouths,   165
But let my soul mount and ascend to heaven.
                        The watch strikes.
O, half the hour is past! 'Twill all be past anon.
O, if my soul must suffer for my sin,
Impose some end to my incessant pain.
Let Faustus live in hell a thousand years,   170
A hundred thousand, and at last be saved.
No end is limited to damnèd souls.
Why wert thou not a creature wanting soul?
Or why is this immortal that thou hast?
O, Pythagoras' *metempsychosis*, were that true,   175
This soul should fly from me and I be changed
Into some brutish beast.
All beasts are happy, for, when they die,
Their souls are soon dissolved in elements;
But mine must live still to be plagued in hell.   180
Curst be the parents that engendered me!
No, Faustus, curse thyself. Curse Lucifer,
That hath deprived thee of the joys of heaven.
                        The clock strikes twelve.
It strikes, it strikes! Now, body, turn to air,
Or Lucifer will bear thee quick to hell.   185
O soul, be changed into small waterdrops,
And fall into the ocean, ne'er be found!

        Thunder, and enter the Devils.

187.1. S.D.] The reference here to '*the* Devils' may be to Mephistopheles, Lucifer, and Beelzebub, in which case they may have exited at l. 103; see note. If, on the other hand, they have remained above throughout the scene (except when Mephistopheles perhaps descends to the main stage to converse with Faustus in ll. 92–103), 'Devils' could here refer to their assistants, played by extras in the acting company, all of whom leave at l. 191. S.D.

O, mercy, heaven, look not so fierce on me!
Adders and serpents, let me breathe a while!
Ugly hell, gape not. Come not, Lucifer!   190
I'll burn my books. O, Mephistopheles!   *Exeunt.*

[v.iii]

Enter the SCHOLARS.

First Scholar. Come, gentlemen, let us go visit Faustus,
      For such a dreadful night was never seen
      Since first the world's creation did begin.
      Such fearful shrieks and cries were never heard.
      Pray heaven the doctor have escaped the danger.   5
Second Scholar.
      O, help us, heaven! See, here are Faustus' limbs,
      All torn asunder by the hand of death.
Third Scholar.
      The devils whom Faustus served have torn him thus.
      For, 'twixt the hours of twelve and one, methought
      I heard him shriek and call aloud for help,   10
      At which self time the house seemed all on fire
      With dreadful horror of these damnèd fiends.
Second Scholar. Well, gentlemen, though Faustus' end be such
      As every Christian heart laments to think on,
      Yet, for he was a scholar, once admired   15

v.iii.5. have] *B1;* hath *B3.*

Whether the devils take the body of Faustus with them is uncertain; presumably he is carried off to hell (as in the A-text), and yet in the next scene his remains are discovered. See next note.

   v.iii.6–7.] If this display of Faustus's remains is made by means of drawing back a curtain, as some editors suggest, such a discovery curtain could also be used to conceal the remains at the end, obviating the necessity for the carrying out of his mangled corpse. Achieving the effects called for by the *Damnable Life* would otherwise pose an interesting challenge for the acting company: 'The hall lay besprinkled with blood, his brains cleaving to the wall, for the devil had beaten him from one wall against another. In one corner lay his eyes, in another his teeth . . . They found his body lying on the horse dung, most monstrously torn and fearful to behold, for his head and all his joints were dashed in pieces' (ch. 63).

   11. *self*] same.

   15. *for*] since.

For wondrous knowledge in our German schools,
We'll give his mangled limbs due burial;
And all the students, clothed in mourning black,
Shall wait upon his heavy funeral.   *Exeunt.*

[Epilogue]

Enter CHORUS.

Chorus. Cut is the branch that might have grown full straight,
    And burnèd is Apollo's laurel bough
    That sometime grew within this learnèd man.
    Faustus is gone. Regard his hellish fall,
    Whose fiendful fortune may exhort the wise   5
    Only to wonder at unlawful things,
    Whose deepness doth entice such forward wits
    To practise more than heavenly power permits.   [*Exit.*]

        Terminat hora diem; terminat author opus.

Epilogue.1. s.h. *Chorus*] Dyce *1; not in B1*.   8. s.d. *Exit*] Dyce *2; not in B1*.

APPENDIX

The First Comic Scene Between
Robin and Rafe (II.ii)

This comic scene appears in the original A-text after Faustus's visit
to Rome (III.i) and a misplaced chorus intended for Act IV. It
immediately precedes a second comic scene involving Robin and
Rafe with the Vintner and Mephistopheles (III.ii). Its location there
is manifestly improbable; Robin and Rafe prepare for conjuring,
exit, and then immediately re-enter to the business of conjuring.
Exits followed by re-entrances of the same characters are generally
rare in Elizabethan drama; the few extant examples suggest textual
corruption, as in the present case. The fact that the Chorus intended
for Act IV is mistakenly inserted into this same gap after III.i plainly
points to confusion about the ordering of scenes.

The B-text supports the impression of textual error by its attempts
at rearrangement. In the midst of what the A-text prints as a long
scene between Faustus and Mephistopheles, II.i and II.iii in the
present edition, the B-text inserts at II.i.166 a brief Chorus intended
for Act III and worded as in the A-text version of that Chorus.
Subsequently, just after the episode of the Seven Deadly Sins
(II.iii.108–74 in the present edition), the B-text introduces its
version of the first comic scene of Robin and Rafe (now named
Robin and Dick) and then an expanded new version of the Chorus
for Act III. The B-text's manifest error of introducing at II.i.166 a
Chorus identical with the A-text's Chorus to Act III, and then
providing a new and fuller version of such a Chorus in its proper
place at the start of Act III, makes it plain that whoever revised or
assembled the B-text at this point did not succeed in straightening
out the A-text's confusion; indeed, the B-text's confusion is its own
and in no way resembles that of the A-text. The same error also
strongly indicates that, in the view of the B-text reviser at any rate, a
break was supposed to occur at II.i.166; that is one reason that most
editors divide the long composite scene of Act II involving Faustus
and Mephistopheles, derived from two separate chapters in the
Damnable Life, into two scenes.

Since the B-text's inclusion of the first Chorus to Act III is
manifestly in error, we have good reason to mistrust the B-text's

placement of the first comic scene involving Robin and Rafe (or Dick) after the show of the Deadly Sins. The argument of this present edition (see 'The A- and B-texts') that two authors collaborated on the original version of the play, dividing their work roughly between serious and comic parts of the play and writing their stints on separate sheets of paper, and that revisions were then added in 1602 and quite possibly afterwards, offers a ready explanation for the misplacing of scenes that we find in both the A and B texts. Virtually all editors of the A-text move the Chorus intended for Act IV from its present position in A1 after III.i to its proper place at the end of Act III. Gill, in editing the A-text (1990 edition), also moves the first comic scene of Robin and Rafe to the place to which it is assigned in the B-text, after the Deadly Sins. In our view, this placement has very little textual authority and is inherently unsatisfactory, though we do agree that the scene needs to be moved. We posit instead that the B-text insertion of a misplaced Chorus at II.i.166 offers an important textual clue as to where the first comic scene involving Robin and Rafe may have belonged. The case is speculative, and indeed some comic material may simply have been lost from the short A-text we have, but in any case the original arrangements of both the A- and B-texts are visibly in error. The arrangement in this present edition of alternating serious and comic action allows Robin and Rafe's (or Dick's) talk of stealing a conjuring book (II.ii) to comment ludicrously on the previous scene in which Faustus has been shown his new book of incantations by Mephistopheles (II.i), and subsequently brings the clowns back for a scene of buffoonish conjuring and transformation (III.ii) just after we have seen how Faustus makes use of his magical powers in the Pope's privy chamber (III.i). See Levin, *Overreacher*, p. 123; Roy T. Eriksen, 'The Misplaced Clownage-Scene in *The Tragedie of Doctor Faustus* (1616) and Its Implications for the Play's Total Structure', *ES*, LXII (1981), 249–58; and Keefer's edition, pp. lxii–lxxvii, for further justification of this arrangement, which has worked well in the theatre (particularly in Adrian Noble's production in Manchester, 1981). Keefer's editorial decision and our own were arrived at independently.

Glossarial Index to the Commentary

An asterisk (*) preceding an entry indicates that the commentary note in this edition adds materially to the information given in the *OED*. Individual words are indexed in the uninflected form; phrases are indexed in the form in which they occur in the text. When a gloss is repeated in the annotations, only the initial occurrence is indexed.

companion, B III.iii.10
compare (sb.), A V.i.30
compass (vb.), A III.i.54, B
    III.ii.22, B IV.i.42, B IV.i.107
concave, A IV.i.82, B III.Chor.12
concave compass of the pole, B
    III.Chor.12
concealed, A I.i.104
conceit, A I.i.80, A IV.i.144
conference, A I.i.70
confound, A I.iii.61, A IV.i.142
confounds hell in Elysium, A I.iii.61
confusion, B V.ii.137
conjunction, A II.iii.63
conjure, B II.ii.17
consistory, B III.i.103
conspire, A Prol.22
Constantinople, A III.ii.33
consumed to dust, A IV.i.49–50
consummatum est, A II.i.74
*continent to, A I.iii.110
contrary circle, A IV.ii.24
contrary to thy promise, A II.iii.91
Cornelius, A I.i.100
corpus naturale, A I.ii.21
costermonger, B IV.i.73
council held at Trent, B III.i.105
counter (sb.), A I.iv.35–6
cozening scab, B IV.iv.34
*crooked age, A V.i.76
crosier, B III.i.88.3. S.D.
crown, A I.iv.34, B III.i.191
cull, A II.i.156
cunning, A Prol.20
curse, B III.i.128
cursen, B IV.v.30
curtsy, B IV.vi.91

dally, B IV.ii.77
dame, A II.iii.92–3
dammed, B V.ii.99
Dardania, A V.i.24
Darius, B IV.i.102.3. S.D.
daunt, A Prol.6
dearest, A IV.i.157
decretal, B III.i.104
deed of gift, A II.i.34–6
deep, B II.ii.22–3
deity, A I.i.65
delicates, A I.i.87

delight, A Prol.18
Delphian oracle, A I.i.145
*demean, B V.ii.10
Demogorgon, A I.iii.19
desperate, A I.i.83
despite of chance, B IV.i.58
determine with, A V.i.11
devil, A I.iv.51, A II.i.116–17, A
    II.i.151, A II.i.155.1. S.D., A
    II.ii.36, A II.iii.92–3, A V.ii.31,
    A V.ii.46–7, B II.i.146.1. S.D., B
    IV.iii.94
devil and . . . his dame, A II.iii.92–3
devil give thee good on't, A
    II.i.116–17
devil's governor, B IV.i.88–9
diametarily, A I.iv.73
diametrally, B I.iv.48
Diana, A IV.i.62–3
dirge, A III.i.75, A III.i.87.1. S.D.
Dis, B V.ii.1
discipulis, A I.iv.16
discover, B V.ii.120.2. S.D.
dismember, A II.ii.12–13
disposition, A II.i.175
dispute (vb.), A Prol.18
divinity, A Prol.15–16
Doctor Lopus, A IV.i.145
dollar, A IV.i.144
dominion, A I.i.62, A II.iii.57
done, A I.i.37
do thee right, A V.i.52
double cannons, A III.i.40
dragon, B I.iii.23.2. S.D.
drawer, A III.ii.6
drawing . . . will, B V.ii.18
drift, A V.i.75
drink, A I.iv.30–1, A IV.i.126
drink of all waters, A IV.i.126
drizzling, A I.iii.2
dunce, A I.ii.19

east, B III.i.15
eat, B IV.v.31, B IV.v.32, B
    IV.vi.110
eat no hay, A III.ii.3–4
ebon, B IV.i.68
ecce signum, A III.ii.2
eclipse, A II.iii.63
elected, B III.i.126